THE

ESSENTIAL

NEW ART

EXAMINER

THE ESSENTIAL
NEW|

Edited by

TERRI GRIFFITH

KATHRYN BORN

JANET KOPLOS

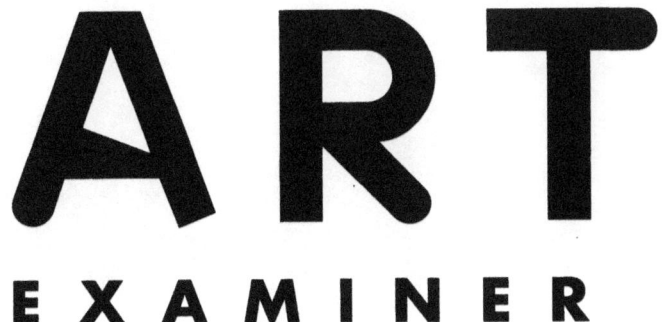

ART
EXAMINER

NIU PRESS / DEKALB

© 2011 by Northern Illinois University Press

Published by the Northern Illinois University Press, DeKalb, Illinois 60115

Design by Julia Fauci

Library of Congress Cataloging-in-Publication Data

The essential New art examiner / edited by Terri Griffith, Kathryn Born, and Janet Koplos; foreword by Kathryn Born.

   p.   cm.

Includes bibliographical references.

ISBN 978-0-87580-662-4 (pbk. : alk. paper)—ISBN 978-1-60909-037-1 (e-book)

1. Art, American—20th century—Themes, motives. 2. Art, American—21st century—themes, motives. I. Griffith, Terri, 1968- II. Born, Kathryn. III. Koplos, Janet.

IV. New art examiner (Chicago, Ill. : 1985)

N6512.E72 2011

709.73'09045—dc23

2011030986

DEDICATED TO **JANE ADDAMS ALLEN** AND **KATHRYN HIXSON**

CONTENTS

Foreword by Kathryn Born—**XIII**

The Way We Were by Janet Koplos—**3**

I DEREK GUTHRIE and
JANE ALLEN FOUNDING EDITORS

*Introduction by Derek Guthrie—***7**

FRANK PANNIER
A Painter Reviews Chicago, Part I
*Summer 1974—***1 5**

FRANK PANNIER
A Painter Reviews Chicago, Part II
*November 1974—***1 9**

JANE ALLEN AND DEREK GUTHRIE
The Tradition
*February 1975—***24**

MICHAEL RABIGER
Letter to Aspiring Filmmakers
*March 1976—***35**

PETER SCHJELDAHL
Dear Profession of Art Writing
*June 1977—***40**

JOSHUA KIND
The Flavin File
June 1977—49

KEITH MORRISON
Art Criticism—A Pan-African Point of View
February 1979—54

LYNNE WARREN
N.A.M.E. at Six—Re-defining the Role of Alternative Spaces
June 1979—71

ED PASCHKE
Speakeasy
February 1982—79

ALICE THORSON
Young Chicagoans Prefer Engagement to Avant-Gardism
May 1982—81

II ANN LEE MORGAN EDITOR

*The New Art Examiner Three Decades Ago—A Memoir by
Ann Lee Morgan—91*

CAROLE HARMEL
The Word vs. the Image—Some Thoughts on Reading Photography
December 1979—97

JANET KOPLOS
Reflection on Glass
Summer 1980—103

MICHAEL STARENKO
A Reader's Guide to Structuralist Criticism
February 1981—111

DONNA AND STEPHEN TOULMIN
Harris Bank Facelift Raises Legal Questions
*October 1981—*121

JANE ALLEN
The (Declining) Power of Review
*November 1981—*126

III **JAMES YOOD** EDITOR

*Introduction by James Yood—*135

JOANNA FRUEH
Explicit—Towards a Feminist Theory of Art Criticism
*January 1985—*139

ALICE THORSON AND JAMES YOOD
Who Follows the Hairy Who?
*March 1985—*147

PETER SCHJELDAHL
'Chicagoization'—Some Second Thoughts on the Second City
*May 1985—*155

HILTON KRAMER
Art Scene of the '80s
*October 1985—*165

CONNIE SAMARAS
Sponsorship or Censorship
*November 1985—*176

THE GUERRILLA GIRLS
Speakeasy
*March 1986—*191

DONALD KUSPIT
The 'Madness' of Chicago Art
*May 1986—*194

IV ANN WIENS EDITOR

Introduction by Ann Wiens—202

ANN WIENS
On View—Chicago
May 1993—207

STEVE HOHENBOKEN
Comfort Cut on the (Gender) Bias—Out of the (Linen) Closet
September 1993—213

HAMZA WALKER
Public Domain—Frank Stella, The Town-Ho's Story
January 1994—217

STEVEN C. DUBIN
Art's Demise—Censors to the Right of Me, Censors
to the Left of Me
March 1994—221

HAMZA WALKER
Please Pay Attention Please
January 1995—232

MARÍA JOSÉ BARANDIARÁN
...In a Place Like This?—What's a Contemporary Art Show
Like 'About Place—Recent Art of the Americas' Doing at the
Art Institute of Chicago?
September 1995—235

JEFF HUEBNER
Bigger, Better, Faster, More?—Chicago's New and Improved MCA
May 1996—243

SARAH VOWELL
On View—Chicago
May 1996—255

V JAN ESTEP EDITOR

A Day in the Life—Editing and Writing for the New Art Examiner
by Jan Estep—259

HENRY A. GIROUX
Heroin Chic, Trendy Aesthetics, and the Politics of Pathology
November 1997—265

DONALD KUSPIT
Art Is Dead—Long Live Aesthetic Management
April 1999—280

JAN ESTEP
Ha Ha Ha—Ray's a Laugh
September 1999—292

MICHELLE GRABNER
Test Family—Children in Contemporary Art
October 1999—299

DAN S. WANG
Kerry James Marshall—Agent of Change
February 2001—308

DAVID ROBBINS
Notes on a Midwest Makeover
May/June 2001—314

Biographies—*325*

Acknowledgments—*337*

FOREWORD

The New Art Examiner was Chicago's only successful art publication. It had a twenty-nine year run, starting in 1973 and ending in 2002, and since its founding by Jane Addams Allen and Derek Guthrie, no other art periodical has survived more than a few issues, or achieved any kind of critical mass of readership.

Yet once it closed, it quickly faded into obscurity among a new generation of artists. However, when Derek visited Chicago in 2008, a year after Jane's death, his mere return spurred a great homecoming and intense discussion about art publishing. A flurry of activity followed; a call for a new publication and a critical look at our current arts coverage, questioning if we were all guilty of what Derek called "boosterism." It was as if suddenly everyone remembered how fun it was to have heated arguments about art, entertaining romantic ideas about throwing critical punches and taking a beating for what you believed.

After his visit, Terri Griffith and I—both active participants in the next generation of online art commentator—were determined to create a simple anthology that would help a new audience understand this phenomena. Many of the magazine's supporters had made efforts to catalog the volumes, but were ultimately discouraged by copyright issues and the sheer magnitude of content. So we settled upon the idea of showcasing representative articles and spotlighting the editors. We chose this concise, "best of" format to catch the high points. It also released us from liability and intense research needed to document the twenty-nine year history of the *New Art Examiner.* Yet this format also omits the chronology, complexities, financials, scandals and personalities that accompany any art magazine. There is more to the story than is contained in this anthology, as Janet Koplos's introduction entitled "The Way We Were" indicates.

Determining even the most basic information—such as decipher-ing the organizational structure behind the magazine's masthead—was more complicated than expected. As we went through the broadsheet version of the first decade, and then the magazine format, it became ap-parent that the masthead was continually revised, and the structure of the organization was periodically overhauled. Titles and responsibilities changed on a yearly, and sometimes monthly, basis. No one served at the helm for more than three years after Derek and Jane left Chicago. In one volume, the title of "Managing Editor" suggested the person at the helm, and in other years, it was the person who ran the operations. There was a period when a new name appeared as the apparent person in charge, only to completely disappear a few issues later. And when the publication created bureaus in Philadelphia and other cities, the masthead became so vast it was difficult to fit all the information on a single page. However, we did find that there were, to a great degree, "eras" of the magazine. A new editor would take the *New Art Examiner* in a new direction. And we feel very fortunate that most of those editors were able to help us by not only writing a personal essay but by selecting articles that tell the story of the *New Art Examiner* in relation to the history of the Chicago art scene.

But note that the essays chosen merely show what was "fit to print" among the feature articles. In meeting the editors, we learned that the real excitement was behind the scenes, as the small publication stood up to the institutions and other powerful bodies. Young artists today have grown up in an era of decentralized media, but the *New Art Examiner* was central to the art scene. This all took place before the word "blog" was ever spoken, so the *New Art Examiner,* although it had an audience beyond the Midwest, was *the source* of news and information for Chi-cago artists. And although there was never an "online version" with a "comment" section, Jane and Derek printed every letter to the editor they received, making the discussion as public as possible, and ahead of their time in regards to un-moderated discourse.

So as the world moves forward, there is no way to simply "bring back" the *New Art Examiner* in the form it was. But this anthology illustrates the universals–great editing, great writing, a feisty staff who changed and adapted as circumstances dictated, and a publication that rolled with the times, and with the art of the times. With their passion, insight, and edi-torial brilliance, they turned a local magazine into a national institution.

THE

ESSENTIAL

NEW ART

EXAMINER

THE WAY WE WERE

Most of the good things in my professional life were not planned. I stumbled into or backed into some fabulous experiences, and certainly the *New Art Examiner* counts among the most rewarding. I was a graduate of the University of Minnesota School of Journalism and Mass Communication and was editing the Minnesota Crafts Council's *Craft Connection* and freelancing art reviews for the *Minneapolis Star* when my then-husband's job necessitated a move to the Chicago area. I said farewell in my last issue of *Craft Connection,* and before we actually left I got a call from Chicago: it was Derek Guthrie, inviting me to contribute to the *Examiner.* That he even saw the little newsprint bimonthly published by a crafts nonprofit organization says something about his interest, intensity and outreach.

I had seen the *Examiner* and felt thrilled to have that door opened for me. I thought everyone there was more sophisticated than I was. Always I was acutely conscious of being outside the city, exiled out in the suburbs, and it was even worse when we moved downstate, to Peoria. But Derek would call and talk about things. When I drove into the city I would go to the *Examiner* office to discuss the shows I should see. There or occasionally accompanying Derek to a nearby coffee shop, I would be introduced to other writers. I was always treated more seriously than I thought I deserved. I was less constantly involved with Jane until I was invited to edit an issue on crafts, which meant spending more time in Chicago. Both of them were completely receptive to my interest in contemporary crafts and my lack of interest in politics; you didn't have to pass a dogma test or a fashionability measure to write for the *Examiner.*

I had no contact at all with Chicago's power structure, and I wasn't even particularly aware at the time that the *Examiner* was subject to hostilities. I just saw and admired it as a feisty periodical reflecting an intellectually aware world that I admired and aspired to. If it was low-budget, well, I had worked on underground newspapers in college, which were no-budget. The kind of energy that now goes into Internet blogs and chats was then channeled into counter-culture broadsheets. The amazing thing is how long the *Examiner* survived.

My association was always with Derek and Jane, and the relationship grew more personal when they moved to Washington, D.C. I stayed with them once while attending a seminar on the language of craft. Then, after a gap of a few years (and moves to Atlanta and then Tokyo), when I was living in New York City and working at *Art in America,* I would regularly visit them in Washington. I even—turnabout!—edited Jane when she wrote a feature for *A.i.A.* on a junket to Indonesia. Busy with other things, I no longer closely followed the *Examiner* in its later incarnations, when they were not involved, although I still thought of it fondly.

From a professional perspective, I valued the *Examiner* because of its breadth of coverage both in terms of subjects and in terms of geography. Even before I came on the scene there was a ceramics editor. Derek, having lived in Cornwall where he knew Bernard Leach, was open to all mediums, and although he had been a painter, he didn't privilege it. The *Examiner* was richly and delightfully unpredictable—following the interests of its writers. Even more important is that it was not New York-based (for a time I thought of its attitude as "anything but New York" and since I am more interested in underdogs than top dogs, I appreciated that). The *Examiner* didn't just trade New York arrogance for Chicago hegemony but proved that art which repaid attention could be found anywhere, not just on the coasts, not just in the major cities, but anywhere. The regional reporting and especially the regional editions supported public awareness and critical dialogue in an amazing number of locations. (Contrast that to the emphasis on the biennial circuits in New York art magazines today, the traveling artists and curators who ship their art or their ideas from one interchangeable city to another.)

Jane and Derek were important to me personally as well—partly because Derek provided that lifeline between Peoria and Chicago and partly because he encouraged me to think ambitiously. I once described Jane as the most intellectual woman I knew, and her independence and integrity made her a model for me. I loved to watch the two of them in conversation on my visits to Washington. Derek was always excitable and Jane seemingly calm. When she talked, she would often close her eyes and speak slowly; when she paused, looking for a word, Derek would usually provide it and she would always pick up the word as if it had bubbled up from her own thoughts, and go on with her serene discussions. They talked about everything; their lives were a constant exchange of ideas, opinions, recommendation and recollections. Their intensity comes across in the pages of this anthology, and I hope their humor does as well. I remember driving to Milwaukee with Derek to see the Peter Voulkos retrospective and laughing so much at his vivid tale-telling that my face hurt!

This book will introduce the *NAE* to a new generation of Midwestern art aficionados, but it will also bring back fond or not-so-fond memories for those who participated in the art world that gave birth to the *Examiner* in 1973 and those who encountered it later. Its changes and growth show in the different accounts of the editors. The emphasis here is on its relationship to its home city. But there is more to the story. It's important to note that the *Examiner*'s "local" emphasis did not make it provincial. Derek is British and Jane had lived in Europe, so their knowledge level was high and the discussion sophisticated. Jane set a fine editorial standard, yet the *NAE* was quite accessible, receptive to new contributors and encouraging of fledgling efforts. The number of national art-world figures who were involved with the *Examiner* at one time or another is astonishing, and it's a story that remains to be told.

Another point that can't be elaborated in this book is the *Examiner*'s interest in the full spectrum of art production. One example is that reviewers were encouraged to list the price range of the works they wrote about. Another is that Derek and Jane moved to D.C. to more closely examine the politics and bureaucracy of the institutionalized art world of the National Endowment for the Arts, making the *NAE* the first publication to give skeptical, even adversarial coverage to the government's changing art policies. Those stories also await telling.

I applaud Kathryn Born and Terri Griffith's work to bring the *New Art Examiner* back into the conversation on art in Chicago. It will fortunately offer a starting point for my own efforts to tell the more detailed story based on interviews and archived documents. In the meantime, read this without fear or favor.

DEREK GUTHRIE and
JANE ALLEN FOUNDING EDITORS

1973–1982

INTRODUCTION

1

The publishing of the best of the *New Art Examiner* is an extraordinary event and bears witness to an important truth, which is that the community has the ultimate power to decide and acknowledge its own reference points of merit and appreciation. In this case the community is led by Kathryn Born and Terri Griffith, who, on hearing stories of the *New Art Examiner* that still linger, discovered with amazement that the copy published decades ago is still vital and has relevance. Their efforts persuaded Northern Illinois University Press to publish this book. This means that the *New Art Examiner* will not be airbrushed out of cultural history, which would have been its destiny if left to the not-so-tender mercies of the art institutions of Chicago.

In making this contribution to the book, my words may well be seen as polemical. If so, I beg the tolerance of the reader. To revisit a life inevitably leads to bitter as well as sweet recollections. I feel compelled to share my experience of Chicago and now am very content for history to follow its course.

2

Jane Addams Allen and I founded the *New Art Examiner* against great odds. It came into existence as an eight-page tabloid in October 1973 without money or sponsors, except for a few brave individuals, because of under-the-table censorship. We had been fired as art critics for the *Chicago Tribune,* without explanation but immediately after publishing a story on problems at the Illinois Arts Council. Soon thereafter, *ArtNews* killed our story on Chicago Imagists going to the São Paulo Bienal just days before printing. That came as a shock to us as previously the excited editor, Milton Esterow, made clear his very unusual decision to run it as a major article a month early.

The explanation is that Chicago's collector/dealer/trustee cabal got *ArtNews* to withdraw the article. The same article appeared in *Studio International* a short while later, suggesting that it was the singers and not the song that was the problem.

This was a disaster for us and made clear that we had no professional future in Chicago. Jane was not prepared to be shut out of her home town and said in simple, practical terms, "If we want to be art writers we are going to have to be our own publisher." A fearsome prospect. But Jane drew strength from the fighting spirit and wisdom of her great aunt, Jane Addams of Hull House, who said, "There is no point in going elsewhere to find greener pastures; what you have to do is to look after your own backyard, and if you do it well, eventually others will notice." I am aware as I write this introduction that linking the historical reality of Jane Addams to Jane Addams Allen will be seen by some as pretentious and opportunistic. Where but Chicago would one be castigated for feeling an obligation to continue the social responsibility of Jane Addams, who died the year Jane was born and for whom she was named? This identity shaped her life.

Jane believed in the best of American tradition. She played songs from Woody Guthrie and also believed in Horatio Alger's boot straps. Jane asked for no favors. She knew her Chicago history and, in detail, the writing of Upton Sinclair, Sinclair Lewis and Carl Sandburg, as well as William and Henry James and John Dewey.

3

Life for the *New Art Examiner* and life in the *New Art Examiner* was difficult; it existed in a state of near permanent crisis. Friends suggested that the *Examiner* should evoke its hidden heritage and seek support from Hull House and other organizations that carried Addams's name. Jane was adamant that she would not exploit her family heritage in this way. I think that Addams's name was never printed in the *New Art Examiner* except once in a slashing attack in the form of a letter to the editor saying that Jane was not fit to carry her own birth name. I saw Jane cry four times and that was the first. Bearing witness was a salutatory experience.

As a young person in Chicago, Jane saw in and around the family Addams's name evoked many times, often with missionary zeal that was lacking in substance. She saw grandstanding self-interest and political social maneuvering. Addams's high mindedness eventually got lost in the thicket of Illinois politics.

Jane, eschewing social work and politics, sought refuge in philosophy, literature and art, maintaining a thread of thinking rooted in American Pragmatic philosophy. Her education at the University of Chicago and the School of the Art Institute completed a home education gleaned informally by little and later not-so-little ears.

Donald Kuspit wrote in the March 2010 issue of *Proof / New Art Examiner,* which is emerging in the U.K., "aesthetic experience transforms alienation into freedom and adversaries into criticality." Those words were not written for Jane but they fit perfectly.

4

As art is a visual language, it can be made and used for all purposes. Whether the purpose at times restricts or damages creativity is an ongoing issue for artists and critics alike, and even art historians.

The *New Art Examiner* worked on the principle that vitality can only come when the writer is following his or her own basic response. Criticism has virtually died in the U.S.—a fact recognized by James Elkins of the School of the Art Institute in his pungent book *Whatever Happened to Art Criticism?* The question is accurate and very relevant; the answer is remote and complex.

In founding the *New Art Examiner* we learned by bitter experience that there is no freedom for criticism or criticality. We understood that critics do not have the last word, so we offered to all artists space to take on or reply to any critic's comments with which they disagreed. Sadly few did, which is an unfortunate testimony to the nature of the art scene in recent years. We believed in discussion.

Again Addams was a model. She made Hull House open to anarchists and Communists to have meetings and discussions, as she simply believed in the priority/prerogative of free speech. In so doing she became a hate figure to some and was categorized as one of the most dangerous people in the U.S. The *New Art Examiner* was treated likewise. We could never understand why some feel that responsible free speech is not only annoying but dangerous. We were encouraging people to have their own perceptions and develop them. Issues of culture are issues of belief, and art criticism at its best deals with that nature and perception of the human spirit as manifested by the artist.

5

The *New Art Examiner* was not a political agent in that it had no political agenda. In fact it was a curious mixture. We believed that intelligent discussion with respect for all participants was the only way toward a full culture.

Unfortunately this was not appreciated by the cultural hierarchy of Chicago, and the *Examiner* could not be accepted as a worthy effort or intelligent as it was not confined by the demands of political correctness—or, in this case, art-political correctness Chicago style.

I remain confused regarding political correctness in Chicago, as to my knowledge the last three governors have been indicted by the federal government and the chief of police as well; most people do not believe that the future offers much that is different from the past.

The fact that the art museums, collectors and art departments are based on insider trading is its own story, yet to be analyzed with authority and/or made common knowledge. Manipulated (art) markets make winners of those who have insider information and losers of those who do not. Museums have inside information at the disposal of the trustees, usually provided by curators and dealers. It may be argued that the art world is a disaster parallel to the political world.

6

There was a heady atmosphere in Chicago when the *New Art Examiner* came into existence. The Museum of Contemporary Art had appeared a few years before and was feeling its own freedom from perceived anti-Semitism that dominated the board at the Art Institute. Chicago always plays the race card.

The first issue of the *Examiner* appeared (in October 1973) with an Editorial borrowing the well-worn phrase, "Without Fear or Favor."

We were so naive in 1973, we believed that if we persevered and developed a professional publication and made it an open platform and if we attained a national reputation for Chicago, that eventually the hostility would cease. It did not. So finally, after seven years, we departed for Washington, D.C. We were without basic income or teaching jobs; even the odd lecture did not come our way. We felt blacklisted and it was claimed many times that we were troublemakers who did not know what we were talking about.

A hilarious and shameful incident happened when a colleague coming to work on the El saw an artist who had just received an ecstatic review in the *Examiner*. Asking what he thought of the review, she discovered rage and exasperation. He said "When are Jane and Derek going to understand they should not ruin artists' centers." He was seeking tenure at Circle campus and felt that our endorsement of his work could be damaging.

Realizing that no matter what we did, our interest, and therefore the *New Art Examiner*'s by default, would be consigned to the blacklist, to keep the *Examiner* alive we left Chicago. Jane and I were the only resources that the *Examiner* had available for necessary expansion and survival. Michael Bonesteel and Ann Lee Morgan and then Alice Thorson, with great professionalism and sensitivity, took over the Chicago office and in doing so inherited the existing budget while we pioneered the East Coast.

7

I think it is appropriate to say now that the *New Art Examiner* was a cooperative. That is, all staff members, whether editor or typesetter, were paid the same. We could hardly pay living wages, and we were all equally dependant on each other. There was eventually a small incremental increase in pay each year rewarding time in employment, as loyalty was our most precious resource.

The Washington experience probably lies outside the interest of this book. However Jane was offered a job on the *Washington Times,* a hated newspaper founded by the Rev. Moon. She ultimately gained considerable prestige and everybody fervently wished that she could work for the *Washington Post.* She won awards, a Pulitzer Prize nomination and an endorsement from Carter Brown, director of the National Gallery, in a public letter to the *Wall Street Journal.*

Again, as so often in the U.S., the ugly side of politics entered into the issue. When Patrick Buchanan, Nixon's presidential speechwriter and adviser and a well-known pundit, attacked artists as degenerates unable to aspire to the state culture like Michelangelo or Mozart, the culture wars had begun.

Jane quietly resigned and we briefly retired to Cornwall. Shortly afterward she gained a Renwick Fellowship from the Smithsonian Institution that brought us back to Washington, but that was cut short by illness. So we returned to Cornwall and Jane spent her last years immersed in the natural world. She faced with inspiring courage three operations for the cancer that eventually caused her death.

She comforted herself with another message learned from family history: "Virtue has to be its own reward."

8

I am so grateful to Jane, who taught me the better side of America, and for her profound reading of art. Her excellent prose, crafted with authority, inspired this clumsy wordsmith to an appreciation of the subtleties and workings of the English language.

Jane started life as an artist and usually drew in a sketch book the pictures and sculptures she was reviewing. This ability, of course, was part of her understanding of the visual image and essential to her writing.

It was her editing that was the cement in the early days; it gave the *New Art Examiner* its high standards. Her patience and commitment to freshman writers so often found original thoughts inside jumbled and mannered prose, and her caring for the budding writer helped many into clear articulation and confidence. So many writers have and will testify to finding their feet or wings in the *New Art Examiner,* and also to a freedom that was not possible elsewhere.

This attention to the individual and the fact that all were welcome were traditions that came from Hull House. Hull House was a refuge for intellectuals as well as stranded individuals, frequently immigrants, dealing unsuccessfully with the demands of the American melting pot and the lack of public health.

One of the most rewarding memories is meeting Peter Schjeldahl circa 1976. We were smarting that week as our friend and early supporter, the important art writer Jack Burnham, had just been asked by staff at the Museum of Contemporary Art why he associated with "that rag." Peter visited the office that week and he observed that there was an intelligence working in the *New Art Examiner* that he wanted to investigate.

9

Conversation with Peter was stimulating and satisfying, as we were recognized as professional. We all shared our observations and discussed the ways and means of the art world and our different tastes. The molding of taste by different backgrounds and circumstances interested us all.

Space does not permit more recall, but in conclusion I wish to leave with one more recollection, an observation made by a Chicagoan who now enjoys an elevated position in the New York art scene. Jerry Saltz, a canny professional, understands, if anyone does, the dynamic of power. He once wrote, "Jane and Derek are the only people I know who wrote their own tickets out of Chicago."

—Derek Guthrie

FRANK PANNIER

A PAINTER REVIEWS CHICAGO, PART I

Summer 1974

It is conceivable that in certain cities most of the major visual statements of the past twenty years have been made within the realms of "pictorial" or "prepresentational" art. However, for the most part, this is not the case in Chicago. Here, through the continual: re-hash of the same old tired "Dada Surrealist" concepts and also through the constant proliferation of simple-minded provincial aesthetics, most "pictorial" art is reduced to that infectious manifestation of visual gonorrhea most clearly typified by the "Hairy Who?" and its many offspring. There are, of course, a few "picture-painters" who are exceptions to this rule.

On the other hand, there is being produced in this city a large and rapidly growing body of fine and important "non-objective" art and despite a currently popular misconception, this work is not historically indebted to New York (or to any other American city). Its beginnings are on its own soil in the 1930s and 40s when major European artists began emigrating to the United States and a few of them (including, among others, Paul Wieghardt and László Moholy-Nagy) decided to settle in Chicago.

While teaching at the school of the Art Institute (and later in life at the Evanston Art Center School) Paul Wieghardt, although himself always a primarily "figurative" painter, introduced several generations of Chicago artists to the concepts that eventually led many of them to work in a totally "abstract" manner as early as the 1940s.

With the founding of the Institute of Design in the 1930s by several of Wieghardt's European colleagues (who had arrived in Chicago at earlier dates) many of the basic concepts and philosophical ideals of the displaced German Bauhaus were continued and further developed. Ex-Bauhaus faculty members (such as Georgy Kepes, Moholy-Nagy and Ludwig Mies van der Rohe) began an open dialogue with the existing art community in Chicago and an era of creative excitement began to unfold.

As a direct result of this cultural influx, Richard Koppe painted in Chicago (in approximately 1938) what are argued by some to be the first truly "abstract" or "non-objective" paintings done in the United States. These canvases which were known as the "chemical paintings" were done at a time when, for example, Adolph Gottlieb, Jackson Pollock, and Mark Rothko were still painting figuratively.

When I began my formal education in art at the University of Illinois at Navy Pier in September of 1964 (after having studied with Paul Wieghardt at the Evanston Art Center, which at the time was a somewhat serious school), I came to personally know Richard Koppe and later John Walley, both of whom had been closely associated with the Chicago "Bauhaus." It is through many conversations with these two men that I have been able to construct the preceding historically sketchy paragraphs.

There exists very little in the way of documentation of this period available for research and with the recent deaths of Richard Koppe and John Walley it is quite possible that a great deal of this information may disappear forever. Unless whatever was written by these men amid the others who shared this era can be located and then made public, we stand to lose a great portion of our cultural inheritance. This is inexcusable.

Today "non-objective" art is entering an amazingly beautiful and prolific period in this city. The work of almost two dozen artists (although infrequently allowed exhibition and almost totally ignored by most "critics") stands as Chicago's finest contribution to the visual arts to date. There currently exists the greatest number of artists manifesting the highest degrees of visual perception and aesthetic excellence in Chicago's history. The city is finally coming of age; a new period is beginning.

The work of Ted Argeropolos, Phil Berkman, Mike Crane, Carol Diehl, Tony Giliberto, Roland Ginzel, Barbara Housekeeper, Martin Hurtig, Michiko Itatani, Vera Klement, Mary Jo Marks, Corey Postiglione, Angels Ribe, Lawrence Soloman, Francesc Torres, Monika Wehrenberg, and (the hell with humility) myself, as well as several other artists, clearly shows the abundance of superior work being done in Chicago. (Footnote: Berkman, Crane, Ribe, and Torres are "conceptual" artists, and their inclusion in the category of non-objective art is my action solely.) But, for the most part, Chicago has traditionally chosen to ignore its best work by championing generation after generation of imitation "surrealism" or even worse.

The seemingly endless glorification of "Chicago funk art" (especially the "Hairy Who?" and its decedents), as well as the enthusiasm
shown for nearly all other visually or philosophically apologetic art: the
inexcusable near-deification of Don Baum, Edward Flood, Art Green,
June Leaf, Gladys Nilsson, James Nutt, Ed Paschke, Alice Shaddle, Karl
Wirsum, and so on; the almost fanatic acceptance of minor ceramics as
major sculptural statements; the lack of interest shown by the city's two
museums and most of its galleries in finding and exhibiting serious alternative art here (the most noticeable exceptions to this practice being the
N.A.M.E., Walter Kelly, and now Richard Gray Galleries), the frequently
published expressions of visual ignorance concerning all "non-pictorial"
art made by most "critics" (this applying in particular and most especially
to Franz Schulze), the highly unimportant pseudo art reviews of Harry
Bouras on W.F.M.T. radio; the remarkably half-assed attempt to fill the
void created in the art section of the Chicago Tribune by the dismissal
of Jane Allen and Derek Guthrie, by hiring Alan Artner for the position
and, in so doing, increasing the initial loss to an even greater degree;
the almost laughable appointment of Paula Prokopoff as Director of the
Evanston Art Center which has predictably resulted in the undermining,
undoing, and otherwise spoiling of most of the far sighted and excellent
work done by the former director William Fejer—all are unspeakably
revolting. But the last (and openly desperate) cries of this dynasty (as it
now begins to die) are finally being heard.

The old ideas that controlled the arts in this city are now starting to lose
hold and a new awareness of the true value of the artistic contribution
to society is being felt. A strong and positive action has begun against
the feudal lords of aesthetic provincialism in Chicago. A generation of
serious work and serious insight is beginning to substitute itself for the
out-house mentality that has so fouled our air these past years.

It is understood that at times art can be the possible reflection of an
occasional mirth which, in turn, may bring forth a degree of sophisticated laughter; but art is not the forum for the kinds of cheap and obvious visual jokes that have been allowed to thrive in Chicago. Most (if not
all) "important" art (regardless of its individual aesthetic philosophy) is
made in conjunction with those very few human qualities that transcend
a basic or excremental level of awareness.

In the past year N.A.M.E. Gallery has added itself to that rather short
list of alternative exhibition spaces that have existed from time to time
(such as "Live from Chicago," which was founded in approximately

August of 1968 by William Fejer with the aid of Ted Argeropolos, a few other artists, and myself, and lasted until January of 1970).

N.A.M.E. Gallery has shown a frequent tendency toward aesthetic bravery and profound statement. But for every new gallery such as this one, there also seem to come a couple (A.R.C. and Artemisia) whose obsession with the shape of their founders' genitals is so totally dominating a factor as to completely destroy their better sense of aesthetics—and, consequently, it is with great infrequency that quality work is shown in either of these galleries. The participating artists therein have not been chosen because of ability, and this is the real shame. Art is a universal that exists regardless of its maker's gender, and it is, perhaps, because of this understanding that most Chicago female artists of note are not connected with those establishments.

Another alternative exhibition space has made itself available in Chicago. The One Illinois Center building has provided such an extensive and varied list of shows that for all practical purposes it has, in fact, become more of a contemporary museum than is Doctor Prokopoff's little club house on Ontario Street (which fails to be very relevant not because of what it shows as much as because of what it does not show). All art does not have to be imported. There could be several major exhibitions of Chicago art held at the MCA each year (perhaps occupying some of the summer months).

While I do not wish to see my aesthetic ideals held universally as those of singular merit and do not wish to substitute a new control for the old, I would most strongly like to see a significant change. I would like to see the city open up very wide and become as mature and as versatile as is the large and heterogeneous body of art that is done here. It truly sickens me that Chicago's international image is the one fostered by Don Baum and presented to the world at the last São Paulo Bienal. There is a more complete picture which strongly deserves attention, Goddamnit.

FRANK PANNIER

A PAINTER REVIEWS CHICAGO, PART II

November 1974

Part I of "An Artist Reviews Chicago" was published in the Summer 1974 issue. It is an independent essay and does not represent editorial policy. We hope other articulate artists will speak out on matters that concern them. The *Examiner* is meant to be a forum for artists and thrives on controversy.

In the first part of this article I began discussing the state of affairs of the visual arts in Chicago. I wrote briefly about the art politics that have controlled this city for several decades, culminating in a well-nourished and masterfully engineered, self-proliferating, pseudo lunatic aesthetic which is evident to varying degrees in ninety-five percent of all work exhibited here.

In further synopsis of the first installment, I offer the following list of individuals, institutions, and other control forces most responsible for this situation.

Collections: Horowitz, Bergman, Shapiro. These chiefly Dada surrealist collections are extremely well-protected by big money and strong political actions such as starting a "Museum of Contemporary Art" and then staffing it with people who won't deviate too much from a central theme.

Collections: Adrian, Prokopoff. These chiefly "Chicago Imagist" collections are protected in value by the influential art occupations held by their owners.

Museums: The Art Institute of Chicago, Museum of Contemporary Art. These institutions simply do not exist at all as show cases for locally produced art that does not conform to the imagist or figurative norm. This year's "American Show" at the Art Institute for example suffered from a slant in favor of figurative art. The "Chicago and Vicinity Show" does not accept much in the way of large scale non-objective art. The Museum of Contemporary Art keeps showing us the "Hairy Who?" This season's installment is the São Paulo bon-bon cooked up by Don Baum.

Galleries: Phyllis Kind. This is, perhaps, the most influential gallery of the contemporary scene in Chicago and the home of the "Hairy Who?"

Critics: Harry Bouras, Franz Schulze. These "critics" are only interested in imagist art and art history.

Critics: Dennis Adrian, Harold Haydon. These critics often lack the courage to be forceful in their writing and work for reform. They are, however, the best and most perceptive available in the local established press.

Critics: Alan Artner, Nory Miller. These critics are total visual illiterates and have no business being art critics at all.

But the blame does not rest with these people alone. Many artists in this city find themselves too fat and content with their self-images of underground artistic stardom, or too overly concerned with divisionism along the lines of sex, age, different life styles, or perhaps, even color of hair, eyes, and skin to form truly professional alliances on the basis of aesthetic philosophy as have the "Chicago Five" (Ted Argeropolos, Lawrence Booth, Martin Hurtig, Vera Klement, and Lawrence Solomon), the Phil Berkman-Mike Crane-Angels Ribe-Francesc Torres conceptual group, "Artists Anonymous" (Carol Diehl, Tony Giliberto, Mary Jo Marks, Corey Postiglione, and myself), and even the good ole "Hairy Who?"

Most of these artists (with the obvious exception of conceptualists) are held together to varying degrees in small alliances and in larger multiple action groups by the fact that they are non-objective artists who cannot accept any further promotion of art as being the exclusive aesthetic in Chicago.

In fact the lack of professionalism beyond the studio practiced by most other artists in this city is probably the single most important factor responsible, until recently, for season after season of unimportant exhibitions of Chicago art and trite unimaginative art criticism. If more artists here were to take their profession more seriously and take some degree of initiative in the extra-studio mechanics which govern the political and economic aspects of art, then, perhaps, Chicago's "art scene" would truly match its potential. Behind the doors of studio after studio some of the most beautiful work that I have ever seen rests in storage.

Currently there is a small but growing number of artists living in Chicago who do not suffer the "closet syndrome." It is primarily through them and the efforts of the people who have worked with them that bang! (almost as if from nowhere) the 1973–74 season in Chicago was probably its most dynamic ever.

The "Chicago Five" held two large and important shows, one at the Time-Life building (Dec. '72–Jan. '73) and the other at One Illinois Center (March–April '73); Artemisia Gallery showed Vera Klement (Dec. '72–Jan. '73); A.R.C. Gallery showed Ellen Ferar (May '73) and Monika Wehrenberg (Oct.–Nov. '73); the Berkman-Crane Ribe-Torres conceptual group participated individually, collectively and in various combinations in over a dozen exhibitions and performances throughout the Chicago area as well as in Canada, New York, Spain and Brazil; Mary Jo Marks had a one-woman show at the State National Bank in Evanston (Oct.–Nov. '73), and along with Carol Diehl participated in the Evanston Art Festival Award Winners show (July '74); Tony Giliberto, Michiko Itatani and Corey Postiglione showed at N.A.M.E. Gallery (April–May '74); and the entire group "Artists Anonymous" came together in an exhibition at Richard Gray Gallery (June–July '74); Sarah Canright had a one-woman show at Phyllis Kind Gallery (Feb.–March '74); outside the city Roland Ginzel had a one-man show at the Madison Art Center (Feb.–March '74) and Ted Argeropolos and Martin Hurtig had one-man shows in New York.

If you don't know who these artists are and if you are not familiar with their work then I suggest that you become as informed as you possibly can and soon because there is a tradition here of excellence splitting from Chicago because no one cares.

The "Chicago Five" will again exhibit together in 1974–75, first at the University of Wisconsin at Milwaukee in Nov. 1974 and then at the Hyde Park Art Center in March 1975; "Artists Anonymous" will exhibit at One Illinois Center in April-May 1975; N.A.M.E., A.R.C., Artemisia and One and Two Illinois Center are planning full schedules for this season.

In addition John Doyle Gallery will soon occupy all three floors of his building and will continue to show excellent work from his exclusively east and west coast stable. Walter Kelly Gallery will move from Bissell

Street and will also expand. The *New Art Examiner* will increase in both coverage and content continuing to make the only serious effort to review what is happening in Chicago as well as giving a forum to artists here.

The M.C.A. has appointed a new curator, Ira Licht, who (because of his involvement with such artists as Carl Andre, Dan Flavin, Sol Lewitt and Robert Morris) at least, seems likely to inject a new point of view, possibly off-setting the current one at the museum, and by so doing make more plausible a dialogue between the museum and local artists. Perhaps he will find it within his power to at long last make that institution live up to its name. If the Evanston Art Center has seen the light, can't there also be a nice sunny day on Ontario Street soon?

As exciting as 1973–74 was for Chicago, 1974–75 seems to hold an even greater promise. N.A.M.E. Gallery has launched its new season with a very remarkable show "We Could Just Tune the Room" (Sept.-Oct. '74) with works by Barry Holden and Barry Foy. Had this show been held in California or New York, it could easily have been an *Artforum* or *Art in America* cover. But here it is ignored.

Currently both One & Two Illinois Center buildings are housing the large exhibition titled "40 Women" which although an extremely uneven show (ranging from the excellent to the idiotic) is an encouraging and necessary one, and except for its obvious exclusion of male artists, is the closest thing we will probably see to a true "Chicago and Vicinity Show" this season.

However, Chicago still faces many problems. Some people (although they now seem to be a dying breed) continue to champion art as a regional contrivance. My anger over this situation is not directed at the privately owned galleries or at those private interest individuals responsible for the never-ending promotion of traditional Chicago funk art. I understand and encourage an individual's complete freedom of choice in this, as well as in all other personal matters.

My indignation relates directly to the fact that non-surrealist art produced in Chicago is almost totally ignored by the "art establishment." This burns me because I feel (and, perhaps, a little too idealistically) that these people and institutions (critics and museums) should not be governed exclusively by private interest mentalities; that they should show art, and encourage art of every aesthetic persuasion as long as the work is excellent. If they cannot recognize excellence when it occurs in an aesthetic which is foreign to their tastes, then they (Alan Artner, Harry

Bouras, Stephen Prokopoff, Franz Schulze, James Speyer, et al) should either seek advice on the matter, or have the decency to publicly admit virtual incompetency in their "professions" and resign.

Chicago is all too vital and too important a city, in terms of the creative people who live and work here, to continue in the hands of the tired, bored, and unimaginative people who control the gears of the mechanism. Once the city was the "Hog Butcher to the world." Then, it became the "cultural butcher to the world." Now, perhaps we will see a city finally aware of its own cultural inheritance, facility, and output.

JANE ALLEN AND DEREK GUTHRIE

THE TRADITION

February 1975

The bulk of this article was printed in *Studio International* in December, 1973. An introduction has been added and some internal changes have been made to bring it up to date.

What happened to the "new regionalism" which seemed in 1973 to be the ground swell of the future? At that time critics and artists vied with each other in pouring scorn on internationalist, formalist New York art. It was a time for true grit, corn pone, anti intellectualism, nostalgia, ecology and a-political funk—a time of cozy artists' get-togethers where outsiders were treated with deliberate rudeness. William Wiley was number one hero and Jim Nutt the heir presumptive. When Chicago imagists were selected to represent the United States at the prestigious Sao Paolo Bienal, art observers here expected the international exhibition to be a springboard to future triumphs for our home-grown school.

Now a scant two years later, Chicago critics Franz Schulze and Alan Artner unhesitatingly label "Made in Chicago" the returned Sao Paolo show "final flowering" or "last gasp" according to their respective points of view. But both consign the Imagist movement per se to an early grave. What happened? The exhibition's notices abroad and in Washington were restrained but not *that* bad. The artists for the most part are still in their early thirties with their best work still ahead of them.

Our best guess is that the profound changes that have occurred in the world and national political situation have radically undermined the premises of Chicago funk art. It was a kind of art that flourished in the repressive atmosphere typical of the Nixon era. In the late 1960s and early '70s the key phrase was "doing your own thing" regardless of larger issues and there was a deep seated distrust of missionary zeal. Immediacies of time and place seemed infinitely more important than formal principles.

In the wake of Watergate and the world oil crisis, how remote that era now seems. Such an isolationist, inward turned position is no longer even possible, let alone desirable. There is a post-Watergate revulsion against hidden values and closet activities that extends even to art. For this reason it is unlikely that any younger artists will elect to follow the lead of the Hairy Who? and post-Hairy Who? artists. Their achievement stands, but the spirit that animated their activity has disappeared. It has now become history to be analyzed and evaluated.

One interpretation of the Chicago choice for Sao Paolo was that the National Collection of Fine Arts, the Smithsonian agency charged with the task of organizing U.S. overseas exhibitions, took to heart John Canaday's suggestion that the agency tailor overseas shows to their foreign locale. For a number of reasons the choice of Chicago artists for the Brazilian exhibition seemed an apt one.

Sao Paolo, a sprawling industrial city, has been called, the "Chicago of South America," and by coincidence is Chicago's "sister city" in the Partnership for the Americas program. Like Chicago it is a tough bourgeois town of unlimited cultural ambition combined with an ambivalent attitude towards its resident artists. According to its first catalogue: the Bienal, founded in 1951 by one of the city's major industrialists, "Ciccillo" Matarazzo, was designed ". . . to place Brazil modern art not just in a mere confrontation, but in a lively contact with the art of the rest of the world, while at the same time an attempt would be made to conquer for Sao Paolo the position of a world art center." The first task was carried out successfully. Brilliant exhibitions in early Bienals of such artists as Picasso, Moore, Chagall, Calder, Pollock and Morandi attracted visitors from all over the world. Important developments in contemporary art appeared in Sao Paolo quickly after their inception so that native artists had firsthand knowledge of current art trends. Yet in spite of this exposure to contemporary art, no Brazilian artist to date has achieved a sizeable international reputation and Sao Paolo remains very much of a provincial center. Observers have noted that the most enthusiastic response of Sao Paolo art patrons is still given to Brazilian naives who characteristically remain indifferent to international trends.

If Matarazzo's ambition was to stimulate Brazilian artists to creative independence his strategy of importing the best failed.

The parallel with the past temper of Chicago is striking. For many years the guiding principle of Chicago's cultural leaders also seemed to be "import the best," be it a 70 foot Chagall for the First National Bank Plaza or the world's largest Picasso for its Civic Center. Rich Chicagoans went first to Europe and then to New York to obtain the art that adorned their North Shore mansions. A book on culture in Chicago written in 1953 reported that Knoedler and other galleries had closed their Chicago branches after World War II when they discovered they sold roughly four times more paintings to Chicagoans for Chicago collections out of New York than out of Chicago even though similar works were available in both places. By 1955 few galleries remained and with one or two exceptions those that did stay showed only out of town works. Artists left Chicago in droves—among others, Leon Golub, Claes Oldenburg, Robert Indiana, Robert Natkin, Jack Beale, Peter Holbrook and John Chamberlain. Literally the only outlets for Chicago artists during the 50s and most of the 60s were art centers, artist-sponsored exhibitions (of which there were many) and the annual over-crowded "Chicago and Vicinity" show at the Art Institute.

That situation has radically changed. There are now at least a dozen reputable galleries clustered near Ontario Street and Michigan Ave, and most show Chicago work regularly. A good part of the credit for the renewed confidence in local talent must go to the artists going to Sao Paolo and to their champion, Don Baum. Eschewing me-tooism, the group, roughly centered around the Hyde Park Art Center which first exhibited their works, evolved a philosophy which ran directly counter to New York mainstream assumptions of what constituted "significant" high art.

The turning point came when in 1969 Baum turned the lower gallery of Chicago's Museum of Contemporary Art into a raunchy basement environment and there, amid old furniture and coal stoves, hung works by 28 artists including 11 of the 12 who went to Sao Paolo and two elderly Chicago natives—Pauline Simon and Joseph E. Yoakum. Titled "Don Baum says, 'Chicago needs famous artists,'" the show and its attendant publicity spoofed all the current requisites for contemporary museum art—the works were small, full of literary subject matter and local color (in both senses of the word), and stacked three and four high on the walls. In effect, Baum and company caught the attention of Chicago patrons by thumbing their collective nose at New York and all it stands for. Assiduously avoiding the journals, they mined local sources and traditions. Instead of competing with local naive artists, they incorporated them into the movement.

There was a good deal of merit in sending a show of this kind to the international Bienal. For it is directly relevant to one of the most chronic cultural problems of the twentieth century—that of the conflict between modernity and regional cultural traditions. Any artist today must decide what he will do about Picasso, about Duchamp, about Pollock, about Oldenburg, even if his decision is to ignore them. But if an artist comes from a third world nation and must also contend with a non-western artistic traditions, his task of finding an identity as a contemporary artist is that much harder. By sending to Sao Paolo a group of United States artists who set local taste above international trends, the Smithsonian clearly gave encouragement to many artists and critics attempting to foster regional styles within their own countries.

The choice of Chicago for Sao Paolo also solved a thorny diplomatic problem. It may well have been an attempt on the part of the State Department to evade the boycotts that have plagued abortive U.S. entries to the past two Bienals. In 1969 the entry arranged by György Kepes, Director of the M.I.T. Center for Advanced Visual Studies was cancelled because of mass defections by exhibiting artists who withdrew their work in a general protest against political repression by the Brazilian government to participating countries not to send "immoral or subversive works" to the Bienal.

In 1971 entry was again cancelled, ostensibly for lack of funds, but clearly in part because the State Department feared a repetition of the 1969 fiasco. In fact when Argentinean Jorge Glusberg attempted to include U.S. artists in a special exhibition, "Art as Idea," planned for the 1971 Bienal, he ran into further protest and was ultimately forced to abandon the plan.

Although the Brazilians have apparently withdrawn the self-censorship request to participating countries, nothing has happened in Brazil that would suggest a more enlightened or more democratic posture. On the contrary, the government in 1972 consolidated its dictatorial powers by incorporating into its constitution a series of institutional acts that confer on the President the legal right to exile persons considered to be a threat to national security, to suspend elections indefinitely, to recess the congress, to rescind any elected official's mandate, and to suspend a person's political rights for periods of up to ten years. The current state of affairs in Brazil reads very much like that of the unnamed South American country which is the subject of Costa Gravas' film, *State of Siege*.

In view of the continuing repression, a group of dissident Latin American artists living in New York formed an organization called "Contra Bienal" the main purpose of which was to disseminate material discouraging artists from participating. As a result of this and other factors, many artists in New York and California even had they been asked to enter the Sao Paolo would have refused.

The world situation is such, in fact, that the whole idea of international exhibitions has been challenged by artists. The most important show of them all, the Venice Biennale, was virtually annihilated by the spirit of protest until it was resuscitated this summer under the title, "Venice Biennale for a Democratic and Anti-fascist Culture" and was devoted to workshops on topical subjects including the repression of Chilean artists.

By contrast there was virtually no likelihood of a Chicago protest. The artists selected for the exhibition are little given to grand gestures and even less to mixing politics with art. (As one painter put it, "Manifestoes seem to us to be in poor taste.") Perhaps, the truth is that artists who matured in Chicago during the 1960s have an ingrained sense of the uselessness of public political or cultural protest. Even when it was announced that "Made in Chicago" would go to fascist Chile, only a few of the artists raised objections and none withdrew their work.

If there is protest in their art, it exists only as an ambiguous undercurrent. In fact there is an esoteric quality to the art—a penchant for in-jokes, for obscure references, for double meanings—all time-honored tactics of people who find themselves in an alien situation or who wish to defend themselves against an alien audience. These strategies may also have found a response in Sao Paolo.

Perhaps, the most significant aspect of the Sao Paolo choice, however, was the fresh evidence it afforded of a new temper affecting artists, museums, and schools as well as the N.C.F.A. Hilton Kramer and other critics have commented at length on the growing decentralization of democratization of the national art scene but an attendant phenomenon almost escaped notice—a recrudescence of the New York-baiting, regionalist nostalgia of the thirties. Like the earlier regionalism, the *bete noire* of the new movement is the effete and intellectual east with its powerful financial and institutional interests, i.e. New York. But where painters of the thirties fixed upon the homely virtues and honest toil of the American farmer and working man as their subject; the new regionalists tend to fasten on vanishing species—victims of the post-industrial world, whether urban artifacts, flora or fauna.

In the case of Chicago it is the urban subcultures of the first half of the 20th century and their living remnants that attracted the artists' attention. If you have ever lived in a unrenewed section of a large city—a neighborhood of homes sporting bay windows with ornamental shades partially obscuring enormous lamps; of old dime stores, cigar stores, lingerie shops, B movie houses, and girlie shows—then you may have some concept of the urban nostalgia animating the Chicago artists going to Sao Paolo. Nostalgia—because such neighborhoods in Chicago are fast falling victim to the squeeze between the expanding black ghetto on the one hand and high class urban renewal (to contain the ghetto) on the other.

What gives Chicago Imagist art its particular flavor is its mix of naive, low-pop and ethnological art sources for imagery and style. This connoisseurship of the vernacular is the twelve artists' most important common characteristic. Their personal collections include such diverse items as children's illustrations; tattoo designs; pinball machines; comic books; picture postcards; ads of treatments for hemorrhoids, varicose veins and unwanted hair; toys; dolls; game boards; circus, striptease and penny arcade posters; naive art; and fine examples of African, American Indian and Pre-Columbian art. Some of these collections become environmental works of art in themselves. In *Fantastic Images, Chicago Art Since 1945* (the most authoritative book on Chicago art after World War II) the author, Franz Schulze states that Karl Wirsum's *magnum opus* may have been his house in Chicago, "an environment affectionately heaped with memorabilia of 1930s lower class America." Out of sensitivity to the formal and informal values of these "trash treasures" came a coherent regional style which lies somewhere in the overlap between the primitive, the naive and popular kitsch: Despite its gritty humor it expresses an attachment to a vanishing way of life.

Almost as important as urban nostalgia in determining the character of the works which went to Sao Paolo was the element of fantasy, particularly fantasy which revolves around sexual themes. In contrast to California regionalist art which is strong on ecology, the Chicago works are piquantly redolent of the great indoors. From the blatant sexuality of Nutt's and Wirsum's figures to the restrained suggestiveness of Christina Ramberg's close-ups of corsets; from the openly (if sadly) provocative Paschke strippers to the covertly Freudian, "Disasters" of Roger Brown, a basic premise for the mix of images in the majority of these works is the primacy of the sexual imagination.

There is nothing obviously regional about that premise, unless of course one takes the fact that *Playboy* too originated in the windy city as proof positive that Chicago is a hot bed of cultural aphrodisia. (As a matter of interest, Kerig Pope, one of the artists who went to Sao Paolo, is the assistant art director of *Playboy* and the magazine regularly draws on this group for illustrations.) In turning to fantasy, however, the artists draw on a long history of Chicago attachment to Surrealism. Ever since the war Chicago patrons and artists have displayed a decided partiality for painters such as Matta, Bacon, Tanguy, Ernst, Klee, Giacometti and particularly Dubuffet. When the latter came here in 1951 for the opening of his exhibition at the Art Institute and delivered his lecture "Anticultural Positions" to a small but enthusiastic audience, the ground had already been well prepared to receive his brand of post-war Surrealism: *art brut.*

One can see the influence of Dubuffet's work on three generations of Chicago painters from the encrusted agonized figures of Leon Golub to the amoeboid fantasies of Gladys Nilsson. But it was his philosophy which most stirred Chicago artists. Both their predilection for painful subjects and their enthusiasm for finding content and artistic values in places and objects usually considered unartistic may be traced to Dubuffet who believed that ". . . the function of the artist is to enlarge the conquest and annexation of worlds hostile to man."

All three generations of Chicago artists are represented in the Sao Paolo show, although the emphasis is overwhelmingly on the third. H.C. Westermann, 51, is the only artist in the exhibition who belongs chronologically with the first post-war generation—a group that also included Leon Golub, Cosmo Campoli and George Cohen. (It was primarily these four who were collectively dubbed "The Monster School" for their tormented depictions of man in the "New Images of Man" exhibition curated by Peter Selz in 1959 for the Museum of Modern Art.) An enigmatic and independent personality, Westermann combines an affection for middle and lower class Americana, past and present, with a cheerfully sardonic view of the mysteries of life, death and procreation. In his case one feels that the prevailing Chicago currents of Surrealism were a liberating force which gave him the confidence to use his gifts as a craftsman in the service of his imagination. For example, his 1957 "Mad House" (included in the show) binds together the most diverse elements in a tour-de-force of woodworking, reminiscent of early American cottage craft cabinetry.

Although Westermann's work received almost immediate recognition in Chicago for its originality and expressive power, his style became a decisive force in Chicago only towards the middle of the 1960s, when it came to the attention of the future "Hairy Who?". James Nutt came into close contact with Westermann's work while assisting in the Frumkin Gallery in 1965–66, the year before the first "Hairy Who?" exhibition, and was immediately struck by its particular blend of elements—its mixture of fantasy and earthy humor; its low pop sources; and its craftsmanlike approach.

Kerig Pope and Ray Yoshida represent the second post-war generation—a much more amorphous grouping than the first and third. Influenced by the more painterly forms of Surrealism, Pope paints gentle, landscape-based fantasies such as his "Two Infants observing Nature" and "Garden of Exhausted Fireworks" in the Sao Paolo show, drawing from such diverse sources as Edwardian children's illustrations, pre-war comics and Chinese landscape paintings. Yoshida paints strangely textured interiors such as "Green Thumpin." Aside from his painting he has been a teacher at the Art Institute for many years; and his influence on students has been a vital factor in keeping the current Chicago aesthetic alive among younger artists of the city.

The rest of "Made in Chicago" is given over to "Hairy Who?" and post-"Hairy Who?" artists. About ten years ago a new spirit began to manifest itself among students at the Art Institute. Where the artists of the "monster school" had been profoundly serious about the condition of man and the second generation paid at least lip service to the ideal of universalism, the new generation went camp. They adopted humor as their weapon and made fun of the ideals of their elders. They regarded manifestoes as poor taste, aesthetics as cant, and art history as beside the point. They were playful and extravagant in dress, paying pennies at the local Salvation Army stores for outrageous garments.

The young artists found a godfather and culture hero in Cliff Westermann. Just as important they found a mentor and impresario in Don Baum, then Director of Exhibitions at the Hyde Park Art Center, a small store front gallery and school on Chicago's south side. In a sense "Made in Chicago" is a Hyde Park Art Center show not only because Baum is curator, but because the majority of the artists made their debut there; and their style is closely associated with the Center. It was Baum, the contemporary of Cohen, Golub, Campoli and Westermann, who saw the connection between the old and new Chicago styles and who gave encouragement and weight to the young artists' efforts to break out on their own. And one suspects that it was Baum who first saw in the young artists a latter-day manifestation of Dubuffet's exploring spirit.

In the first "Hairy Who?" show in 1966, which introduced the work of Karl Wirsum, James Nutt, Gladys Nilsson and three others, the seeds sown by Westermann came to fruition. Wirsum's and Nutt's paintings had the supersmooth paint surface and careful textures of the naive artist; the loose and unsettling graphic style of graffiti and the hard-edged sado-masochism of Dick Tracy. Add to this mix, verbal and visual puns, a strong sense of the decorative and the odd amputation or two and you have some idea of the new Chicago art. It was cruel, gritty, crass, nostalgic and somehow fulfilled the image of Chicago as immortalized by Nelson Algren, Al Capone and Mayor Daley. To the surprise of "The Hairy Who?", Chicago patrons liked it!

Following on the heels of the success of the "Hairy Who?" other groups with similar interests showed at the Art Center. While none had the verve and *Chutzpah* of the trail blazers each exhibition contained a few artists who attracted gallery and critical attention. Paschke and Flood from the "Nonplussed Some;" Brown, Hanson and Ramberg from "The False Image" and Barbara Rossi from "Marriage Chicago Style."

Gradually the fame of the Hyde Park Art Center and the kind of art it was sponsoring began to attract national attention. Besides the "Famous Artists" show in 1969 a show of the "Hairy Who?" was mounted in the Corcoran Gallery of Art in Washington and the artists appeared en masse in "The Spirit of the Comics" exhibition in Philadelphia.

The 1973 N.C.F.A. choice for the Sao Paolo Bienal would seem to indicate that the Chicago art had definitively arrived. But where? The new regionalism was not a style but a pervasive state of mind that accommodated many styles. In its broadest sense it was a world phenomenon as well as an American phenomenon, born of disillusionment with the search for universal values and a profound distrust of missionary zeal. It was a "do your own thing" and "dig in your own garden" state of mind which said that immediate time and place are more important than formal principles. John Canaday reflected the spirit of this regionalism when he said that N.C.F.A. should tailor its overseas exhibits to suit the locale. The Chicago artists were regionalist in their indifference to the Brazilian political situation. And in the art world, the new Chicago school was only one of many assaults on the assumptions of the New York mainstream. For example, California artists living in and around

Mill Valley and Sacramento shared with the Chicago group a determination to mine local resources and reflect local color; and a profound distaste for the elitist intellectual atmosphere of the New York art world. (Interestingly enough James Nutt, Gladys Nilsson and Karl Wirsum all moved to Sacramento.) No doubt other groups with similar ideas were to be found in Texas, in Minneapolis, in St. Louis.

The regionalist state of mind in Chicago, however, resulted in a very particular product with its own particular strengths and weaknesses. At best it is strong, crackling and gutsy with a fine decorative feel for materials and color, and a grassroots quality which is appealing. In "Made in Chicago" Nutt's "Nose Jam"; Paschke's "Heavy Shoes"; Nilsson's "Very Worldly" and "Recycling Black-veenus Rabbit"; and almost all of the Westermanns have these qualities. But at its worst Chicago art is precious, campy, ingrown, and suffers from a myopic and defensive view of art. The irony of Dubuffet's influence is that with each succeeding generation, the area of conquest has been narrowed rather than enlarged. Two of the youngest painters going to Sao Paolo—Ramberg and Hanson—were almost exclusively concerned with slightly out of date, Midwest, lower middle class taste. The Acid sentimentality of Hanson's "Country Club Dance" and "Yellow Lily" suggest that he fell into the trap of using Dubuffet's invitation to annex hostile worlds as an excuse to play taste games.

Critics have differed widely in their estimation of the "Hairy Who?" and post-"Hairy Who?" art that makes up the bulk of this exhibition. In his review of the "Chicago Imagist" exhibit mounted in 1972 by the Museum of Contemporary Art, Lawrence Alloway praised their vitality and lively use of color. Amy Goldin, on the other hand, has slightingly referred to the new Chicago style as "greasy kid stuff." Chicago critics are equally divided. Harold Haydon has bitingly attacked the campiness and ersatz naïveté of the post "Hairy Who?". Franz Schulze was a powerful booster but in his review of the return show speaks of a "Final Flowering." However, Whitney Halstead (who wrote the catalogue to "Made in Chicago") feels that Chicago Imagists are a significant new force on the national art scene.

There is no question that as a strategy and state of mind, the brand of regionalism fostered by Hyde Park Art Center in the late 1960s was brilliantly successful in giving Chicago artists increased confidence and a sense of identity. But as a style and a school of the 1970s it suffered from Chicago's perennial blight—the exodus of the strongest artists from the city. H.C. Westermann has long since settled in Connecticut. Nutt, Nilsson and Wirsum have moved to Sacramento, and one can see evidences in their most recent work that they are moving steadily away from the local references that abounded in the first "Hairy Who?" show. What remains of their gutsy spirit in Chicago are memories of the heyday of the Hyde Park Art Center and a jealously guarded tradition that has become a strait jacket for younger artists.

The evidence is that Chicago no longer needs a single all-pervading style and school to inspire collectors and critics with confidence in local art. But even in a re-evaluation of the Imagists' position, we shouldn't forget that they were the trail blazers in a city where art was something you went out of town to find.

MICHAEL RABIGER

LETTER TO ASPIRING FILMMAKERS

March 1976

The last decade has seen a tremendous growth of film study. Much of it is half-baked, but it's sure that "the 20th century art form" is catching on. Some declare cynically that interest in film is related to the decline in literacy. Be that as it may, it seems that film has become the fashionable means towards self-discovery and self-expression.

To develop a critical response is relatively easy, but to then meet one's own expectations as a film maker is a very different matter. Learning to use film means also learning how one perceives, how one's consciousness actually works.

If you set about trying to be a film maker there are several roads to becoming professionally competent. You can sweep floors in a film company and learn apprentice fashion. Few such chances exist. You can buy your own equipment and learn out of books. It's equally safe to buy your own aircraft and fly by printed instructions. The expensive independent film-makers' packages of used equipment always for sale are mute testimony to many a lost shirt. Or you could take courses. That costs money, so things are getting serious. What's it to be *for*? Maybe you'll shelve that question, and figure out what to do with your skills when you have them.

If you live in the big city, you'll probably have two kinds of choice; technical film school or arty film school. The former is meant to put you on the lower rungs of a long ladder leading (for those with stamina and some flair) to the film industry. This means films for TV, industrial films, educational or advertising films, and beyond these possibly unexciting prospects, there is the Golden Fleece itself, the impossible dream you hardly dare divulge even to your best friend—Hollywood, Calif.

Taking that direction is a long stony road. It offers uncertainty and threatens to subject you to grey disciplines and greyer personalities. Understandably, those emerging from the educational treadmill are in no mood for more "discipline." They crave an atmosphere that promises to gratify their ideals and longing for individuality. Many aspiring film makers (young ones in particular) who don't immediately have to support themselves, find what they know about art school much more attractive than what they know about the craft oriented school, which carries sordid trade and commerce associations.

Unfortunately, important decisions are often made with only such stereotypes available. It would be better if you could sit through a day of material produced by students of the two different kinds of school—a typical day's screening, let us say.

The craft school films may strike you at first as pedestrian, juvenile in conception, or over-earnest. Often they will be deficient in their story line, or mistaken in conception so that they are abstruse. In their failings they are easy to disparage, yet it is unusual that one does not get a feeling about the makers. Most of these films succeed in some way, somewhere, and almost all communicate human concerns and evoke feelings. As the students become more advanced, one sees an increasing mastery of the means and tools of the cinema—the use of light, the use of the camera, of subject matter and actors, of composition, of the elements and rhythms of sound and of visual rhythm in editing.

A day's footage in a fine art film school cannot but strike you differently. Concentrating heavily upon visuals and dense, repetitive visual techniques, the footage by comparison seems abstracted, tells no story but is often attractively evocative by moments. The emphasis is upon color, form, movement and non representational imagery. When one does discern what the images are (a bicycle hub? A bathtub drain?) they seem to be used in an evanescent symbolical way which leads the mind outwards and then leaves it, lost. A day of such film will probably leave you bewildered and feeling that you have to learn much about art history and experimental film philosophy before you understand what the film makers said about their work. You might also feel that though the makers *spoke* of the feelings that motivated their works, the works themselves merged into an impersonal stream of flashing light which refused to yield up either the individuality of the makers nor the feelings they saw incorporated into their films. You would probably conclude that there were some fairly massive rites of passage before you could *see* in the way the initiates saw. You might find the emphasis on personal values, the unwillingness to pass value judgments, and the atmosphere of tolerance, of sincerity and genuine desire to strike in new directions, and the atmosphere of avant garde research all very attractive.

Whatever you chose as a film school now would depend on whom you identified with and what kind of work you wanted to produce. Even if you felt uncertain about experimental film, you know that ultimately you would be licensed to teach as a consolation prize if you don't make it to artistic stardom.

However, in examining the activities and output of the fine art film school, you might be forgiven for seeing them some sort of Hassidim of the film world, perpetuating their own mysterious and traditional values and denying the existence all around them of the State of Israel. Something is very wrong, and it isn't just a Chicago problem, or even just an American problem—though the enormous wealth and cultural clout of US institutions makes the situation more pronounced. To put it baldly, large numbers of people are being supported to make large numbers of films that no one likes. Although their efforts are intellectually, democratically, morally and aesthetically defensible in all kinds of ways, the fact is that they connect with almost nobody outside the sect. Even the Midwest Film Center, which is affiliated to the Art Institute Film School, avoids so-called experimental cinema because of its poor drawing power. Yet personal appearances by the charismatic Brakhage and other independent film makers pull in large audiences of young people.

Perhaps the most striking difference between the two kinds of film sensibility is the very different way that the makers' egos are at work. The craftsman type regards himself as a necessary link in a process of communication. He is someone using his skill and his sense of values to put an audience in touch with the essence of a story or (in documentary) with an actuality. If in doing it successfully people start to call him (or her, of course) an artist, then he is pleased and flattered. Often he will reply by paying tribute to those who worked with him in his collaborative medium.

The independent/experimental film maker however seems to start off with the conviction that, simply by having chosen to be, he *is* an artist. The self concept he works toward comes straight out of a 19th century mold. He is an individual who can only work alone and in a sort of purified seclusion; he cannot compromise his vision by partnership or unenlightened patronage; he carries the torch of civilization but expects in his lifetime to be ignored or rejected.

The concept of the artist as an autonomous being may work for writing, painting and sculpture, but breaks down when it comes to practicing in theater, music and dance, all of which are collaborative media. Most filming, by the nature of the equipment and the subject matter, is also a collaborative medium.

Why then do art school films always seem to be made amateurishly by one person? The answer appears very simple: they are dominated by people whose minds are conditioned to think that the highest form of visual art is painting, so that painting history and painterly values form the choices and assumptions of those who teach. The result is an unerring concentration on what is familiar (color, form, composition, texture, symbolism etc.) and an unerring avoidance of everything that isn't covered by the traditions. This runs up a formidable list of no-nos to the unwitting film maker who just blew in off the street, fresh from a background of American and European cinema. Hardly a whiff of that, unless it's sanctified and toothless from age. Anything narrative is out (though film, proceeding linearly through time is unavoidably telling a story, however haphazard); boring old representative images are out unless you can fuzz them around and make them obscure; sound will only be tolerated as a menial supportive element. If you want to be noticed you'll have to dream up a technique no-one else has been able to think of—perhaps a permutation of scratching, flickering, dyeing and multiple printing on the optical printer.

Ultimately, the significance of the film has to be decoded by its maker, so that the film functions not as something complete in itself, but more as an organ of publicity for its maker. It is the means of illustrating what would otherwise be a less commanding verbal presentation of self. Here the artist joins the showman in self-importantly indulging that particularly American love of undiscriminating self-exposure. It's a real shock to hear young and inexperienced people talking about their artistic odyssey like visiting celebrities.

How experimental are the experimentalists? Those I have seen (and I too crave alternatives to standard fare) may intend an experimental philosophy, but the execution is usually wretchedly inadequate. To experiment, you must first master what exists before declaring you will extend it. Film students, at the Art Institute regularly prospect for basic skills in other schools, because the Art Institute has yet to realize that significant film can only be obtained through mastery of the tools, and mastery of the aesthetic disciplines that direct the use of those tools. This is not to suggest that the Art Institute alone suffers from this attitude. Independents from elsewhere show a similar disregard for skills implicit in what, passively, they take for granted in others' work, and omit in their own. To lack mastery of the medium is to produce something random—and randomness is the prevailing impression.

The most depressing thing is that large numbers of agreeable young people seem to feel no real interest or responsibility for the world around them, and regard art as a privileged and apolitical therapeutic activity. Film makers intent on generating a separatist language, who look inward at self and patterns of self, who abandon even the idea of reaching out to an audience are out of touch with what art is all about—changing people by communicating something important.

DEAR PROFESSION OF ART WRITING

June 1977

My crummy benefactor, how can I not be grateful?
For 12 years fount of my sustenance, social identity,
claim to fame,
without you where would I be today?
Teaching?
Teaching what? I don't know anything
but you, Profession of Art Writing.
Would I be more a poet than I've become?
Maybe, but at what cost? That much closer
to complete physical, and psychic collapse, or beyond it already,
an unhappy memory, another scalp
on the belt of drug abuse and cultural devastation,
gibbering in some Rocky Mountain ashram,
understood to have had a good mind, some adventures,
a wad of lyrics poignant arid obscure . . .
I would not at any rate be sitting here
smugly, at this desk, this typewriter,
as baby daughter capers in next room
and cat suns on day bed. A picture of total contentment.
I must be a jerk not to regard you more highly;
Profession of Art Writing, my lucky charm.

Or perhaps like a clumsy teenage suitor shocked
to have conquered, I find you hard to "respect."
You did favor me awfully readily.

A rhetorical knack—what else did I bring to you?
Abysmal ignorance, slovenly habits of thought, star-struck
narcissism, a starved and sneaky ego . . .
Yet success came my way in cozy degree.
I get top dollar when I'm nervy enough to demand it.
I get frequent opportunities to decline,
with secret glee, offers to write or speak.
Still, I have craved in vain the approval of my betters,
the ambitious toilers, the scholars, the committed,
from whose difficult harvests I gleaned at random
whatever I've provided of food to the mind.

Not that I lose any sleep over that. What's ghastly
is that on occasion I mistook my hand-me-down taste
for the light of election, and poured ink on the worthy.
I still blush, hotly, for those occasions,
yearning for a large bomb to fall directly on my head.
Like that supercilious dismissal of William Baziotes—horrible!
And Laszlo Moholy-Nagy, for God's sake, I patronized
your venerable ghost! And Susan Crile, estimable painter,
what full moon was shining when I sat down to review you?
Also Stanford University, and redoubtable scholar Albert Elsen;
I sneered at your splendid museum,
behaving just like a paranoid's dream of a New York chauvinist,
oh shame! James Brooks, you didn't complain
those years ago, but even today you could flay me with a look.
Jim Dine, how could I, and Joan Snyder, how could I
denigrate your indubitable value in the (unpronounced) name
of (non-existent) standards of acceptability?
Richard Hamilton, where did I get off
welcoming you to America in that disgraceful fashion?
And Gio Pomodoro, though you never will be to my taste,
that was no excuse for behaving like a fat-mouthed provincial!
All these atrocities in the Sunday Times, each in a million copies
just whizzing off the presses, fanning out over the land,
alighting in libraries—*microfilm*, oh God!!!—
unkillable and infamous words! Just let me
take this knife and . . .

But no. (Puts knife back in drawer and closes it.)
Already I feel a little better . . .
So back to you, Profession of Art Writing,
whose fool I've been: who needs you anyhow?
What loosens the purse strings of the journalism business
to finance the bad conscience of louts like me?
The imperatives of commerce, is it?
Capitalism? The art-buck megalith and entertainment combine?
Are we all just lackeys?
Seemingly so. But then who isn't, here and now?
(If we aren't bourgeois, then what the hell are we?
as James Schuyler once said something like.)
But is the artist, for instance, a lackey,
upon whose peculiar habits the whole industry turns?
The artist, our dream god or goddess of freedom,
free to act crazy in public, free to send his craziness forth
in the tidy receptacles of his work
which, though inexorably they reach the iron museum,
stir souls on the way—don't they?
(*FUCK!!!*
You see, I can do that because I'm a poet.
Poet, *n.* a currently negligible species of artist,
an atavistic survival like painters,)
Many art writers, as I did, hopefully start out
expecting to be the friends and peers of artists,
participants, even, in grandiloquent studio illuminations—
this before we. encounter the artist's reticence,
artist's pettiness, desperation, gloom,
the artist's uncanny resemblance to just about anybody
nine-tenths of the time, and in the tenth tenth
the artist is off somewhere, unavailable,
working.

In the meantime one has written a number of things
embarrassingly adulatory, partaking of the second kind of sin:
the fawning rave.
(Not as bad as the first, because all that get hurt
are the sensibilities of the sensible;
these heal in time.)

The other sin, disgruntled and malicious,
follows as night to day,
or at least it did in my own impulse-ridden zodiac.
Then for some of the ambitious and bright ones (not me, need I say)
comes the tabernacle chorus of formalism,
of solicitude only for the work, which suddenly starts behaving
with a small, humorless but pertinacious mind of its own—
like a set of well-trained lab assistants in this old favorite
of mine: "Frank Stella's new paintings investigate
the problem of shape as such." Ouch!

Strung out between such crystalline insanities
and the utter murk of creative reality, art writers
commence to be furtive, neurotic, displaying
by their tics and funks and struts, their introvert theatrics,
what might be the superfluous disorder of an artist's mind.
The sleep of art produces reason,
vague and excited mental movements in the night
before the deadline. Even as we meet here,
an art writer somewhere is in heat,
smoking, spilling coffee, squinting at illegible notes,
studying for the 20th time a slide irritatingly too red
in which he sees, or did yesterday, a late spasm
of Constructivism. "Bullshit, bullshit," whispers
his most hated and most reliable inner voice,
leitmotif in a fevered subjective babble, e.g.,
"What is this work? Who made it? What did he or she intend,
portend? What influences, contexts, matrices apply?
What does this work do to my cherished notions?
What to my enemy's cherished notions? Is it any *good*?
If I like this, how can I like what I liked last week?
I guess I really am a lightweight, what the heck.
I'm also in a rut:
this is the second time this month I've reviewed this gallery.
Well, can I help it if Leo Castelli is a-genius?
On top of everything else, I'm supposed to be *fair*?!
Hmm, do you suppose I have to insert a definition of Suprematism?
Probably. Gotta think of the amateur audience,
bringing it up to my own midget educational level.

Drink deep, or taste not . . .
Fortunately I love art, or I'd be a real phony after all.
I'm not just a Lipton Tea taster, I'm a Lipton Tea lover!
But do I love the art here at hand?
Do I want to persuade others that they ought to love it, too?
Don't people have enough guilt without feeling responsible
to some paint-spattered sheet metal?
Well, that's their lookout, this stuff is terrific,
and I'm making such analogies!
So pretty, they can't help but be wrong,
If the footnote critics ever read me, which I doubt,
they'll start snorting with disgust just about here.

Poetic drivel! they think, I think.
But can only art be beautiful?
Can't I be a little beautiful, too?
The cookies were lousy, but the box was delicious.
Jeez, I sure hope somebody is going to read this.
It is an eventuality one would do well to anticipate.
Let's see, how many s's are there in Lissitziky?"

And so he taps on into the perfervid night,
ending at last in a daze of self-satisfaction—
after retyping, the best part,
that's where he puts in the jokes and finesses,
chuckling to himself (heh heh, you smart aleck!),
making the paragraphs shapely, the transitions neat—
then a number of stiff drinks, then sleep.
We will pass over in silence, draw
a merciful curtain on, the subsequent second thoughts,
sudden doubts, the cold sweat over an inapt
or impolitic phrase now irretrievable, inconsolable fits
of self-loathing; then later the scream of anguish
over editorial meddling, followed shortly by a taste of ashes:
another product of his sweat arid blood come and gone
like spit on a griddle, unremarked,
no feedback, useless, as if it never happened;
then the check in the mail, a sigh, and on to the next.
Peace to all that. We won't; even mention it . . .

Profession of Art Writing, you were not always thus.
When before, for one thing, has your seedy self
so long held the exquisite attentions of a poem?
(Wow, I'm even original!)
Once strictly a gentlemen's or partisan's occupation,
or the busman's holiday of an academic,
except in France, of course, whence sprang the poet-critic tradition:
Baudelaire and Apollinaire inspiriting Frank O'Hara
inspiriting me, a tradition
that is today justly, alas, in disrepute.
A poet who insists on behaving like one
is good about art mainly when everybody else is determined
to be extremely excited.
The license poetry gives to feeling, not to mention the mean streak
nourished by a career of deprivations,
does not make the poet a dependable wide-ranging thinker—
except in France, of course, where everyone is doomed
to be smart about everything, I hate them!

Anyway, then came the postwar American ebullition—
"crashing waves of paint," as Schuyler put it—and greatness
out walking in the street and drinking at the Cedar,
and Rosenberg and Greenberg, and world leadership,
and secretly CIA-funded exhibitions, and journals, symposia,
The Club! "the Irascibles"—*Life* magazine, unbelievable!
who's in, who's out? the color this year is purple!
did you hear what de Kooning did to Joe Hirshhorn?
and Hirshhom collecting, and people-actually collecting,
and Ad Reinhardt warning on corruption—isn't he cute?—
and Katie-bar-the-door here comes Nelson Rockefeller!
Money! veritable long green, not right away but soon,
and gosh everyone wants to be there
if not to field at least to spectate—and the parties!
Then they had this big party and called it The '60s.
I was there. Weren't *you* there, chum? Too bad!
So anyway, art writing no longer seemed such a tacky job.
It was practically compulsory. And me,
what with my dynamite way with words, y'know,
I got into it, and then it wouldn't let me go,

though it gradually became not nearly so glamorous again
and here I am fit for nearly nothing else. Hello.
Hello 1970's, as dramatic as an overexposed phonograph.
Hello, have you heard photography's the thing now;
(Jesus, I don't know an f-stop from a flapjack eraser.)
Fading fast here, folks. Fading fast, Profession
of Art Writing, you really have been incredibly good to me.
I've traveled—around town, and once to Chicago—
and met so many interesting people!
I have elicited monosyllables from Andy Warhol
and been stared at like I was some kind of moron
by Robert Motherwell. Been in a videotape by Les Levine.
Alex Katz cut me out of aluminum.
Portrait painted by George Schneeman and by Peter Dean.
A noted critic give me heartfelt counsel:
"It's all public relations," she said nonchalantly.
(Speak for yourself! I've wished ever since I'd replied;
boy did I hate that! though it was truer of me at the time
than not true, I'll allow.)
Thomas B. Hess asked me the best question, truly,
that can ever be asked of an art reviewer—
like all great questions, unanswerable.
Saw de Kooning drunk and saw him sober, dazzling man!
Delighted in the friendship of, besides those
already mentioned, artists Bill Barrell; Jennifer Bartlett,
Lynda Benglis, Joe Brainard, Rudy Burckhardt, Scott Burton,
Robert Dash, Donna Dennis, Martha Diamond, Rafael Ferrer,
Jane Freilicher, Mike Goldberg, Frank Owen, Yvonne Jacquette,
Tom Kovachevich, Doug Ohlson, Larry Rivers, James Rosenquist,
Herb Schiffrin, John Seery, Michael Singer, Arlene Slavin,
Jim Sullivan, Neil Welliver, Nina Yankowitz
and others too numerous, etc.
The art world drew me insensibly away from poetry
and the company of poets—not a bad event.
I could not have lived long, what with my vertigo,
on that precipitous slope. (Here I direct your attention
to the present day mountaineers, my heroes,
whose feats make non-boring poetry conceivable:
Ginsberg, Kock, Ashbery, Schuyler, Padgett. Up there, hello!)

Since we seem to be into the credits now, reeling,
let us turn to the career critics, your captains
and minions, Profession, without whom . . .
but here they come in dancing array!
Inspiration, let us call them by their qualities:
Lucy R. Lippard of the portable moral authority;
Hilton Kramer the abhorrent, who makes art sound as appealing
as a deodorant enema; nice-making John Russell;
Harold Rosenberg, honey-tongued blowhard (but great, why not?);
charmingly repellent John Coplans; David Bourdon, cub reporter;
Robert Rosenblum, hosanna king; Donald Kuspit, avid bore;
Peter Plagens, aging whiz; Brian O'Doherty, or
can you whiz forever?; Carter Ratcliff the cornucopiate,
from whom I steal all my ideas; schizzy and impeccable
Michael Fried; inexplicably diffident Irving Sandler;
Leo Steinberg, a bit too smart to be Kenneth Clark,
and regrettably in the wrong country; Clement Greenberg,
worm-eaten colossus, our Father,
who taught us that art is not virtue, but power;
egregious claque-flack Kenworth Moffet;
William Rubin claque-flack of undeniable gifts;
Linda Nochlin, lead on!; anxiety-prone Amy Goldin
who rejoices my heart; Diane Waldman, sedatives in prose;
absurdly talented Sanford Schwartz, so mellifluous sometimes
I want to beat him up: honorably obsessive Joseph Masheck
and earnest Roberta Smith, to your bright futures I would tip my hat
if I had one; excruciatingly mild James Mellow;
Gregory Battcock, 'nuff said, and 'nuff-said Mario Amaya;
John Perreault John Perreault; Peter Frank—Peter Frank?!;
Walter Darby Bannard of the chronically misdirected energies;
Barbara Rose, educator and discourager; Robert Pincus-Witten,
lunatic savant of St. Theresa and tautology;
Dore Ashton; enthusiast: Hayden Herrera of the kind heart;
Elizabeth C. Baker—hi Betsy!; Phyllis Derfner kindly shape up!;
Nicolas Calas, surrealist warhorse; sweet Franz Schulze
and sour Dennis Adrian—Chicago Taste; Sam Hunter of the dollar;
Jeremy Gilbert-Rolfe, totally crackers; Lawrence Alloway,
sanitation engineer; Rosalind Krauss and Annette Michelson,
let me out of here!; John Canaday, ugh; Marcia Tucker,

may she relax and enjoy; Jack Burnham, eek!, and David Antin,
yawn, and Robert Hughes, ho hum, and Douglas Davis, ugh;
Emily Genauer, triple ugh; Max Kozloff,
I'll make up my insignificant mind about you eventually;
Thomas B. Hess, *il miglior Fabbro.*

(Anyone inadvertently omitted here
may apply for insult in later editions.)

More charming than a cannibal tribe, this bunch,
and rather more stimulating than a dentist's convention:
a tidy guild on the fringe, of useful human endeavor.
I cannot regret having made their acquaintance.
And I will not regret our years together; Profession;
I neither enriched nor eroded you, as others have,
but I would hope I've done my bit for pleasure,
a fleeting kind that is sweet to the serious.
I intended no harm. May my sins be forgotten.

THE FLAVIN FILE

June 1977

"Flavin is either a genius or nothing at all."
—B. O'Doherty (1970)

"I know of no occupation in American life so meaningless and unproductive as that of art critic."
—D. Flavin (1965)

"When the Gods wish to punish us, they make us believe our own advertising." —D. Boorstin paraphrasing Oscar Wilde (1962)

It may be the case that any anger at Flavin's work becomes suspect in a fairly knowledgeable brain because of the uneasy sensation that this frustration is easily likenable to philistinism. But Alan Artner's fine phrase aside, "Flavin has weathered the changes in the American art climate better . . . than many of his Minimalist brethren," the work both graphic and light, has always bugged some people and the problems and the puzzlement are now clearly seen by many.

It is truly astonishing just how frequently Flavin's fluorescent light arrangements have been used by the "professional art world" to present and "test out" the tenets of an era—call it Post-Modernism if you will. In one year, for instance 1970, Flavin appeared in three New York exhibitions, in Paris, Munich, and Cologne—in one-man shows while also appearing in group exhibitions in Minneapolis, Turin, Paris, Cologne, and of course New York. It was not an unusual year except that there were no one-man museum exhibitions: In 1969, the Canadian Museum network hosted a large travelling exhibition; in 1972 the Albright-Knox in Buffalo, and the Rice University Institute of Arts offered exhibitions of Flavin's work; and of course here in Chicago as early as 1967–68, Flavin was Jan van der Marck's emblem of modernism in the second exhibition at the MCA with 8 foot pink and gold fluorescent tubes disposed about the first-floor walls there.

So that one source of Flavin's well-attested-to arrogance is his establishment position in the world of gallery and museumdom; still another is broached in Lawrence Alloway's response to a Flavin letter (*Artforum*, Sept. 1974) complaining about shabby critical treatment; Alloway writes,

> The giveaway in his letter is his complaint that he hasn't read "much published sympathy" from me in the past so why am I writing about him now? His choice of term for art criticism . . . shows clearly the unctuous flattery that he expects art criticism to be. He has grounds for sanguine expectation in the past record of admiring critiques in this magazine . . . typical of Flavin's mix of humbleness and vanity is his pious loquacity concerning himself . . . it comes on as a cry for justice but turns, as you read, into an account of his international exhibition schedule . . .

The exhibition held in April and May at the Art Institute of Chicago, organized earlier by the Ft. Worth Art Museum, was but a further example of the continuing omnipresence of Flavin—and also the continuing arrogance of both museum and artist. The Ft. Worth exhibition was entitled "Dan Flavin: Drawings, Diagrams, and Prints from 1972–75." Here in Chicago, via a gift from the Society for Contemporary Art, three light sculptures were mounted in the Montgomery Ward Gallery, both as filter and climax for the rather meaningless collection of graphic work in the travelling show. Flavin's linear control is inelegant, and he is apparently uninterested in developing it. He himself had previously explained, "My drawing is not at all inventive about itself. It is an instrument, not a resultant."

So then why, as the artist, allow that body of work, for the most part pragmatic and unaesthetic, to be displayed? One answer, discussed below, is that Flavin's work is for him ostensibly his life—not that unusual an attitude anymore—and thus courts the danger of "Emperorizing his clothes," i.e., no detachment.

One wonders also at further *chutzpah* of museums to host this exhibition of all the travelling exhibitions abroad throughout the U.S. crying out for space. Isn't it late in the game of "modernism" for professionals in the artworld to be cowed by reputations; by clichés—both connections and styles? Maybe not.

And it is not as if no one has spoken to the issues. Although Flavin's critique-record in *Artforum* may be B-plus, or even A, as early as 1970, B. Vinklers wrote in *Art International* (April),

> . . . but one weakness of the exhibition was the inclusion of an unnecessarily large number of Flavin's drawings . . . which lack the quality and significance of the neon work . . . it seems that Flavin has made all the original statements he can with the neon tube (read fluorescent) and is now on the verge of insignificant variation that he might avoid by taking this retrospective as a milestone beyond which there should be a new direction.

Jack Burnham, in the best extended piece on Flavin (*Artforum,* Dec. 1969), offers explanation partially based on biography: Flavin's early identification with the Joycean-Mallarmean tradition of symbolist and hermetic, pristine clarity may have lead to Flavin's obtuse and defiant stance. My own feeling in this area is that the death of a twin brother 15 years ago, at the start of his artistic career, may have freed the artist from hesitancy and further instilled his aggressive drive for self-realization— apparently a problem for twins.

In the work, this sense of self may have made the art a very "literary" thing for Flavin. Obviously aware of the spatial implications and the color qualities of his installations, Flavin nonetheless came to fruition as an artist in the Minimalist era, with a ready-manufactured light fixture and bulb as his medium. Ultimately and inherently, this resultant simplicity, an *a-complexity,* is an exasperating aspect of both his compositions and his color choices.

His works in their smug self-referential state seem really to express— thus perhaps their inbuilt antagonistic stance—the on-going life of Flavin; they mock us with not their success, but rather *his* success. It is as if the work is beside the point in the face of "all the rest": the triumphant organization of yet another exhibition; the acknowledgement of friendship—that literary, biographical thing perhaps—in the dedication of one of the pieces to the Art Institute's curator of Prints, Harold Joachim; just so, the entire exhibition here at the Art Institute is dedicated to a recently deceased Italian friend. Flavin has done this often before. Elizabeth Baker expressed her unease at this practice in *Artforum* (Feb. 1971), about a work for Barnett Newman: "There is something vaguely offensive about dedicating pieces of visual art to the deceased; it is perhaps like sending candy rather than flowers to a funeral . . . the show was a reminder that Flavin lives . . ."

The relative silence hovering about the work of other Minimalists may exempt their work from this particular kind of antagonism.

But then there is the question whether that stylistic designation will suffice. Flavin's works are full of reference to lots of stuff: Like a stage director, he posits positions which are then played out by installerelectricians; his medium is "ready-mades;" his compositions are "Constructivist;" his color is "environmental" and rarely "structural;" his titles are most often poetical and personal; a Pop art immediacy hovers about the work despite all because of those kitchen and bathroom connotations—both fixture and bulb-wise. Minimalism by that time has receded far into the distance.

Barbara Rose got into the problem (*Artforum*, April 1967): "I am defining didactic art as art whose primary intention is to instruct. The pure didactic work then has no aesthetic content. Both Morris' and Flavin's work are mixed type of didactic work because they have some formal value . . ."

I argued in *ArtScene* (April 1968) that "Flavin's work has value because it causes us to question our ideas about art (and life). It should be admitted that the 'ideas' are more interesting than the art itself . . ." In other words, this particular tack acknowledges that "literary" quality that seems so much a part of Flavin's endeavor, and may indeed be a major source of the consternation his work has produced over the course of his exhibition career. Like a concept artist without Thesaurus.

Although Flavin himself may seem to speak to this aspect of his work: "I don't want to impose separate sculptural ego dumps as public works. I don't want to rival architecture and public spaces insistently grandiosely."

He may be judiciously avoiding the real issue by insisting, as here, on the humble, ephemeral aspect of his art. After all, given his materials, no matter how grandiose his dispositions, his works have to read as humble. (While I was at the exhibition, a 10-year old ran into the light area, yelled "Broadway!" and began a dance step.) If Flavin can be read as someone who "hedges his bets," who is really not at all the "Emperor with New Clothes," that is, unconscious about the fragility of his art—then I think that while smiling at the kid's appreciation, he would be inwardly nervous: uncalled for perhaps, but nonetheless the image of Nixon holding on to those tapes comes to mind. The crime here may be "Art."

KEITH MORRISON

ART CRITICISM

A Pan-African Point of View

February 1979

Are there ideas native to Black artists that critics overlook? The question has been asked many times before but the answers have not led to change that the overwhelming number of Black artists would consider to be even remotely satisfactory. The shortage of published criticism of the works of Black artists would lead to the assumption that there are no art ideas—no aesthetic tradition characteristic of Black people and that therefore, that which is commonly known and written about a handful of Black artists is all that needs to be known. Because of the assumed absence of a Black art character, most critics have felt free to judge Black artists, according to the traditions of American-European art criticism.

The problem is that there continues to be no consistent publication of art criticism in major art journals written by Black critics, interested in art from a Black person's perspective. No doubt, White critics have the ability to write about ideas' that relate to Black culture, but very few have the interest.

A recent article in the *Village Voice* (Sept. 11, 1978, p. 113) explores the effects of this problem, by pointing to the continued scarcity of exposure of art by Blacks and stating that less than half a dozen Blacks are spread among the best known New York galleries. The author, April Kingsley, states that "the majority of the recent work that I've seen by Black artists is powerful." Ms. Kingsley comments on the great number of major Black artists who are without a gallery anywhere and states bluntly that as good as their work is, no one will care until it is shown at Marlborough, Emmerich or Tibor de Nagy. In speaking of sculptor

Mel Edwards, she states that "Nothing comparable to Edwards' dense, masklike reliefs out of welded tool and automobile parts has been done since the early work of David Smith, and there is no counterpart to the rhythmic coordination of counter-balanced masses in his large sculptures, with their intimation of vernacular architecture despite the level of their means. Most work in this vein (by Michael Steiner, Joel Perlman and Tony Rosenthal, for example) is technically good, formally pleasing, but emotionally empty. Edwards' work, however; is rich in metaphor, implication, and connotation, with no loss of plastic vigor."

And so the article goes on, cataloging many Black artists without critical or gallery support. What is the reason or reasons for this disinterest in what Black artists do? It is racism (conscious or subconscious) to be sure, but it is also more than that. I believe that much of the reason lies in the fundamental assumptions underlying the very basis of art criticism. The assumptions have to do with the notion that art is culture-free, and it is these assumptions that have led to an inadequacy of modern American art criticism.

I believe that all art, including "Modern Art," is culturally based and that will probably seem absurd to the great multitude who have been indoctrinated with the notion that all great art is "universal." I wish to challenge this doctrine of universality since I do not believe that it is based on universal evidence: It seems to me that what is called universal is most often a cultural dominance, rather than synthesis of two or more cultures. American and European-controlled art publications commonly hold that Michelangelo and Picasso are universal, though nobody has bothered to ask the Eskimo whether he agreed. And, of course, so-called "modern art criticism" (a term that is full of arrogant implications) is based on traditions and reactions to Western art criticism and culture.

Any art history book makes this point excruciatingly clear. I mean, does it not seem an odd coincidence that no non-Western artist is among the most famous one thousand artists you ever heard of? Does it not seem an odd coincidence that the only non-Western cultures to make good art are either dead cultures or ones that are economically poor and politically non-threatening? Does it not seem an odd coincidence that no non-Western people alive today can produce art that is as good as American or European art? When was the last time that you saw a contemporary Pakistani artist on the cover of *ARTnews*? Obviously, God in his infinite wisdom has bestowed all of the world's talent on White people.

Modern art criticism continues to ignore the horrendous fact that it is fundamentally *White* art criticism—and mostly middle-class White male at that. A few respected critics such as Lucy Lippard (see *Changing Dutton,* NY, 1971) and Amy Goldin (see "American art history has been called elitist, racist and sexist. The charges stick," *Art News,* April 1975 pp. 48–51) have been writing against the tide, but the ocean of modern art criticism continues to flow. One is left with the realization that our Western critical framework does not provide for a comprehensive understanding of the values of the Black artist.

So I dismiss the notion of universality as being unworkable or, at best, premature. I submit instead what seems to me to be a more workable hypothesis, the idea that art exists essentially in a cultural context.

I do not use the word culture in the strictest Margaret Mead (bless her!) sense, since few if any people continue to live in the same total isolation of yesterday's Samoa. Nowadays, there is obviously much cross-cultural fertilization and neutralization throughout the world. So what I mean by "culture" are the remnants of culture that continue to set groups of peoples apart. These remnants of culture continue to provide substance for artistic differences in points of view and aesthetic sensibility and "taste."

Aesthetics, of course, is not taste, but that branch of philosophy that analyzes the nature of taste. Principles of aesthetics may be universal but taste is regional or cultural. From their own cultural contexts people involve themselves in matters of aesthetics; the hierarchy of preferences that they evolve is what is considered taste. The phenomenon of describing and analyzing taste is what we call art criticism.

Art criticism—unlike aesthetics—must be made useful. Art criticism has no value unless it is meaningful to the culture as a whole. Art criticism must therefore describe objects in a broad enough way so that a large group of people or a culture as a whole can find the description useful. This is because the ultimate aim of art criticism is to promote ideas for the artists and audience of a culture to act upon.

It should therefore seem that I consider art criticism to be an aspect of sociology, and I do. However, sociology in its broadest sense is a passive science, the analysis of systems of how people behave. But art criticism is not passive, neither is it a science. Instead, it is a culturally biased construct designed to elucidate points of view that are of central interest to the cultural values of its origin. Rather than being sociology, art criticism is a social activity and as such it is an aspect of politics.

When I say that art criticism is an aspect of politics, I do not mean that it is the result of an elected mandate, but that it is a public (rather than private) function and that it is useless unless it promotes a point of view that can have a common meaning for a large group of people or a culture as a whole. Further, I should distinguish between art criticism and propaganda (although it is often difficult to tell them apart). Art criticism is honest interpretation of relationships between art objects and a culture's values: propaganda is a willful distortion of that relationship.

Yet it is obvious that we live in a time when most cultures are aware of one another and of their influences upon one another, and this, of course, has come about because of the facilities of modern communication and because of the analyses of modern sociology. But in spite of the modern factors that have caused cross-cultural fertilization, the impact of many cultural differences remains dramatically evident in many aspects of life and art. Although modern communication would suggest that a synthesis of art—at least abstract art (but more on that later)—should come about, and that a universal art could be achieved, this has clearly not been the case, judging from the limitations of our dominant critical framework over the last one hundred years.

For example, the 19th century French artists were strongly influenced by aspects of Japanese prints that relate to flat space, color and composition cropping similar to the then-emerging art of photography. In other words, the 19th century French were interested in the Japanese print to the extent that French and Japanese cultural values coincided. However, there remained many aspects of Japanese art to which French art criticism was apathetic. And of course, some of the art ideas that they had in common they each used for quite different reasons. Certainly, the spatial characteristics of the Japanese woodcut did not result from an interest in light and photography.

A similar analogy is found in how Western Africanists such as William Fagg have interpreted West African objects as "cubist" sculpture, or in how just about every major Western art critic, following in the context of Braque and Picasso, have put West African objects on the static pedestal to be viewed like a traditional European statue. It is only with the recent interpretations of scholars such as Robert Ferris Thompson's *African Art in Motion* (U.C.L.A. Press, 1974), that African objects have been written about in an African context.

I am saying that European art criticism has been self-centered. However, this is neither unusual nor undesirable—if you are European. To the contrary, history suggests that ethnocentric art interpretation is not only the norm but an apparent prerequisite for definition of a culture's character. The Renaissance greatly admired Greek art but redefined it to fit aspirations of 16th century Italy. Michelangelo turned Greek realist images into super-Christian figures and Raphael turned a pagan Aphrodite into the Holy Virgin. In the 19th century, Gauguin's visions of the South Seas were really an imposition of a European sensibility upon exotic subject matter.

Similarly, Americans built Washington D.C. according to their interpretations of the pure, white visage they fantasized to be the glory of ancient Greek architecture. They were ignorant of the fact that ancient Greek architecture (and sculpture) had been painted many bright colors and had jewel inlays, and that time had washed away the paint and thieves had stolen the jewels. It is a cruel joke of history that rain and thieves should have laid the foundation of the nation's capitol.

It is bizarre to imagine the White House daubed with orange and blue paint, or the statues of Washington and Jefferson mired and gold with green inlay eyes. The notion ridicules the very image of North America and the structure of temperance and restraint upon which so much modern American art criticism is based. A red and green Thomas Jefferson would symbolize that the United States had become a pagan state. Nixon would resurrect Watergate and the Daughters of the American Revolution would stage a shootout. All of which is why the old concept is still maintained as the basis of much of America's attitude toward art and thought, though North Americans now know what ancient Greek architecture and sculpture looked like. For the old concept fits better into the value structure that has been built than does the authenticity of history; America is America and Greece is Greece and ne'er the twain shall meet. I am not saying that American or European art criticisms are lies, but rather that they are designed to suit values of Americans or Europeans. And this is an attitude that would seem useful to any culture's better understanding of itself.

As I have implied, the art criticism of all cultures is self-serving and a culture's tendency to make its ideas dominant over other ones seems natural enough. It is this dominance-seeking nature that causes criticism of one culture to select from another and to put values of the exotic culture into a framework of its own. If I may paraphrase Voltaire, criticism is the Professor Pangloss of art for it allows us to rationalize our values as those which exist in the "best of all possible worlds." Indeed, you can create for yourself a "best of all possible worlds" when you control all major art publications, movies, television and radio. With that kind of control you have the perfect guarantee that you can hear only what you wish to hear, whether this is what you intend or not.

I am not building a case for a White conspiracy, but for a better understanding of the causes of political and biased criticism which seems to be a natural condition of all cultures, even those cultures that are tolerant of other ones. We should note that tolerance and acceptance are not the same. For while it is easier to tolerate the presence of exotica as harmless objects, the interpretations of this exotica into a framework of art is a more formidable task. It is interpretation that is the dominant force that gives an object its definition as "art." In other words, interpretation always falls within a cultural context, as Marcel Duchamp well recognized. For a urinal becomes art only in the context of a museum established by people who are preoccupied with the problem of whether art is form or function. And the problem of Duchamp and his urinal has been a regional problem, not a universal one. If artists in Uganda are interested in that problem, it is most probably because they have had to read *Art News* to pass courses in White American universities. If the editors and boards of governors and financiers of *ARTnews* and *Art International* were Black or Vietnamese, rest assured that the face of "universal" art criticism would not be painted just White but also Yellow and Black.

The overwhelming of one art criticism by another with more communications media control has been acceptable because people of different cultures lived farther apart in the past and had no reason or basis to test theories of cultural supremacy or universality. But in today's world, when cultures have come in conflict, cultural comparisons and hypotheses about universality are put to the test. For the first time in history there are many different peoples with similar formal education and therefore a more meaningful basis upon which to test the existence of a truly universal hierarchy in art. Today, for the first time, the conditions widely exist for two persons with similar academic education but different cultural biases and political interests to look critically at the same art object and arrive at two different and equally valid kinds of criticisms about it.

Note that I have not said different in degree: I said different in kind. For at the heart of the matter is not simply whether an object might be interpreted as good or bad but whether it might be interpreted as art by one culture and be totally meaningless as art to another. The problem, therefore, has to do with recognition of pluralistic dialectics in art criticism.

It is at this juncture that recognition of some of the neglected values of Black art lies. Perhaps it is easier to understand this neglect in relation to figurative art. For example, an easy answer to the question of why American criticism has ignored Charles White might be that White people do not care to see the Black faces that he draws hanging on their walls. But the problem seems more subtle in relation to abstraction, since the assumption has been that abstraction is non-objective, without subject matter. The ultimate question, therefore, is whether an abstract shape can have different meaning to different cultural contexts. I believe that it can and does. I believe that what we perceive to be the non-objectivity of Mondrian is really our respect for a revelation of an ultimate Dutch formalist tradition. I believe with Duchamp that inside the White American-European museum his urinal becomes a formalist proposition and outside the museum it remains an ultimate symbol of malfeasance. Ironically, Duchamp's urinal is more "universal" outside the museum than within it. And so my proposition, of course, is yes, that abstract shapes can have different meanings to people, in different cultural contexts.

Many of the neglected aspects of Afro-American art are based on ideas which are used in a similar way by most Black artists throughout the world. This seems true in figurative art as well as in non-figurative art, although I am writing only about non-figurative art. This common linkage is what I would call a Pan-African heritage since the obvious source is Africa from which all Black people have come. And so by Pan-African I mean that which has been called the "Black Diaspora" or scattered existence of Blacks all over the world who share common cultural linkage.

If Pan-African abstraction has had no written identity in major publications it is only because it has not had the means for its own advocacy. Pan-African abstraction has been invariably put into an American-European context rather than one of its own. This follows the tradition that says that the ideas of Saul Bellow or Jean-Paul Sartre are truly universal but those of Richard Wright or Chinua Achebe are regional, since Black life and experience lacks the potential for universal thought. In art, for example, during the 1930's Elizabeth Catlett's angular sculptures were said to have been derived from Picasso and both were interpreted in the context of a modern European art. From a Black person's point of view, they both should have been put in a Pan-African framework for both of their ideas came from Africa. Black critics of the time, such as Alain Locke and W.E.B. Du Bois exposed that kind of cultural distortion very eloquently. However, it should be noted that not all Black artists can be thought of in this way. For example, I am not aware of anything particularly "Pan-African" in the work of Richard Hunt or John Dowell. And of course Black artists are influenced by other ideas just as anyone else. I myself have been influenced by Stella, Kelly, Rothko and a host of European associations. So I make a case not for total reassessment, but for an art criticism that includes and gives parity to Pan-African characteristics.

As I said, I am here restricting my scope to abstract painting, though strong arguments could just as well be made for figurative painting, sculpture and other aspects of the visual arts. But space being limited, this abstract painting framework is presented merely as an example of the possibilities of a Pan-African character. The characteristics of Pan-African abstract painting that seem to me to be most pronounced have to do with the following four associations: silhouetted two-dimensional form; use of textile as direct means of expression; expressive pattern and a preoccupation with bright color. These categories are my own and are necessarily broad in a paper of this limited scope.

Early in this century, Afro-American artists realized that their works still retained strong African qualities, and coming out of the bitter disillusionment of reconstruction, Black artists agreed that they had to look to their African ancestry for identity. In the 1920's and '30's, many Black thinkers and scholars articulated views that confirmed the idea of Africanness. A few of these were W.E.B. Du Bois, James V. Herring and Alain Locke who were professors at Howard University, poet Langston Hughes and Hon. Leopold Senghor of Senegal who developed ideas about "Negritude." Locke, the first Black Rhodes Scholar, was perhaps the most prolific writer of that time on the subject of "Negro Art." His articles appeared in many publications including the *American Magazine of Art* (Sept. 1931); *Opportunity Magazine* (Dec. 1925); *Encyclopedia Britannica* (14th and 15th eds.); and *The Arts* (Feb. 1927). However, it was in his landmark book, *The New Negro* (Boni, New York, 1925; reissued by Atheneum, 1969), that he developed a philosophy of art in which the concept of a "Black aesthetic" was first articulated. In his now classic essay in *The New Negro*, "The Legacy of the Ancestral Arts," Locke argued for an Afro-American aesthetic based on a return to an African legacy. Many Black artists and poets of the time had already been doing this and now they embraced their ideas with even more fervor.

To my mind, the most significant early return to Africanness in painting had to do with a redefinition of silhouetted form. Among the many artists of the 1920's and '30's whose works characterize the early interest in two-dimensional silhouette were such artists as Horace Pippin, Aaron Douglas and Richmond Barthe (the latter in his relief sculptural forms). One could use Douglas's art of the period as a model example of the idea of silhouetted form. This silhouette sensibility has, as its essence, flat shapes that appear as though they were shadows on a flat surface, relating to one another in lateral and horizontal patterns. The use of this kind of silhouetted form is something that Douglas mastered. In recent talks with Douglas, I was fascinated with his continuing fervor about the supremacy of what he referred to as Egyptian-type design. Like so many Black intellectuals, he continues to think of Egyptian ideas largely as indigenous African ideas.

This point of view is conspicuously absent from most White publications and an interesting Black response to it is Chancellor Williams' *The Destruction of Black Civilization* (Third World Press, Chicago, 1974). Black intellectuals are always symbolically conscious that the Nile flows *north;* that ideas as well as materials emptied into the Nile Valley from the Black South and across the Sahara from the Black East. Whites have so often written without serious regard for this fact and therefore without much recognition that Egyptian ideas might have more naturally traveled from the middle of Black Africa to the Nile Valley. In fact, for centuries White authors developed theories about trade and thought patterns in Central West Africa on the assumption that the great Niger River flowed Westward. The White world was therefore shocked a little after the year 1800 when a young Scots surgeon named Mungo Park explored his way through the Sahara to the upper parts of the Niger River and then wrote in triumph that he had seen the Niger " . . . as broad as the Thames at Westminster, and flowing *slowly to the Eastward.*" The italics were his own (see Basil Davidson, *Lost Cities of Africa*, Little, Brown & Co., Boston, 1959).

Black scholars long have been aware that the more than two thousand African Rock paintings that have been found in such regions as Tassili, Fezzan, Tanganyika, Zimbabwe and the Kalahari, preceded Egypt by thousands of years and were the obvious force behind Egyptian two-dimensional design. Many White scholars agree and have done research to confirm this view and at the forefront of these has been Leo Frobenius and, more recently, Burchard Brentjes whose book *African Rock Art*

(Clarks N. Potter, Inc., N. Y. 1970) argues the case resoundingly. Black intellectuals are ever aware that so many other things about Ancient Egypt including people and rulers were Black, as opposed to the Hollywood image of a Nefertiti who looked like Elizabeth Taylor, of pharaohs who looked like Richard Burton and Rex Harrison and of a Nile, flowing south from an Egypt which was a Eurasian movie set on the tip of Africa.

It is in this perspective of a Black intellectual view of Africa that the early work of Aaron Douglas falls. And consistent with this view, Douglas saw Egyptian two-dimensional painting as being directly related to West African two-dimensional design.

In the silhouette, Douglas saw not only a two-dimensional device for expression of his figurative imagery, but a visual schema in which the background became an equally silhouetted and plastic shape in such a way that it was difficult for the viewer to consider the background of the painting less important than the foreground. In this way, Douglas succeeded in creating a truly comprehensive abstract arena in spite of his figurative subject matter. For what was most dramatic about Douglas's work was the poignant and mysterious character of his shapes which evoked a psychology of rhythmic tension. Douglas's strongest achievement was to make the psychology of the silhouette the potent expression of the subject matter it portrayed. As such, he made the psychology of the silhouette its own characteristic expression.

Horace Pippin, too, was interested in the silhouette, although in a less severe way than Douglas. Nevertheless, it is the silhouette that Pippin used as the pictorial device to organize his paintings. The tradition of the silhouette has been explored by succeeding generations of Black artists including Jacob Lawrence, William H. Johnson, Ellis Wilson, Charles Alston and Romare Bearden. Of these, Lawrence is closest to Douglas in the sharp angularity of his shapes, the simplification of his compositions, and the dramatic supremacy of the silhouette, used in such a way as to make foreground and background equally important and dynamic. While William H. Johnson was also preoccupied with the silhouette, he developed a sense of linear abstraction that broadened the scope of Pan-African two-dimensional art.

Along with Jacob Lawrence, Romare Bearden remains one of the two most distinguished Black painters whose figurative images strongly relate to a tradition of two-dimensional abstraction. Bearden uses the silhouetted shape and the background-foreground reversal dynamic to give his photographic images a simultaneity of existence that literally and ironically mirrors Black life from New York and Mississippi through the valleys of the Niger and the Nile. Bearden has done quite a bit of writing himself, but more on that later.

Many of my own interests in the silhouette are allied with the ideas of Douglas and Lawrence, for they remind me so much of the forms that are so prevalent in the West Indies where I grew up. Some aspects of the works of many other Black painters seem to fall in this tradition, including Malcolm Bailey, Bernie Casey, Emilio Cruz, Alvin Hollingsworth, Joe Overstreet and Thomas Sills.

I consider the use of textiles as a direct means of expression to be another characteristic of a Pan-African abstraction. By this I mean a conscious focus on the aesthetic possibilities of cloth itself. In so many works by Blacks throughout the world one sees cloth itself being elevated to a level of fetish object. For example, in Lagos, New York or Kingston today it is common to see Black people fascinated with the garments they wear because of what they consider to be the expressive power of the cloth surface and the color. For many Blacks, cloth is not just a serviceable necessity, but a kind of plumage.

I see this association most strongly in the work of Sam Gilliam. This statement will probably surprise those who have always considered Gilliam's cloths "Gothic Drapery." That Gilliam's ideas are far-reaching enough to encompass Gothic associations is no doubt a testament to his brilliance. However, it should take away nothing from Gilliam to recognize that his ideas manifest sensibilities that are a very common and visible part of the Pan-African vernacular. Gilliam himself chooses to let his work stand as it is usually interpreted, so this present interpretation is mine, not his. However, Gilliam does point out that Black people tend to find great spiritual empathy with his work, and that they compare it with West African fabric design, with Kente' cloth and tie-dyes. That is what I mean by the relationship between Gilliam's art and a Pan-African vernacular art based on the usage of cloth.

I see Gilliam's ideas largely in this context, as a marvelous revelation of the essence of a Pan-African fascination with the magic of pure cloth and pigment. The draped sense of Gilliam's cloths, of course, allows for movement, like the fleeting and imprecise view of an image. The movement creates elusive macabre fantasies, like the colorful drapery of the African medicine man and dancer or the Jankunu dancer in the West Indies. Gilliam's ideas are beyond the specific but retain their vernacular sensibility and make sense in the context of Thompson's *African Art in*

Motion, mentioned earlier. Thompson articulated how West African art was one of motion, with dancers, actors, charmers, sculptures, cloth and other objects all participating in an experience of movement, rather than the passivity of the museum environment.

A third characteristic of Pan-African abstraction is what I call expressive pattern. In Western Art, the notion of pattern is usually thought of as decoration or embellishment and is most often considered excessive or extraneous to the otherwise functional quality of the art object. Thus, it is said that Louis Sullivan was a great architect in spite of his ornate embellishments, and that Matisse understood form and shape despite his decorative tendencies, and that the Alhambra is a great complex of sophisticated engineering, though overly decorative, as opposed to the Parthenon which is understated in its austere balance, or the Seagram Building in New York which is a prime example of the concept of less is more.

But what is often characteristic of Pan-African abstraction is the notion that more is more. Decorativeness is sought after and the decorative shape itself becomes the object of expression. This is distinct from the way in which the history of Western art looks at shape. To the strictly Western sensibility, a shape is a defined bit of space that creates a tension with another defined bit of space. Westerners (traditionally in their art criticism) see shapes not as ends in themselves, primarily, but as utilitarian forces that work together to make a composition. In a sense, the history of Western art has been an exposition of the possibilities of composition. Recent notions of compositionless art represent a withdrawal from a traditional Western sensibility.

Black people the world over have always been affected less by composition as a totality (with beginning, middle and end like a sonata) but rather with pattern as a random sequence of shapes whose ultimate relationship is not the finiteness of composition but to the expressive infinity of a continuum. The sonata is a good example to illustrate a Western concept of art, though it is in music. Mozart's "Jupiter" symphony has strict sections that follow a sonata form. There is an introduction, development, exploration then finally recapitulation. Compare that with the approach of a traditional African drummer. He begins a sequence, adds other ideas to it and after he has exhausted an exciting enough pattern he stops. He is satisfied without a recapitulation; the notion of a tight composition is irrelevant. Again, musically one could make a similar comparison between Stravinsky and John Coltrane.

Black artists create visual art in much the same way. I am not saying that their-work is formless (for you must start and end somewhere), but their work deals with the notion of pattern as an expressive possibility in itself which can be primary and needs no other aesthetic basis for its support. One such artist whose work is prominent in Black America today is Joe Overstreet. Overstreet's patterns obviously derive a great deal of influence from West African masks and their rhythmic patterns. While Overstreet does not paint masks, as such, he uses similar types of shapes. Also in America Ben Jones obviously uses the mask-type pattern as a part of his visual sensibility. Jones takes heads and legs and decorates them lavishly. In another way, Twins Seven Seven in Nigeria relies heavily on decorative mask-like forms.

Many contemporary African artists have a similar sensibility toward pattern. Among them is the distinguished Sudanese artist Ahmed Shibrain whose art seems to derive largely from the calligraphic qualities of Arabic decoration that have adorned Sudanese buildings for centuries. In fact, Shibrain titles some of his works "Calligraphy" and has pointed to the visual effects of the Koran upon his work.

There is a widespread African relation to Islam and its deletion of figurative imagery and reliance upon abstract symbolic surfaces to express aesthetic meanings. For years Alma Thomas' ideas were not taken seriously, because they were considered too randomly decorative. Later, as painters such as Frank Stella and Kenneth Nolan developed, White critics saw her work in the context of field painting. Thomas' strength had to do with her affirmation of the primacy of pure decoration and for me that is enough. I would imagine many White critics would find that hard to accept.

My fourth category of a Pan-African abstraction in painting has to do with bright color. It used to be popular for Whites to say that all Black artists were in love with garish color, although this kind of statement would be indiscreet today. Well, it is true, I think, that Black people usually love bright colors. It makes sense that they should.

Africa, South America, the South of the United States and the West are the areas from which most Blacks traditionally come. The sunlight and colors in these parts of the world are bright, by comparison with the less sunlit Northern regions from which most Whites come. It is, therefore, natural that the colors that so many Black artists prefer would be colors of their traditional lands, since over centuries aesthetic preferences develop in relation to the environment that one experiences. In his book *Mies Van Der Rohe* (Penguin, 1968) Peter Blake tells how the architect was shocked by the brightness of the light the first time he went to Italy from his home in Germany. He thought Italy was bright! I have often, wondered what might have happened had Mies' first trip south been to Accra or Port-au-Prince.

So many Black artists thrive on really bright colors, and have the visual capacity to easily absorb and tolerate one bright color after another. Black cultures being of the tropics also tend to be more out-of-door cultures and have greater association with sunlight. A bright color is the intensity of the tropical sun scintillating from a cocoa leaf or a blood red Poinciana tree. He who can appreciate bright colors earns the right to look into the sun. So it was with the Impressionists who went out-of-doors.

William T. Williams is a major Black artist who has experimented with a variety of pigments in search of more color intensity. Williams has been considered by some to be a Black Frank Stella and, as such, he has been criticized for straying beyond the Stella mold with his exuberant color. But Williams is not really a Black Stella—at least not insofar as his color is concerned; rather, his apparent exuberance is really an excellent example of a Black artist's fascination with color.

White pioneers into aspects of bright color have been influenced primarily by non-Western associations. That was true of Veronese and many other Venetians of that time who came in contact with Middle Eastern and African cultures. Few if any Europeans used really bright color until Delacroix, who again was influenced by Middle Eastern cultures. The Impressionists worked out-of-doors to attain their sunlit palettes, so too did Bonnard; Rousseau, Gauguin, Matisse, Marc and Kandinsky borrowed heavily from non-Western associations. Of course, many other White artists in recent times have used bright colors, being influenced by urban experiences of electric lights and mechanical colors on the one hand and the 20th century visualization of psychology through color on the other. One could catalog a long list of these from MacDonald-Wright, Stuart Davis, Pollock and Hoffman to Nolan, Newman, Stella and Vasarely. But still a tendency to use saturated color is really not pervasive in the culture as a whole. On the other hand, the overwhelming number of Black painters that I have known have been interested in bright color.

The question remains as to whether the spirit of a Pan-African culture can be caught sufficiently by Whites for them to write criticism about Blacks that is meaningful to Blacks and my answer, resoundingly, is yes.

Yes *if* they are capable or willing to look beyond their own cultural biases and to realize that simply because they have controlled the forces of international criticism does not mean that their criticism is just in relation to other peoples. Whites will have to stop excusing themselves for ignorance of Black culture. Most Black artists who have been through graduate school are expected to know the history of White civilization. Ignorance by a Black of the agonies of Jackson Pollock and Mark Rothko or the sober vision of Edward Hopper would be considered disgraceful but the reverse is not true. White colleagues will admit almost boastfully that they have never heard of Charles White, Henry Tanner or Norman Lewis. Until Whites recognize their deficiencies toward Black culture to be that of true ignorance they will not be in a position to assess its merits meaningfully.

Most of what has been written about Black artists by Whites has been predicated on White values from the outset. This is true of the most recent book in that regard, Elsa Fine's book, *The Afro-American Artist* (Holt, Rinehart & Winston, N.Y., 1973). Fine's book draws heavily from material previously written by Alain Locke, James Porter, Cedric Dover and others, but is conspicuous in its omissions of information readily available at several Black universities and museums. In addition, she argues her case always using values of White artists as her ultimate criteria in her endless comparisons of relationships between Black artists and their White counterparts.

Any study of Pan-African art will reveal the paucity of critics and critical journals in the field. Someone must be willing to publish you before you can be heard from. Blacks have not had much success in this venture. If Black critics were editors of major art publications, what I have said in this essay would be common knowledge.

A fellow Black artist, knowing that I was preparing this paper, questioned whether indeed the artists I mentioned considered their work as I did. I told him that I hoped so, but that what the artist consciously means is not always the basis of art criticism. Criticism is not about the language of artists but the language of art. One doubts that Botticelli would have agreed with Berenson, or Grunewald with Wölfflin. We know how fiercely Whistler disagreed with Ruskin, how Albers disagreed with Greenberg and how all of contemporary art disagrees with Tom Wolfe. And on the other hand, of course, are the legions who do agree with Berenson. Wölfflin, Ruskin and Greenberg. But agreement or disagreement with criticism has never stopped criticism in the past. Criticism has always been advocacy and a path or alternative for consideration by artists and audiences. So it has been with major criticism of American and European art. So it should be with criticism from a Pan-African point of view.

Bibliographical Information

One of the earliest Black critics in the field was Alain Locke. I have already spoken of some of his writings including the *New Negro*, published in 1925. Yet it is important to recognize that since the time of Locke there have been comparatively few Black critical writings published. After Locke, the next significant critical landmark on the subject was written by James Porter a professor of art and art history at Howard University. Porter's book *Modern Negro Art* (Dryden Press, 1943, reprinted with an "introduction" by Walter Pach, Arno Press, 1969) has long been a classic. It received wide review then fell into oblivion to the White art world, though held as a sacred source book by Blacks. Porter's book traced origins of Afro-American art through works done during slavery to the nineteen thirties. In 1965 Porter updated an essay called "One Hundred Fifty Years of Afro-American Art," which previously appeared in *Presence Africaine* (Djon, 1958), as the main text of a catalog called *The Negro in American Art* (U.C.L.A. Art Galleries, 1966). "One Hundred Fifty Years of Afro-American Art" reviewed the history of Afro-American art and pointed to a new affirmation of African consciousness.

Another book which lists more than 100 artists and many extensive bibliographies was Cedric Dover's *American Negro Art* (New York Graphic Society, 1960). But Dover's book borrows most heavily from Porter's, involved little new research and omitted a great number of younger artists.

Black artists have traditionally had to do much of the writing about their own works. That was the case with Porter. Romare Bearden has himself done quite a bit of writing since the 1930's. "The Negro Artist and Modern Art" by Bearden appeared in the December issue of *Opportunity* and also in *Journal of Negro Life*, 1934. In the October 1948 issue of *Critique* Bearden published an article called "Problems of Negro Artists." Later he published "The Artist's Imagination," *Pyramid Club Annual* (May, 1956); "Rectangular Structure in My Montage Paintings," *Leonardo* (Jan., 1969); "The Artist and His Education," *Harvard Art*

Review (Spring 1969); and more recently a book co-authored with Harry Henderson, *Six Black Masters of American Art* (Doubleday & Co., 1972) and a bibliography on Horace Pippin (Phillips Galliers, 1977).

Another artist to have written extensively in the field has been Elton Fax. An artist of international reputation he has written several books which presented thorough biographies of many artists. His books include *17 Black Artists* (Dodd, Mead, N.Y., 1971) and *Black Artists of the New Generation,* (Dodd, Mead, N.Y., 1977).

There have been a number of bibliographical studies and bibliographies including Carroll Greene's and Warren Robbins' *The Art of Henry O. Tanner* (Museum of African Art, Washington, 1969); Carroll Greene's *The Evolution of Afro-American Artists 1800–1950* (City Univer. of N.Y., 1967) which accompanied an exhibition by Greene and Bearden. Also Greene's *Romare Bearden: The Prevalence of Ritual* (Mus. of Modern Art, N.Y., 1971); Edmund B. Gaither's *Afro-American Artists: New York and Boston* (Museum of the National Center of Afro-American Artists, Boston, 1970); Robert Doty's *Contemporary Black Artists in America* (Whitney Museum, N.Y., 1971); Evelyn S. Brown's *Africa's Contemporary Art and Artists* (Harmon Foundation, N.Y., 1966); Ulli Beier's *Contemporary Art in Africa* (Praeger, N.Y., 1968); Rosalind R. Jeffries' *Directions in Afro-American Art* (Johnson Museum of Art, Ithaca, 1974); David C. Driskell's *Amistad II: Afro-American Art* (United Chess Press, N.Y., 1975); David C. Driskell's and Earl Hooks' *The Afro-American Collection Fisk University* (Fisk Univ., Nashville, 1976) and again by Driskell: *Art by Blacks: Its Vital Role in U.S. Culture* (Smithsonian, Oct., 1976). Other writings have been done by such people as Samella Lewis, E.J. Montgomery, Lois Mailon Jones, Adolphus Ealey, Guy McElroy, Allan Gordon and myself.

However, it is David Driskell who has emerged as perhaps the primary authority on Afro-American art today and it is from him that much of the bibliographical information contained herein has come. His distinguished scholarship would be an invaluable source for anyone who seriously wishes to gain better information about the field.

N.A.M.E. AT SIX

Re-Defining the Role of Alternative Spaces

June 1979

> "I thought how History has a two-fold effect, viz.,
> intellectual pleasure and moral pain."
> —**Emerson**

My friend Jeff has a very provocative theory about the art world and co-operative galleries, or, to be more precise, "artist-run alternative spaces." His theory goes something like this: Alternative spaces founded and run by artists are "contexts for the insecure." This phrase means simply that those persons (artists) who have no standing in the art world are the people likely to start or be involved in an alternative space. Through such acts, these people garner the recognition they crave from what I shall call "the establishment art world" or EAW.

These artists are not motivated to become involved with an alternative space because their particular types of art works are unsuitable for presentation or absorption by the EAW, as the common myth has it. It is obvious that there are many "establishment artists" around who do untraditional works that are difficult to show in a gallery or museum setting—Burden, Christo, Oppenheim, and Serra, for example. In fact, many contemporary artists do work of this nature, and untraditional work is in reality a valuable calling card when courting the EAW.

Nor do these artists become involved in alternative spaces for the other reason so often cited: that although their work is in traditional, "gallery-prone" modes—painting, sculpture, and the like—it is in a *style* not in demand or sanctified by the art marketplace of the moment. Thus, even if such artists wished to work with the establishment or show in a commercial gallery, they would be excluded because of their unsuitable style.

This cannot be so. Looking at the artists who have shown in alternative spaces, one is immediately struck by the large numbers who quickly leaped into the EAW after initial exposure, and further have become acceptable and even successful. Artists whose work is truly not in demand or truly unacceptable to the EAW would have no such luck.

Thus, through the development of a *context* in which to be viewed, for themselves and their art works, alternative-space artists have a more confident facade behind which to hide their personal and artistic insecurity. They simply "create" their own art world. This is a great danger, according to my friend, because he feels that the EAW has become quite dependent on the art put forth by the alternative spaces, and that this art, because it is produced in a context of insecurity, is inferior. He finds even more disturbing the EAW's willingness to leave the job of taking the risk out of "new art" and new artistic thoughts—a burden he feels should be shared by all—to the alternative spaces.

Subscribing to this rather radical viewpoint, one can see why my friend saw the flowering of the alternative spaces as one of the worst things that could have happened to the Chicago art scene. However it is virtually a tenet of dogma that the alternative spaces were one of the *best* things that could have happened to the Chicago art scene.

Last month N.A.M.E. Gallery, celebrated its sixth anniversary (its fifth on Hubbard Street) with a show documenting its history along with the publication of a limited-edition portfolio featuring six gallery members and four rather more renowned artists. In light of the attention that N.A.M.E. has focused on itself for this anniversary, it seems suitable to single it out for an examination of the entire phenomenon of artist-run spaces in Chicago. Why did they come about in the first place? What kind of effect did they have on the EAW? How did they define themselves, and what role did they actually play? What is in store for the future?

"It was through a network of friends who got together at studios to talk," says Phil Berkman, a founding member of N.A.M.E. Said Jerry Saltz, a second founding member, in a 1974 interview published in the *New Art Examiner*: "We were meeting together and talking—at first just individuals who happened to be artists getting together to see what it was like." It is hard to get any concrete statement from the N.A.M.E, founders[1] on why they got together to form a gallery in the first place. The time seemed right; there was constant talk of change, alternatives. A.I.R., a pioneering alternative space, had been having an impact on New York's art community since 1971.

It is noteworthy, however, that all but one of the N.A.M.E. founding members (Berkman) were students at the School of the Art Institute (SAIC). The School has an incredible hold over its students. Highly dependent relationships form with instructors and fellow students. Going out into the big wide world when one is not particularly well prepared for it is terrifying. So it is not entirely flippant to suggest that N.A.M.E. was founded as a sort of club for graduating SAICers.

Of course there was also plenty of idealistic rhetoric: N.A.M.E. was going to provide an alternative to the entrenched and difficult-to-break system artists in Chicago were forced to go through to show their work. As a city, Chicago had only recently acquired, at long last, a style with which to identify itself, namely Imagism; and in its proud mother flurry over this elder child, it ignored the younger artists who did not do Imagism (not to mention the older abstractionists). Clearly, something had to be done.

So it was this particular group, out of Lord only knows how many eager young dreamers, who decided to *do* something. This particular group had among its strengths two movers and shakers—Holden and Saltz—whose bureaucratic abilities enabled them to get not-for-profit status, a tax exemption, initial contributions, and later grant money. But for the first year, anyway, all members paid $15 a month dues, pitched in with all the work, met as a group to make decisions, and hung exciting if not widely-seen shows. After a year at Wells and Lake in a dark third-floor loft with a scenic vista of the Ravenswood elevated tracks, N.A.M.E. moved to its current home at 9 West Hubbard. Now was N.A.M.E. to have an impact. Now was the "Hubbard Street Scene" to be born.

In 1975 N.A.M.E. took in six new members, swelling its ranks to twelve. Filmgroup, a corollary to N.A.M.E., was having success with an exciting film program. Performances and jazz were bringing in yet another segment of the audience. N.A.M.E. began to receive wide notice in the local press as well as mentions in *Artforum* and even *Time* magazine. But the inevitable internal friction had also reached a high pitch, caused not least by the large number of members. Come 1977, only four of the original nine founders remained.[2]

Then, in 1977–78, N.A.M.E. was awarded five CETA positions, and hired, among others, a gallery director (Krystin Grenon, an artist formerly based in Detroit), a bookkeeper, and a maintenance person. N.A.M.E. also surprised the Chicago art community with large, guest-curated group exhibitions, bringing in such well-known art-world personalities as Ellen Lanyon. The gallery also mounted a popular performance series, organized by Linda Novak, which culminated in the ambitious *Encyclopedia of*

All Art, by Peters-Gottlieb-Despota (certainly one of the most significant works of the last few years to be totally ignored).

Many of the artists N.A.M.E. had showcased in earlier years had become quite successful—Don Sultan, Nancy Davidson (both one-time members), Mary Stoppert, Andrea Blum, Tom Kovachevich, to mention but a few. N.A.M.E. had spawned Chicago Filmmakers, formerly Filmgroup, which now occupied a space across the street, shared with the women's co-op ARC. Artemisia Gallery had been an upstairs neighbor for a couple of years, and a dance center, Cloud Hands, occupied the third floor of the 9 West Hubbard address. West Hubbard Gallery (formerly East Hubbard Gallery) was gaining recognition down the street as a sort of "bastard foster child" to N.A.M.E. A video co-op also joined the scene. N.A.M.E. couldn't have seemed to have been more successful, basking in the light generated by the alternative energy it had drawn to Hubbard Street.

But there remained a problem: money and acceptance by those with the money, namely private collectors and patrons. "Art looks different on the walls of an alternative space than it does on a museum wall. The context of an alternative space to some extent nullifies the value of the art in the minds of EAW critics, curators, and especially collectors." I'm taking the liberty of paraphrasing, but essentially this was what Krystin Grenon, N.A.M.E.'s CETA-funded director for the last two years, said to me.

Like it or not, the context in which we see art is nearly as important as the art object itself. N.A.M.E. had recognized its separate and not entirely equal relationship, of course, not long after opening, but nothing much was ever said, let alone done, about exactly how to remedy this situation.

Looking back to the request for not-for-profit status generated in 1973 by N.A.M.E. founders and put into proper bureaucratese by Barry Holden's father, a professional copywriter, one finds this interesting statement: "N.A.M.E. feels that by offering the people of Chicago an alternative and/or addition to the established and conventional art forms, it will be adding an important new dimension to the community's *awareness and appreciation of the creative act.*" (My emphasis.) So it was not the *product* of the creative act, i.e. the art work, it was the *act* itself that N.A.M.E. founders wished to promulgate to "the people of Chicago." Did N.A.M.E. consider itself, a sort of open kitchen in which the creative act was to be observed cooking, while the community partook of sanctioned art works out in the dining area of the EAW?[3] It was hard to determine in 1973.

But Guy Whitney and N.A.M.E. members, writing some five years later in the *New ArtsSpace,* published by a conference at the Los Angeles

Institute of Contemporary Art, finally acknowledged and addressed this difficult, unsolved dilemma: "The artist's economic well-being has become an increasing concern: for being able to sell a piece of art is as *real a kind of support* (my emphasis) as giving someone a show." Whitney and friends go on to mourn that "Chicago collectors do not generally seem willing to risk buying local new art."

So even if N.A.M.E. would make the radical turn to promoting and handling sales of art works (a labor deferred to the artists themselves in the present system), how would N.A.M.E. attract the well-heeled local collectors who still do most of their shopping on Ontario Street? How can one make a rebellious political statement by founding an "alternative space" in the first place and still expect the support of the monied patron who is firmly plugged into the very aspect of the art world that the concept of an alternative space attempts to debunk?

As everyone knows, when Jewish "new money" collectors found themselves ostracized by the Old Guard WASPs at the Art Institute, they founded the Museum of Contemporary Art—and look at the difficulty the MCA has had in reconciling its brash upstart self to the scorned and wounded giant. It is this same process that is going on with N.A.M.E. and the last unseduced virgin in the EAW, the collector and patron.

Now these subtle issues are not often on the minds of idealistic young graduates of art schools, but they soon enough manifest themselves in the real world. So in 1979, N.A.M.E.'s publication of a limited portfolio might be correctly seen as a gesture of conciliation toward the collector-patron. There is icing on the cake in the form of established names—Ron Gorchov, Lynda Benglis, William T. Wiley, and Jack Tworkov—and the fact that it was printed by Landfall Press.[4] By coming up with this portfolio and a fund-raising program (the main feature of which has been a slick mailing piece funded by a grant from McDonald's Corporation asking for patronage and support), N.A.M.E. has confirmed the suspicion in many people's minds, that it never was a "true" alternative space. Whatever the discrepancy between original, idealistic purpose and subsequent reality, in three or four short years N.A.M.E. has become a major conduit through which many younger artists entered the art world. Indeed, now it has become almost mandatory for a young artist to show on Hubbard Street before breaking into commercial galleries or museums. And so quite ironically, N.A.M.E. has merely extended the system of the EAW. If N.A.M.E. ever once was a "true alternative," it did not remain one long.

All of this may seem like so much splitting of hairs, but it is of extreme importance when considering the role of N.A.M.E vis-à-vis the expectations and perceptions of the community. As much as one has to admire the democracy of N.A.M.E.—all members still meet weekly, and decisions are made by majority vote of the group—at the same time one longs for a central personality upon which to fix a "leader" if you will, who charts a clear direction. Saltz and Holden, by dint of their particular personalities, had become identified as the "spokesmen" for N.A.M.E. throughout its formative years. Now that neither is associated with the gallery, the community seems to be waiting for someone to lay out a comprehensive five- or ten-year plan for the future.

Is N.A.M.E. intending to take the part of a little MCA? Certainly it seems to be moving in a museumish direction. The fact that it has a paid staff of five makes N.A.M.E. look less and less like an artist-run space (though it still certainly is) and more and more like a museum. N.A.M.E. seems to have a lot of money to work with, expanding from a mere few thousand in '73 to $33,000 in '77 to a projected $95,000 this year.[5]

It is worthwhile noting at this point that N.A.M.E. has always seen its existence per se as a major justification. "The most important thing is that this place stays open," said Saltz in 1974. Stays open *as what* is the unspoken question. And it is the perception of N.A.M.E. as an institution which carries the connotations common to artist-run spaces that is the delicate creature being bruised by N.A.M.E.'s growing and changing. But the altruistic and idealistic are still involved in N.A.M.E. in the form of new blood.[6] Pamela Burgess, an artist formerly based in Boston, said that her attraction to N.A.M.E. was as a place more to give to the community than to get from it: "It's easy to get a show; but involvement at N.A.M.E. supports it as a place to talk and meet. It's a stepping stone," she says, echoing the words of the founding members back in '72 and '73.

Though it might be a context by which the artistically insecure define themselves, and may indeed hide a festering of inflated egos, N.A.M.E. really does offer a haven for those who wish to disassociate themselves from the EAW for whatever reason. It further offers hope to the art student, as well as a slightly strange harbor for the EAW to explore.

There is no question that N.A.M.E. vastly changed the face of Chicago's art scene. Was it for the worse, as my friend would argue? Is there something inherently dangerous about the EAW relying on alternative spaces to point the way and show "new art" without accepting those same alternative spaces as equal partners in the art world?

N.A.M.E. has had an astounding success rate, not only in promoting young artists to higher elevations in the art world, but also in promulgating a way of artistic life. Through its auxiliary programs—film, music, performance—N.A.M.E. has proven that there is an audience for such events, and besides spawning new alternative spaces like Chicago Filmmakers, has fed music and performance programs at art-world establishments like the MCA. In other words, N.A.M.E. has created its own little "culture gulch" and taught the Philistines what they should desire.

Granted, there is always a certain danger in institutionalization. Not only art students, but a whole generation of critics and curators have come of age with N.A.M.E., and alternative spaces are an integral part of their thinking. The real danger here seems to lurk in the old and vulgar question of whether the art alternative spaces give to Chicago is "good" or "bad." The assumption that artist-run spaces will show "good" art because the members, being artists in the first place, will have a more highly developed sensibility is one that N.A.M.E. does not deny. But is this necessarily true? Will history look back at the particularly fecund period spanned by N.A.M.E. and dismiss much of the work as the self-absorbed play of art students who were still wet behind their ears? This does not seem a far-fetched possibility.

Are Hubbard Street and N.A.M.E. just too "easy," and artists who exhibit there insufficiently forced to refine and distill their vision? Probably. But while one might lament that the community is being deluged with a great deal of mediocre work, one might also say that because the community is being exposed to so much, it will develop more exacting standards. Looking and learning for ourselves, taking risks and standing back up after falls, seems a more viable way of artistic life than blindly following the EAW, who in turn were led by New York tastemakers, as was the situation before the advent of N.A.M.E.

The future, as always, is fraught with danger. There is some question—on both philosophical and financial grounds—about how many alternative spaces Chicago can support. Last year's loss of government grants by the dance collective, MoMing, sent a ripple of concern through the alternative spaces. The disinclination of the spaces to work together more than they do (the annual "4/4 Show" seems a token to many) is disturbing. The idea that alternative spaces are in competition is distasteful as it is antithetical to the very idea of an alternative space. But the two-year-old West Hubbard co-op has been perceived by some as attempting to inherit and compete with N.A.M.E.'s legacy. Also, the fact that West

Hubbard is able to mount exciting programs and exhibitions[7] with virtually no government money makes many wonder why N.A.M.E. can't do more with the nearly $100,000 it has to work with.

Last year the Museum of Contemporary Art celebrated its 10th Anniversary; this year the Art Institute is mounting a Centennial Celebration. In their celebration of anniversaries, these institutions point back with pride to their "institution-hood"—their accomplishments, their position in the community, their plans for the future. In an interesting and revealing contrast, *The N.A.M.E. Show: A Portfolio and History,* mounted to celebrate the six years of N.A.M.E.'s existence, seemed strangely tentative—indeed almost apologetic. The April 11th opening of *The N.A.M.E. Show,* which was meant to kick off a fund-raising effort, was essentially like any other N.A.M.E. opening save for the fact that a sum of money was spent on a tuxedoed waiter to serve drinks—a standard practice of the Museum of Contemporary Art.

Is N.A.M.E. afraid to stand up and point to its own "institution-hood"? Does N.A.M.E. somehow feel that because of its initial identification in the eyes of the art community as an "alternative space," it is all right to redefine its goals and pursue new audiences only as long as the process is not discussed openly, almost as if it were some shameful disease?

Anniversaries are the proper times to acknowledge and let go of the past and make plans for the future. N.A.M.E. Gallery should not be embarrassed or reluctant to do either.

NOTES

1. Along with Berkman and Saltz, Othello Anderson, Bill Brand, Michael Crane, Barry Holden, Marty Long, Amanda Perry, and Guy Whitney.

2. Anderson, Whitney, and, not insignificantly, Holden and Saltz.

3. Interestingly enough, Jerry Saltz, in the aforementioned 1974 NAE interview, used a food analogy, although in support of an entirely different viewpoint: "First we get some new cooks in the kitchen, [then] we get some more people to eat that food."

4. Apparently N.A.M.E.'s portfolio, with a pre-publication price of $1200, is selling quite well; 15 have been spoken for at press time.

5. Roughly half of this figure is CETA monies for manpower, a quarter is NEA funds, and the remainder is from the IAC and various revenues (admissions, showing fees, and the like).

6. In the last year, N.A.M. E. has taken in four new members: Pamela Burgess, Michael Brakke, Terry Karpowicz, Paul Krainak.

7. Like last year's ambitious contemporary European photography show which traveled to West Hubbard from a Texas museum and the affiliated Chicago Books artist's book organization.

SPEAKEASY

February 1982

Each month the *New Art Examiner* will invite
a well-known, or not-so-well-known, art world
personality to write a "Speakeasy" essay on a topic
of interest—whatever it may be.

New York Uber Alles: Pluralism. The critics and curators have all but buried it. Before laying it to rest consider: in its diversity and lack of distinction, it may have been the ultimate metaphor for the seventies. Its multiplicity was an extension of the ME generation—of divergent interest groups all shouting for equal rights—of individual morality demanding "get down," "do your own thing," and "I need my own space." It was a personification in paint, plastic, plaster and, yes, "works on paper," of non-judgmental, non-hierarchical sub-cultures proclaiming "I'm O.K.—you're O.K."—and "anything I call art is art." Literary, narrative, collage, mixed media—it was the essence of a society stuffing satin shirts in denim pants and pay as you go. How do you define pay? What is the value of anything . . . What is someone willing to pay for it? What is all this business about justice and fair play? There is always force (of course).

Manhattan has 20 blocks to the mile. New Yorkers seem to spend the better part of their time in an area of maybe 40 or 50 blocks. To them the "territory" sounds impressive, but it's only 2 ½ miles, a distance any non-New Yorker travels for even the most mundane, self-supporting reasons. Granted, there's a lot compacted on the bedrock of the island—one big experience is going on in that compressed mass of humanity. It is, in a sense, a city full of semifinalists. A marketplace in which peddlers descend to hawk their aesthetic and practical wares. But how are the natives responding? Do they see more of life? Or do they shut themselves off—sensory overload—and become provincial and smug. Historical tunnel-vision as concept.

How would Leonardo feel about his Mona Lisa as a billboard—wearing Koss stereo headphones? We live in an era of embryonic, computerized lifestyles . . . pathetically domesticated and shriveled instincts. Regeneration is a universal phenomenon. To eliminate from one's life the natural processes in the name of seriousness is to indulge in self-deception.

Where have all the people gone? Electronic shadows of their former selves watching video screens, ignoring the right of refusal.

Or perhaps they are driving up in their new Mercedes' and BMW's to buy German Expressionist paintings. Do the ladies clutch their Gucci's as they strut in Claude (not Joe) Montana and shell out for the newest European cultural imports?

Perception, or what we experience through our sensory apparatus, is being affected by the rapid acceleration of media-related technology. Our view of the world is changing as the "global-environment" expands through media accessibility and the information reservoir gets deeper. My belief is that these elements (good or bad) have woven their way into the collective fabric of our lives. I also believe that any artist always works within the context or conditions that are indigenous to his or her own time and, in doing so, reflects the energy, temperament and attitudes of that climate.

Paint may seem like an outmoded medium but the human imagination is endless.

A L I C E   T H O R S O N

YOUNG CHICAGOANS PREFER
ENGAGEMENT TO AVANT-GARDISM

May 1982

The following article is based on interviews with 13 young Chicago artists. I would like to thank Deven Golden, Stephen Reynolds, Paul Krainak, Bill Cass, Olivia Gude, Luciano Franchi de Alfaro III, Marcia Weese, Fred Holland, Susan Sensemann, John Phillips, Fern Shaffer, L.J. Douglas, and Dan Reynolds for their time, hospitality, and ideas.

"There are many rumors going on that more people are interested in what Chicago is doing . . . There's a feeling in this town that wasn't here, originally."
—**Stephen Reynolds**

The past decade has seen a tremendous surge in Chicago's prestige and importance as an art town. Manhattan dealers have "raided" Chicago lofts (See NAE, May 1981), while, at the same time, numerous Chicago artists have emigrated to New York and made it. Currently uppermost in everyone's minds is the third annual Navy Pier Show, the five-day, commercial extravaganza which has gained a reputation as the most prestigious dealer art fair in the country.

Never, it seems, has the energy level run so high in Chicago. The past few months alone have seen the opening of half a dozen new galleries, while enterprising individuals have managed to organize major shows on shoestring budgets (Larry Lundy's "Loop Show"; Margaret Tinguely and Margo Rush's "Some Girls"). The alternatives are still going strong, and every six months or so an "art party" brightens the social scene.

Given the current, international vogue for expressionistic, idiosyncratic, figurative art, there is an overall feeling that the tide is turning our way. On the surface, everything is rosy. But how do Chicago's young artists feel about the current state of affairs? Beneath the optimistic fanfare, is Chicago truly perceived as an ideal place for the artist to live and work? Or does it still remain the Second City, the halfway house, the cheap hostel on the road to glitter and fame of New York?

> "I'm going to stay in Chicago. I can't see moving to a city where I'd have to spend as much time as would be necessary to support myself in virtually the same style. I'd be working at least two times as much."—**Fred Holland**

At present, it seems the artist's primary motivation for living and working in Chicago is economics, pure and simple. Horror stories about New York's high cost of living (particularly the astronomical price of loft space—$2000 a month!), combined with rumors of crowded conditions and the difficulty of obtaining employment, pose a tremendous deterrent to even the most ambitious Chicago artist. Here, according to John Phillips (who spent six months in New York as a Whitney fellow and then returned to Chicago), "your dollar goes farther, there's less unemployment, and places are still cheap."

On the practical side, for the artist, Chicago clearly has New York beat, hands down. After economic viability, space appears to be Chicago's most important commodity—space, not only in terms of square footage, but space in terms of artistic elbow room. According to Fern Shaffer,

> I find Chicago stimulating. I think there's enough room here for people to have the good ideas. I don't know how much room there is in New York because [there] you're playing against people who have been playing a long time. If I were to start to go into performance, I'd go to The Kitchen. I'd have to be competing against Vito Acconci because he's still working out of The Kitchen. I don't know if they would let me play.

Although no one would deny that the artist in Chicago faces some stiff competition, neither could one deny that the odds of getting lost in the shuffle are not nearly so great here as in New York. Particularly for the younger artist, who has not yet acquired the competitive edge that accompanies financial success, the possibility of being a big fish in a little pond is a definite plus for Chicago. As Deven Golden expresses it, "I like that it [Chicago] is a little bit backwards. I feel that my personal impact is greater. In New York, I either become a superstar or nothing. Here, not even being the superstar, you can exert quite a bit of pressure and get ideas that you have accomplished."

By contrast to the "compressed mass of humanity" of Manhattan Island (Ed Paschke, "Speakeasy," NAE, February 1982), many artists feel that, at times, Chicago's "space" poses a bane to communication. Despite the fact that Chicago's "loft district" stretches from the shopping malls of the North Shore to the steel mills of Indiana, accessibility, as this writer discovered, is simply not a problem. If Chicagoans are not necessarily gregarious, they are certainly friendly enough once they're approached. As Paul Krainak points out, "You can get around and meet everybody. That's the strange thing about Chicago. There's not a lot of communication, and yet if you're willing to go find the people you can find them. It's easy."

Some feel that it is precisely the dispersed nature of Chicago's art community that renders it so conducive to artistic individuality. Painter and University of Illinois-Chicago Circle instructor Susan Sensemann sees it as a "positive thing." From her standpoint, "That's the reason I really like being in Chicago—because I don't feel pressured to do anything other than what I want to do."

The meaner side of art politics seems thwarted by Chicago's extra elbow room—almost as if much of its energy were exhausted merely in trying to locate the objects of its attention. After spending several years in New York, working in a studio in the Bowery, Marcia Weese says she moved back to Chicago because "I could concentrate on my work, more than on the politics involved . . . I could see, laid out in front of me, my next five years. I could see being held in check by this group of people, and not being able to go ahead because of that group of people. It was so oppressive, as much as I loved it."

> "You tell someone you're an artist in Chicago and you think they say anything? They go, 'Oh, that's nice. What do you do to support yourself?'"
> —**Deven Golden**

Regardless of the numerous practical advantages offered by Chicago, most artists agree with Susan Sensemann who admits, "I guess I do believe that if you're going to make it, it has to be in New York, ultimately." Generally speaking, those artists who visit New York experience a sense of dissatisfaction on returning home. John Phillips recalls, "When I was in New York the discussions were much different. People felt more pressure to know, to be up on, what was going on. And here there's not that pressure." Deven Golden, whose studio is adjacent to Phillips' in an old warehouse on Haddon Street, betrays a similar impatience with Chicago's less-than-dynamic involvement in art. He complains,

> In New York, people are aware of art; it's part of their everyday existence. Every apartment I walked into, people had very nice collections and they thought about their collections. In Chicago, when someone puts a painting on the wall, it's there for 25 years. That's it—they put the painting there, the room is decorated. In New York, they have ten pieces on this wall, five on that wall. This year they'll sell two of those, buy three more. It's an active thing. More than the intellectual atmosphere, I think there's just more acceptance there. If you tell someone you're an artist there, they don't ask you how you feed yourself, they're not interested. Here, it's just the natural question. Because they don't believe it.

Fortunately for the walls of Chicago, Reaganomics has not proved conducive to grandiose dreams of fame and fortune in the Big Apple, and current attitudes of young Chicago artists toward meeting the New York exodus range from xenophobic rejection of the whole trip to wary apprehension. Fern Shaffer comments,

> I'm not going to New York. I really have no intention of picking up and moving to New York for five years and being in another gallery and fighting. Whatever I do is going to be here, and the ideas and concepts that I'm working on are going to be here. The fame and glory will come if it's going to come at all: It may never come. What's important is that I feel that I have ideas that are strong enough to support myself and to influence society in some way.
>
> The people who left here and went to New York—I don't know where they're at. I don't hear their names, I don't know what shows they're in. Do they get eaten up in the game of survival? I'm not interested in that, I'm interested in making art.

Despite differing attitudes toward the prospect of packing a bag and leaving, one issue on which Chicago artists are unanimous is the primacy of the art. If one can eat, one can work—and location be damned. According to Luciano Franchi de Alfaro III, "The main criterion is that you have this need to do this work. And you have to do it. And you're going to do it whether you're famous or not."

Perhaps it is the very perspective afforded by an "outsider" mentality that makes young Chicago artists suspicious of stereotyped definitions of success and wary of the spiritual impoverishment success often breeds. As Marcia Weese explains,

> To be an artist you have to work all your life. It's a slow process. We're in a really funny time when you can be famous when you're 28. But you might be very confused and not know what it is you're doing. It's a dangerous game in terms of artists' expectations of themselves. They'll start taking shortcuts, they'll start getting lazy about all this crap they have to go through.

Olivia Gude, an artist who lives in Chicago's historic Pullman district and is finishing an MFA at the University of Chicago, registers a similar apprehension about the possibility of corruption. She confesses, "In some ways I'd rather make this shit and pile it up in my basement . . . I'm real afraid of how the environment that you work with changes you and changes your work."

> "A lot of Chicago artists are suddenly being shown in New York. They're exactly what's happening right now, and they've been doing it for so many years, and suddenly they're in the limelight. So there's really no excuse for the lameness of getting the art out in print to the people and educating the people about art."—Marcia Weese

Outward bravado notwithstanding, the Second City syndrome is still alive and well. However, the past several years have witnessed an important shift in the locus of Chicago's inferiority complex. As Chicago artists achieve international acclaim, an increased confidence burgeons at home. Few artists would disagree with Shaffer's assessment that, "The work being done here is terrific." Rather, the source of their disappointment is the support system—the museum, gallery, and critical network that seems to have lagged hopelessly behind the artistic vanguard: Thus, Shaffer remarks, "We have some major museums here, it's too bad they're very closed. They're not supportive—they don't take somebody in their own city and give them a show or retrospective." Similarly, Deven Golden wryly asks, "Support is one thing, but who's qualified to decide on the support? . . . If you [the city] have $150,000 to spend, do you have the right to spend it on ten Chicago unknowns, or should you safeguard the city's money and buy one Miro?"

Particularly since so many Chicago artists have garnered outside recognition, impatience with the conservative nature of native institutions has been mounting. A look at art-world institutions reveals that provincialism is still rampant in Chicago—and not the good-natured, aw shucks provincialism of a young, ignorant cow-town, but a more deadening, insidious provincialism that expresses itself in a lack of confidence and a refusal to gamble even when the dice are loaded.

Is it over-simplifying to suggest that a working-class town exercises a working-class caution with regard to supporting art? That fearing risks, it hedges its bets by investing in big-time sculpture by big-time modernists, instead of tapping the fertile resource of its native talent? As Deven Golden observes, "New York makes capital by creating the investments in the first place. We are followers here. We are not creators. We're not making something that is going to be taken for the Chicago scene, even though we have the artists."

> "People generally are afraid to make a judgment on their own, so the name of the gallery, or the name of another critic, or a collector who has done something with the work always influences anyone who is writing about art. I think that most critics are chicken."—Susan Sensemann

The seventies were difficult years for critics, despite the fact that criticism (thanks to a shot in the arm from French structuralism) was in its heyday. At the beginning of the decade, under the rubric of conceptual art, artists attempted to usurp the critic's role. Shortly thereafter, critics found themselves adrift on a sea of pluralism, without a theoretical anchor.

Those critics who attempted to save themselves by retaliating with ever more effusive streams of verbiage found themselves accused of intellectually patronizing their audience, and, in the end, merely served to convince their readership that, as Luciano Franchi de Alfaro III expresses it, "Sometimes the artists just say what they have to say much better." Even now, as the pluralist dust appears to be settling a bit, critics are still feeling the aftereffects of those frantic years.

For example, when questioned about her feelings on Chicago criticism, Sensemann responded, "I don't read much of it to tell you the truth . . . The little bit that there is—it's inconsistent, it's based on not looking at art or thinking about it." She adds, "I don't think that's true just of Chicago though."

Sensemann's response raises the question of whether years of visiting galleries filled with conceptual and minimal art have dulled the critic's visual sensibility beyond repair. Certainly, the theoretical exegesis which was invented as a substitute for narrative and figurative content never found a comfortable home in Chicago; for, at least when it comes to critiquing works in the Imagist tradition, such theoretical breast-beating appears largely unnecessary. Worse yet, it appears as a way of dodging a visual encounter with work that has visual import extremely important to its effect. Perhaps for this reason, Chicago artists are particularly virulent in their critique of criticism and critics.

Contrary to popular myth, Chicago artists are not anti-intellectual; rather, they are "anti" intellectual-bullshit, or "anti" the pseudo-intellectual filter which serves to distract from and deflect the direct impact they seek. If the art is approachable, the criticism should be too. According to Luciano Franchi de Alfaro III, "I think that criticism should be a learning experience for the reader . . . When it becomes so esoteric that only the writers know what they're talking about, I just don't see what the purpose is. It's almost like: art for art's sake; then, criticism for the critics."

But, for the most part, while artists in New York are busy trying to unravel the intellectual intricacies of excessive verbiage, Chicago artists find themselves in the opposite predicament—confronted by a dearth of criticism and elusive critics. As one artist relates her experience, after mounting a major show of her work, she "tried everything. I called up all these reviewers—the four major newspaper reviewers . . . and I felt as if even if I had been established in Chicago for five years, they still would have to really think it over, about coming or not. It's a terribly pompous attitude. It's no longer the art they're interested in, it's whether you're important enough so that they can get a pat on the back for having written an article."

Most young artists agree with Krainak that, "We need some sort of reasonable, mature, glossy art magazine, and we also need one or two art journals." But, is the paucity of critical coverage a symptom or a cause of what is perceived by artists as a deplorable lack of discourse and criticism within the artistic community itself?

Perhaps it is this very dearth of discourse, compounded by the obstacles posed by physical distance, that infuses so many young artists with the desire to connect, not only with the members of their own community, but with society at large. It is this impulse, rather than a particular set of stylistic tenets, which seems to form the core of a "Chicago sensibility."

> "By a really conservative estimate I have this $25,000 art education . . . It seems like there's this really strong pressure that what you do with your $25,000 education is make work which is only accessible to people who have $25,000 educations."
> —Olivia Gude

The idea of a specifically "Chicago" sensibility is often rejected by artists as too limiting. Recently, it was characterized as "an anti-intellectual, anti-formalist, anti-corporate attitude that proclaims the primacy of idiosyncratic expression, without the necessity for any rationale or dogma beyond the activity of making art" (Jane Allen, "Intellectual Art Dead in New York," NAE, April 1981). But conversations with young artists reveal that Allen's definition still holds up. Chicago artists were never enthused about the reductive sterility of a modernism stifled in theory.

As Deven Golden explains it, "Art is about seeing, it's about visual impact. It's not about ideas about it. That's something else. That's for art historians, that's for critics, that's for everyone else to talk about. It's not for artists. I think it's important to know those things, but I don't think that that makes a painting."

Chicago art—visual as opposed to cerebral? Rarely. In Chicago, anti-intellectualism does not mean anti-ideas. It reflects the belief that ideas and theories are a poor substitute for experience. Here, ideas are relegated to the planning stages; they don't show up with a frame around them.

Chicago's young artists strongly protest the division of the artistic sensibility into formal- and content-related concerns. Here, even when form ostensibly is content, the artist's intention stretches far beyond modernism's dialogue with itself. For example, Phillips says he intends his huge, abstract paintings as "a narrative in which the viewer has to put together a story." Similarly, the creator of such formally elegant sculptures as Marcia Weese insists, "The whole reason that I work abstractly is so that I can grasp the essence of something and then put it out there so that someone can almost unconsciously have a revelation." Weese's work and Deven Golden's, for instance, with its concern for psychological content, are miles apart stylistically. Yet, in terms of sensibility, in their desire to directly affect the viewer at a subconscious level, they tread common ground.

Thus, the old myth that Chicago is hostile toward abstraction is eroded by a new sensibility which does not recognize abstraction, per se, because, figurative or abstract, everything is subordinated to the desire to make contact. It is at this point that even those artists who are stylistically at odds with the Imagist heritage can relate to the Chicago tradition.

> "After a period of art that was basically about art,
> you just have to consider yourself humanity."
> —Bill Cass

If the seventies appeared as a repudiation of the counterculture creed, the eighties are once again quietly reabsorbing its ideas, securely integrating them into the social fabric. No longer torn between a tacit commitment to radical social consciousness and the inexorable momentum of modernism's self-fascination, art in general is now striving to play a different role, a role Chicago art has tended to play all along.

Stephen Reynolds points out that the current feeling is "Let's get energetic" as opposed to the last phase of cerebral, intellectual "cool" art. It seems that, almost instinctively, artists realize that the time for cerebration is past. Currently, the artist cannot afford to be uninvolved, to abdicate his responsibility as a molder of consciousness, or to hide his sensibility under an intellectual or decorative veneer at the risk of decreasing his effectiveness.

The showing of Chicago artists en masse, banners flying, at the April 10 peace march offered yet another demonstration of a commitment to human values which is ever-present in their work. In spite of an art-world power structure nurtured on avant-gardism—which persists in casting them as purveyors of fashion—Chicago's young artists accept the mandate of their native tradition and insist on their role as purveyors of consciousness.

ANN LEE MORGAN EDITOR

1979–1982

THE NEW ART EXAMINER THREE DECADES AGO

A Memoir

Sometime in the late winter or early spring of 1979—more than thirty years ago, as I now look back—I first entered the *New Art Examiner* office at 230 East Ontario Street, just off Michigan Avenue. In the heart of what was then Chicago's gallery district and just down the street from the original Museum of Contemporary Art, the quarters appeared dingy and cluttered. Tidying up obviously took a back seat here to other priorities.

Presiding that day, Derek Guthrie welcomed me with disarming enthusiasm. At that point, I had been in academia all my life. I went straight from college to graduate school to earn a Ph.D. in art history, and subsequently I'd taught for ten years—American art, primarily, but also modern art and the history of photography, as well as the inevitable surveys. Although always intensely interested in contemporary art, I'd never written about it. I could not have guessed it that day, but my experiences at the *Examiner* would prove instrumental to my evolution toward a new professional identity as a writer, editor, and, eventually, an independent scholar.

Before I showed up that day at the office, I'd been reading the *Examiner* for several years. Of course, its coverage of Chicago exhibitions and features on local artists interested me. But something else meant more.

Modest as was its format, the countercultural *Examiner* fearlessly offered a thought-provoking, often refreshing alternative to New York-based commercial publications.

Designed as a non-profit (which it surely was!), the *Examiner* operated under the aegis of the New Art Association—also created by Derek and his partner Jane Addams Allen. (Jane appeared on the masthead as editor; Derek was listed at various times as associate editor or as publisher.) Its statement of purpose, reprinted in every issue, succinctly defined the *Examiner*'s goals, which had little to do with art as a marketable commodity. It is worth quoting in its entirety:

> The New Art Association is a not-for-profit organization whose purpose is to examine the definition and transmission of culture in our society; the decision-making processes within museums and schools and the agencies of patronage which determine the manner in which culture shall be transmitted; the value systems which presently influence the making of art as well as its study in exhibitions and books; and, in particular, the interaction of these factors with the visual art milieu.

Founded in 1973, the *Examiner* paralleled—and fostered—a burgeoning local art community, as Chicago began to assume the identity of a distinct regional art center, rather than a backwoods satellite of New York. From the beginning, the *Examiner* intended to expand the critical discussion, both locally and nationally, to a more cosmopolitan view of Chicago art than had been common. Previously, from the late 1950s the art press had focused on the undeniably original but raucous work of Chicago Imagists. The *Examiner* opened the discussion to Chicago's other tradition of abstraction and formal invention, as nurtured particularly at the Institute of Design (originally the New Bauhaus), founded by László Moholy-Nagy and later known particularly for its photography program in the hands of such masters as Harry Callahan and Aaron Siskind. In addition, the *Examiner* took note of Chicago's involvement with varied sorts of representational painting, with forms of craft expression, and with large-scale public sculpture, as well as its ongoing role as a leader in architectural design. New galleries—including a number of important artist-run spaces—opened in the 1970s, and the Museum of Contemporary Art began to acquire a permanent collection for its first purpose-built space. The Art Institute of Chicago, which was much smaller then, before ambitious renovations and expansions, continued to host annual exhibitions of Chicago-area art, as it had since the late nineteenth century, while also starting more often to recognize recent and contemporary work in general. In 1980 the advent of yearly Navy Pier exhibitions—at a time when such regional, gallery-oriented fairs had not yet become common—was widely celebrated as a coming-of-age moment for Chicago art.

For its community of readers, the *Examiner* provided a nexus of communication. Artists were not only reviewed when they exhibited but often asked to write. A monthly invited "Speakeasy" column gave an artist, critic, or other art world luminary an opportunity to speak his or her mind on a topic of the writer's choosing. The *Examiner* published every letter it received. Although this policy occasionally devoured valuable print space, it signaled the *Examiner*'s respect for its readers and insured that no one could accuse the journal of protecting a biased point of view.

That spring, I wrote a review or two and occasionally stopped by the office for an energizing conversation with Derek and/or Jane. More often Derek. Of the pair, he was the talker. Jane could hold her own, but at the office she was largely focused on the editorial tasks of copy-editing, conferring with writers, and determining the layout of the next issue. To my surprise, near the end of that season, they asked me to join their editorial team the next year. (I was not totally unprepared for this job, as I'd earlier had some journalistic experience.) The salary wasn't much, but I jumped at the chance to become involved. We agreed that I would work full time in Chicago for a week each month, helping to edit reviews and articles in the run-up to publication, and the rest of the time, if my services were needed, I could work from home—which at that point was in Champaign-Urbana. Because I needed a place to stay during my Chicago stints, Jane and Derek offered me a bedroom in their capacious, if somewhat threadbare Hyde Park apartment. Thus it was that I became a part-time member of their household, which included also Jane's thirteen-year-old daughter Sarah (today, as Sarah McQuaid, a singer-songwriter well known in England and Ireland), as well as another staff member, Annie Markovich, who worked mainly on the business side. As a result, during these monthly interludes, I found myself immersed in non-stop, wide-ranging and highly informed discussion and argumentation. Generally I had the kitchen to myself at breakfast (sometimes Sarah, the other early riser, joined me), but from the time we left together for the office in Jane and Derek's jalopy until bedtime, we three were together at work, at home, and for dinner. The contentious conversations could become exhausting, even exasperating, but the couple's intellectual intensity, idiosyncratic thinking, and imaginative élan dazzled.

I mention these memories because I think they are not incidental to the *Examiner's* success—and perhaps also to some of its shortcomings. This level of discourse—and the pair's back-and-forth on practically every issue imaginable—provided the publication's bedrock and energized its purpose. True, despite their warm-hearted and generous personalities, from time to time their sometimes confrontational style and disinclination to compromise on principle alienated some in the local art community. Nevertheless, Derek and Jane formed a remarkable team. Born in England and trained there as a painter, Derek was the more intuitive and impulsive of the pair. He was a font of ideas. His irrepressible enthusiasm recruited writers, built an audience, and kept the Chicago art world on edge. A Chicago native, Jane had both a more academic background (she earned bachelor's and MFA degrees at the University of Chicago) and a more practical nature. A fine writer (who won awards for her essays in the *Examiner* and elsewhere), a superbly analytical thinker, and something of a perfectionist, she never let writing out of her hands as "good enough," but demanded precision and logic. Derek could be inspiring, but I held her intellect in awe.

In the summer of 1980 Derek and Jane moved to Washington, D.C., which had no significant art voice of its own. They intended to expand the *Examiner* to fill that void, but more important, they wanted to be closer to the country's political center. At that time, the federal government played a larger role in the art life of the nation than it does today. Particularly through the National Endowment for the Arts and—to a somewhat lesser extent—the National Endowment for the Humanities, funding was made available to individual artists, as well as to museums and other exhibition venues, community arts groups, and state arts councils. Jane and Derek always nurtured a particularly acute sense of the power structures that affected art production and reception. "Keeping them honest" motivated the *Examiner's* nationally admired investigative reporting on many aspects of the art world's institutional structure, including those in Chicago. The Washington location provided a better perch to observe the flow of money and power.

With their departure and the increased complexity of our operation, I agreed to spend more time in Chicago. (For another year, I continued to live in the Hyde Park apartment, along with Annie Markovich and Michael Bonesteel, a writer who for a year served in the position of Chicago

/Midwest editor before I assumed that title.) Jane and Derek retained editorial control, but I oversaw production in Chicago. We began to publish two editions, one for each city. These were in most respects identical, but they carried different exhibition reviews. The *Examiner* in those days retained a newspaper format. Its unbound pages therefore allowed insertion of the appropriate reviews section into each edition. Jane and Derek continued to commission many of the features, but I still worked with Jane on editing. In those days long before the internet and email, we took advantage of an earlier cutting-edge communications technology: Federal Express. Its deliveryman appeared at our door almost daily to deliver and pick up essays and reviews that Jane and I traded back and forth. In Chicago the *Examiner* had its own typesetting machine, so I was responsible for overseeing the work of our part-time typesetter and doing most of the final proofreading. Computerized production was still in the future, too. Our designer pasted the typeset material into page-sized facsimiles. Then, once more I went over the pages before they went off to the printer (where they were prepared for reproduction with a photographic process). It was all a bit cumbersome, but with the telephone (our bill ran toward the exorbitant in a day when long-distance calls still incurred individual, extra charges) and the expedited mail service, we managed.

I look back on those days with some pride in what we accomplished and with gratitude for the opportunity to have been there. I learned a lot. I recall frustrations, as well. Some issues were better than others, but—like most editors, I suppose—I regret that the compromises sometimes necessitated by a monthly production schedule prevented attaining a higher standard every time. Still, as I scan copies of the *Examiner* from that time, I'm pleased to see how many articles and reviews stand up. We were supported by subscriptions, advertising (mostly from galleries), and grants, but money was always a problem. It was difficult to pay writers and keep the lights on, too. Still, the *Examiner* provided an invigorating atmosphere, and one has to appreciate any job where there is rarely a dull moment.

I left the *Examiner* in the fall of 1982 for another editorial position, this one with a book publisher. Through the 1980s, I continued to write occasionally for the publication, but after I departed Chicago in 1990, I wrote only a few more times, and later ceased my connection altogether. By then, the editors and many of the leading personalities of the Chicago art world were unfamiliar to me. I saw Jane a couple of times in Washington in the early 1990s, but we did not meet again after she and Derek moved to England soon thereafter.

For this essay, I have chosen to concentrate on my personal experiences at the *Examiner*, rather than the issues that absorbed the art community in those days. (Hints of those may be gleaned from the articles reprinted in this volume.) In addition to describing something of how the *Examiner* was put together each month, I have written at length about Derek and Jane for two reasons. First, it occurs to me that almost no Chicagoans under fifty years of age remember them in their most vital and consequential years. (A few younger people have met Derek on infrequent visits to Chicago, but Jane died of cancer in 2004.) Second, to my mind, during the period when I was at the *Examiner*, Jane and Derek were inseparable from it, maybe indistinguishable. Scores of people contributed in important ways, but the founders' vision controlled and sustained it. And earned its national recognition. The very premise of the *Examiner* rested on a broader purpose than chronicling Chicago and Midwest art—which, of course, it did, and very well. Derek and Jane's curiosity about all forms of visual expression, their deeply-felt appreciation for the esthetic, their insistence on holding local art to national (and even international) standards, their passion for exploring the cultural values of art, and their keen eye for art's infrastructure of finance and power gave the *Examiner* a recognizable and potent voice that spoke to readers everywhere.

—Ann Lee Morgan

THE WORD VS. THE IMAGE

Some Thoughts on Reading Photography

December 1979

> "To speak of what is seen presumes the complementarity of language and pictures."
> —Frederick Sommer, *Pictorial Logic*

Only two years ago, Susan Sontag's now notorious *On Photography* ripped into the curious silence surrounding photography and opened the way for the photographic community to think about photographic images in ways that included more than mere investigation into formal values—ways that included the historical and cultural contexts out of which the images came. We are now seeing the publication of collections of criticism, such as A.D. Coleman's *Light Readings*, selections of his writings which appeared in the *Village Voice* and *New York Times*, and Max Kozloff's *Photography and Fascination*, essays mostly from *Artforum*. Photographers have brought words into the gallery, forcing a confrontation between word and image and emphasizing the importance of theory. For instance, Barbara Jo Revelle's *Reading: a 91-Day Performance Installation* this summer at Columbia College, included 91 articles about photography along with photographic images. (See Candida Finkel's review, *NAE*, Summer 1979.)

I predict that we are at the beginning of an onslaught of words "about photography" that will make the recent proliferation look positively frugal. Hopefully, out of this barrage will come what is sorely lacking now—a coherent theoretical basis for thinking and writing about the photographic image.

What is the bridge between words and images? Many artists have felt that there is no bridge, that the two forms of communication exist as separate languages, that to speak of art is to lessen it. Modern artists have resisted the authoritarian and limiting nature of words. Words define or prescribe boundaries. they reek of analytical thought processes and the Establishment. In painting, the figurative, art of the thirties was "silenced" by the Abstract Expressionists, seeking through pure form, process and emotion to silence the Word forever. And yet, as Tom Wolfe pointed out in *The Painted Word,* abstract art led directly into a new confrontation with words, where theory became all-important and understanding of the theory was initial to understanding the art.

More recently, as typified by the Revelle *Reading* show this summer, photographers have come to incorporate language somehow in their work. Yet the great antagonism on the part of photographers towards words and that of many writers towards images (as typified by the controversy over Sontag's *On Photography*) shows that if there is a potential complementary relationship, it is at present an uneasy one at best.

What is needed in writing about images is a very basic examination of what occurs when the experience of picture-viewing is verbalized. Toward this end, the concept of "reading" could be particularly helpful. Whereas "reading" may be used generally to mean a close examination of an image, file term specifically relates to the work of Minor White published in *Aperture* during the 1950s and early 1960s.

In his attempt to form a coherent theory of "reading," White borrowed from several sources. One of these was I.A. Richards, whose book, *Practical Criticism,* became a text for the so-called New Criticism of literature. Richards called for a close attention to the words on the page, rather than social and historical contexts. Another extremely important source was the idea of "equivalents," as practiced by Alfred Stieglitz, who, like White, was one of the most influential theoretician/practitioners of photography. For Stieglitz, an equivalent was a photograph which functioned as a work of art because it evoked feeling states. Other sources were in the East: Tao and Zen ideas, of passive (as opposed to active, analytical) knowledge and Sumiye painting. In the latter, a painting was seen not as self-expression, but as an expression of the harmony of the universe. From these and other sources, White saw "reading" as a close attention to images. He sought to avoid value judgments, to suspend critical evaluation, and to focus on information given by the photograph itself. The strengths of this approach were that it loosened criticism from its ties to traditional fine art aesthetics on the one hand, and on the other took the viewer beyond seeing a photograph as pure subject matter—as a transparent window on the world. Although White is often charged with lapsing into mysticism, I feel that his work will offer one of the most fruitful sources for future criticism of photography.

The concept of "reading" images has been used by Barbara Revelle in a very different way than White, but the introduction of verbal thinking (as opposed to icons or images) into the gallery owes much to the general photographic atmosphere spawned by White. Her recent show at Columbia College juxtaposed images of personal diaristic nature by unedited contact sheets shot in response to articles about photography and/or newspapers. The articles, the newspapers and the images were hung together in the gallery space, forcing a confrontation between these different modes of communication-prose writing, photographs, and the instant transmission of newspaper information.

Whereas Revelle's stated intention was to show how reading affected the way she took pictures and to give the viewer a structure of her process, she also raised important questions about these different modes of communication. For instance, the inclusion of unedited contact sheets shows the viewer more of the context, the in-between moments of shooting, as opposed to the "decisive-moment," that perfect conjunction of events in the Cartier-Bresson tradition. This way of viewing photographs is more like "reading" in that it involves a process, an unfolding in time, closer to the temporality of film than to the snapshot. The newspapers, on the other hand, show us images pre-packaged in verbal wrappings, telling us what to think about the images rather than leaving the translation up to the viewer.

The inclusion of the articles themselves as objects in gallery show that, at the very least, we can no longer accept Hollis Frampton's dismissal of still photography as a "headless corpus." The photograph is no longer asked to be mute. It is asked to speak, to think and to search out its relationship with words and thought processes. Overdue in this respect, photography trails behind self-reflexivity in the other arts such as literature and painting.

Within Revelle's 91 articles, there was a heavy emphasis on semiological method. Filmmaker Jonas Mekas said of semiology, "It sounds like half of something." Semiology can be seen as an extension of Minor White's concept of "reading," although with a much more rigorous, scientific method. Semiology, or the study of signs, has grown out of linguistic analysis, and is being used extensively in film theory by writers such as Christian Metz and Peter Wollen. It is only beginning to be used in the study of photographs, or the individual image, by writers such as Leroy Searle. Since these names, and indeed semiology itself, are unknown to most readers, I will attempt here a very simplified explanation of this new area of analysis.

As semiology is the study of signs, we may first ask: What *is* a sign? A sign is a basic unit of meaning, comprised of a "signifier" and a "signified." The signifier is what we first grasp with our senses: a word on a page or the patterns which form an image. The signified is the meaning attached to these letters, the patterns. There may be multiple meanings. For instance, the letters R-O-S-E may signify a flower, at another level they may signify passion or other conventions associated with that flower.

Charles Sanders Peirce, one of the originators of semiology in America, defined three kinds of signs: iconic, indexical and symbolic. In an iconic sign, the signifier structurally resembles its signified, such as a photograph (A photograph of a rose resembles the actual rose). In an indexical sign, the signifier is existentially linked with the signified. An example of an indexical sign might be an imprint of a body in the snow, which signifies the actual body. A symbolic sign is one in which the signifier is linked to its signified by cultural convention (e.g., the case of words and verbal language).

These three divisions—iconic, indexical and symbolic—are not, according to Peirce, mutually exclusive. In fact, they often overlap. This point is extremely important for critical readings of images. The "meaning" of an image is often multiple and layered, and thus a semiological "reading" need not, as many fear, be reductive.

For instance, in Revelle's photographs, the image of a dog appears over and over. On one level this image is iconic in that what we see on the paper, those patterns of light and dark; signify the word "dog." At another level, it has a symbolic meaning in that because of the posturing of the dog and its context with other images, we read these patterns also as freedom, animal vivacity, exuberance, or the like.

Poetic images like Revelle's are more difficult and open-ended than photographic images in advertising. Advertising relies heavily on the conventional quality of signs. For instance, the icon of a seductive woman is used to sell products. Photographers such as Revelle work against the conventions, but at the same time rely on them to get across their own messages.

A code is a system of signs. In a body of work such as Revelle's, one sign, such as the dog, may be repeated over and over, thereby becoming a code. In the society at large, the image of a woman, used as sexual object, may be seen as a code, immediately understood to mean availability or desirability. Advertisers take advantage of this code to sell objects.

Semiology is a complex tool and one which is only beginning to be investigated as a means of talking about images. It is an extremely analytical tool and because of this, many artists react against it. Whereas I have based this essay on "reading" as part of a current tendency toward analytic thought, I must also point out the counter-tendency, the tendency of some artists to subvert language at an analytical level. Words have been brought into the gallery by Revelle and others, but on the level of art objects, I believe, to attempt to make language more intuitive.

In the Revelle show, for instance, in contrast to the immediate impact of the images, the articles hung covered and mute. Since no casual gallery-goer had the time to read this over-abundance of riches, the presence of the articles was a taunt—words which would not be read. Nor were they aimed at the serious scholar. Many of the articles were not dated, nor their sources cited. There was no bibliography from which those who were interested could look up the articles on their own. In short, the exhibition was not set up to encourage verbal "reading" on the part of the audience.

Rather than integrating or showing us new insight between the two modes of communication (words and images) they existed as strangers to each other, offering rather than new clarities but only greater mysteries. Another example of this tendency is the work of Duane Michals, whose photo "*narratives*" include handwritten phrases along with the images, but the phrases are language only at the most personal level. Rather than cutting through language to the "thing itself," language is itself mystified.

White encountered the same stubborn dichotomy in his work, and never completely resolved it. He has been severely criticized for trailing off into subjectivity and mysticism. White was limited by the milieu of thought that nourished the Beat Generation—Kerouac, Robert Frank and the underground romantic tradition that placed the individual outside society. Thus, White's "reading," for all the attention it focused on the photographic medium, rested ultimately on the myth of the individual consciousness disengaged from society.

I would suggest that there is an important link between White's "reading" and contemporary semiological analysis, and that semiology might be the means for overcoming the limitations White encountered. White placed his emphasis on the individual. Semiology seeks to go beyond the individual to the structures of communication, which tie the individual to the society as a whole. Critics and other "readers" of images might, through semiological analysis, come to question their own hitherto unconscious structures, so that rather than "evaluating" an image in terms of the unconscious biases, the new reader would use the image as a locus of meanings—open-ended rather than closed and as a method for exploration.

JANET KOPLOS

REFLECTIONS ON GLASS

Summer 1980

Studio glass is still in its literal adolescence, having only escaped from the confines of the factory after Harvey Littleton's pair of workshops at the Toledo Museum of Art in 1962. Before that, there had been utilitarian glass, decorative glass and so-called "art glass"—all produced by skilled factory workers according to a designer's specifications. Littleton, then a professor of art at the University of Wisconsin, saw glass as a field for artistic expression, but that expression was dependent upon a complicated technology which had to be adapted to the needs of an artist working alone.

Littleton had developed the rudiments of a small furnace suitable for a studio rather than factory use. But the first workshop was still nearly stumped by technical problems in melting the glass. Dominick Labino, then vice-president for research for Johns-Manville Fiber Glass in Toledo, contributed pre-formulated glass "marbles," which would melt evenly at temperatures Littleton's small furnaces could achieve. There, after 4,000 years of utilitarian production, were the materials and the techniques. What had to follow were the ideas that would justify contemporary labors in the ancient medium—the ideas that would make it art. From this beginning, the balance between technique and concepts has been the major problem of studio glass.

The tradition of using glass for function or decoration had been pulled in a new direction when Louis Comfort Tiffany produced his first "art glass." He found the material ideally suited to the curving, languid lines of Art Nouveau. Organic forms, resulting from gravity and the rotation of the blowpipe, come easily to blown glass. Yet, other art glass resulted from different and completely contradictory properties of the material, such as the sharp and prismatic character of cut glass.

Glass is an abstract material, and represents many dichotomies of character: besides organic or prismatic it can also be opaque or transparent, highly colored or colorless, fragile or shatterproof, ductile or rigid and so on.

This abstractness allows the artist working in this material an extraordinary leeway. The exploration of this freedom, the search for form, dominates the studio glass movement today. Of course, the production of beautiful objects in the decorative tradition continues.

Art Nouveau and gem-faceted styles sell as well as ever and have become, in fact, almost a trap for the movement. So lovely, so popular, so much easier than breaking new ground, these objects—in every glass exhibition—demonstrate that Littleton's dictum, "Technique is cheap," has not found universal understanding. And they demonstrate the widening rift within the medium between traditional artisanry which concentrates on execution and artwork (whether functional or nonfunctional) which concentrates on the expression of ideas.

The studio movement is concerned with finding new imagery, expanding the limits. Indeed, current work is so varied in character that the mere fact that all these objects use glass as a basic material is becoming increasingly insufficient as grounds for comparison and exhibition. Glass is no longer any one thing. As it approaches maturity as an art medium, it has become a medium and a vehicle for the expression of an artist's ideas rather than an end in itself.

Large-scale exhibitions, such as the recent *8th Annual National Invitational Glass Exhibition* at Habatat Galleries in Detroit (500 works by 92 American artists), and the Corning Museum of Glass's *New Glass: A Worldwide Survey* (273 objects by 196 entrants from 28 countries) demonstrate the increasingly divergent groupings, expanding outward like some supernova, into separate systems of work that would be better served by thematic and contextual shows. Glass has simply outgrown the confining expectations of its name.

A separation has always existed between stained glass and blown glass, in history, purpose, esthetics and technique. There is some crossing of the breach, however. Many stained glass artists are developing greater-than-traditional relief, and much interesting work by glassblowers is very flat, although glassblowers have avoided the selection-and-assembly approach of stained glass.

The blown glass field is so evolving, so open, that any list of significant work includes not just some, of the "old masters" of the movement, (those whose pioneering involvement goes back to the early 'sixties) but also students of the third generation whom are newly graduated from the major glass programs, such as those of the Rhode Island School of Design and Illinois State University. The field is also so new that each discovery or elaboration of technique tends to be applauded for its potential in broadening the expressive capabilities of the medium. Such advances in technique have tended to be the focus of more attention than advances in concept, which are more difficult to discuss.

It's interesting that the maturing of the field has meant letting go of some of the characteristics unique to the medium. A prime example is transparency. At first work in studio glass tended to fix on the ability of a blown form simultaneously to reveal both interior and exterior patterning. If one imagines a stereotypical early 60's piece, it would be an expressionistic and organic abstract form with surges of color overlapping and light transmitted through the entirety of the form.

Joel Philip Myers, for one, has progressively moved away from the use of transparency and now has abandoned it entirely. Three years ago, his vessels were wrapped in meteoric streaks of overlapping color that nearly made the form visually impenetrable. But there were still slits of transparency and the entire form was encased in clear glass. His more recent *Contiguous Fragments* series used only a shallow transparency. The form itself was opaque, but collage-like grafts of color sometimes retained a modicum of transparent depth.

His most recent works are black, sandblasted and opaque and abandon even the slightest suggestion of transparency. Color is still important, but it is opaque; enamel-like color in small quantities. The vessels achieve a sense of density and mass uncommon in glass; they absorb light and energy into their blackness to suggest a monumentally far beyond their restricted physical dimensions. Because of its small scale, glass seldom achieves a strong, presence. Transparency has prevented it from achieving even the attention-demanding density of Joel Shapiro's tiny, floor sculptures for example. However, Myers has surmounted the problem.

These vessels also embody a sculpture/painting paradox. They are emphatically objects in space and undeniably' three-dimensional. Although they emphasize mass, they are not solid. By abandoning transparency, using a simple traditional vessel form and placing all his focus on surface design, Myers treats the object as a shell with little regard for its space-occupying quality. It is a curved canvas, a collage in the round, a painting with no front or back.

By contrast, Eric Sealine, new to prominence in glass, uses transparency to emphasize the abstract and ambiguous positioning of his paintings in space. He enamels transparent plate glass with simple shapes, such as a few overlapping rectangles or a river-like pour of color. The paintings seem to hover in the indeterminate space barely identified by the freestanding plate glass. He fixes the painting in space by inscribing on the glass horizontal or vertical. But these are very fragile spatial anchors. They say nothing about depth. Because the transparency of the ground, the paintings seem to have no real depth and to be only floating fragments of illusions. The visionary quality is compounded by a cast shadow which repeats the color of the painting in an elongated form.

Sealine is using the glass in much the same way Duchamp did in his *Large Glass*. However, there is none of the machine symbolism, and Sealine is unlikely to consider his work finished when it cracks, as Duchamp did. Some of Sealine's imagery is rationalist-Minimalist in its geometry, and some uses a much more Abstract Expressionist approach. However, all his imagery is restrained, simplified and ultimately reductionist. The glass is important for its visual absence, for its non-complication, allowing the painting to exist, isolated, in space.

Steven Weinberg also explores the use of transparency, in blocky cast forms. The severe, simple exterior planes of the forms contrast to an interior that is a Chinese puzzle of positive and negative space, access and closure. Interior surfaces are opaque and striated. Apparent space and real space within the block are sometimes precisely the opposite of what they seem. Handling a Weinberg piece can be embarrassingly disorienting, as what looks to be an exterior surface may in fact be held to the inside by the ghostly presence of transparent glass, and what seems to be a clear surface may in fact be empty space leading to interior hollows or shapes. The pieces often suggest models of contemporary architecture, but the ability of glass to define outer planes while revealing inner structure makes them a concentrated, complicated and surprising perceptual experience.

Marvin Lipofsky, like Joel Myers, goes back a long way in glass. Lipofsky was the first MFA from the first U.S. college glass program, established by Harvey Littleton at the University of Wisconsin after those 1962 workshops. Like Myers, he has given up transparency when the effect suited his needs. He has also struggled with the limitations of blown glass scale (a physical limitation due to the weight of the molten mass at the end of a blowpipe and the size of annealing ovens). Non-transparency contributed to the sense of mass but did not answer the question of scale, so Lipofsky did a series of blown forms which were presented in their own environments—within plexiglass boxes—to expand their effective scale. His work is also unusual in the contemporary glass arena for its persistent sexual symbolism.

Lipofsky has worked and studied at European glass factories, and many of his pieces use the carnival-stripe colors of Italian Murano glass. Perhaps it is because of the European factory experience that he has been willing to have some of his works executed by someone else. This is a live issue in any craft medium, because it seems the nature of crafts to require the direct mind-hand-object continuum of creation.

Until the studio movement began, nearly all glass—functional or decorative—was designed by one person and executed by another. The history of the medium and its complicated techniques were presumed to necessitate such a separation of responsibility. The studio movement's rationale was a one-to-one correspondence, the artist executing his own work. There are many cooperative glass studios, and many glassblowers use assistants, but Lipofsky went a bit further than that, using an attitude more parallel to the commercial fabrication of Minimalist or monumental sculpture than to most craft efforts (with the exception of large-scale architectural fiber pieces).

Lipofsky's most recent works mark a middle ground in his abrasive pushing of the limits of the medium. In his *Small California Loop,* a series of bulbous blown forms connected by twisting tubes, he experiments in copper plating the blown glass forms, concealing the primary shaping material. His sexual reference continues in forms that suggest breasts and nipples. The forms are natural to blown glass, but in copper they seem less obvious, more measured and reasoned—a choice on the part of the artist. They also suggest California kelp, and gourds, growth and movement.

Those organic qualities are also an important part of the statement of Dale Chihuly works. Some years ago, Chihuly struggled with scale by creating a neon environment. His more recent works have followed quite a different course, making two significant contributions to glass: the practice of borrowing imagery and forms from other media, and the concept of multi-piece groupings.

Glass, like clay, is strongly influenced by its vessel tradition. A large number of contemporary artists still draw on this tradition—Myers, for instance, or Dan Dailey (who will be discussed below). Chihuly's most recent series does not refer to the historical glass vessel but adapts the form of basketry. The difference between the softness of collapsing baskets and the brittleness of glass might seem insuperable, but Chihuly has bridged it with the common characteristic of fragility. Molten glass is soft, and the shapes of Chihuly's basket series retain the memory of that softness. The receptive suggestibility of the basket is emphasized by the extreme lightness of the glass (some pieces weighing less than an ounce), by the subtle colors, and by the range of deformation in the groupings of basket forms, reflecting idiosyncratic organic collapse.

These groupings also alter the usual nature of multiples in glass; they are not sets. Groupings imply a much looser bond, stressing differences rather than similarities, and drawing the viewer's attention to subtle color, volume and form variations, and to spatial relationships. A grouping, as opposed to the repetition of sets, makes a three-dimensional statement larger than any one part can provide, and this is a useful addition to the vocabulary of form in glass.

Dan Dailey also employs the vessel form but, in a sense, he uses it in a less neutral way than Myers does. The vessel tradition provides a sort of "eternal" context for his imagery. He uses an identical vessel form, or blank. The imagery is not directly related to the form in the way Myers's abstract lines comment upon his vessels' forms. Dailey's most recent work employs preliterate symbolism, that is, the kind of stylization that might presage writing. His symbols are drawn from the environments he experiences, such as simplified verticals of urban buildings below a texture of stars.

A particularly effective series is drawn from the landscapes of the Pacific Northwest, such as slashing diagonals representing rain, chevrons for the sea, and long and short clumps of vertical lines for marsh grasses. This imagery is not at all specific to glass; it deals with abstract ideas rather than the nature of the material. One sees traces of Oriental brushwork, Islamic geometry or Egyptian hieroglyphics. The visual references are familiar, but ageless and nonspecific, as are the forms of his blanks.

Dailey's vessels seem to speak of broad eras of time and to connect our day to others. Time is a very strong reference in the works of Mary Shaffer, but it is a much more specific time: the passage of the glass piece from a cold state, to a hot state that deforms it, and back to cold again, recording the transition in altered form. Her glass reflects moments of violence, a destructive course interrupted, and it reflects natural forces, such as gravity. It can take a subtle form, as in a bundle of five plate-glass sheets which are just beginning to slump at the top, to a much more savage connotation in mirrored glass drooping and beginning to tear across four particularly brutal-looking hooks. The former viscosity of glass is particularly eloquent in Shaffer's pieces; the lines of flow are gentle, poetic and emotional. However, each piece includes hooks or chains or cutting, constricting wire, spelling out a raw contrast that reveals the natures of the materials with utter clarity. These works emphasize process; they are Cartier-Bresson's decisive moment translated into glass. Because of the character of the medium—heavy, brittle, hot—the works also address the idea of danger in the process.

Several young artists are fascinated by that danger. Robert DuGrenier has exhibited massive sheets of glass joined by some remarkable glue and perilously suspended by thick ropes. Bruce Chao joined plate glass in great V's and hung them in mid-air by means of suction cups (one thinks of Loren Madsen's suspended beams of brick—which is the worse threat, being squashed by the massive beams or shredded and punctured by the nearly invisible but equally lethal glass?). Thermon Statom has also toyed with this threat, in an arch composed of triangular sheets of glass held apart by glass cones but held together by nothing except the keystone principle.

Jack Schmidt also uses plate glass, but in a less threatening and more elegant approach than these young artists He focuses on the repetition of line through movement, tension and gradation. Schmidt's work, in fact, is more akin to other works of twentieth-century sculpture than to other work in glass, except that it is not monumentally scaled. It is easy to imagine his pieces with the rhythmic but tense metal structures of Linda Howard or Kenneth Snelson, for example. Yet Schmidt still achieves an exploration of the visual qualities of glass. He uses beveled-edge sheets of gray glass combined with bases of stainless steel which are punctured visually and literally by the sharp edges of the glass. He fans out the glass to overlap rhythmically, and the piece evolves from transparency at the edges (looking through a single sheet) to opacity and reflectiveness toward the center. The fans emphasize movement with a particular grace, sometimes suggesting a slow-motion camera or a graphic schematization of change.

Besides the directions indicated by these artists, current work in glass is exploring three-dimensional pictorial depth; a kind of funk flashiness, archeological symbolism, color studies, gritty specimens of life today, arrested motion, forms and surfaces inspired by ceramics and other directions. The spark has been struck in this medium of light, of vision, of illusion, of reflection.

Glass needn't look for its own voice or its own metaphor, because it has many. The future holds recognition of this multiplicity and movement beyond the "protection" of glass galleries and associations. Not only numbers but prices have increased astronomically in the last few years. Glass work is ready for wider recognition.

MICHAEL STARENKO

A READER'S GUIDE TO

STRUCTURALIST CRITICISM

February 1981

> "This 'I' which approaches the text is already itself a plurality of other texts, of codes which are infinite or, more precisely, lost (whose origin is lost)."
> —Roland Barthes, S/Z (1970)

In spite of—or because of—their intense mutual dependency, art critics and their readers, like couples in a Tom Stoppard play, derive a great deal of satisfaction from insulting each other. At the moment, the main source of their mutual irritation seems to be the issue of difficulty. Readers insult critics for being unreadable, or at least, for being too difficult to read. Detecting here a double standard, critics retort that written criticism must be just as difficult as its objects. They ask: if difficulty is the most desirable attribute of modern art (and what, they ask rhetorically, is modern art if not objectified difficulty?), why should readers expect criticism to be easy? Both sides, of course, are right—and wrong.

Critics certainly have good reason to feel insulted when readers give up on their essays after the first page, claiming that the critics' arguments are "inscrutable," when, point of fact, the readers' attention span is no more than one page to begin with. However, television, the usual scapegoat in discussions of the decline of "book" learning and general literacy, is not the only cause of this new illiteracy. Evidently, our system of education, particularly art education, appears to have done little to train people in the art of reading criticism. By the same token, art criticism is often un-necessarily difficult to read. In addition, the readers' familiar complaint that critics write mainly to better other critics, or that they write about issues that only other critics could appreciate, is well-founded. In any event, a new critical method called, loosely, structuralism has made these genuine complaints seem relatively insignificant in comparison to its claims to self-reflexive difficulty.

Why is it important that readers (and critics) understand structural-ism? To put it as simply as I can, structuralism, a human science based on a model provided by linguistics, shows why the relationship between reading and writing, which is always mediated by a "text," is paradigmatic of the far more complex "intertextuality" of human life in general. What is more, since we commonly understand criticism as the "translation" of one text (a painting, a building, a photograph or a performance) into yet another text (writing or criticism), any new theory of language can be expected to have a significant impact on what we, as writers and readers, believe criticism should be all about. As for the contrary belief that all art, or the best work of certain artists, is ineffable—incapable of being expressed in words—that, of course, is the source of considerable and sometimes extreme animosity between writers and (anti-) readers. A demand for silence is the sharpest insult that anyone can hurl at a critic. Nevertheless, to the extent that an individual is a reader of criticism, he or she must consider even the finest art open to "translation." There is, however, still a tacit assumption on the part of readers that the critic "won't go too far—won't try to explain it all."

To the uninitiated reader, structuralist criticism often seems to trans-gress this assumption. Moreover, the technical jargon of structuralism (e.g., "diachrony," "index," "metalanguage," "simulacrum," "syntagm") has no doubt turned off a great many readers who might otherwise be interested in what structuralism has to offer. In the interests of the bemused but potentially sympathetic reader, I shall try to unpack some of the essential terminology of structuralist art criticism, and in doing I shall argue that structuralism does not so much explain away the "mys-tery"' of art as raise the ante for what is at stake.

And what, exactly, is at stake in all of this? Well, in a curious way, so-called objectivity is at stake. While we all think of art as fictional or highly imaginative in some sense, structuralist criticism argues that many of our most cherished beliefs about art are, in practice, expectations about its "real" character, about our belief that art somehow goes beyond mere appearances to real reality. While agreeing with formalist criticism that "surface" is everything in art (and non-art), structuralist criticism out formalizes formalism by arguing that everything about human culture is artificial—hence is art.

The absolute presupposition of all structuralisms (which, since they exist in many fields of human inquiry, are confusingly numerous), is expressed in the following formulation: the relationship between the signifier and the signified is arbitrary. Now, this might not sound like such an important distinction, but then again, that was also what many of Copernicus's contemporaries said of his claim that the Earth is not the center of the universe. Also, what Copernicus is to astronomy, Ferdinand de Saussure is to linguistics, and thence to structuralism. Around the turn of the century, Saussure, a Swiss philologist, became disappointed with the then dominant view that language is best studied by tracing the meaning of words back to their origins (with the "divine language of things" the point of language's origins). He came to the conclusion that for the individual user or performer of language, "origins" are irrelevant to communication—all that matters is the dynamic interrelationship (or "intertextuality," as Julia Kristeva would later expand upon it) of words (or phonetic units, to be more precise) with one another.

Saussure's theory of language can be found in his *Course in General Linguistics,* a collection of lecture notes published in 1916, three years after his death. Perhaps the most important passage in that seminal work is the following: "**In language there are only differences**. More than that: a difference normally presupposes some positive terms between which it is established; but in language there are only differences **without positive terms**." For Saussure, then, the adjective "flat" is a term of difference; that is to say it is defined (as in a dictionary) by reference to other words. Even nouns, like the proverbial "tree," are defined this way, although they are more readily **identified** (and identification is the doctrine of all idealisms, of which realism is but one) with a positive term: the so-called actual tree, the—mythical tree itself. Now, the word "tree" is a sign composed of two elements: a signifier (the word-concept "tree") and a signified (the thing-concept tree). The relationship between them is arbitrary, which means that it is not naturally given, but symbolically designated.

Yet, to claim that the relationship between "tree" and tree is arbitrary is not to claim that it doesn't matter if one calls, trees rocks, as young children are prone to do when they give **things** the wrong **names**, but that, insofar as society (which is rather oblivious to the needs of the individual ego) is concerned, all that matters is that we can **agree that** a given phonetic unit (the sound-concept) refers to a given thing or action (thing-concept) in a given context (also agreed upon). In language—and indeed in all sign systems that depend on systems of agreed value (pertaining between given signifiers and given signifieds)—value, or meaning, or, intention, is always **assigned**. That which is assigned is arbitrary. Saussure conceived of value in terms of an economic metaphor, where a given unit of currency has the same value regardless of whether it is coin or paper money—again, all that matters is that we agree upon its value. As in a game (one of the privileged metaphors of linguistics), without agreement, language breaks down into meaningless noise and scribbles, hence there is no such entity as a private language, expressionists notwithstanding. This latter point is made emphatic by the stark terror one feels in a country where one does not know the language. Not surprisingly, the usual home of structuralism in university departments is comparative literature.

At this point, the reader might well object that all this explication, while relevant to the study of literary art, is practically irrelevant to the visual arts, especially to so-called autonomous or non-representational visual art. Then again, structuralist art criticism does not take kindly to the belief, absolutely essential to the *raison d'etre* of abstract art, that art objects or any other kinds of objects, possess a value **in and of themselves**—a point of view to be found, for example, in a modern classic of formalist criticism, Clement Greenberg's *Avant-Garde and Kitsch* (1939):

> The avant-garde poet or artist tries in effect to imitate God by creating something valid solely on its own terms, in the way nature itself is valid, in the way a landscape—not its picture—is aesthetically valid; something given, increate, independent of meanings, similars or originals. Content is to be dissolved so completely into form that the work of art or literature cannot be reduced in whole or in part to anything not itself.

It is interesting that Greenberg makes such a sharp distinction between the intrinsic validity of a landscape and the implied imitative effect of a picture of a landscape; for what is a landscape if not the attribution of "picturesqueness" (another human construct) to a geological formation?

As soon as representation is seen not simply as a copy of reality, but as a "copy of a copy," this has the inconvenient tendency of undermining defining presuppositions of formalism. In his early, Marxist essay of 1937, *Nature of Abstract Art,* the art historian Meyer Schapiro wrote:

> The abstract painter denounces representation of the outer world as a mechanical process of the eye and the hand in which the artist's feelings and imagination have little part . . . These views are thoroughly one-sided and rest on a mistaken idea of what representation is. There is no passive, "photographic" representation in the sense described; the scientific elements of representation in older arts—perspective, anatomy, light-and-shade—are ordering principles and expressive means as well as devices of rendering.

In order to defend the claims of "pure art," formalist art criticism has little option but to defend the claims of "realism" in some other artistic style or medium—which has come to be, namely, photography. Ironically, by making abstract art available to critical scrutiny (through art historical slide archives and book reproductions), photography has simultaneously rendered that art obsolete. Even more disconcerting from the point of view of formalist criticism is the Pandora's Box opened when photography's prior truth-claims are debunked by both "photography-as-art" and structuralism's critique of all realisms, "photographic" or otherwise.

Although an early, "anthropological" variant of structuralism was marginally applicable to abstract art (witness the "mythological" structuralism of Jack Burnham's *The Structure of Art*), structuralist criticism today is largely uninterested in abstract art, including almost the entire medium of painting. Nothing much is at stake in the powerless "discourses" (increasingly privatized) of the Fine Arts Tradition, which has been "marginalized and rendered impotent" by its progressive "kenosis" and by the "Mega visual," to borrow Peter Fuller's famous formulations. To the degree that abstract (or, more popularly) decorative art has become divested of social value, it is more likely to be found on the walls of corporate headquarters. For structuralist criticism, the social issues of truth, representation, "what- goes-without-saying," human nature—in short, reality—lies in the "metadiscourses" of photographic and video images. For example, whereas it hardly matters to the market system what people think about painting or sculpture, **it matters** what people think about photography, since most advertising or promotional messages (which depend on a truth-claim: X is better than Y), are delivered as photographic or video images. Furthermore, photography and film are "metadiscourses" that comprehend (in its literal sense) and comment upon other "discourses" or sign systems (e.g., human faces, clothes, architectural interiors, paintings, public events, etc.), which thereby become sign system signifieds within the photograph or film—"in the same way that a critical analysis of a literary work requires a metalanguage in order to analyze the 'language-object' under scrutiny," wrote Paul Willemen in *Screen* (Spring 1972).

The late Roland Barthes was structuralism's greatest debunker of "what-goes-without-saying." He took Saussure's signifier/signified concept and re-fashioned it into a connotation/denotation concept. Barthes showed why all representations, verbal or pictorial, can be analyzed as an implied relationship between **codes** of connotation (what common sense calls the figurative meaning) and **objects** of denotation (the literal meaning) where the latter is privileged over the former. In *S/Z* (1970), his line by line reading of Balzac's novella *Sarrasine*, Barthes argues that there are ultimately only codes because objects possess meaning only to the extent that they are thing-concepts or "texts" in relationship with a vast plurality of other "texts":

> Structurally, the existence of two supposedly different systems—denotation and connotation—enables the text to operate like a game, each system referring to the other according to the requirements of a certain **illusion**. Ideologically, finally, this fame has the advantage of affording the classic text a certain **innocence**: of the two systems, denotative and connotative, one turns back on itself and indicates its own existence: the system of denotation; denotation is not the first meaning, but pretends to be so; under this illusion, it is ultimately no more than the **last** of the connotations.

Barthes' claim that denotation "is ultimately no more than the last of the connotations," has rather broad ramifications, to say the very least, for formalist or conventional art criticism. "It is as impossible to reconcile this project with formalism," wrote Rosalind Krauss in the current *October*, "as it is to revive within it the heartbeat of humanism. To take the demonstration of the de-originated utterance seriously would obviously put a large segment of the critical establishment out of business."

As the reader should have guessed, the underlying motive of contemporary structuralist criticism is decidedly Marxist in character. Like structuralism's founder, Saussure, the practitioners of this kind of criticism can't quite seem to get that economic metaphor out of their minds. Every time they trace the paths of codes of connotation through a novel or around a photograph, they inevitably encounter a peculiar class of signs: dollar signs. Everything has its price.

In the best general account of structuralism that I know of, *The Prison-House of Language*, Fredric Jameson wrote:

> The deeper justification for the use of the linguistic model or metaphor must, I think, be sought . . . outside the claims and counterclaims for scientific validity or technological progress. It lies in the concrete character of social life in the so-called advanced countries today, which offer the spectacle of a world from which nature as such has been eliminated, a world saturated with messages and information, whose intricate commodity network may be seen as the very prototype of a system of signs.

As Jameson correctly observed, whatever can be said, pro and con, for the technical points of structuralism, its most sobering discovery is how our "intricate commodity network may be seen as the very prototype of a system of signs." Thus, especially for many younger critics influenced by the New Left movement of the sixties, structuralism offers the last remaining glimmer of "adversariness" available in advanced—and rapidly advancing—industrial society. As the early class-oriented critiques of classical Marxism are perceived as too "crude" by most structuralist critics, the Marxist character of structuralism has become rather Nietzschean in tone. Structuralists call only for criticism, and ever more criticism. What is more, because structuralist critics consider Individualism **the** ideology of advanced capitalistic society, the debates are now moving off the streets and into the bedroom. The term "post structuralism" designates the return to Freud on the part of structuralists who have, after the fashion of Jacques Lacan, "rewritten the unconscious in terms of language."

At this point I must break off this account because, as Lacan often puts it, "I am getting ahead of myself." However, suffice it to say that the present horizon of structuralist criticism is becoming increasingly interested in the Individual or the subject. Like the surrealists, structuralists increasingly conceive of freedom ("the play of the signifier;" "the pleasure of the text") not in grand political action, but rather in **preventing** any more unfreedom. Which is to say, "salvation" lies not in some future class-less society (and the future has come to be envisioned as a hellish apocalypse), but rather in models buried under the wreckage of capitalism's "Progress." As was the case with the extraordinary Walter Benjamin, structuralist criticism is awash with historical "melancholy." An air of *fin de siècle* Vienna currently blows through structuralist criticism like so much decorative painting through the art world. As Leon Botstein aptly put it in a recent issue of the *New Republic:* "The absence of politics, a gradual social fragmentation in our nation, the decline of America as a world power, the retreat into self, a selective reclaiming of tradition, nostalgia, aestheticism, and a deeply passive pessimism now draws us near to fin de siecle Vienna."

Finally, I am inclined to agree with Jameson, that as I trust is clear to the reader, "There is a profound consonance between linguistics as a method and that systematized and disembodied nightmare which is our culture today."

A Short Bibliography of Structuralist Criticism

While America exports some art and a great deal of popular culture to Europe, the means for their interpretation are, ironically, imported from Europe. Though small in financial value, structuralist criticism is an important export for proud European intellectuals—especially if they live in Paris! And like Moutarde de Meaux mustard, which is not available in every supermarket, journals and books of structuralist criticism cannot be found in shopping center book stores. Nevertheless, the interested reader can find all of the following structuralist literature in most university book stores and libraries. First, the journals.

The foremost English-language journal of structuralist criticism is England's Screen. In the late sixties, a tiny group of more or less Marxist film critics and filmmakers formed an educational society, with Screen as its house publication. The development of theory in Screen over the course of the seventies is an encapsulated history of structuralist criticism—from crude Marxism to semiotics to post-structuralism. Two of its writers, Rosalind Coward and John Ellis, have written *Language and Materialism* (London: Routledge & Kegan Paul, 1977), a brilliant synthesis of Marxist esthetics, Saussurian linguistics, and Lacanian psychoanalysis. As this book is likely to intimidate the uninitiated, a short book by another Screen writer, Peter Wollen's *Signs and Meaning in the Cinema*

MICHAEL STARENKO A Reader's Guide to Structural Criticism **119**

(Bloomington: Indiana University Press, 1972, third edition), particularly its third chapter, is as readable as anything ever written on structuralism.

While some "mainstream" art journals in America, notably *Artforum*, publish an occasional, watered-down structuralist essay, the only American art journal with strong editorial support for structuralism is *October*. Co-editors Rosalind Krauss and Annette Michelson, founded *October* (published by MIT Press) shortly after they resigned as co-editors of *Artforum*. *October* is at present the preeminent American journal of art criticism and theory. Highly recommended are its special photography issue (*October* 5) and Craig Owens' essay "The Allegorical Impulse: Toward a Theory of Postmodernism" (in *October* 12 and 13). Other important American journals of highly theoretical character are *Critical Inquiry, Diacritics, Glyph, New German Critique, Semiotexte, Social Text, SubStance,* and *Yale French Studies.*

Invariably, the essays published in the above journals presuppose a certain familiarity with the major works of structuralism in particular, and of Western philosophy in general. Saussure's *Course in General Linguistics* (Cambridge: MIT Press, 1974) is required reading, as is Fredric Jameson's Marxist critique of structuralism, *The Prison-House of Language* (Princeton: Princeton University Press, 1972).

As the historical and theoretical dissemination of Saussurian linguistics is a matter of interest mainly to specialists, let me say simply that structuralism, as it pertains to art criticism, begins with French anthropologist Claude Levi-Strauss's *The Elementary Structures of Kinship* (Boston: Beacon Press, 1969) first published in 1949. This and subsequent books created quite a stir in Parisian intellectual circles in the fifties (for a polemical account of this sensation see Susan Sontag's essay "The Anthropologist as Hero" in Against Interpretation). Following Levi-Strauss, Roland Barthes, formerly a drama critic, published *Mythologies* (New York: Hill and Wang, 1972), in which he wrote: "I wanted to track down, in the decorative display of what-goes-without- saying, the ideological abuse; which in my view, is hidden there." This book marks the politicization of structuralism by turning it to the unmasking of ideological "myths." While all of Barthes' many books (Hill and Wang have published nine to date) are relevant to art criticism, his *S/Z* (1974) and *Image, Music, Text* (1977) are especially relevant. For a general overview of "politicized" structuralist criticism, see *The Structuralist Controversy: The Languages of Criticism and the Sciences of Man* (Baltimore: Johns Hopkins University Press, 1970), a sophisticated reader edited by Richard Macksey and Eugenio Donato.

Beginning in the early sixties, Freudian psychoanalysis has been increasingly "grafted" onto Saussurian linguistics, and this has had the effect of moving structuralist criticism into the realm commonly considered outside of social critique—namely, the individual ego or self. Called post-structuralist criticism, this is the subject ("the theory of the subject") of considerable contemporary interest. The crucial figure here is Jacques Lacan, whose writing is setting new standards of difficulty. The best general introduction to Lacan and art criticism is *Textual Strategies: Perspectives in Post-Structuralist Criticism* (Ithaca: Cornell University Press, 1979), a collection of essays edited by Josue Harari. Moreover, at the back of this anthology is a very complete bibliography of structuralist and post-structuralist criticism. Very highly recommended.

DONNA AND STEPHEN TOULMIN

HARRIS BANK FACELIFT
RAISES LEGAL QUESTIONS

October 1981

The mutilation of portraits is an old story. It has been done both by owners and by painters themselves. Whistler defaced his own portrait of Lady Eden in a quarrel over the fee. It is rumored that, in the basement of Emerson Hall, there is a group picture of the pre-World War II Harvard philosophy department in which the likeness of George Santayana has been replaced by a row of bookshelves. So, the recent scandal over the transformation of Martyl's portrait of former Harris Bank president, Paul Russell, from a human being to a harlequin, is nothing new.

The story broke on the front of the *Chicago Tribune* Business Section for July 6, 1981. It had been the bank's tradition to commission portraits of its chief executive officers, and Martyl was invited to produce this painting without any particular limitations on her treatment of the subject. At first, all went well between artist and patron. On its completion, the painting was warmly praised by the chairman of the board, and by Russell's family and friends. However, problems arose when the bank decided to hang the portraits of all the bank's presidents in chronological sequence.

Given this "rogues' gallery" treatment, Martyl's painting put all the others in the shade; and the bank asked the artist to "make the background more mellow." She demurred on painterly grounds, arguing that any problem had been created by "an unsatisfactory grouping" of the portraits, and that darkening the background would not improve matters, since her technique on the entire canvas was so different from that used in the other paintings. "Any change," she warned in a letter answering the bank's request, would affect the whole picture "and almost certainly ruin the portrait." A better solution would be to hang the Russell portrait separately. Nothing more was heard from the bank, until rumors began to circulate that it had arranged for someone else to make the changes it had requested; and, as matters turned out, the portrait had indeed been ruined. Not only had the background been sanded down and repainted a "patent leather" black, but all marks of maturity and character in the face and hands had been crudely over painted.

In recent years, there has been much discussion among artists and lawyers about legal protections aimed at securing for artists two distinct interests: a share in the proceeds from lucrative resales, and some kind of control over the attribution, publication, conservation and restoration of their works. (For cases and materials, see J.H. Merryman and A.E. Elsen, *Law, Ethics and the Visual Arts,* 1979.) In the present episode, only issues of the latter kind are involved. What kind of interest, then, do artists have in protecting the integrity of their own works? What is to happen when this interest comes up against the right of patrons to do as they please with "goods" that they have ordered and paid for? The Harris Bank story clearly illustrates how such conflicts can arise, and how little the law can help in resolving the disputes that result.

The problem of preservation affects artists working in different media in quite different ways. Architecture is one extreme case. There, the scale of the patron's financial stake is usually so large that it can outweigh the architect's hope of seeing his conception scrupulously executed, let alone preserved. This can lead to very rough justice—e.g., in cases where the architect is replaced at a late stage in a major construction project, as happened with the Syndey Opera House. However, there is probably no country in which an architect has an enforceable "right" to carry through a brand new building at the owner's expense, once the patron has decided to withdraw the commission. So, as a general rule, the owner's right to use, and change, a building as he pleases can be restricted only once that building has been accorded landmark status. At the other end of the spectrum, copyright and the use of guild contracts give the work of writers and musicians a measure of protection that is not available to architects. Painting and sculpture fall between these two extremes; and it is there that the hardest cases arise.

French law has traditionally recognized that, on selling one of his works, an artist retains a pecuniary interest in this work (the *droit de suite*); and further, that he embodies in his own person certain moral rights (the *droit moral*) as a creator. (See Russell J. DaSilva's recent thorough discussion of artists' legal rights in France and the United States, in *Bulletin of the Copyright Society of the U.S.A.*, October 1980.) In theory, therefore, it looks as though in France the artist should emerge victorious from any disagreement with his dealers or patrons. However, that is not how things always turn out in practice. For instance, if artists seek to exercise the right to take back a work they have sold or otherwise published (*droit de retrait*), they must repurchase the work at its current value, which only well established artists can afford, and, after such a withdrawal, they can republish or resell the retracted work only if they first offer it to the original purchaser at the original price. Still, the cornerstone of the *droit moral* remains and is a powerful protection: the French courts have been very reluctant to limit the exercise of the artist's right to preserve his works from alteration or mutilation (*droit au respect de l'oeuvre*). If the episode of the Russell portrait had taken place in Paris, the painter could thus have obtained a court order to prevent the bank from having the picture altered behind her back.

In the United States, there have recently been several moves toward giving artists some of these protections—partly through novel state legislation, partly by the extension of existing common law categories, such as those of defamation and privacy. For instance, California's new Art Preservation Act (1979) seeks to prevent the intentional "physical defacement, mutilation, alteration or destruction" of a painting, sculpture or drawing for up to 50 years after the death of the artist. However, the Act by no means resolves all problems. It applies only to "fine art," which it defines as "original painting, sculpture or drawing of recognized quality"; but it specifically excludes "work prepared under contract for commercial use by its purchaser," and it leaves it to the courts to determine "recognized quality" on the basis of opinions from the artistic community, i.e., collectors, curators, critics, and dealers, not just artists themselves. (Finally, only limited protection is given to works of art that are attached to buildings.)

On the common law front, most attention has been paid to the doctrines of defamation and privacy. Any publication of a mutilated work of art is then seen either as defaming the artist's reputation, or alternatively as placing him "in a false light" in the public eye (which counts as invasion of privacy). However, both these doctrines focus on the individual artist's personal interest in his reputation, and they carry with them no protection of the artist's property rights over the work of art itself. In consequence, the remedies available under these two doctrines would do nothing to ensure restoration of an altered work to its original state. At most, they could be relied on to stop further publication and to compensate the artist for any emotional or financial harm.

Most significantly, perhaps, for an episode such as the present one, the American courts have never been happy about intervening in situations where there is only the threat of a defamatory action, without any actual defamation. So, the law of defamation—protective as it is toward reputation, rather than actual works—gives artists only limited protection. Even the most certain evidence that a patron was planning to have an art work altered would do the artist no good; since, ironically, First Amendment objections to "prior restraint" on a patron's "freedom of expression" would mean postponing any legal action until after the damage was done. Again, as in California and France, such limited protections as these seem to be available only to artists who already have established reputations to protect, not to novices or to those who are critically unsuccessful. A classic double-bind: artists are unable to protect their work because they have not developed a sufficient reputation, yet they may be unable to develop a reputation just because they are unable adequately to protect their work.

The weaknesses of the law in this area reflect the more general shortcomings of reliance on litigation and "legal" remedies. The relations between artists and patrons, dealers and museums should ideally be relations of confidence, respect and mutual understanding; and any resort to "adversarial" proceedings is itself a sign that those relations have broken down. Where any difference of opinion arises about the terms of a contract, for instance, it is the course of wisdom and prudence alike—as every banker knows—not to race off to court but to call in an arbitrator; and this is just as true in the case of contracts between artists and patrons as it is with those between business corporations. By their very nature, arbitration proceedings seek to avoid adversarial confrontations, and deal with disagreements by working out adjustments that are acceptable to all parties. And one precaution that both artists and patrons might be wise to consider, as a way of guarding against any further Russell portrait episodes, is for them to agree in advance on arbitration procedures in case of disagreements over the subsequent execution of a commission. After all, if any particular clients were to refuse this proposal, it would at least tip the artist off that—in the immortal words of a Harris Bank executive—"What we wanted was a portrait, not a work of art."

Where could suitable arbitrators be found? Here, the professionalism of corporate curators becomes a matter of high importance. At a time when large corporations are taking over the leading position as purchasers and collectors of works of art, their curators have a special responsibility to act between, and "protect the equities" of, both the artists from whom corporations buy and the corporations themselves. When misunderstandings arise between artists and their corporate patrons, this intermediary position is one of special delicacy; and, in the light of the Russell portrait scandal, the new professional society of corporate art curators might well consider how to play a constructive part in any similar future episodes.

It may be a bit late in the day to say so now, but if the Harris Bankers had been thinking a little more coolly, they might at an early stage have called on the art curator at (say) First National for disinterested advice about their differences with Martyl. In this way, they could have spared the painter much professional anguish and themselves some bad publicity.

Certainly, there is little help that any law court could—or should—have provided in this wretched affair. The courts do not pretend to be, nor have they ever been, particularly skilled in arbitrating delicate matters of interpretation and taste. Still, less are they equipped to serve in the front line as defenders of the Arts against the blunders of the Philistines.

THE (DECLINING) POWER OF REVIEW

November 1981

The following was delivered as an invited lecture
on October 2 at a symposium on "Criticism and
Contemporary Art" at the Virginia Museum of Fine
Arts in Richmond.

When I first received the suggested topic of this talk in the mail, it distressed me. "The Power of Review."—Somehow, it did not quite agree with the way I thought of myself. The "Power of Review" suggested something military to me. It called up the image of a cinematic sergeant striking fear into the hearts of a row of straggly conscripts.

As a critic, I did not envisage myself as a tough-minded professional soldier getting the troops in order. If anything, my view of myself as editor of the *New Art Examiner* has been rather anti-institutional—say the keeper of an underground railway station, helping runaway slaves escape from the domination of the plantation system. Decidedly, the title "The Power of Review" did not appeal to me.

But then I thought, "this talk is not for me." The mere fact that this is the topic reveals a good deal about the current state of the art world. This is the way critics are seen, and perhaps, I should examine the truth of that perception.

Certainly there are critics writing today who keep alive the military metaphor. Hilton Kramer of the *New York Times* is one, and with that paper's vast circulation and influence he can afford to be more than military. I noticed in the catalogue for the *Art of Our Time* exhibition that curator I. Michael Danoff at one point makes a reference to one of Hilton Kramer's articles, the title of which is, *"The Best Paintings Jim Dine Has Yet Produced."* That's not just a sergeant speaking. That's the pope.

Most critics writing today have neither the power of Hilton Kramer nor, perhaps, even the inclination to acquire it. In fact, a growing number of critics want neither the perquisites nor the inconveniences of power. A few years back when I talked to Carrie Rickey, then an up-and-coming art critic who wrote for the *Village Voice,* she told me she never answered her phone because she could not stand the pressure from artists and dealers. Her phone number was unlisted, she said, but she still got 15 to 20 calls every evening. Since then, she has given up art writing and become a film critic.

The fact is there is a large discrepancy between the way critics are perceived and the way they perceive themselves. Most critics think of themselves as responsive intellectuals, coping as best they can with the plethora of material that the vastly extended art world presents to them. They attempt to keep faith with their own values, but also to evolve them in response to the evolving art they see around them. For the majority of critics, Lionello Venturi's definition of criticism still holds true. He asks, "What is criticism if not a relationship between a principle of judgment and the intuition of a work of art or of an artistic personality?"

This relationship is not always easy. Particularly in the twentieth-century, the critic had to be something of a masochist. In our era of the "tradition of the new," the critic not only has his values continuously challenged by the individual work of art or by the outrageous assertions of the artists. He or she must embrace this challenge as part of the job.

As Leo Steinberg recently pointed out in a lecture at the Art Institute of Chicago, critics usually can only take this kind of punishment and integrate it into their critical value system for a limited number of years. By and large, new art demands new critics who can empathize with the artists because both are at approximately the same stage of emotional and intellectual development. Your developing Turners demand new Ruskins, your budding Delacroixs, new Baudelaires, who will not only sympathize with the new work, but will develop vocabularies and a world view to match it. This is criticism at its highest level, and it will continue to be the standard so long as we remain romantic in our conception of culture.

However, besides the dilemma of the romantic critic who rides the crest of the wave and then is thrust aside by the forces of history, critics today face other problems unique to the past decade. That is what I want to focus on—what happened in the seventies to undermine the self-confidence of critics vis-a-vis art and the art world and to erode their function as intermediaries between new art and the public.

In the 1930s and 1940s and even the early 1950s before the market for American art was developed, before art had acquired its current role as the last refuge of the entrepreneurial spirit, critical discussion took place in cultural and political arenas, not in the shadow of Wall Street. It is truly hard to imagine, but in 1939 when Clement Greenberg wrote his famous essay on the distinction between avant-garde and kitsch, the monetary value of the work of art did not enter into his argument. He assumed that avant-garde culture needed the patronage of the rich; the idea that the rich would get richer through the speculative promotion of avant-gardism never occurred to him at that time. In fact, he states flatly in the essay that "Capitalism in decline finds that whatever of quality it is still capable of producing becomes almost invariably a threat to its own existence." Good left rhetoric but poor prophecy.

Reminiscing later on, Greenberg said of the period when that article was written:

> The artists I knew formed only a small part of the downtown art world, but appeared to be rather indifferent to what went on locally outside their immediate circle. Also, most of them stood apart from art politics if not from political politics. Worldly success seemed so remote as to be beside the point, and you did hot even secretly envy those who had it. In 1938 and 1939, I was attending life classes run by the WPA, and when I thought of taking up painting as seriously as I once half-hoped to do before I went to college, the highest reward I imagined was a private reputation of the kind Gorky and deKooning then had, a reputation which did not seem to alleviate their poverty in the least.

Part of the attraction of Greenberg's critical prose came precisely from his sublime confidence in the morality of his motivation, springing as it did from the intense discussions of a small group of friends, all equally poor. At that time there were no worldly rewards for writing as he did, and if a friend gave him a painting, he did not calculate its potential increase in value as opposed to real estate or money-market certificates.

A second source of Greenberg's confidence came from his dependence on an already well-established European tradition introduced to this country in the Armory show of 1913, but virtually obliterated by American indifference and the Depression. By 1939, the European avant-garde had been in existence for half a century and had a recognized cast of heroes and a critical literature to support them.

Out of this originally disinterested commitment and the tradition of a social and cultural world view came the real moral and esthetic authority of Greenberg—and not just Greenberg. Rosenberg and Steinberg too, those other mountains of twentieth-century American criticism, carried the same disinterested authority. It became the norm for our expectations of criticism. Succeeding generations of critics during the sixties built on the critical language and tone of high moral seriousness established by these three.

The publication that most consciously capitalized on those expectations was *Artforum*. Its clean, sober format, in which the ads were rigorously separated from the editorial copy, the length of its articles, its preference for monographs all contributed to its air of authority. Founded in California during the early sixties, the magazine had the distinction of inflating critical currency to its highest degree in the late 1960's and then presiding over its collapse in 1976 when editors John Coplans and Max Kozloff were fired by the publisher, Charles Cowles.

If there ever was a time when the phrase "the power of review" applied, it was to *Artforum* in the late sixties. Power seemed literally to emanate from its shrewdly designed horizontal format, from the full-color reproduction on its cover, from the somber, pretentious fervor of its articles. I remember waiting for it each month to see what artist would be canonized on its cover, thumbing through the pages to look at the reproductions, putting off reading the formidable-looking prose. It was both supremely attractive and utterly repellent, and I was sure that its corruption fully matched the power and glamour it represented. Certainly, it seemed to represent a world completely inaccessible to me and to the artists I knew.

In his article "*Ten Years Before the Artforum Masthead*" printed in the February 1977 *Examiner,* Jack Burnham did a beautiful job of summing up the feelings of the regional artist in academia, which was precisely what I was:

> *Artforum* vis-a-vis academia personified the perfect example of a Freudian love-hate relationship between parents and children. First it symbolized an almost omnipotent authority. It had taken a few dozen relatively

young East Coast artists and had devoted incredible amounts of space and color reproductions to their work—something no other art magazine had done with the same éclat. It implied that New York City in the 1960s was the seat of an artistic revolution of considerable proportions. *Artforum* lionized the youthful artists in a way that dug at the core of each young artists fantasies for approval and love. And in the midst of all this youth-oriented egalitarianism *Artforum* generated a clannish in-group atmosphere of suffocating proportions. For the art student *Artforum* was the gate to nirvana, one that seemed incredibly inaccessible, if for no better reason that that it rarely conceded that artists outside New York were even worth reviewing.

But even at the time of *Artforum's* apogee, doubts about the American critical enterprise were growing. I have mentioned my own skepticism. My colleagues and I in Chicago suspected that advertising played as great a role as quality in *Artforum's* choice of artists to feature on the cover and that the yards of serious prose masked all sorts of financial and sexual liaisons. I think now that we were wrong or, at least, not as right as we thought we were. Our doubts were vague and unproven, and we were far from the center of power.

The internal doubts that wracked the critics of *Artforum* were more serious. In 1967, Max Kozloff, then contributing editor of *Artforum* (for which he still, incidentally, writes), made a plea for professionalization of the critic's role. In retrospect, it seems prophetic. Cynically, he listed in *Renderings* the different kinds of activities that have been called criticism—daily journalism, partisanship for one's friends, "riposte against change, discharge of vanity, occasion for philosophical theorizing, annunciation of the good and true, and erection of esthetic superstructures." "I can find nothing satisfactory in the format of any of this," he said. And a little later, in his essay titled *"Psychological Dynamics of Art Criticism in the Sixties,"* came the real kicker. "It is sentimental to think of artists as friends, even if one is praising them, and it can be said that one has vested interests when devising, power systems of which works of art are the pawns." What a devastating indictment! What a total dissolution of that cozy world of bohemian artists and intellectuals called up by Greenberg.

As Kozloff's stark assessment indicates, the convergence of critical power with market forces gradually eroded critical confidence. I think it is fair to say that the general anti-establishment fever that pervaded the country during the Vietnam and Watergate crises finished it off. Actually, it is still very difficult for me to write about the critical scene of the seventies with any detachment because I have such a stake in it. But I think that politics played a large role in the splintering of critical opinion, a far larger role than is usually accorded it by apostles of pluralism. The turn-off from the gallery/collector market system, which was seen as inextricably connected with the larger political and financial corruption, was very widespread. It was no accident that Coplans and Kozloff were fired as the result of the uproar they had caused with their frankly political attacks on the structure of museums and the way in which art was marketed.

It was a revolution—a non-violent and ultimately abortive revolution—but a revolution nonetheless. It took all sorts of forms and encompassed many shades of political opinion, but essentially it functioned as a massive withdrawal of spirit and energy from what had hitherto been called the mainstream of American art and the market system which supported it. The seventies was a decade obsessed by corruption of the human spirit and by pollution of the landscape. Often the latter becoming a metaphor for the former.

Some art critics, such as Jack Burnham and Douglas Davis, supported art that sought to redeem the human soul from its state of alienation through various forms of non-static art, performance, video, body art and the like. The artist was to play the role of shaman to society's psychic ills. Others, such as Lucy Lippard, found redemption through feminism. Still others, such as Max Kozloff, Rosalind Krauss, and Susan Sontag, took refuge in consideration of the, as yet, untainted resources of photography. There was a virtual explosion of new publications, regional, political, esthetic and artist-initiated, all claiming to bypass the corrupt ties between advertising and editorial copy in the New York glossies.

In the general attack on hierarchical values and claims to authority, the very act of writing criticism itself became suspect. John Cage, a major cultural influence in the seventies, told critics they were wasting their time. The best criticism, he said, would be to do your own work.

Even *New York Times* critics were not immune to the general frenzy of agonizing reappraisal. In 1977, Peter Schjeldahl, now critic for the *Village Voice,* read a poem to members of the Society of Contemporary Art at the Art Institute of Chicago, a fragment of which I would like to repeat here:

. . . . . . What's ghastly
is that on occasion I mistook my hand-me down taste
for the light of election, and poured ink on the worthy.
I still blush, hotly, for those occasions,
yearning for a large bomb fall, directly on my head.
Like that supercilious dismissal of Baziotes—horrible!
And Laszlo Moholy-Nagy, for God's sake, I patronized
your venerable ghost! And Susan Crile, estimable painter,
what full moon was shining when I sat down to review you?
Also Stanford University, and redoubtable scholar Albert Elsen,
I sneered at your splendid museum,
behaving just like a paranoid's dream of a New York chauvinist,
oh shame! James Brooks, you didn't complain
those years ago, but even today you could flay me a look.
Jim Dine, how could I, and Joan Snyder, how could I
denigrate your indubitable value in the (unpronounced) name
of (non-existent) standards of acceptability?
Richard Hamilton, where did I get off
welcoming you to America in that disgraceful fashion?
and Gio Pomodoro, though you never will be to my taste,
that was no excuse for behaving like a fat-mouthed provincial!
All these atrocities in the *Sunday Times,* each in a million copies
just whizzing off the presses, fanning out over the land
alighting in libraries-microfilm; oh God!!!
unkillable and infamous words! Just let me
take this knife and . . .

—*New Art Examiner,* June 1977

You might have thought from the forgoing description that during this period of avant-gardist retrenchment, critical doubt, and rejection of crass market values that the art market would shrink.

If you did, you would be mistaken. In fact, it went through an unprecedented expansion. Not just in New York, but in Chicago, Houston, St. Louis, and in Washington, D.C. The number of galleries doubled and tripled. With them tripled the number of advertising dollars available for art publications and the number of art writers publishing.

There are two main reasons for the expansion of the art world in the seventies. One has to do with a great deal of pump-priming by the

National Endowment for the Arts. I heard a figure the other day which put this into focus for me. During his five-year tenure as director of the Visual Arts Program, James Melchert dispensed 27 million dollars on various visual arts programs and projects. By comparison with military expenditure it's nothing. By comparison with public monies spent on the arts in previous decades, it's a lot. A good deal of this money, as much of it as Melchert could manage, went to the support of contemporary art and artists.

Now Melchert, along with many others, was interested in promoting alternative (i.e. non-market) systems for the support of contemporary art. He funded "alternatives" (non-profit galleries, such as N.A.M.E., Washington Project for the Arts, and P.S. 1, and non-profit publications such as the *New Art Examiner* and *Afterimage*), he gave out millions in small and large artists' fellowships, he encouraged schools and universities to establish visiting artists' programs, to build galleries, and to start exhibition programs. He also encouraged museums to increase the number of exhibitions devoted to contemporary art and to set aside special areas for the informal exhibition of experimental art by younger artists.

The strange effect of all this was to build up a service industry and an audience for art that fed directly into the market system. The more money was poured into alternatives and non-profits, the more the market boomed. (Perhaps Reagan should study this phenomenon.)

However, there was another less quixotic reason for a booming art market. The seventies was the decade in which the public at large suddenly realized the profitability of collecting. At the beginning of the decade, a landmark was the much publicized Robert Scull auction in which Rauschenberg saw paintings which he had sold to the collector for a few hundred dollars sold for hundreds of thousands of dollars. The *Wall Street Journal* began to tout art as an investment, a hedge against inflation. Collectors' clubs at museums proliferated.

Now here is the interesting point I'd like to make. Do these collectors clubs invite critics to talk to them about art and to advise them on choices? Occasionally. But much more frequent choices of speakers are dealers and curators, for very practical reasons. Particularly in areas outside of New York, dealers and curators are in a much better position to predict future swings in the art market. They know what major exhibitions being planned in museums across the country would enhance the value of certain artists' work. They know what the hot numbers are in the New York and European markets.

There's no question that the "power of review" still exists. Young artists are still desperate for that first review that will recognize their existence in the art world. Middle-aged artists still tend to measure their success in terms of the number of pages devoted to their work in New York publications.

However, the game has fundamentally changed. Dealers no longer need the intermediary critic to sell new work to a reluctant public. In the heated-up market of present-day New York, shows sell out before the critic has time to lift his pen, sometimes even before the show opens. The consumer, not the critic, is king.

It seems to me that critics have not yet caught up with this situation, so different from the fifties and sixties when critics manned the front lines and were the last authority on the "significance" of a work of art. We are still sorting it out, still trying to understand what it means, and trying to maintain our belief in the intrinsic spiritual value of art, while recognizing that market forces are far more potent persuaders than our words.

Perhaps, however, this turnabout is a blessing in disguise. In many respects, the era of the omnipotent critic was an historical aberration, a function of America's long-deferred reception of modernist art. When Greenberg began writing, he had no institutional or financial support, but he had behind him a half century of tradition. He conceived as his mission the selling of his own unique interpretation of modernism to the American public, and he was spectacularly successful in doing so.

Critics now have been relieved of the necessity of selling contemporary art. It is being done more effectively elsewhere. They have time now to think, to observe, even to criticize, to look at the whole of society and the relationship of the visual arts to it and to reform their ideas. One might say that the critic/intellectual has landed right back down at the base of the art-world pyramid along with the artists. And perhaps that's where the critic belongs.

JAMES YOOD EDITOR

1984–1987

INTRODUCTION

Oh, the *New Art Examiner*, I'm all over that, first I wrote for it, then I worked for it, then I edited it, then I wrote for it, then I was on its board of directors, and probably a day still doesn't pass that I don't have some cause to think about it. The *NAE* suited me just fine; if Chicago is the annoying little brother of American culture, contemporary art's disloyal opposition, not quite in harmony with the dictates and aspirations of our cunning coastal cultural capitals but loud and big and filled with enough talent to assert its incredible independence even if it's largely ignored by the rest of the contemporary art scene, then I was pleased to work with a magazine that similarly seemed out of tune with the go-along-to-get-along realpolitik of American culture, and that always took the "yes, but . . ." position while all the other art mags seemed to march in giddy lockstep. Chicago has always had a bit of chip on its shoulder and so did the *NAE*. It was a magazine that continually privileged independence over consensus and that challenged authority and power not because of contrariness but because that was where the bodies were buried, where the culture industry made its sausage.

In a shorthand manner I'd divide the history of the *NAE*—only in terms of its relationship to Chicago, mind you; the whole history of the mag would be another story—into three phases. The first would cover the foundation and early years of the *NAE*, when Jane Allen and Derek Guthrie created the context of the magazine and determined its format and the timbre of its voice. The second phase would cover the years after Derek and Jane moved to D.C. in 1980, the years of the Chicago editorship of Alice Thorson, myself and Jean Fulton, sort of from 1982–1992. And the final phase would be the editorships of Allison Gamble, Ann Wiens and Kathryn Hixson. (I'm already desirous of immediately descending into caveats and counter-arguments. Words such as "editorship" imply a sort of pa- or matriarchal authority or trickle-down control that really didn't exist—I've never worked at a more egalitarian place than the *NAE*. Everyone had the same base salary, and we each did a bit of everyone else's job—if you phoned the mag in 1987 because you had a problem with your subscription, I assure you that it's very likely I answered the phone and took care of it, or at least tried to. Still, the editors did make most of the initial decisions about content, though things often had a way of intriguingly careening out of control. I'll never forget Derek telling me, "Jim, you offer them [by which he meant writers or invited guests for things such as the Speakeasy or Art Press Review columns] an opportunity and then if they want to hang themselves, it's their business.")

The editors of this compendium, I'm informed, are including an article I co-wrote with Alice Thorson on the subject of neo-expressionist painting in Chicago in the early 1980s and its relation to some specific aspects of the history of art here. I haven't read the article since shortly after it was published. Writers, like sharks, must always move forward, and I rarely read pieces I wrote a long time ago. But I remember a great deal about the context of the article, the feel of the time, what Alice and I were trying to explicate. I remember our divvying up aspects of the article, and several afternoons and one long evening when we cobbled the whole thing together. I particularly recall the chart that juxtaposed specific aspects of neo-expressionism and Imagism in Chicago. That was my Wölfflinian bit, borrowed from Frederick Hartt's survey textbook on Italian Renaissance Art, where he did the same for the Renaissance and Mannerism.

Trying to understand what Chicago actually is as an art center, what its place is in contemporary art, what, if anything, makes it distinct from elsewhere, was and still is a bit of a cottage industry for local critics. For most May issues in the 1980s, to run concurrently with Art Chicago, we would invite some respected national voice (Donald Kuspit, Peter Schjeldahl, Eleanor Heartney, etc.) to take a crack at trying to define the attitudes and tendencies in Chicago art. I hope a few of those have made this compendium. The enormous shadow of Chicago Imagism, the work and position of artists such as Roger Brown, Ed Paschke, Gladys Nilsson, Karl Wirsum, Jim Nutt, Barbara Rossi, Christina Ramberg, Phil Hanson, Hollis Sigler, Robert Lostutter, Phyllis Bramson, Ray Yoshida and many more, came to define both locally and nationally what Chicago was about. While this isn't the place to get into all the niceties of the argument, I think it would be fair to say that it was in the DNA of the *NAE* to take its usual "yes, but . . ." position, to challenge the dominance of Imagism, not disdaining the art or the artists themselves, but attentive, possibly hypersensitive, to how the local power brokers in our galleries and museums seemed to kowtow to Imagism and overlook everything else. The *NAE*'s interest in groups such as The Five and in abstract art in Chicago was, I would propose, never anti-Imagism but was part of its independent refusal to get on board the Imagism train and its effort to broaden the scene here.

As we got to the mid 1980s, when the Imagists were more or less in their mid 40s, at the height of their skills and influence (10 of the 12 artists listed above were—and some still are—local professors), the conversation began to shift from examining alternatives to Imagism to positing successors to it, trying to identify what might be the next wave in Chicago art. If we had waited a few more years, until the end of the 1980s, Alice and I might have examined the new group of conceptual artists that then emerged out of the School of the Art Institute of Chicago. But from our vantage point in 1985 the energy and bravado of the recent neo-expressionists, particularly the painters, seemed part and parcel of the dynamic growth of the art community, a kind of pictorial impetuosity parallel to the understanding that Chicago really did have an art world that was exciting and diverse and open-ended. I continue to admire many of those artists today.

When I'm asked about the *NAE*, the questioner always seems to assume that we sat around most of the day talking about Hilton Kramer or Lew Manilow or Phyllis Kind, etc. The reality was that at least 50 percent of our time was spent on running the business of the *NAE*, and for much of that it could have been an auto parts magazine. I remember hundreds of conversations with printers, distributors, advertisers, suppliers, sales representatives, board members, potential funders, bankers, etc. We were almost always on the brink of financial collapse—sometimes more, sometimes less, but never was there a comfort zone of knowing that you could make payroll every two weeks or be able to pay the printer. The grinding pressure of producing a magazine every month finally wore me out and I moved on, but I would give a great deal to be back on Ohio or Grand Street one more time on that day each month when we shipped the final boards of the mag to the printer (always around 6 or 7 p.m.), to spin around with Alice and Andrea Greenfield and Bill Ortleb and Joel Davies and Elizabeth Hoxie and Andrea Silverman and Janet Magnuson and Jean Fulton and more, attending to all the final details and fixes, seeing to the crescendo that last hour or two before pick-up. But no can do; magazines are history on the fly, snapshots that try to be reflective and analytical but are completely time-stamped, more *of* than *about* a moment in history. That's what makes them valuable, and there is probably no better single way to understand Chicago as an art center in 1978 or 1986 or 1993 or 2000 than to leaf through the issues of the *New Art Examiner,* not just the articles, but the ads, the classifieds, the letters from readers, the editorials, the reviews, the snippets just as much if not more than the lead articles. And such fun, too!

—James Yood

JOANNA FRUEH

EXPLICIT

Towards a Feminist Theory of Art Criticism

January 1985

Like Marxism and structuralism, which receive due attention, feminism has altered the content and constructs of art history over the past 15 years and continues to do so. However, many art historians, like their compatriots in other academic disciplines, view the adoption of a feminist perspective with suspicion. Simply put, detractors claim that feminist art historians and critics are narrow and self-indulgent and that they distort and polemically misread images and material, thereby undermining art history.

Actually, feminists serve both art and art history: by seeking knowledge about the overlooked meanings of art; by examining our own unacknowledged assumptions and biases and those of previous and contemporary art historians and critics; and by developing ways to write about art that will serve as new models for art critical discourse.

Art history and criticism are frequently divorced: you practice one or the other. Basically, the myth is that art historians aim for objectivity by gathering data that will prove the "truth" about various aspects of an artist's life and career or of a particular period's aesthetic mentality. By keeping their distance, art historians supposedly maintain intellectual neutrality.

Traditionally, art critics, whose function and pleasure is primarily writing about the art of their own time, also seek "truth." However, many of the best critics have been, and are, highly subjective. For Diderot, the first modern art critic, criticism was an empathetic occupation. In fact, he demanded passion from art so that he could feel it. In 1766 he wrote, ". . . move me, surprise me, rend my heart; make me tremble, weep, shudder, outrage me; delight my eyes afterwards if you can."

Traditional art historical methodology answers certain questions about art: who made it? When? Where? How? Whys are often unsatisfactorily answered through stylistic analyses or investigations of iconography and patronage?

But whys also demand analyses and interpretations of social and conceptual contexts. Because it involves discernment, criticism is a more inclusive activity than historical study which focuses on the recording, analysis, and interpretation of events. Pursuing old questions in new ways, as feminism does, extends art historical methodology and makes connections between historical context and culture. Such a pursuit turns the historian into a critic.

Feminist art critics join the supposedly incompatible modes of art historical and art critical practice, wedding deep responsiveness to art with factual information, such as biography, sources of an individual artist's work, and stylistic connections with other artists and movements. Many traditionalists find such a marriage wanting in intellectual neutrality, but feminist historian/critics like Arlene Raven believe in intimacy with art. As Raven writes in the first sentence of an essay on Harmony Hammond, "I enter Harmony Hammond's works." Raven is speaking of complete identification: being at one with the art, and through it, the creator, another woman. Thus, subject, Raven, and object, the art works and another human being, are not detached at all. The object no longer exists. In this kind of criticism, the term art object does not make sense, and a subject to subject relationship replaces the standard subject to object one.

Utter involvement without loss of self is the outcome of this new critic-to-art connection, which is discourse as intercourse: entry into another's body (of art). Feminist criticism of this order belongs to an art criticism of overtly personal engagement, which has waxed and waned in appeal during the past two centuries. After a period of disfavor, for most of the twentieth century, it is now on the upswing. In a 1979 issue of *Art in America*, Nancy Marmer wrote about "the . . . critic's openly subjective interpretation of art" and stated that "the expressive possibilities of a personalist prose have once again become highly attractive."

Moreover, Marmer noted that "such criticism weaves the fabric of its content out of the critic's subjective, psychological response to the work—thus absorbing the artist into the critic's mental universe." Feminist critics do this and more, for a penetrating study of art, being physical as well as mental, requires that the penetrator, as poet and thinker Robin Morgan has said in *The Anatomy of Freedom,* "feel with the brain and think through the body." Penetration, then, should not be viewed as phallic, an insertion of self into other (subject into object). Rather, penetration may be understood in terms of mutuality, a diffusion of (my) self into (your)self into (my)self. In this way, the study of art becomes even more emphatic than it was for Diderot. Although it has some exemplary practitioners, e.g. Carol Duncan, Lucy Lippard, Rozsika Parker, Griselda Pollock, and Arlene Raven, feminist art criticism is woefully unevolved. Far more sophisticated than feminist theory and scholarship is feminist literary criticism. Consequently its development in the 1970's and methodology serve as useful models for an understanding of feminist art criticism.

Three "critical" stages exist in recent feminist literary criticism. The first has been a resurrection of lost or ignored women writers and works. Concurrently, feminists in art have been rediscovering women artists and works. H.W. Janson's classic survey text does not mention one woman artist. Therefore, scholars such as Eleanor Tufts, in *Our Hidden Heritage: Five Centuries of Women Artists,* and Linda Nochlin and Ann Sutherland Harris, in *Women Artists 1550–1950,* redress this omission. Also, through such a comparison as Artemisia Gentileschi's and Caravaggio's versions of Judith beheading Holofernes, in which a woman boldly treats the same subject as the man from whom her style of dramatic realism derives, feminist critics can prove that women, unlike what male-engendered myth would have us believe, are fertile and productive in other ways than simply as sexual creatures and mothers.

First-stage scholarship has been important, by showing that women are a part of art history and thereby providing women artists with a sense of belonging. Also, unlike traditional art history, which generally examines "major" monuments by venerated "masters," first-stage feminism shifts the focus of study to "minor" works by artists whose skill has not been deemed consummate. Dealing with "secondary" artists and objects fleshes out the skeletal "truth" of art history encouraging us to create new bodies of knowledge. Such "bodybuilding" strengthens art history.

Despite the accomplishments of first-stage efforts, they are often reformist rather than truly re-visionist; for they exemplify scholars' interest in new subjects, but with a continuing employment of standard art historical tools. As Rozsika Parker and Griselda Pollock write in *Old Mistresses,* the "determination to relocate women in art history on the discipline's own terms" is "subscrib[ing] to a slightly modified, but nonetheless conventional notion of art history; its system of values and criteria of significance . . . a radical reform, if not a total deconstruction of the present structure of the discipline is needed in order to arrive at a real understanding of the history of women and art."

Second-stage critics have considered the possibility of a women's tradition either counter or related to the male literary tradition. They have examined a "female imagination," their counterparts in art a "female sensibility." When we think of Eva Hesse's and Sol Lewitt's minimalist sculptures, can we say that the pieces reveal the sex of their creators? Is Hesse more involved in a visceral response to materials, indicative of women's perhaps socialized awareness of their bodies, both inside and out? Is Lewitt more concerned with rationalizing the materials, ordering them in an evenly systematic fashion?

These questions and their implicit answers are simplistic. Nonetheless, in the mid-1970's female sensibility was a burning issue, and the following hypothesis, among others, was presented: women's art is obsessive and often characterized by central core imagery. But are Alfred Jensen's works any less obsessive than Joyce Kozloff's? Or are Barnett Newman's voids any less symbolic of a central core (a cunt, a womb) than many of Georgia O'Keeffe's flowers or Judy Chicago's *Dinner Party* plate images?

Despite the superficiality of such hypotheses, they were significant attempts to think about the differences between female and male art. Perhaps Newman sees the central core as a void (as a gross generalization: for the male, the womb is empty, the vagina something to be filled), whereas O'Keeffe and Chicago see the central core as full (for the female, the inside of her body is complete in itself).

Second-stage questioning also revealed the class aspect of art world sexism in the distinction between high (men's) and low (women's) art. Crafts and decorative objects made by women were reconsidered as fine art, proving the absurdity of labeling Mondrian's or Rothko's paintings as high art and, say, a reductively composed and colored Amish quilt as low art, for all are examples of non-objective design.

However, because the first two existed within the avant-garde, intellectualized framework of modernism and the quilt was created for use in the everyday world, the paintings could be praised for their denial of merely decorative (in other words, frivolous) effects and for their absolute aesthetic integrity. Indeed, it is their "immaculate" conception that assured their value to viewers and critics.

The exposure of classicism also opened the way for women and men to make use of pattern and decoration in their art, and Miriam Schapiro's deliberate use of fabric and floral and geometric designs in many works of the late 1970s demonstrates a "low" art, "feminine" aesthetic transferred to a "high" art context; for Schapiro exhibits and is written about in the art world dominated by male-identified authority figures.

Third-stage feminism is more theoretical than the first two and centers on gender analysis of literature or art, and thereby the interconnections among text or object, historical context, and culture. Here, critics reassess the values placed on art in regard to content as well as function. What would previously have been viewed as just "feminine" sentimentality in, for example, the heart motif of some of Schapiro's "femmages," is reinterpreted in several ways: society has relegated women to the degraded sphere of emotion; feeling, however, is powerful and beautiful; sentiment, then, can expose the heart of the matter (of life), which is Love; and Love emerges from and leads to both intellectual and emotional exploration.

Third-stage critics also reappraise men's art, the gender implications of which have been either ignored or considered innocently intentioned because of the creator's supposed pure, serious, commitment to Art. Most art critics and historians, however, fail to discuss the power of images to inform and educate the viewer.

A feminist perspective does not replace traditional art historical methodology. Rather, the new complements and amplifies the old, for fresh analyses and interpretations of style and iconography show that art is not value-free and that previous scholarship has not taken this into consideration.

Feminist art criticism is significant and necessary because it challenges what feminist literary critic Annette Kolodny calls the "dog-eared myth of intellectual neutrality." Such neutrality presupposes the neuter status of the mind; as if gender imbalances did not exist in scholarship. For the most part, male-identified minds study art, and as feminist philosopher Mary Daly understands, the sexist products of such intellects affirm what she terms Methodolatry, which is the worship of method, the devotion and faith in "the rite of right re-search."

I turn again to the model of feminist literary criticism, in Kolodny's article—"Dancing through the Minefield: Some Observations on the Theory, Practice and Politics of a Feminist Literary Criticism," for an

argument against Methodolatry. Kolodny offers three pertinent proposi-
tions. (I have substituted art terms for literary ones): (1) Art history (and
with that the historicity of art) is a fiction; (2) insofar as we are taught to
see, what we engage are not objects but paradigms; and, finally, (3) that
since the grounds upon which we assign aesthetic value to objects are
never infallible, unchangeable, or universal, we must reexamine not only
our aesthetics but as well, the inherent biases and assumptions informing
the critical methods which (in part) shape our aesthetic responses.

Kolodny is proposing what Adrienne Rich calls re-vision; and feminist
art critics re-view and re-vise by looking at well-known works in fresh
ways and seeing what art historical "authority" has taken for granted or
made invisible. Even those mainstays of traditional art history—style,
iconography, and patronage—can illuminate a work from a re-visionist
perspective.

Embedded in Gustave Courbet's *The Source* (1868), for instance, is
the deep-rooted notion that woman is nature. Both the subject—a naked
women at a spring—and the theme—woman as origin of life—are conventional, but Courbet's conflation of woman and nature is unusually
deft. A fleshy woman sits by a stream. One hand holds on to a branch,
seems almost molded to it, as if she herself were part of the tree; and
her contours, from the buttocks up, are eaten by shadows, so that nature
absorbs her flesh, is actually one with it. Her lower left leg and right foot
are submerged, so that she and the water are also one; more so, because
Courbet creates an equivalent sensuousness between her dimpled thighs
and the rippling water. Woman and nature literally mirror one another
for the material of the female body is the material world.

Not only does this equation cast woman as body, as opposed to man
as mind, which, of course, is analogous to culture; but also, because
Courbet is a master at making paint read as the texture of whatever it
describes, landscape and woman reverberate with one another's physi-
cality. Water feels like flesh, dense, smooth, heavy; and flesh feels like
water—surely it would "give" with pressure. Courbet elaborates this
bonding in various ways: the spring gushes from the dark vegetation
much as the nude emerges from it; the water pours over her left hand,
and light dapples skin and liquid; lush greenery reads as a metaphor for
the lushness of the body.

All in all, woman symbolizes fecundity and lack of consciousness. But
who is this nude? She is the single, anonymous woman who represents
all women, not as a social group, but as Woman—Female of the Species

in one aspect of the Eternal Feminine: Earth Mother/Mother Earth. This myth of Woman is not necessarily repugnant. However, it is only a fragment of reality, an ideology through which we should not expect to see what any individual woman genuinely is.

Courbet painted *Woman with White Stockings* (1861) for Khalil Bey, a wealthy one-time Ottoman ambassador in St. Petersburg, who settled in Paris. In the painting a seated young woman pulls a stocking over a bare foot balanced on an already stockinged, raised knee. The view, from below, angles up, making her genitals a focal point. Patronage indicates where aesthetic, economic, and political power lies, bluntly, who can "own" people and things. The artist owns the image as a creation, but the buyer owns the art as an object of aesthetic and/or monetary value and the image as an object of desire.

Most likely, Khalil Bey did not want the painting primarily because, as Jack Lindsay writes, "This is a masterpiece in its organization of form, making of the nude a compact unity without parallel." According to Lindsay, Khalil "kept it locked in a sort of tabernacle or cabinet." Thus he enforced his power as purchaser of two "sacred objects": the painting and the woman, who Khalil "has" (to himself). She, of course, is woman, whose being is locked up in *her* tabernacle, the genitals. Lindsay disengages her from any selfness, for she is only "a brilliantly original piece of patterning, with the body a single solid mass, yet with the limbs clearly articulated in a rhythmic structure balanced on the slit of the genitals." That slit! It is the pivotal point: not only of composition, but also of an art historian's interest, probably of a rich collector's purchase, and of the myth that Woman is a cunt and no more.

If feminism is about freedom, then feminist art criticism strives for the accomplishment of mental freedom. I use the word mental rather than intellectual because the latter is generally thought to be the power of rational thought as distinguished from the power to feel or to will, and the former relates to the total emotional and intellectual response of an individual to an environment.

Notions of intellect discount the possibility that knowledge can be gained through the body, the emotions, or wishes. Consequently, intellect, alone, confines the critic by denying not only the usefulness, but also the worth and relevance of her/his desire to use her/himself fully. Exclusive emphasis on intellect denies a critic's being, the fact that s/he lives: on many levels and in many modes, and in an aggregate of social and cultural conditions.

From Duchamp's *Bicycle Wheel* to Johns's *Painted Bronze (Beer Cans)* to Chicago's *Menstruation Bathroom,* modern and contemporary art have dealt with, to paraphrase Robert Rauschenberg, the gap between art and life. The interplay between the two, demanded by their disparity, involves the feminist critic as much as the artist. It is as a participant in this interplay that s/he can truly penetrate the art and it her/him, that s/he can know it as subject.

REFERENCES

Brookner, Anita. *The Genius of the future; Studies in French Art Criticism: Diderot, Stendahl, Baudelaire, Zola, the Brothers Goncourt, Huysmans.* London: Phaidon, 1971.

Daly, Mary. *Beyond God the Father: Toward a Philosophy of Women's Liberation.* Boston: Beacon Press, 1973.

———. *Gyn/Ecology: The Metaethics of Radical Feminism.* Boston: Beacon Press, 1978.

Frueh, Joanna. "Crucibles of Beauty: Occult Symbolism and Seven Chicago Women." *The New Art Examiner,* 8, No. 2 (November 1980).

Kolodny, Annette. "Dancing through the Minefield: Some Observations on the Theory and Practice of a Feminist Literary Criticism." *Feminist Studies,* 6, No. 1 (Spring 1980).

Lindsay, Jack. *Gustave Courbet: His Life and Art.* New York: Harper & Row, 1973.

Marmer, Nancy. "The Performing Critic." *Art in America,* 67, No. 8 (December 1979).

Morgan, Robin. *The Anatomy of Freedom: Feminism, Physics, and Global Politics.* Garden City: Anchor/Doubleday, 1982.

Parker, Rozsika and Griselda Pollock. *Old Mistresses: Women, Art and Ideology.* New York: Pantheon, 1981.

Raven, Arlene. "Harmonies: An Essay on the Work of Harmony Hammond" (Chicago: Klein Gallery, 1982).

———. *Picture This or Why Is Art Important?* Houston: The Judy Chicago Word and Image Network, 1982.

ALICE THORSON AND JAMES YOOD

WHO FOLLOWS THE HAIRY WHO?

March 1985

Artists make art. It is critics who concern themselves with the question as to when a group of artists constitute a movement or collectively define a style. Such categorization is inevitable; no matter how individualistic a certain artist may be, no matter how entrenched our notion of the primacy of a single artistic vision, no artist is larger than his or her own time, and inevitably an artist will reflect the urges of the moment in which he or she lives.

Chicago has not been immune to this drive towards aesthetic generalizations, and its recent artistic history has been marked by movements like the Imagists, the Monster Roster, the Zombies and the Hairy Who?. These "tags" function as touchstones to larger truths; one may or may not find it helpful to think of Leon Golub as a member of the Monster Roster, but such a term helps fix him in a particular cultural climate and aids us in assessing his relationship to his contemporaries.

The movements mentioned above are specific to Chicago. But much confusion exists as to what constitutes each movement, often the invention of one critic, and what their relationships are to one another. Infighting among critics in an attempt to establish a definition has had a pervasive effect on the cultural dynamics of Chicago. Imagism is a case in point—some critics have attempted to define it as *the* signature Chicago style in painting.

The limits and heritage of Imagism have been hotly debated, and this debate has all but precluded any serious consideration of new painting in Chicago. In fact, an examination of some recent trends in Chicago painting reveals the coalescence of an aesthetic that not only challenges

Imagism, but more importantly forces a reassessment of issues that have marked cultural discussions here over the past few years.

The October 1984 *New Art Examiner* featured a "Speakeasy" by Russell Bowman, curator of the Milwaukee Art Museum and an ardent admirer of Chicago Imagism. In his essay Bowman contended that the Imagists have been given short shrift by Chicago critics since the mid-1970s, citing numerous instances of their mistreatment.

Most notable was the *Chicago Sun-Times* critic Franz Schulze's perceived defection from the Imagist camp: Schulze suggested in a 1975 article in the *Chicago Daily News* that Imagism had passed its prime. Coming from the author of *Fantastic Images,* the book that laid the groundwork for the codification of the Imagist aesthetic, this was criticism that smarted. In Bowman's view, Schulze added insult to injury in his 1983 article in *Art in America,* "Made in Chicago: A revisionary view," by unfavorably comparing the decorative refinement of current work by Imagists Roger Brown, Jim Nutt, and Ray Yoshida to the high moral seriousness of Monster Roster artists Leon Golub, June Leaf, and Cosmo Campoli.

Responding in the December *New Art Examiner* to Bowman's charges, Schulze reiterated his belief in the superiority of the Monster Roster and carried his argument further, challenging Imagism's pedigree by repudiating the theory that there is "a lineal descent from the immediate postwar Chicago generation to that of the present day."

In contrast to Schulze's rejection of stylistic continuity are the theories of the two most vocal supporters of Imagism: critic/collector Dennis Adrian, who posits a set of stylistic characteristics peculiar to Chicago art, and Chicago Sun-Times critic Christopher Lyon, who sees in Chicago art a continuity of style that can be traced back to Ivan Albright's work in the 1920s.

In the catalogue for his 1983 exhibition titled *Some Other Traditions* Adrian outlined a set of characteristics endemic to Chicago art: a "high number of formal incidents," a penchant for "organic abstraction," the "use of linear elements to circumscribe and define form," "techniques which avoid heavy impasto effects in painting," "scrupulous finish, and painstaking attention to detail."

In "Coming in from the Cold" (*Chicago Magazine,* May 1984) Lyon traces a direct line of descent from Albright to Golub to the Hairy Who? to "post-Imagists" Hollis Sigler and Phyllis Bramson. Lyon's version of Chicago's art history takes Adrian's codification of the Imagist aesthetic and applies it to the past, forcing it to fit Monster Roster artists whom Imagist supporters can then cite as a pedigree.

At issue here is more than mere aesthetic preference. For better or worse, Imagism has given Chicago its artistic identity. When curators come to town scouting work for national shows, they rarely leave without an Imagist work or two—the most recent example being the Hirshhorn's *Content* show, where three of the five artists chosen to represent Chicago art from the past *ten* years were Imagists. Local institutions, both mainstream and "alternative," have been supportive as well: The Museum of Contemporary Art, which mounted *Don Baum Sez Chicago Needs Famous Artists* in 1969, has gone on to give one-person exhibitions to Roger Brown and Karl Wirsum, and is the promised beneficiary of Dennis Adrian's extensive collection which includes many important Imagist works. In the past two years N.A.M.E. Gallery, Randolph Street Gallery, and the Renaissance Society have given mid-career retrospectives to Ray Yoshida, Gladys Nilsson, and Ed Paschke, respectively.

Whereas New York's identity (and importance) is vested in its omnivorous appetite for the new and untried, Chicago resists wholeheartedly embracing those artists who venture too far from Imagism—as if acknowledging a new aesthetic would mean the loss of its artistic identity. This reluctance has contributed to the creation of a myth of Imagist hegemony that far outstrips reality—in fact, Chicago has produced outstanding artists working in a variety of other styles and genres.

But Imagism is "The Tradition" to which all other styles are referred; geometric abstraction is "The Other Tradition"; organic abstraction is "Some Other Tradition." We have seen the rise of post-Imagism in the work of Sigler, Bramson, and Prussian (NAE, October 1978); highlighted in last year's *80th Chicago and Vicinity Exhibition* was a diluted and deluded form of "neo-Imagism." Thus, Bowman's complaints with regard to the mistreatment of the Imagists must seem ironic to those Chicago artists who work in their shadow.

In his 1982 year-end review for the Reader, Christopher Lyon noted a painting renaissance in Chicago. After chronicling a series of shows that "seemed to sum up the Imagists' achievement," he launched into a review of the achievements of Chicago's younger painters. "Neo-expressionist" is the tag Lyon used to sum up their collective direction. Singling out Mark, Jackson, Jim Brinsfield, Clar Monaco, Will Northerner, and Lance Kiland, he concluded "a major shift in painting has occurred." Earlier in the year and referring to much the same phenomenon, Alan Artner had described a number of Chicago's younger painters an "aggressive zombies" in the *Chicago Tribune*. Michael Bonesteel more sympathetically discussed this group, along with Auste and Darinka Novitovic, in a story for the *Reader* titled "Zombie Parade." Schulze, in his 1983 *Art in America* piece also recognized a change in painting's direction, alluding to "the recent emergence of a group of self-conscious primitivists and punksters."

Lyon's discerning of a shift in Chicago's painting was echoed two years later in Bonesteel's 1984 "year in review" for the *Reader,* where he stated, "If there was an overwhelming aesthetic evident among gallery and museum shows in '84, it was the dreaded neo-expressionist, or, if you will, New Image look adopted by more and more artists locally, nationally and internationally." His list of local artists exhibiting an expressionist persuasion included Northerner, Brinsfield, Jackson, and Monaco, overlapping markedly with Lyons 1982 list; he extended it to include Wesley Kimler, an artist from Minnesota, and Linda King, an ex-Californian recently settled in Chicago.

One might add to Bonesteel's list other "expressionist" painters who made career strides in the past year, including Michael Zieve, Hannah Dresner, Gary Gissler, Matt Straub, Michael Hoskins, L.J. Douglas, Robert Pollack, Erik Hanson, Janet Cooling, and Arnaldo Roche. Individually, each has received a degree of critical recognition, but as a group their reception has been decidedly mixed and rarely energetic. Pigeonholed, often mistakenly so, as "neo-expressionists," Chicago's new painterly painters have been developing without the support of establishment critics and institutions. For example, in his catalogue essay for *Some Other Traditions,* Dennis Adrian acknowledges Chicago's new expressionist trend (as well as important minimalist, conceptualist, and performance artists), but excluded all of them from the show on the grounds that "the artists concerned have deliberately adopted stylistic points of view and attitudes about art which are not indigenous to Chicago, but which have been formulated elsewhere, say in Europe or New York." In an art town that prides itself on having its own distinctive, hometown aesthetic, this is a damning observation.

Adrian's criteria exemplify the kind of regional parochialism that has long marked Chicago—an "us against them" kind of town. As a focus for action, this manner of thinking might be a good way to keep lights out of Wrigley Field; when applied to art, it is reductive and chauvinistic. For many in Chicago, the term neo-expressionist has come to signify "out-of-towner," or defector, or agent of the hated New York, or disloyal to one's roots. It was easy enough for viewers, dealers, and critics to place abstract artists into "the Other Tradition," but the young figurative artists had to be put in their place, dismissed as ephemeral phenomena.

The "effect of this dismissal has been the virtual suppression of a new non-Imagist aesthetic in Chicago painting—the shift Lyon identified (and subsequently declined to treat in any incisive fashion) in 1982, and which by 1984 had begun to take on the definition of a movement. Among the many young figurative artists in Chicago who work in a painterly, at times neo-expressionist style, one can detect a distinct commonality of intent and execution in the work of Michael Hoskins, Gary Gissler, Hannah Dresner, Wesley Kimler, Linda King, James Brinsfield, Will Northerner, Arnoldo Roche, and to a lesser extent Michael Zieve and L.J. Douglas. While this is certainly not an exhaustive list, these painters are representative of a stylistic and attitudinal shift which departs radically from Imagism. In terms of their relationship to a Chicago tradition, it is the Grandfather Principle that holds sway here. Certainly one must allow for the differences in experience between a generation that grew up in the sixties and seventies, and one which grew up in the thirties and forties; nonetheless, in examining the work of these young painters, one discovers an approach that is noticeably similar to the one Schulze described in his 1983 discussion of the Monster Roster: "Each has always taken experience, whether personal or mythic, as the primary energizing factor of his art, and then sought to transform it metaphorically into painting or sculpture."

Hailing as they do from different galleries or lacking gallery representation altogether, and displaying a degree of cosmopolitanism that would have been difficult to achieve for a Chicago artist a decade ago—before the gallery boom, before the maturation of those Chicago institutions which regularly bring outside art into the public eye, and before the annual onslaught of international art in the form of Art Expo—these young artists resist easy aesthetic codification. However, it is possible to outline a set of shared characteristics which emerge not only in their work, but also in the work of many of their contemporaries.

In addition to the obvious shift toward a more painterly mode of execution, one observes in these painters a distinct change in attitude from the coolly ironic stance and intentional "psychic distance" of Imagism. There is an emotional immediacy and a quality of vulnerability in the prone, twisted female torsos which inhabit Dresner's paintscapes; in King's naked figures who huddle or confront each other in the glow of protective fires; in the reclining male atop a bier in Gissler's *Support*; and in Roche's embracing couple, who meld together in total self-abandonment, like the lovers in Edvard Munch's *The Kiss.* The faceless, shadowy, hulking form which haunts Hoskins's work exudes anxiety; he is poised as if waiting or as if suddenly surprised. Kimler's favored motif, a young hunter posed with his "kill," also emanates expectation; his youthful pride seems tinged with anxiety—perhaps a need for approval.

Vulnerability is implicit in the uninhibited embrace extended by the winged female who repeatedly appears in Brinsfield's recent work. In *Yes to Yes, No to No,* that impression is heightened by the fluttering, heart-shaped leaves that radiate out from a glowing central orb. In contrast, the frantically outlined, knife-wielding figure in Northerner's *Angry Muse on a Control Circuit* attempts to mask his vulnerability with an aggressive pose—a spectre of death looms behind him; a real knife threatens to invade his painted domain.

The central figure in Zieve's *Atla,* twisted and contorted with an outward show of strength, elicits our empathy; Confrontation is also evident in L.J. Douglas's *Three Men,* where two pudgy males appear to be abducting a third whose arms are pinned behind him; one has the overwhelming sense of witnessing a crime, perhaps a kidnapping or an impending drowning.

While these artists vary in their approach—from mysterious narratives involving several figures to centralized iconic motifs—and each has evolved a highly personal vocabulary, they are united in their desire to use the human figure to express human anxieties and emotions. In each of these paintings, the artist's strong identification and sympathy with his/her protagonists is apparent, from Zieve's and Northerner's aggressively macho males, to Dresner's defenseless, expectant females and Douglas's hapless victims.

In contrast to the Imagists' concern with scrupulous finish, for these artists, creation is as much a process of discovery as it is the visual realization of a preconceived idea. Much of their work displays a layered effect, with the various stages of production preserved in the final painting; evidence of accident, serendipity, and other formal "happenings" remain.

It is often difficult to discern the precise subject matter of much of this work at first glance—figure and ground, figure and figure, all seem to overlap and interpenetrate. Because few of the figures wear clothing, we are deprived of the opportunity to assign them either a temporal or a geographic niche; most are faceless by virtue of cropping, lighting, or rendering, forcing us to deduce their emotions and reactions from their postures alone. Even those figures who are endowed with facial expressions are strangely anonymous. They are not personalities but symbols, vehicles for deeper psychological and emotional truths. Monumental in scale, and distorted almost beyond recognition, a number of these figures are only marginally human, as if they have been boiled down to those essentials necessary for the communication of a particular message.

Purposeful ambiguity extends to the setting of these dramas as well. The figures exist in open, unspecified locations, in direct contrast to the seedy urban milieu and claustrophobic interiors which have become hallmarks of Imagism. References to architecture, the man-made world—to anything which might lend these images an identifiable context—are scrupulously avoided in favor of generic symbols of nature or natural forces, and murky atmospheric effects. The figures, for the most part, are enveloped by their settings, veiled or captured in environments of rubbed, smeared, scumbled, or piled-up paint. A limited palette, usually dark and tending toward the neutral range, reinforces the feeling that these figures inhabit a netherworld—the world of the psyche and of myth.

These figures, which both enact and elicit primal fears, anxieties, impulses, and desires, seem light years away from the street-wise actors of Imagism. But, in the final analysis, one is struck by these new painters' preoccupation with the time-honored "Chicago" themes of sex and violence, and by their tendency to suffuse their figures in an aura of menace—a favorite device of the Imagists. The psychological edge of this work constitutes yet another affinity with Imagism.

Examining these new painters individually, one discovers a selective culling from the Imagists; elements are chosen and then combined with other influences. Thus, even for artists who can be seen to collectively pursue a vastly different aesthetic, Imagism is a point of both reference and departure.

But these painters have attempted to maintain in Chicago a sense of introspection, a highly individualized humanism, a belief in the essentially optimistic, communicable power of picture making that bears a more genetic resemblance to the artists of the Monster Roster; the new Chicago painters have both expanded and galvanized the notion of an indigenous, but not insular, Chicago brand of art. Their accomplishment is already worthy of note; as to their place in Chicago's art history . . .

	IMAGISM	NEW PAINTING
ATTITUDE	cool, ironic	emotional immediacy
	detached, humorous	committed, involved
	analytical	introspective, moral seriousness
TECHNIQUE	linear	painterly
	flatly painted	textural; scumbled, malerisch
	scrupulous finish	records process of creation
	attention to detail	purposely ambiguity
	calculated; idea precedes	evolves, receptive to accident,
	process	chance effects
CONTENT/THEMES	social	personal
	contemporary urban life	primal fears, anxieties, impulses
	images from popular culture	and desires
	sex, violence, menace	mythic, autobiographical images
		sex, violence, menace
COMPOSITION	closed	open
	emphasis on pattern	emphasis on painterly effects
	decorative appeal	primacy of emotion
	scale of figures small in	figure fills picture area
	relation to picture area	
SPACE	claustrophobic, flattened	expansive, infinite recession
SETTING	specific, identifiable	non-referential, ambiguous
	man-made, architecturally	nature; occasional introduction
	of defined	landscape elements
COLOR	light palette, dominated by	dark palette, dominated
	primaries	by neutrals
	color areas circumscribed by	color areas loosely described
	line	

At the risk of oversimplifying some very complicated issues, the above table presents a distillation of some of the tendencies which mark Imagism and the New Painting in Chicago.

'CHICAGOIZATION'

Some Second Thoughts on the Second City

May 1985

    When I was asked to give this lecture (given to the Society for
Contemporary Art, at the Art Institute of Chicago, March 20, 1985) it
was suggested that I speak on the phenomenon for which I seem to have
coined the name: "Chicagoization." My first impulse was to say no, for
the reason that I think that all uses of this little Frankenstein-monster
term of mine are misunderstandings. As much as any other critic, I
would love to go down in history as a phrase-maker. I remember the
sixties, and the unspeakable glamour that invested Lawrence Alloway
then for having invented "Pop Art"; as a kid critic, I figured that naming
an artistic development would entitle me to die happy. But in this case
at least two mistakes stand between me and footnote glory: my own, in
hatching the word, and that of other people, in quoting it. It appeared in
parentheses in a *Village Voice* column I wrote more than four years ago
about the veteran New York painter George McNeil. I was discussing the
rise to fashion of expressionistic painting, an event still fresh and uncharted then. I wrote: "Expressionism is the definitive bad neighborhood
in the city of modern art, often associated in America with the wacky/
nasty 'Imagist' tradition in Chicago. (The Chicagoization of New York is
a large and, in New York, still largely unmentionable topic.)"
    Re-reading that passage today, I wonder what in the world I could
have been thinking of. It had to be one of those blinding insights that
occur in the delirium of writing for a deadline, when there is no time
for the second thought that would reveal their fishiness. I do remember

feeling that I was onto something and being immensely pleased with myself, in consequence. But now I cannot imagine any significant way in which my term could, on the face of it, be true. Granted that, at the time, the expressionistic tidal wave was bringing with it a modestly heightened interest in Imagism, and granted that a new crop of Chicago emigrants was making its mark—part of the endless inflow of promising talent to New York, the pride and the despair of outlaying art communities—granted all that, I could not have been aware of a meaningful influence of Chicago-style on New York-style, if those entities can be said to exist at all, because there was no such influence. "Chicagoization" might as well have been a typing error.

On the verge of rejecting the proposed subject, however, I reconsidered. Given that the word may be meaningless, might I not be free to use it as arbitrarily as I pleased? Like an algebraic expression, say, by which we can take "a + b" to represent anything at all plus anything else at all, or as a swing-barreled poetic metaphor. More to the point, I became intrigued by the question of why anyone—myself to begin with, and others, thereafter—would *want* "Chicagoization" to mean something. Why is it satisfying to imagine the artistic spirit of one city invading the spirit of another? Why, to take it a step further, is it satisfying to think of any city—a jumble of playgrounds, coffee shops, and police cars—as having a "spirit" that somehow issues in artistic idiosyncrasies? Reflecting on this, I got excited by the possibility that at last, after some muddled attempts in the past, I would find something useful to say on a bedeviled subject: the center and the margin, centrality and provincialism, mainstream and periphery, the whole psychology of geography in contemporary art.

This is a disreputable subject for a number of good reasons, among them that it tends to spark a discourse remarkably gross. In this discourse, if it can be called that, raw feelings confront insulated ones—defensiveness confronts snobbery—and everybody gets either mad or maddening. It is a subject that, as a lover of art, I would like to see simply go away. What could be more vulgar than the confusion of geographical rooting interests with art production? It is all very well for citizens of a place to feel passionately about their institutions, whether these be museums or sports teams—as I need not remind a city that boasts the Art Institute and the ongoing Shakespearean tragedy of the Cubs. But I would prefer to think that a fundamental error is made when this spirit of identification is allowed to embrace the actual work of actual artists—unless, perhaps, they are indigenous naive artists (a peculiarly Chicagoan question, which I will get into later). Conscious, sophisticated art of all times has a profound independence from places, and the places that host it show the peculiar dissociation, the gregarious impersonality that we call "cosmopolitan." When we look at the sites of great artistic moments, at least within the Western tradition, I think we see that what they have in common is a certain negative virtue, not a team spirit but a disinterested though passionate curiosity. I get tired of talk about the possibility of art in this or that place, feeling that the only question that matters, as Harold Rosenberg suggested, is of whether art is possible at all.

Now, if we were creatures of transcendent reason, we could leave the matter right there—but we aren't, and we can't. Place-patriotism is as strong today as ever—maybe stronger, even—despite a century notable for cosmopolitan experience and internationalist hopes. In America, even the inexorable forces of full-tilt geographical mobility, mass communications, and popular culture have failed to homogenize it out of existence. Place-patriotism is capable springing up overnight in jerry-built communities from New Jersey to Orange County. How much less effaceable will it be, then, in a city as densely traditioned, as proud, and as grouchy as Chicago? To personalize this, I will note that in examining myself—a person determinedly loyal to the cosmopolitan ideal—I find a positively primitive attraction to the mystique of place, an attraction no less electric for being unplugged. So my own lofty sentiments are ambushed from within.

In any case, the fact that I was able in 1981, for even a moment, to associate the expressionistic painting then newly rampant in New York with Chicago *had* to indicate a yearning in me to do so. I repeat that no visible basis for such a comparison was present, Expressionistic painting in New York, then as now, tended to be big, loose, and painterly. Chicago Imagism tends to be easel-scaled, tight, and lapidary. Even the preceding work of the Monster Roster, as is brought home by the early paintings in Leon Golub's current retrospective, had a conservative scale and a tendency, despite its roughness, to relatively restrained surface and color. Extravagant gesturalism was a New York bag in the fifties, and one might say it was honored in the breach by the fanatically cleaned-up abstract styles of the sixties, only to emerge once more—with a big boost from some Italians and Germans—in the late seventies. As for Golub, his recent great paintings were made possible by, if anything, a de-Chicagoization, an assimilation of aesthetic lessons from New York-type abstraction and of iconological lessons from New York-type Pop art.

So the meaning of "Chicagoization" cannot be deduced; it must arise, if at all, through free association. Pursuing the latter process in my own mind, I come up with something like a Principle of Antagonism. Chicago is, of course, a net exporter of antagonisms, strangely mixed with enthusiastic geniality. In no other city I am familiar with are people, in general, more openly friendly up to a certain point and more obstreperous beyond that point. By contrast, New York is rude through-and-through, though marked by cosmopolitan tolerance. In New York you are given every *right* to exist—for all the good it does you. The same goes for styles and fashions, which are often paid the compliment of being resisted in Chicago while being languidly embraced in New York, because change itself, if not progress, is New York's most important product. These generalizations are flimsy, I know, and I don't want to make a central point of them. The point may simply be that, in the art world of 1981, I caught a whiff of some un-New Yorkishly combative contradictions on the level of style. An urge not just to change but somehow to *violate* stylistic agreements, and perhaps by extension social agreements of other kinds, seemed to be erupting, and the idea of an urge to violate made me think of Chicago.

By what right do I claim significance for my thoughts of Chicago? My answer is autobiographical. I grew up in small towns in Southern Minnesota. I am, I have come to believe, a Midwesterner in my bones—or in whatever part of me it is that, after 20 years of strenuous effort, I have been unable to alter. I assumed that I hated the Midwest until it dawned on me that the quality of my assumed hatred might be as Midwestern as corn, an expression of the automatic sullen reflex that is the shadowy side of Midwestern wide-openness. Chicago, as the somewhat tarnished Emerald City of the Midwest, played a big role in my youth. It was on visits here that I made a quantum leap in my capacity for behaviors and pleasures that, though not all of them were against the law, were certainly against my Lutheran upbringing and common sense. Incidentally, I count it a stroke of luck that my first exposure to the Art Institute—my callow first love of Caillebotte and de Kooning, to name my early touchstones—got mixed up with feelings of sinfulness. (I rather pity anyone who has been indoctrinated with the arid illusion that art is "clean.") Then I became persuaded that a city of even more dubious fulfillments lay to the East, and I made for New York at a dead run, intending never to look back. When one refuses to look back at something, of course, one is pretty certain to collide with it somewhere up ahead.

The cardinal feature of my story is its typicalness. It is an old American story of the city as the place where country kids go to scrape off their innocence. Chicago, as the capital of worldliness in the nation's heartland of naivete, is a time-honored stage for this drama, generation after generation, in its starkest forms. What all this has to do with art—as you may legitimately be wondering—must entail a willingness to see the face of art in any particular place, and by this I mean not art *of* a place, but imported art, museum art, art in general—to see that face as a mirror of that place's particular meanings. Such a willingness goes against the grain of the academic, institutional, commercial, and otherwise professional systems that organize our encounters with art, but I think there may be wisdom in granting it, wisdom of a type theoretically obtainable from a Rorschach Test. In New York, which may be only technically a place at all, the local attitude thus revealed is cosmopolitan, the dream of being one of the gang in the boiler room of world culture. In Chicago, I suspect that the attitude is one more of absence than of presence, more in the nature of a frustrated wish that is, nonetheless, full of special dynamism. At any rate, it will be an attitude that slides into and out of synch with attitudes elsewhere, at some point perhaps sliding in with a *click* that makes a New York critic, despite himself, suddenly open a parenthesis in what he is writing and insert the ugly and interesting word "Chicagoization."

By "attitude" here, I obviously do not mean *conscious* attitude. I mean a darkly rooted world view, the distillate of local history, politics, ethnic makeup, religion, power structure, social class, and so on. In Chicago, most of these factors are very highly charged, of course. This is a city of extremes, a city in love with Utopia, as seen in its famous architecture, and irresistibly drawn to the underside of life, as seen in its equally famous journalism. Those are clichés, I know. But I am not especially afraid of clichés, which are simply large truths that have gotten encrusted with use. I would just as soon try to restore some shine to them as to strain after the very small amounts of communicable truth that, at any given moment, have yet to be spoken for. In the interests of crust-busting, then, I am going to recite my views of Chicago's art culture—views guaranteed sincere, though hardly original and probably tactless. My aim is to hold up the imperfect mirror of my sensibility to your reality, in hopes of causing some mutual reflections.

Between Utopia Chicago-Style and Chicagoan nostalgia for the gutter, most of the best Chicago artists have never wavered in their preference for the latter. It's as if creative people here were born under the constellation

Anthropology, and the city were a Field Museum without walls. The peculiarly smart and discriminating local love of local naive art is unique to America, so far as I know. People in most cities get embarrassed and sulky when you express interest in their region's untaught artists; they want you to concentrate on their *real* culture, which generally turns out to be a spanky-clean gallery handling David Hockney lithographs. Primitives are not condescended to here; they are granted mythic force and actual influence. This is not an entirely good thing perhaps. It comes with a form of narcissism. But it's alive, and its emanations have proved vitalizing again and again. In my sense of it, the real author of the glory that was H. C. Westerman was as much this city as the man himself. And if ever Chicago infiltrated New York, it was through Claes Oldenburg, who said of his art, "I made it all up when I was a little kid." The Chicagoan aura can even work retroactively, annexing Joseph Cornell, for instance. Cornell's work makes a kind of sense to me here that it doesn't anywhere else.

As for Imagism, it remains for me easily the outstanding achievement of visual art in Chicago, embodying more of this culture's special strengths and, most important, its special contradictions and antagonisms that anything else—except perhaps the plays of David Mamet, a world-class genius who might at a stretch, be called a theatrical Imagist. It is a minor style, essentially illustrational and, even when done big by Roger Brown or Ed Paschke, essentially miniaturist in spirit. But it is authentic. It strikes me as a style of frozen hysteria, a style for consciousness driven back by its own revulsions while remaining half in love with them. My memory of being a sensitive misfit in the Midwest approves. At the same time, for all its maniacal cartooniness and low-life fixations, Imagism is not really a vernacular style, let alone a form of Pop art. Its particular historical inspiration in the middle 1960s was to leapfrog the styles of New York in order to assimilate the precise European influences—surrealism and expressionism—that New York seemed to disallow. Making surprising use of the lessons Dubuffet brought to Chicago in 1951, Imagism gave local sensibilities something trans-local to chew on.

I do not imagine that Imagism, which will soon be 20 years old, is exactly a burning issue in Chicago right now. So: What has happened in Chicago art since then? Nothing very much, as far as I can see. And with that undoubtedly irritating remark I return to the psychology of center and province in contemporary art, a psychology that dominated American art discourse in the 1970s. Remember the 70s? In that most confusing of art decades, in which everything was tried and nothing seemed to work, the second most prevalent buzz-word, after "plural-ism," was "regionalism." To use computer language, New York was *down*. Though still the hub of art's market and communications, Manhattan was as befuddled as anywhere else about what the important questions were in current art, never mind answers. Thus it came to seem logical that the long-suffering provinces would exploit the power vacuum to come into their own. Like a lot of other New York critics, I pilgrimaged to art scenes around the country—including Chicago's, which I wrote up for *Art in America*—in anticipation of the regionalist Renaissance.

It didn't happen. In retrospect, the expectation appears wishful and foolish, a mirage born of political right-thinking rather than analysis. It was blind to history, which shows that the cultures of "second cities" thrive in direct proportion to those "first cities." Artistic vitality is not a zero-sum game, by which one place's loss is another's gain and vice-versa. Think about this: The three and only really distinct successful regional modes since Grant Wood—Chicago Imagism, Bay Area Figuration, and the L.A. Look—occurred precisely while New York's art world was most prestigious and intimidating. That is no mere coincidence. Even more damning about the regionalistic mentality is that an authentic local ex-pression may be the last thing it really wants, whatever lip service is paid to the idea. In the seventies I was startled to find that Chicago's *New Art Examiner*—by a long shot the best of the regional tabloids that sprang up then—was disdainful of Imagism, preferring to support second and third-rate, truly provincial versions of abstract styles that were a dime a dozen in New York. Such things taught me to be skeptical of the most common complaint of regionalistic rooters: "We have no good critics here." Most of the people who said this, if Heaven sent them a good critic, would have crucified him or her within a week.

With this memory-capsule of a mentality that is, thank goodness, on the wane, I mean to convey the banality of letting civic and geographic interests affect our thinking about art—unless (and this is a big "unless") art itself forces the issue. Art did indeed force the issue a few years ago, but the development popped out of an entirely different mouse-hole than the regional ones we were dutifully watching. In a reprise of much earlier decades of this century, it came pouring across the Atlantic, re-versing a flow of influence that had prevailed since Jackson Pollock. It was at that time—while I was getting my first full doses of the Italians and Germans and of a new breed of European-influenced young Ameri-cans—that I saw fit to unveil the momentous secret of "Chicagoization," a notion immaculately wrong. What could have possessed me to write such a crazy thing? Well, craziness was ambient in that moment when the geography of art was undergoing an earthquake—at least seven or eight on, so to speak, the (Gerhard) Richter Scale. And crazy people sometimes rave profoundly.

I think I may, in that moment, have had a subliminal flashback—not to art in Chicago but to the way art appeared to me when I was haplessly, crazily young in Chicago. And still does somewhat in Chicago. I mean art as symbolic of *elsewhere*, charged with the pathos of distance and exile. The sudden mysterious force of a new European art briefly destroyed my sense of New York's separateness from the American mainland, collapsing the miles I had carefully put between my urban maturity and my boondock roots. Fumbling for a word to express the sensation, I might more rationally have hit on "provincialization," because it was a sensation very much of occupying a center that had abruptly been kicked to the margin of something *more* central. But such a negative-sounding term would not have done, because the sensation did not feel negative; it felt proper and full of energy, an exciting break in the miasma of the seventies. So instead my mind reverted to Chicago, where as a provincial kid I had experienced art as a life-changing seduction, a magnet for yearnings that were drawing me away from everything I knew toward everything I didn't know.

I do not mean to suggest that Chicago is merely a great place to be *from*, though it is certainly that, as witness its celebrated sons and daughters. I mean something more complicated, which is that the particular flavor of marginality that pertains in Chicago may be a strength rather than a weakness, if only it can be regarded as such. The present situation in art dramatizes the fact that Chicago, for all its symbiosis with the American South and West, is still in some ways the westernmost outpost of Europe. (To go any nearer the setting sun is to enter a more or less totally American reality.) In cultural terms, it is the Continental Divide, marginal (if you will) in every direction, a center for marginalities. That isn't nothing. It also nicely situates Chicago to gauge the American tremors of a nationalistic era.

The strongest underlying impulse of artistic expression in the eighties is *national*, reflecting a worldwide surge of religious, racial, and historic nationalisms that is at once thoroughly dangerous and, in the short run, all but impossible to oppose effectively. The irritability of peoples is at a peak: global Chicagoization, if you will. Or Beirut-ization, to see the phenomenon at its most nightmarish. In such a moment, Europeans are bound to shine. For once in modern times, their heaped histories are resource rather than burden. Thus we see Francesco Clemente, though living in New York (nothing may be more Italian than leaving Italy), communing with the Neapolitan Baroque. And we see Anselm Kiefer reconstructing a German tradition, piece by charred piece. We Americans have a tradition, too, of course: a tradition of the void, of what isn't here. Many of the great symbols of our literature are literally empty: the open road, the sea, the prairie, the river, the Whiteness of the Whale. We might expect to see, in this present, an American art symbolic of lacking and wanting, and, in the work of some excellent young artists, I think that is exactly what we see.

We see these young artists mainly in New York, which makes sense, once again, not only as the center of art's market and publicity—in a moment dominated by commerce and publicity—but as the historic port of entry for European influence and as the world capital of homelessness. But one must leave New York to find the meanings that these young artists are galvanizing, because the meanings are pre-eminently national, undermining the modernist internationalism that used to reinforce the impression that New York was a nation apart and aloof from the United States. The individualism and commercialism of the current art world are national values incarnate, as is, in its own way, a widespread, reactive hatred of those same values. To put it as melodramatically as possible, the soul of the nation is in convulsion right now, and the fact may be far more naked in, say, Chicago than in the cocoon of Manhattan. Whatever is good and bad elsewhere in America often seems simultaneously better and worse in Chicago, which seems more innocent and more cynical than other places. It is certainly a city I associate with *wanting:* Even leaving out a certain prevalence of flat-out greed, it is a vacuum-cleaner of a place that sucked the blues up from the South and the beef in from the plains, and whose art collectors, as a group, are the most all-around aspiring in the world.

I am nearly through torturing your city for my rhetorical purposes. I will let you have it back in a minute. But first I will return to the initial retroactive significance I found for "Chicagoization": a spirit of antagonism. The culture of the Midwest—my culture, deep down—is positively defined by antagonism. It is a culture that literally does not agree with itself. On the one hand, an ache for principles of certainty; on the other, a democratic resentment that wants to level everything.

More clichés, of course. My aim in polishing these chestnuts is only to suggest how a habit of looking *elsewhere* for the drama of capital-C Culture, the constant projection *elsewhere* of cultural angels and demons that is characteristic of provincialism, an alternating current of reverence and malice—how this whole, old, dumb syndrome might, in a flash of inspired self-consciousness, be seen to generate authentic meanings. It may be the poetry, as well as the curse, of this place.

THE ART SCENE OF THE '80s

October 1985

On May 9, 1985, the Chicago New Art Association and the School of the Art Institute of Chicago co-sponsored a lecture by Hilton Kramer, which is re-printed below. The Chicago New Art Association is a not-for-profit educational organization that sponsors visual arts-related activities such as lectures, seminars, and the publishing of the *New Art Examiner*.

Hilton Kramer is the editor of *The New Criterion*. He was formerly the editor of *Arts Magazine* and the chief art critic and art news editor of the *New York Times*. He is the author of *The Age of the Avant-Garde* (1973), a collection of critical writings on the art of the modern period. *The Revenge of the Philistines*, a new collection of art criticisms from the years 1972–1984, will be published by the Free Press this month. It was a pleasure and an honor to welcome Mr. Kramer to Chicago.

Nowadays there are many people like myself who, in observing the art scene of the 1980s and seeing it in a perspective reaching back to the 1960s and even the '50s, cannot but have the impression that we are living in a distinctly new period. Not merely because of the passage of years, but because of the issues that characterize the life of art at the present moment, we feel that we have entered a new era.

This sense of a new period haunts not only the art of our time, as we see it, but also the discussion of the art of our time, the whole surrounding world of analysis—the world of ideas, the world of gossip and criticism, and the world of commerce: in other words, everything that has now attached itself to the life of art and made it something of a mainstream experience in American cultural life.

The question that is often asked about a period that makes itself felt as something new, as a new historical development, is: What accounts for it? How can we really explain these changes in art as well as the changes in our response to it?

We know pretty well what the usual explanations offer us. Some say: Well, it's fashion. It's like hemlines. It's the cultural equivalent of women's fashions, or indeed, for that matter, men's fashions. Or we are told that it's all the result of shrewd and cynical dealers, or that it's all the result of influential museum curators and influential critics. In short, the usual explanations come down to a kind of conspiracy theory in which money and the market, in collusion with the media, shape our cultural life and account for these significant changes in taste—not just minor ones, not just passing ones, here today and gone tomorrow, but the really significant changes in taste and in standards that we see taking place.

Now only a fool would deny that all of these things—fashion, dealers, critics, the media, money, the market—play a role, and a fairly obvious role. But in my view they do not really play the fundamental role that is customarily ascribed to them in accounting for the real changes in taste that we are observing and reeling from, the changes that induce this sense of a new period.

When we consider the nature of the changes that come into art, I think it is always a great mistake to omit the key figure responsible for those changes, the figure who tends to get left out of all these conspiracy theories about changes in the art world—the figure of the artist, who is in my view the key figure.

It is really the artist who stands at the center of all fundamental change in art. So the question really comes down to: What induces an artist to initiate a change, a really fundamental change in art?

I want to attempt to answer that question, to begin with, in two parts—first, with a quotation, alas from myself, from something I wrote in the *New York Times* in April of 1981, and then with an anecdote. The article from which this passage is drawn was the first review that I wrote of the paintings of Malcolm Morley and Julian Schnabel, whose work was causing a tremendous commotion at the time, or at least beginning to cause a commotion that has gotten to be tremendous.

> Nothing is more incalculable in art or more inevitable than a genuine change in taste. Although taste seems to operate by a sort of law of compensation, so that the denial of certain qualities in one period almost automatically prepares the ground for their triumphal return later on, its timetable can never be accurately predicted. Its roots lie in something deeper and more mysterious than mere fashion. At the heart of every genuine change in taste there is, I suppose, a keen feeling of loss, an existential ache, a sense that something absolutely essential to the life of art has been allowed to fall into a state of unendurable atrophy. It is to the immediate repair of this perceived void that taste at its profoundest level addresses itself.

One of the experiences—it was a key experience for me—that brought me to think about this question of change in these terms was one that I had early on in the '70s. It would have been about '74, as I recall. I was visiting for a couple of days one of the major art schools in the East—not in New York. And what I found there left me rather shaken and curious. I couldn't put my hand on what was wrong with what I found there at the time, but the meaning of this disturbing experience was finally revealed, I believe, some years later, by developments in the art of the late '70s and the '80s.

When I visited this school, it was at that time still very much in the grip of the influence of the art of the '60s, of course; that is, Color-field painting and Minimalist art were still the dominant styles. By that time, Pop art, which was the other major new development in the '60s, was pretty much on the wane, at least as an influence, and most of the painting students, in the work they were doing in their studios, were still very much under the influence of Color-field painting and Minimalist art. Some of it was very accomplished in the way of imitative student work, but it was not the painting in the studios that left me with my most vivid impression of this particular school.

There was a lounge area which the art students had created for themselves. It was a long, narrow room that had chairs and couches lined up along each wall so that you faced the person opposite as you were sitting there. This is where the students drank coffee and Coke and smoked cigarettes and other things.

What was extraordinary about this room was that one of these long walls was papered from floor to ceiling with color photographs of nude girls. And some were really wild photographs. They weren't your garden-variety *Playboy* centerfolds. They seemed pretty far out.

The wall opposite was papered from floor to ceiling with photographs of nude boys, also pretty far out, all of the subjects generously endowed and in extraordinary postures. The students sat around, chatting with each other and with me in what I took to be a highly charged atmosphere, quite as if this was just the ordinary sort of wallpaper they had grown up with at home. What was so strange to me was this disjunction between the highly charged iconography, if you will, of the coffee lounge, and the utter blandness and unadventurousness of the paintings being created in the studios. This left me with a very disturbed and vivid impression of this particular school.

After all, it was a place where new art was being created or attempted. A place where students were devoting their lives to being trained in art. Most of them had at least the illusion that they were going to become serious artists, and for these few years of their lives, in any case, they were concentrating all their energies and mental faculties on attempting to create something. That in itself ought to make for a highly charged atmosphere, but on this occasion it didn't.

It was particularly interesting, this experience, in another respect. And that is that well into the '70s, the principal influences still operating on these art students, as indeed they were still the principal influences operating on the kinds of exhibitions of new art that were being organized in museums that devoted themselves to contemporary art and the kinds of art that were still being paid the most protracted attention in the art journals and the art press—that is to say, Color-field painting, Minimalist art, Pop art, and various amalgams and variations of them—that well into the early '70s, the basic modalities of contemporary art still all derived from the Kennedy period. Very little had really entered into artistic thinking, certainly into painting, that made it significantly different from the paintings one saw, say, in the period 1960 to 1963. The paintings got bigger, thinner, more decorative, more expensive, certainly, but the fundamental artistic modalities were still those of the Kennedy period.

Now if we think back about what happened between 1963 and 1973–74 in American society, in American cultural life and in American social life in that decade—what happened outside of art—we cannot help but be acutely aware of the tremendous uproar that those years brought into our lives. Beginning with the civil rights movement, the Berkeley free speech movement, going to the anti-war movement once the United States got into the war in Vietnam, the emergence of the counterculture, the whole social revolution, the drug culture, the dropout culture, and so on—all of these really tremendous transfiguring changes in American society and in American experience in those years made absolutely no dent on the kind of art that was created between 1963 and, say, 1974.

It was as if there were certain prohibitions imposed upon art. Of course they were self-imposed. They weren't imposed by any person or group dictating these matters. But certainly prohibitions were observed to such a degree that they functioned as a new orthodoxy that defined what was permissible in art and what was forbidden. The boundaries of acceptable taste for '60s art all came to be clearly recognizable. The attribute that was most admired was, in fact, the very attribute of clarity.

Sixties art, whether it was Pop art or Color-field painting or Minimalist art, boasted of clean surfaces, hard edges, a kind of instant legibility, an easy transparency, an image of perfect order—and these attributes were so established as defining the boundaries of taste in art that any evidence of, or, as we might say, incitements to feeling, to the overt expression of emotion, came to be looked upon as a kind of vulgarity, as somehow uncouth. We were invited to believe that we lived in a sort of Ellsworth Kelly universe which allowed, around the edges, an emotion no stronger than a Lichtenstein kind of irony.

While the world was exploding, when every issue involving politics, morals, the spirit, and the body was being subjected to one of the greatest upheavals of this century, the world of art was observing this new orthodoxy, which shut out every possible consideration of any of these issues. As happens with every new orthodoxy, the art of the present began to reshape our conception and our judgment about the art of the past, including the recent past, too. It was in this period, rather than in the '40s or '50s, that certain members of the Abstract Expressionist generation were elevated to a new position of mastery. I think particularly of Barnett Newman and Ad Reinhardt, who, in the '50s, were not particularly regarded as leaders of the Abstract Expressionist movement. If you go back, for example, to Tom Hess's book, published in the early '50s, *Abstract Art: Background and American Phase,* which was the first book any critic devoted to the Abstract Expressionists, you will not find a single reference to Barnett Newman in it. Many years later, Hess organized the Newman retrospective at the Museum of Modern Art and wrote what is still the basic book on Newman's art. That is the kind of event that simply would not have occurred without this new orthodoxy of the '60s establishing itself.

It was in this period, too, that a painter like Malevich, and indeed the whole Russian avant-garde with its concentration on geometrical and constructivist abstraction, emerged from the shadows to take a place in the foreground of twentieth-century art history. The art of the present, having defined a new orthodoxy, played a definitive role in reshaping our sense of the earlier history of art in the twentieth century.

In contrast to this, in 1966, there was a retrospective exhibition at the Museum of Modern Art in New York devoted to the work of Max Beckmann, the German Expressionist painter. And with the exception of myself, that was an exhibition that fell, so to speak, on deaf ears and blind eyes. It was like dropping a stone down a well and never hearing it hit bottom. You can't even say that the Beckmann retrospective was not well received in 1966. It wasn't received at all. It was an exhibition that one never heard discussed. It was never talked about. It was a non-event. The whole outlook on what was possible in art and what was not possible succeeded in shutting it out.

Last year, 1984, there was another Max Beckmann retrospective. It was organized by three museums—in Berlin, in St. Louis, and in Los Angeles. And there were months in New York, certainly, when one could hardly hear anything else but the Beckmann retrospective discussed. People were trying to decide whether to go to Berlin to see it or to go to St. Louis to see it. And I know that dozens of artists went to considerable personal trouble and expense to see the exhibition in one place or the other. Something had happened that conferred a new visibility upon Beckmann's work, and suddenly he was now recognized once again as the great master I believe him to be.

I take this changed response to Beckmann as a sort of emblematic event in the art of the '80s which, as I see it, is clearly an attempt to repeal the aesthetic prohibitions of the '60s. And in that attempt at repealing the prohibitions of the '60s, the revival of the expressionist impulse in art has played a central role.

Expressionism in art does not lend itself to tidiness or detachment or the kind of easy clarity and transparency that was so much valued, so much prized and praised, in the art of the '60s. Expressionism tends to be hot rather than cool. It tends to favor the visionary and the irrational over hard-edged specificity and easy clarity.

Expressionism tends to look upon the canvas as an arena of subjective discovery and exploration, and its characteristic impulse is to exult in the physical properties of painting—and not only in the physical properties of painting but in the other powers that painting is capable of, particularly its power to encompass symbolic images and even to tell stories, at least stories of a kind.

Now it seems to me that one of the "stories" the art of the '80s has taken upon itself to tell us is the history of that whole realm of altered historical experience that was up on the walls of that coffee lounge in that art school and that I could not quite grasp the significance of at the time. For it seems to me that one of the things that the art of the '80s has been determined to accomplish is to take—not literally, of course—the images of those nude girls and nude young men from the walls of that lounge and bring them into the studio and do something with them. This transfer, so we might call it, has turned out to be one of the central issues of the art of the '80s.

All those elements of altered consciousness that came into American experience with the '60s, all those residues of the drug culture and the sexual revolution, or the counterculture and the political conflict that came into the bloodstream of American society at that time, despite all the social changes that separate us in the '80s from the '60s, all of these elements remain very much a part, if not always an immediately visible part, of American experience today.

I don't think there's any other way of accounting for the tremendous changes that define the art of the '80s as distinct from the art of the '60s. I don't think there's any other way to account for this momentous historical shift except as it is an attempt to encompass, to come to terms with, these upheavals and experiences which were systematically shut out of the art of the '60s.

If we look to European art in the '80s, we find that theory pretty much confirmed. An artist like the German painter Anselm Kiefer, born in 1945, seems to have devoted all of his major work to an attempt to come to terms with the period of German history that came to an end the year that he was born. Without a sense of this search into the German past—particularly the Nazi nightmare, but also the resonance which that had in the entire fabric of German history and the role of myths and violence and the impulse to domination—without some sense of this background, a painter like Kiefer is simply incomprehensible. There's no way to make sense of his work except as a searching critique of the German past.

It's not the '60s that Kiefer is in search of, but something earlier, although the very nature of his painting, the very attributes he brings to painting, would have been quite unimaginable except for certain elements of the German equivalent of the counterculture which emerged in the '60s when he was a student.

I think that it is this altered mode of experience, this attempt to encompass a new historical inheritance, that lies at the center of the changes that have taken place in the art of the last six, seven, eight years. But the art that has been produced as an effort to encompass this altered mode of experience is created and has its life and its intercourse with us, in an art world and in a cultural world that is itself greatly altered, so that everything that this art attempts to do is now amplified and modified by the circumstances in which we experience it.

The most crucial change that has taken place in the art world, and in that part of the larger social landscape which encompasses the art world, is a matter of sheer numbers. That is, the new art of our time is created in a situation in which there is more of everything—more artists or people claiming to be artists; more people interested in looking at art and even buying it; more people interested in being dealers and exhibiting art and selling it; more museums; more exhibitions per museum; more attention from the media; more attention from the academy; more attention from the government. There is just more and more of everything in the life of art today than was really conceivable when I was a student.

The first museum I ever went to was the Museum of Fine Arts in Boston. It was around 1944 or thereabouts when I wandered into that precious place for the first time, and did so as a kind of accident. None of my teachers had ever told me it existed—because art, even in its respectable form, that is its established form, in a city like Boston in those days was way out on the margin. And in those days indeed, you could spend an entire afternoon in the Museum of Fine Arts in Boston and never see another person—not even a guard, because art hadn't yet acquired the kind of visibility which attracts the interest of thieves. I mean, if they had stolen something, what could they have done with it?

Today, since the new wing was built onto the Museum of Fine Arts in Boston, the biggest problem is trying to find a place in the parking lot. They seriously underestimated the size of the parking lot when they built the new wing. I mention that contrast because I think that gives us a graphic sense of how sheer numbers have totally altered the social medium in which art of any kind functions today.

Partly as a function of these altered numbers, there is also another new factor that is perhaps more crucial. And that is what might be called the limelight factor. Art today either functions in the limelight, which is merciless, or it functions in the shadows. There appears to be very little space between the one and the other.

In the limelight, which is capacious—that is, there's room for plenty of people in that too, though it's in the nature of the limelight that there isn't room for everybody, of course—but under limelight conditions, an artist is observed like a specimen under a microscope; that is, there's nothing about him—whom he marries or doesn't; how many pictures are produced; what size; what is served for dinner; the artist's sex life; his drug life, etc.—that goes unreported. Everything about an artist's life and work is, under limelight conditions, public information. As a result, the artist is inevitably transformed into a kind of celebrity, whether he wants to be a celebrity or not—and I've never met one who didn't.

His production—that is, the work he actually produces in his studio—is therefore created under quite different conditions. Among other things, no mistakes are allowed, no failures are allowed; that is, they're not acknowledged to be failures. Of course, when we go to the exhibitions, we see plenty of failures. But as the price of a failure is the same as the price for a success, there is no differentiation made. And it's left to disgusting critics to make these invidious comparisons between good pictures and bad—and that's one reason why criticism is particularly unwelcome in a limelight situation, because what the limelight calls for is attention; that is, words, but not critical words.

It is also a characteristic of this new situation that the art of the '80s, which is still, I think, for the most part an art that owes its spirit and basic character to the whole modernist outlook—but it's one of the characteristics of this period that this art has come into existence at a moment of extreme breakdown in the whole modernist tradition.

We have seen in the last decade or so the revival of, and indeed the extravagant praise and support for, a great many modes of art that it would have been unthinkable to have revived in the '50s, in the heyday of the Abstract Expressionist movement. I refer to all that nineteenth-century Salon painting and Academic painting. In New York, for example, at the Andre Meyer Galleries at the Metropolitan Museum, along with Cézanne and Manet, right next door you can go look at Gerome and Bouguereau—a condition of propinquity that would have nauseated Cézanne and probably have made Manet stop painting.

If you look at a book like Robert Rosenblum's recent *Nineteenth Century Art,* which is clearly intended to be a textbook and is indeed now widely used as a textbook, you will find a book that is deeply corrupting to any sense of what quality in art is. Along with attention paid to all the greatest painters in the nineteenth century, equal time is given to many of the worst painters in the nineteenth century. In this altered atmosphere, a sense of quality is not just denigrated, it becomes non-existent. The whole identity of what the modernist tradition was in art is nullified by elevating to a position of parity all of those moribund traditions that it was the function of Modernism to bury.

The academy—that is, the colleges and universities, the classrooms— also play a role in this altered cultural situation by paying such close and unremitting attention and such instant study to absolutely everything that occurs in the art world. It was only a few years ago that a museum like the National Gallery of Art in Washington had a rule that prohibited the purchase of any work of art by an artist who had not been dead at least 50 years. Remember, too, that even in the early days of the Museum of Modern Art, in the '30s, when Alfred Barr and his colleagues were assembling that great collection of modern masterpieces, the museum was not organized at that time on the principle, as you might say, of having to buy the fish fresh every day. The greatest works, which were acquired in the '30s by the Museum of Modern Art had certainly been painted before 1930. Many of them had been painted before 1915.

In the classroom at that time, it would have been unimaginable to study a painting as art history while it was, so to speak, still wet—but now that is the preferred mode of study. And so the academy too plays its role, it too contributes its power and its pressure to this limelight factor that now is, in the view of many, such a disfiguring element, such a distorting element, in the art scene of the '80s.

Finally, the sense of this new period that we are in is also a sense of a period without a center, of an art scene without a specific direction or rationale. I suppose that's what we mean by the art situation being an "open" one today or a "pluralistic" one. It is an art scene of many talents and no masters.

It seems from the empirical evidence that an art situation which is rather narrower in its conviction about what is possible at any particular moment seems to have a greater power to produce mastery than an art situation in which everything is permitted with an equal blessing.

And to end on a really gloomy note, I think we have to consider the question of whether this situation of increased numbers, this situation in which the limelight plays so great a role, in which the sense of quality becomes so problematic, in which even the schools (which exist, after all, to teach us what is good or great as distinguished from what is worthless) find it problematic to discharge their function. We have to ask ourselves whether this is really the ultimate end in the life of art that is brought about by its increasing democratization and institutionalization. This is a question that all of us are obliged to worry about, particularly those like myself who have a deep conviction in favor of the democratization of high culture and even in favor of institutions that are a part of that democratization. But today, it's not enough to declare oneself in favor of democratization of art. We also have to worry about the consequences, and today we are living with them in a very vivid and troubling way.

The solution, however, insofar as there is a solution to these problems, is not going to be provided by the art market, or by a new fashion, or by a curator, or even by a critic. The solution, the turn to new modalities in art, and changes in our relationship to art, are going to be determined, above all, by artists—for it is, after all, what artists do that, even in this alarming but extremely interesting art situation of the '80s, still determines what we think about art and what we experience as art.

SPONSORSHIP OR CENSORSHIP

November 1985

Since the late 1960s, Hans Haacke has emerged as one
of the most influential and progressive political artists
in the twentieth century. Born in Cologne, Germany,
in 1936, he has lived since 1965 in New York, where
he currently teaches at Cooper Union Haacke's earlier
works dealt with natural systems, paralleling his interest at that time in General Systems Theory. Working
first with physical systems, he constructed kinetic and
multi-media works that also dealt with biological and
social systems. Since the late '60s, Haacke's work has
been concerned almost entirely with social issues. A
long-time critic of corporate sponsorship of the arts,
Haacke has constructed a number of searing works
that unveil the dark side of corporate support. Media
and style are dictated by content, and often his work
is produced for the particular context in which it is
to be shown. With an elegant sophistication, Haacke
packages his message by mimicking the "appearance
of [his] opponent." Because of his outspokenness
both in his art and in his writings, Haacke's work is
rarely seen in U. S. museums, although he exhibits
extensively in Europe.

This interview WAS conducted at the Detroit Institute of
Arts, where Haacke was a guest lecturer, in May 1985.

NAE—In 1970, the Guggenheim Museum invited you to give an exhibition of your work. Six weeks before the opening in 1971, the director of the Guggenheim, Thomas Messer, canceled your show. He felt that the work you had proposed, analyzing the ownership of slum properties in Harlem and the Lower East Side, was libelous to the museum, despite the fact that you culled all the information from public records.[1]

Haacke—The legal argument, which is not backed by experts in the field, served as a smokescreen for an ideological determination that the pieces were "inappropriate" for showing in a museum. According to Messer, museums should exhibit only those works that are "self-sufficient" and lack what he called an "ulterior motive." If he were to take this doctrine seriously, he would have a hard time filling his museum. Messer saw himself as the bright knight who warded off an "alien substance" from invading the citadel of art.

NAE—Then they wouldn't have offered you a show at that time had your work dealt entirely with social systems?

Haacke—No doubt. However, I believe Messer hoped for some sort of tame "ecological" show (I had been working with water, air, animals, and plants in the second half of the '60s). He probably thought of a romantic evocation of green grass and chirping birds.

NAE—It's commonly thought that the reason the Guggenheim canceled your show was that there are slum landlords on the board of trustees.

Haacke—No. As far as I know, there is no link between the board and the two real estate groups I looked at.[2] I find it quite remarkable, though, that people are ready to suspect the museum board members of having a connection with slum properties. It means that one expects all sorts of dirty things from trustees.

NAE—Have you had an individual exhibition in a major American museum since?

Haacke—No.

NAE—But you have had a number of one-person shows in Europe?

Haacke—In Europe, yes . . . in museums in Germany, Holland, Belgium, England, Switzerland.

NAE—You grew up in Germany when Hitler was in power. Your parents refused to join the Nazi Party. Does your background have a direct bearing on your work?

Haacke—Not directly; perhaps at a more removed level. If you grew up in Germany after the Second World War, even though you were not implicated in the atrocities and the repression of the Nazi period, it does haunt you. We carry this mortgage. Many people in my generation feel they have a responsibility to make sure that things like that will not happen again. In that sense, maybe, the history of the country where I was born has a bearing on the direction of my work.

NAE—Have you ever had legal action taken against you?

Haacke—There have been attempts which, I believe, were intended to intimidate me through legal arguments. The Mobil Oil Corporation has tried to interfere with the dissemination of information on works that I had made about the company's activities. Last year I had a show at the Tate Gallery in London. A substantial catalogue was published by the Tate, together with the Stedelijk van Abbemuseum in Eindhoven in Holland. About half a year after its publication, the Tate Gallery and the Dutch museum got a letter from Mobil objecting to three works and to an interview with me in the catalogue. Because I had incorporated the Mobil logo in these pieces, Mobil claimed I had infringed on their property rights. They also claimed I had violated the privacy of their officers, because their names and signatures appeared on my Mobil stock certificate, which I had used as the base for a piece with the title *Upstairs at Mobil: Musings of a Shareholder* (I had bought 10 Mobil shares for this purpose). The Tate Gallery's lawyer called Mobil's claims "frivolous and insubstantial." In the U.S., Mobil doesn't have a case either, although it based its attack on U.S. law. I therefore saw no reason not to use the Mobil logo again in a recent piece. I am a "repeat offender," so to speak. However, since the European museums cannot easily evaluate the legal situation here, they withdrew the catalogue from distribution as a precautionary measure. This is probably what Mobil was banking on. It's clear to me that Mobil couldn't care less about what it claims to be infringements of property and privacy rights. The content of my pieces bugs them.

NAE—But despite the fact that the lawyers from both the Tate and the Dutch museum were aware that this was simply a coercive tactic on the part of Mobil, they still withdrew the catalogue?

Haacke—People, and particularly institutions, like to be cautious. Even though you may be right and win in the end, in the meantime you can lose a lot of money on legal fees, particularly if an arrogant and aggressive giant like Mobil is breathing down your neck. Sometimes this is the way we enjoy our freedom of speech.

However, what may also have played a role—I've nothing to substantiate such a suspicion—is the fact that Mobil had sponsored shows at the Tate in the past and that the museum may like to get support from Mobil again in the future. It is conceivable that the Tate fears Mobil's "*largesse*" might be contingent on its "good behavior." Who knows?

NAE—That's something you've discussed in your writings—the pitfalls of corporate support of museums.

Haacke—Yes, if such considerations had indeed played a decisive role at the Tate, it would be a classic case of self-censorship, prompted by an institution's addiction to corporate funding. For obvious reasons, it is rare for such deliberations behind closed doors to become public. It is therefore easy for institutions to simply deny that they consider the interests of their corporate sponsors, and that these "benefactors" are, in effect, being granted veto power over the institution's programs. To admit this publicly would tarnish the image of the corporations whose support they seek, and the institution would not look too great either. People from the museum world occasionally tell me, in private and off the record, that this assessment is correct. They also tell me that those among them who have not naively or cynically internalized this mode of operations chafe under it or feel thoroughly alienated. They say in many institutions the development office is calling the shots. Sherman Lee, the former director of the museum in Cleveland, is among the few who publicly deplored this dependency. He was quoted as saying: "By deciding what they will support and what they won't, corporations pull a negative string in terms of what we as professionals think should be supported."

NAE—In the exhibition you just had at the John Weber Gallery you showed a piece titled *MetroMobilitan* (1985). That's a great piece; could you talk about it?

Haacke—Like many of my pieces, *MetroMobilitan* has several layers. On the one hand it raises the issue of material support for the South African government's apartheid policies. With more than $400 million worth of assets in South Africa, Mobil is one of the largest U.S. investors. The South Africans consider oil a "munition of war." It has been estimated that Mobil is the source for about 20 percent of the fuel needs of their military and police. In other words, the armored personnel carriers that move into the black townships to suppress the rebellion against racism are fueled by Mobil. And so are the helicopters that carry South African sabotage commandos into neighboring countries. When Mobil was challenged by a coalition of church groups over its involvement with the repressive forces in South Africa, it officially gave the answer that I quoted on the left and right banners of my piece. The company shows a remarkable sense for "responsible citizenship."

The banners, of course, mimic those with which the Metropolitan Museum graces its facade to advertise the latest blockbuster, over the logo of its sponsor. Behind the banners, the viewer in the gallery can make out a wall-sized photograph of a black funeral procession in South Africa. In a magazine reproduction, it is impossible to reconstruct the three-dimensional situation which allows for the investigation of what is covered up by the banners. The photo for the photo-mural was taken in March by Allan Tannenbaum, a photographer of the SYGMA photo agency, at the Crossroads shantytown near Capetown. Women carry two children's coffins. They are followed by a number of adult coffins on the shoulders of black men. On the left side of the picture, one can see a white photographer with several cameras dangling around his neck.

The central banner alludes to an exhibition of Nigerian art which Mobil sponsored at the Met a few years ago. Nigeria is a country where Mobil has extensive interests. I am sure it also did not escape the company's PR officers that association with a show of African art may play well with the black community in this country. They may have speculated that, under the cover of promoting the art of black people, it would be easier to go on with business as usual in South Africa. Please note that the Tanda sculpture on the banner lost its arms.

I designed the "superstructure" as a somewhat abstracted version of the entablature of the Metropolitan Museum. Running around the entire facade are these peculiar androgynous Victorian heads, half Walkyre, half Greek hero, flanked by horns of plenty. The plaque in the center carries a quote from a brochure with which the museum recently addressed the business community: "Many public relations opportunities are available through the sponsorship of programs, special exhibitions and services. These can often provide a creative and cost effective answer to a specific marketing objective, particularly where international, governmental, or consumer relations may be a fundamental concern." The pamphlet had the telling title *The Business Behind Art Knows the Art of Good Business—Your Company and the Metropolitan Museum of Art.*

NAE—You've referred to the art world as an industry, specifically a "consciousness industry." Essentially corporate sponsorship of the arts serves as an advertising tool.

Haacke—Clearly, it is not product-oriented. It is not meant to sell more gas or convert people to smoking cigarettes. Its function is to open doors. That's what counts! It is a goal that the general public rarely understands or, for that matter, would be worried about. Gaining access to the movers and shakers, however, is at least as important as the bottom line at the end of the year. In the long run, of course, it has a lot to do with the company's profits. By creating for itself a favorable climate through its association with the arts, business can operate less inhibited by environmental concerns, by health and safety regulations, by taxation and political problems. Also, union busting is easier under this cover. It insulates industry from critical scrutiny and it helps the passing of legislation favorable to its interests. The significance of a good climate is often underestimated. This, however, is what public relations is all about. A whole industry has grown to serve this purpose. A Mobil officer once described his company's support of culture as a "good will umbrella," which allows them "to get tough on substantive issues."

In other words, the acceptance of the corporate dollar turns the museum into a lobbying tool, with potentially far-reaching consequences for public policy. We don't realize that our love for art is being co-opted to serve interests that have nothing to do with the things we want to see in the museum, and that these interests are potentially in conflict with our politics, with our moral beliefs and what might be good for us and the community. The more the interests of cultural institutions and business become intertwined, the less culture can play an emancipatory, cognitive, and critical role. Such a link will eventually lead the public to believe that business and culture are natural allies and that a questioning of corporate interests and conduct undermines art as well. Art is reduced to serving as social pacifier. Let me add a footnote: I am sure that many corporate art advisors and funding officers as well as their counterparts in the development offices of museums genuinely believe they are working as advocates for the arts, rather than seeing themselves carry out a cool business strategy. They are as brainwashed as the target group of this strategy.

NAE—In addition to the conservatism and self-censorship that is bred by corporate sponsorship (you once quoted somebody as saying that a good measure for dealing with corporations is "no nudes, no politics"), the National Endowment is also becoming quite conservative. Could you comment on that?

Haacke—Well, theoretically perhaps, the NEA could've been a counterweight against the influence of corporations. Certainly, under the present political constellation, you can write that off. Furthermore, the policy of matching grants from the "community," which means in practice predominantly from business, has the opposite effect. In all fairness, one must say, though, that this policy predates Reagan. What is new is the deliberate attempt by the government to relinquish entirely its responsibility for the culture of the country to nobody. It is also an innovation of the Reagan Administration that recommendations made by panels of professionals are overridden for political reasons, not only at the NEA, but, as we have seen recently, in the Serra case, also at the General Services Administration.

NAE—Well, whereas corporate sponsorship of the arts serves the corporate world, the NEA serves the Reagan Administration or whatever administration is in office the same way.

Haacke—Of course, each president has the opportunity to appoint members to the National Council for the Arts. That body plays an advisory and, to some degree, a supervisory role at the NEA. A lot depends on the quality of these appointees. As in other agencies, Reagan's choices for the National Council for the Arts are decidedly conservative. In fact, among them are members who are unabashedly pushing an ideological agenda. One of the more conspicuous victims is the program of grants for critics. Hilton Kramer and his publisher, Sam Lipman, who is a council member, seem to have had a hand in this. One of Kramer's complaints had been that the grants had gone to people who were "opposed to just about every policy of the United States government." Not only is this claim sheer humbug, behind his argument is a rather peculiar understanding of the guidelines according to which a government agency is to withhold a grant in a program set up by Congress. I assume that this line of reasoning is the norm in the Soviet Union. Will it now become a *new criterion* in this country?

NAE—Doesn't Hilton Kramer caution the NEA from funding the avant-garde as well as socially concerned art? My understanding is that he perceives the avant-garde as a dangerous thing to foster because the artist symbolizes the potential everybody has for change and unpredictability.

Haacke—He certainly argues against the funding of anything that makes even faint reference to social issues. In his view of the history of modern art, the artists' challenges to the social norms of the day are reduced to anecdotal significance and dismissed as extra-artistic ambitions, if they are not portrayed as utterly foolish or dangerous aberrations. He discounts the critical role modern art has played beyond the artificial boundaries of the art world, particularly in some manifestations of Dadaism, Constructivism and Surrealism and their more contemporary descendants. The edges are rounded off and we are left with an account of history that relegates art to the drawing room. In effect, he would like art to be sequestered in the world of genteel connoisseurship. While on the face of it that appears to keep politics out of art, it is, in fact, an ideological and, by implication and consequence, a decidedly political stance.

In fact, a political agenda is being pursued here, under the guise of purported liberation of art from political passions. Their assessment that culture is an integral part of a society's ideological fabric and that it is therefore important for them to shape it along neo-conservative lines, if neo-conservatism is to dominate the ideological landscape, is absolutely correct. But in view of the American public's suspicion of ideologues, it is tactically wise for Kramer to present himself as the proponent of an "independent high culture" and to claim a position of "critical disinterestedness." Who cares whether this claim is philosophically tenable or, for that matter, in view of his writings, intellectually honest?

Kramer has frequently argued against the post-war avant-garde; his attack aims to discredit its exploratory and, at times, almost activist role in the shift of social values towards greater emancipation. It would be interesting to hear whether he locates Julian Schnabel, one of his favored contemporary artists, at the "cutting edge" (notice the shift in metaphor) where other supporters, of Schnabel put him, or within his sanitized version of modern art. Kramer complains a lot about the loss of "standards of quality." So one should assume that Schnabel, in his eyes, is among the few lonely defenders of such standards. Certainly, the most he breaks is plates.

N A E—In his recent review of your show at the John Weber Gallery, Gary Indiana mentions that your piece *U.S. Isolation Box, Grenada, 1983* sent Kramer into orbit and prompted a lengthy attack in his journal the *New Criterion*.[3]

Haacke—Yes, he was quite incensed. All of a sudden I found myself in the company of a great number of illustrious artists who had earned his disdain in the past. Didn't he accuse Pollock of "provincialism," "tedium," and of being "an artist driven by aspirations which cruelly outdistanced his talents?" Visiting a Pollock show was for him a "dismaying experience." Duchamp did not fare better. Kramer's summary judgment: "resplendent triviality." I could go on quoting from a long list of remarkable evaluations. They were presumably all passed as part of the task he had set for himself, namely "to apply a new criterion to the discussion of cultural life—a criterion of truth." So you can imagine that I am tempted to carry his opprobrium as a badge of honor.

The article covered a sizable segment of recent art that deliberately refers to contemporary social issues. Quite a number of established institutions and individuals, even Donald Kuspit, came under attack, because they had either produced, exhibited, or are critically supporting such work. For years Kramer had been fulminating against art that concerns itself with the social and political environment of its day. But there was a new twist to this article: the terminology of his condemnation. Lurking in all this he discovered the "Stalinist ethos"! He warned his readers, and, by implication, funding agencies and private donors against being suckered into underwriting "Stalinist-colored liberal ideas" which could lead us down the path to the "eventual acquiescence in tyranny." A forgiving interpretation of this tirade would view Hilton Kramer as still being caught in the battles of the *Partisan Review* of a bygone era. I am afraid it is, in fact, a bit more sinister. These are no longer squabbles of a bunch of New York intellectuals. It is a raw power game.

By associating the individuals and institutions that had provoked his rage with the Gulag, the article amounted to a red-baiting crusade.

Once a link with the worst excesses of Soviet history is established in the public mind, particularly in Washington, where Kramer has powerful connections and where such nonsense is cherished these days, those who have been so decorated with Kramer's red star would lose all moral standing and the witch hunt could begin. This ploy and the mentality behind it reminds me of the reign of the lunatic fringe of the right in the '50s.

It is not entirely surprising to find such attitudes, which are in conflict with the best traditions of America, from the editor of the *New Criterion*. They are consistent with the ideological company he keeps. Hilton Kramer's journal is generously subsidized by three wealthy right-wing foundations. For the years 1982 and 1983 alone he got about three quarters of a million dollars. Anyone familiar with publishing knows that this is an awful lot of money for putting out a journal that doesn't carry illustrations other than advertising. These foundations, whose declared goal is to address questions of public policy, are tax-exempt, which means that you and I are indirectly chipping in. It is relevant to note this, because one of Kramer's arguments has been that public money should not be spent to support socially inspired artworks or writing.

These same foundations also rank among the major benefactors of the Heritage Foundation, a powerful right-wing organization in Washington which is well-known for supplying the Reagan Administration with policy papers and personnel (it also advertises in the *New Criterion*). One of the three, the John M. Olin Foundation in New York, is the "philanthropic" arm of the Olin Corporation, a company which produces ammunition and other war material.[4] The *New Criterion* started off in the company's headquarters on Park Avenue. In the '70s, the Olin Corporation was found guilty by a federal judge of having illegally supplied its arms and bullets to South Africa. Also, in other respects it has a noteworthy record. It includes the illegal dumping of mercury, price fixing, strike breaking, and questionable payments to foreign government officials. Among the Fortune 500 chemical companies, it is the only one that is bidding, at the moment, for a government contract to produce poison for gas warfare. The foundation's president was recently listed by the *New York Times* among the individuals who are collecting money to bankroll the Contras, the soldiers of fortune who are hired to overthrow a foreign government and leave a trail of murder, pillage, and rape behind themselves. Under the cover of a purported fight against tyranny the *New Criterion* is, in fact, allied with forces that are the enemy of human rights.

NAE—Given your politics, you must be faced constantly with difficult decisions in establishing boundaries for the distribution of your work. For example, with your work *Der Pralinemeister,* you refused to sell it to the subject of the work, German chocolate manufacturer Peter Ludwig, and sold it instead to Detroit collectors Gilbert and Lila Silverman.[5] Why did you make this decision?

Haacke—At the time when Ludwig wanted it, I didn't see anyone else waiting in the wings to buy it. I knew for sure that no German museum would take it—neither in West nor in East Germany. Ludwig has friends and has gained considerable influence in institutions on both sides of the German divide, and he has demonstrated that he is willing to exert his power.

In East Germany he is more obliging, because he is dependent on the good will of its authorities for a profitable expansion of his chocolate business. In fact, he has become a lobbyist for East German art in the West. By denying the sale to Ludwig, I risked sitting on this piece for a long time. However, it did provide an opportunity to show that Ludwig's money can't buy everything. I had two reasons for not selling to him: I didn't want to run the risk of his pulling the piece out of circulation, and I thought it would undercut its bite if he decided to parade it around in a show of tolerance or as a tribute to his vanity.

NAE—Do you refuse to sell to those corporations whose practices you are critical of?

Haacke—That hasn't been an issue yet.

NAE—Who does collect your work? Collectors who share your political beliefs, investors?

Haacke—Canadian and European museums have some in their collections. I have a few private collectors. In one or the other case they may sympathize with my point of view: people and institutions collect for a great variety of reasons.

NAE—In your work the materials are very important.

Haacke—Yes. The materials, their textures, colors, etc., a variety of print-ing processes and typefaces, velvet, gold-leaf, and so forth, also the sculptural or painting approaches that I choose in particular cases; all of this has not only an important visual quality, but has a bearing on the content as well. One should not underestimate the power of the cultural history that is inscribed in these elements. If not consciously, it is subliminally registered by the viewer. I get sensuous pleasure from manipulating these things. After all, this is one of the reasons why people gravitate towards art. I also want to have some fun.

NAE—In the mid-70s, Peter Fuller wrote a review of your work analyz-ing the chronology of owners of Seurat's Les Poseuses (Small Version) between 1888 and 1975. He said you demonstrated that, over time, the meaning of the painting was eclipsed by the importance of the object as an investment commodity. He also said that your work was doomed to the same fate for putting it into the form of art rather than criticism or theory.

Haacke—His objection applies to practically anything that survives the day. It gets archival value and is endowed by all sorts of other values and connotations that it didn't have before. If you are looking for an original Heartfield today, you have to put a lot of money on the table. There's nothing that can escape this wear of history. This is not really surprising if one believes, as I do, that the context in which an art work or, for that matter, a piece of critical writing appears determines a great deal their meaning, their potential consequences, and their monetary value.

NAE—But the content in your work is so direct that it seems to me that it would have a better chance of surviving.

Haacke—Perhaps my stuff has a slightly longer life-span. But eventually it also becomes academic. Whether it is worth speculating in it, who knows? This discussion reminds me of an episode during my wran-gling with Thomas Messer. When we were arguing over the inclusion of the three works in my show, my lawyer said to him: "Well, what about Russian Constructivism? You show Russian Constructivism in your museum. Isn't that revolutionary art?" Messer's response was: "Yes, but that's history."

NAE—Thus, is your concern to have an effect on the immediate his-torical circumstance if, in effect, the subversive quality of the work dissipates with time?

Haacke—I don't have delusions about immediate and demonstrable effects. If my stuff has repercussions, they remain largely immeasurable. However, there is a chance that, together with many other people, one may have an influence on the social climate, both within the art world as well as beyond its assumed parochial boundaries. That climate is a composite of many factors—the work of many individual artists, of critics, of institutions, and others in the consciousness industry and elsewhere. They are all interacting. What happens in the art world rubs off elsewhere. It is wrong to think of the art world as an enclave all unto its own. If that were the case, the media, the government, and corporations would not pay attention to it, and there would be no reason to pour money into the *New Criterion*.

NAE—Why do you think that there's such great antipathy to art that deals with political issues? So many artists themselves are insistent that art and politics do not mix.

Haacke—A lot of things play a role. Politics is assumed to be a dirty business, while art, according to a popular notion, is pure and holy and could only be ruined by contact with politics. Neither of these assumptions makes a lot of sense, nor do they help to understand the two interacting spheres. They rather foster the bewildered and passive acceptance of what appears to be incomprehensible forces beyond one's influence. Another problem is that a lot of work done with a political intent does not measure up to the professionalism of other types of work or, to be more precise, because it is "deviant," its imagined or real shortcomings are viewed more critically than the failures of "normal" art. That gives the whole enterprise a bad name.

NAE—Why do you think that the quality of a lot of political art is inferior?

Haacke—It is not taught. I should add, though, to avoid misunderstandings, that I am not advocating the indoctrination of a particular line. There is also a lack of constructive criticism. People in this field are often so embattled that they hesitate to criticize a few examples of such work and rather close ranks in order to survive—a natural reaction, but one that does not help to develop more sophisticated strategies. Let me say, as a footnote, that I always cringe a bit when I hear the term "political art." It ghettoizes it and falsely implies that "other" types of art do not have a political dimension and political consequences.

NAE—In order to be effective, a political artist must have a sophisticated understanding of politics in addition to a sophisticated understanding of aesthetics.

Haacke—Absolutely. Merely using currently popular political terms is like dropping names, it means nothing. Another dampener is the lack of encouragement from institutions, funding agencies, collectors, critics, and employers—as problematic as this might be under certain circumstances, if it occurred. Therefore, the go-getter kids in particular follow their instincts and steer away from what they perceive as a losing proposition. Many of them are quite sophisticated. It's not easy to convince these Yuppies that their first priority should not be fame or money. Who wouldn't like to live off the fruits of his or her work?

NAE—There are so many stumbling blocks for artists wishing to do socially engaged art that is also good art. Do you see things changing at all?

Haacke—Perhaps. Surprisingly, since about three or four years, there is an increasing interest for such work on panels, in magazines, and even in a few galleries and institutions. For about eight years after the end of the Vietnam War there was nothing of the kind. I think the recognition Leon Golub is finally receiving is significant. I am happy that also among the younger artists there are now some very good ones with a wide range of approaches. And they are even getting a bit of media attention. It's terrific.

NOTES

1. In addition to the two works dealing with Manhattan real estate holdings, Messer also objected to a poll Haacke was proposing of the museum's visitors. According to Messer: "The poll appeared to us inappropriate and the polling under museum auspices of a public that by and large comes for other purposes than to divulge its income, its political convictions, and its attitude toward extra-artistic issues seemed an imposition to be avoided." Thomas Messer, "Gurgles around the Guggenheim," *Studio International*, June 1971, p. 249. Curator Edward Fry, who had proposed the one-person show of Haacke's work, was fired for publicly disagreeing with Messer.

2. According to Haacke, Sol Goldman, a partner of one of the real estate groups, was recently "dragged into court for perjury. He has been mentioned in the context of the illegal demolition of two buildings in midtown New York. The demolition was carried out a few days before a new law went into effect that would have prevented the type of development for which these properties were slated by their owners. They were in such a hurry that even the gas lines were not cut before the wrecking ball hit the buildings. It was all done after hours, without a

permit. A prominent art collector from New York seems to be implicated in the scandal too."

3. Gary Indiana, "Art Objects," *Village Voice*, May 21, 1985, p. 109. Based on a description he read in the *New York Times* and later verified with the reporter, Haacke reproduced an "isolation box" used by American troops in the recent invasion of Grenada. On one side of the 8' x 8' x 8' box is stenciled "Isolation Box, as used by U.S. Troops at Point Saline's prison camp in Grenada." Prisoners must crawl though a knee-deep trap door. The use of these boxes was in violation of the Geneva Convention rules on prisoners of war. The piece was installed in the City University Mall in New York as part of the 1984 *Artists Call Against Intervention in Central America*. Upon inspecting the installation, Haacke found the box pushed into an unlit corner of the mall with the writing turned to a wall.

4. The other two foundations are the Smith-Richardson Foundation and the Carthage Foundation (Richard Mellon-Scaife).

5. *Der Pralinemeister* (*The Chocolate Master*), 1981. Seven Diptychs. Multi-colored silkscreens with photographs and packaging of assorted chocolate bars pasted in. The text juxtaposes statements about German chocolate manufacturer Peter Ludwig's corporate practices with descriptions of the expanding power base Ludwig is acquiring in the West German art scene, particularly in the city of Cologne.

6. For a reproduction of this work see: Hans Haacke, *Framing and Being Framed*, Halifax: The Press of the Nova Scotia College of Art and Design and New York: New York University Press, 1975.

SPEAKEASY

March 1986

Each month the *New Art Examiner* invites a
well-known, or not-so-well-known, art world
personality to write a "Speakeasy" essay on a topic
of interest—whatever it may be. Here we reprint
a missive sent to us by The Guerrilla Girls, a New
York-based organization dedicated to fighting art
world sexism.

GUERRILLA GIRL #1

I'M A GUERRILLA GIRL AND I'M NOT ANGRY. WHY SHOULD I BE
ANGRY THAT ONLY ONE MAJOR NEW YORK CITY MUSEUM HAD
AN EXHIBITION BY A WOMAN ARTIST LAST YEAR?

GUERRILLA GIRL #2

I'M A GUERRILLA GIRL AND I'M NOT ANGRY. WHY SHOULD I
WASTE MY TIME GETTING HOT AND BOTHERED ABOUT THE
FACT THAT SO MANY MAJOR NEW YORK GALLERIES SHOW LESS
THAN 10% WOMEN? WHAT DO I CARE ABOUT BLUM HELMAN,
MARY BOONE, GRACE BORGENICHT, DIANE BROWN, LEO CAS-
TELLI, CHARLES COWLES, MARISA del RE, DIA FOUNDATION,
ALLAN FRUMKIN, MARIAN GOODMAN, PAT HEARN, MARL-
BOROUGH, PACE, TONY SHAFRAZI, SPERONE WESTWATER, ED
THORP OR WASHBURN? WHY SHOULD I BE FURIOUS THAT MOST
OF THE OTHER GALLERIES DON'T DO MUCH BETTER?

GUERRILLA GIRL #3

I'M A GUERRILLA GIRL AND I CERTAINLY DON'T THINK THERE'S ANYTHING TO GET ANGRY ABOUT. SHOULD I HATE THE MALE ARTISTS WHO ALLOW THEIR WORK TO BE SHOWN AT GALLERIES THAT SHOW HARDLY ANY WOMEN? I'M SURE THAT CLAES OLDENBURG AND BRUCE NAUMAN HAVE MADE IT CLEAR TO LEO CASTELLI THAT HE MUST SHOW MORE WOMEN. I KNOW THAT DAVID SALLE HAS OFTEN DEMANDED OF MARY BOONE THAT SHE AT LEAST TAKE ONE WOMAN ARTIST. WITH THE MOST SUCCESSFUL MALE ARTISTS ALL TELLING THEIR DEALERS TO TAKE ACTION, WHAT DO I HAVE TO BE ANGRY ABOUT?

GUERRILLA GIRL #4

I'M A GUERRILLA GIRL AND I'M NOT AT ALL INCENSED THAT THE MUSEUM OF MODERN ART SHOWED ONLY 13 WOMEN OUT OF 169 ARTISTS IN THEIR INTERNATIONAL SURVEY OF PAINTING AND SCULPTURE. OR THAT THE CARNEGIE INTERNATIONAL HAD ONLY 4 OUT OF 42. I KNOW THESE FIGURES OCCURRED SIMPLY BY CHANCE: THERE WAS NO SEXISM—CONSCIOUS OR UNCONSCIOUS—AT WORK.

GUERRILLA GIRL #5

I'M A GUERRILLA GIRL AND I'M NOT ANGRY AT THE CRITICS WHO WRITE LESS THAN 10% OF THEIR ONE-PERSON SHOW REVIEWS ABOUT WOMEN ARTISTS. I ADMIRE AND RESPECT DORE ASHTON, EDIT DeAK, THOMAS LAWSON, KIM LEVIN, GARY INDIANA, IDA PANICELLI, ROBERT PINCUS-WITTEN, PETER PLAGENS, CARTER RATCLIFF AND VALENTIN TATRANSKY AND I HOPE THEY USE THEIR 10% TO WRITE ABOUT ME THIS YEAR.

GUERRILLA GIRL #6

I'M A GUERRILLA GIRL AND I'M NOT ANGRY THAT THE ART WORLD IS ADMINISTERED ENTIRELY BY MIDDLE-AGED WOMEN FOR THE BENEFIT OF VERY YOUNG MEN. AFTER ALL, WOMEN ARE ACCUSTOMED TO BEING WIVES AND MOTHERS. WE KNOW HOW TO BLOW THEIR NOSES!

GUERRILLA GIRL #7

I'M A GUERRILLA GIRL AND I THINK THAT THE ART WORLD IS PERFECT AND I WOULD NEVER THINK OF COMPLAINING ABOUT ANY OF THE WONDERFUL PEOPLE IN IT. AFTER ALL, WOMEN ARTISTS MAKE FULLY ONE WHOLE THIRD OF WHAT MALE ARTISTS MAKE, SO WHAT'S THERE TO BE MAD ABOUT? I MEAN, IT'S NOT NICE TO GET ANGRY, NICE GIRLS DON'T GET ANGRY. I WOULDN'T DREAM OF GETTING ANGRY. THANK YOU SO MUCH FOR TAKING TIME OUT OF YOUR BUSY DAY TO LISTEN TO THIS.

THE 'MADNESS' OF CHICAGO ART

May 1986

As I begin to write about the "Chicagoness" of Chicago art—as though it is possible to give an essence to what has a vigorously diverse existence—I am in dread of incurring Franz Schulze's wrath. Schulze took Russell Bowman to task for arguing that "the central concept of the Chicago Imagists was that commonplace imagery, and vernacular, kitschy imagery in particular, could be sources for intensely personal expressions" (*NAE*, October 1984). Schulze retorted: "That characterization hardly fits Chicago art of the period 1945 to 1965. Campoli, Petlin and Statsinger were either indifferent or consciously hostile to kitsch and the vernacular, preferring to explore themes more nearly mythic or universal in intent" (*NAE*, December 1984). Schulze will no doubt feel I am guilty of even greater misapprehension of Chicago art than Bowman—of overlooking even more of the details of its history. For in a calculated attempt to avoid all the clichés about it, the redundant, hackneyed, Procrustean terms in which Chicago art has come to be discussed—"prodigal funk," "*retardataire* and provincial pastiche of Pop and Surrealism," "exacerbated figuration," "monster roster"—I want to change the terms of the discussion by locating Chicago art in a larger context of understanding than is customary. It is in fact the largest context: I want to understand its place, function, and "philosophy" in modern art as a whole.

Such an enterprise is no doubt filled with the pitfalls (pratfalls?) of overgeneralization—although it promises to end the usually defensive character of discussions of Chicago art (or else put it more on the defense than ever). But it seems the only way of breaking the stranglehold imposed by the conventional categorization of Chicago art, which has unexpectedly made it seem banal by too vigorously insisting upon its way-outness. (For wayoutness is the most habitual, banal characteristic of modern art.) I believe Chicago art has a truly extraordinary position within what Harold Rosenberg called the "tradition of the new." I would like to generate a fresh respect for Chicago art, create a new perspective from which it can be appreciated. It is an important innovative art; but the implications of its novelty for modern art as a whole have not been spelled out. Critics have been too busy defending its right to its "difference" to examine the full meaning of that difference.

For me Chicago art is a special demonstration of the troubled character of modern art—more particularly, of two problems that have shaped it from the start. First, its profound dissatisfaction with and distrust of all modes of articulation, which keeps it restlessly on the move inventing novel modes of articulation, all of which remain haunted by the aura of inarticulateness, that is, by the suspicion that they are futile as articulations of reality and subtly inarticulate or confused in themselves. Another way to state this is to say that the most serious modern art has always thought of itself not only as art but as anti-art, the viper which grows within its bosom—yet that is what makes modern art "modern." For anti-art expresses the "nihilistic" relationship of art to the modern world. That is, its devaluation or deprecation of itself in the very act of making itself is its internalization of its "inferior" status in the modern scientific world, an implicit acknowledgement of its doubtful reason for existing in this world. In overt anti-art, we see art banalizing itself into another dumbly "positive" material fact of the modern world in the very act of asserting its triumph over—negation of—that world. Modern art is full of morbid self-doubt. While it makes a virtue of its self-doubt, uses it to drive itself towards ever more revolutionary articulation, this Faustian pursuit of revolution is itself a sign of the rot/rottenness brought about by self-doubt. Second, as a correlate of this, modern art is profoundly uncertain as to whether art has anything to say in the modern world. For implicitly the modern world is, because of the scientific outlook which makes it modern, indifferent to art, regarding it as essentially trivial ("decorative"). From the positivistic point of view, art belongs with religion and metaphysics to the childhood and adolescence of mankind. It is inherently beside the point of reality and presumably has nothing to do with developing a "reality principle."

The one is a methodological anxiety, the other an anxiety about meaning, involving art's uncertainty about its relationship to reality. It does not know what "stand" it should take to modern reality—how it should locate itself within this reality, as a major recognition of or witness to it, yet at the same time offer critical resistance to it. Methodological anxiety about the proper mode of art-making leads to art's restless preoccupation with basic values—a perpetually changing sense of what is formally significant, leading to an awareness of stylistic relativism, coincident with a constant expectation of aesthetic revolution. Anxiety about meaning leads to art's insecurity about its "message," even doubt that it has any. (Its defiant proclamation of its "uselessness" simply acknowledges a social fact.) I have in effect restated the "dissociation of sensibility"—the schizoid separation of thinking and feeling—that T.S. Eliot thought pervaded modern art, infecting the conception as well as development of it. (It is perhaps worth noting that from this perspective Postmodernism is simply another statement of the modern double-edged anxiety about art-making, rather than a solution to it.) The dissociation is perhaps most succinctly expressed in Bernard Berenson's distinction between stylistic and illustrative values in art. (Reformulated by Clement Greenberg as the distinction between aesthetic and literary values.)

This distinction has become commonplace in contemporary art-thinking. It has come to be regarded as normative, controlling our understanding of art, and has become hierarchical, controlling our sense of artistic value. An art in which stylistic/aesthetic/ formal concerns dominate is regarded as inherently superior to one in which illustrative/literary/message concerns dominate. I think this distinction, and especially its hierarchicalization, represents a major tragedy for art—a major loss of unity of purpose. I think Chicago art is an important response to the dialectical insecurity and frustration implicit in the distinction. Chicago art is an important attempt to rearticulate and at the same time overcome it.

In an upfront way—it is this "indiscreteness" which may be responsible for the way Chicago art has offended many people—Chicago art is fraught with the complex anxiety of modern art: stylistic restlessness, insecurity about message (doubt that art is a privileged cognition of reality, implying a special relationship to it), and the realization that the only way to lay these anxieties to rest is to reconcile the vital opposites of thought and feeling they represent. But Chicago art offers no premature, Utopian reconciliation—another reason it is offensive to modern art lovers. Its continuous agony is the expression of its implicit recognition that the world historical situation—the external condition necessary for reconciliation—promises no reconciliation of thought and feeling, and of the antagonisms that generally animate the world—and so no "sanity" for art. Chicago art knows the world offers no pastoral possibilities, and that the condition of hypostatized contradiction in which it exists is hardly a condition of peace or reconciliation. How can the internal contradictions of art change when the external contradictions of the world seem unchangeable? How can art lose its anxieties about itself when the world still arouses profound anxiety? The internal contradictions must be lived with, however much they continue to bring the nature and stability of art into doubt. This is the "philosophy" of Chicago art.

Thus, Chicago art is to some extent "mad." One way of living with contradiction is by going mad—a seeming rebellion against contradiction which in fact articulates it and the anxiety it embodies more fully. (Madness, with its hardened frustration and disbelief in the possibility of any reconciliation between the opposites that constitute the contradiction, is the extreme opposite of utopianism, which believes in inevitable, if historically postponed, reconciliation. Utopianism, I think, unconsciously motivates more modern art than madness, for utopianism seems to bring contradiction under control—reconciling us to it as mad art refuses to do.) Chicago art is *the* example of a deliberate if risky attempt to make "mad art." It is an artificed "outsider art." Chicago art acknowledges the self-contradictory, anxious condition of modern art by refusing to accept stylistic repression of its anxious self-doubt. It operates with no fixed sense of style; it tends toward a condition of stylelessness rather than stylization. This helps generate a sense of its "drivenness." Hence its so-called "eccentricity." Paradoxically, the deliberate attempt to be mad in art makes the repressive stylistic structures all the more visible by "bending" them. Thus Chicago art reveals the inner contradictions of modern art with special flair and intensity.

I want to look at Chicago art from the perspective of these ideas not only because I think they are key ideas for understanding modern art in general, but once and for all to get beyond the essentially dead distinction between sophisticated cosmopolitanism and provincial regionalism. This distinction once permitted a New York critic to speak of Chicago artists as "Midwestern eccentrics." Why should Midwestern eccentricity be any more or less credible than German eccentricity, or the eccentricity that was central to modern art from the start—that in retrospect can be seen to be inseparable from its nature? Or rather, the sense of eccentricity—reflecting uncertainty about norms, even a sense of their arbitrariness—that has pervaded the modern sense of reality, and that Midwestern eccentricity is another articulation of.

Expressionist-type art has usually been labeled as eccentric, while Cubist-type art has usually been regarded as normative, but this distinction—Greenberg's—is false, arbitrary, and political. It shuns critical awareness of the issues rather than expounds them. It conventionalizes one type of art at the expense of the other in an attempt to give it social status, to signify that it is the approved type; but such conventionalization represses recognition of the complex distinction that underlies it. Indeed, the moment such an absolute distinction is established, it begins to rot. Several scholars have argued for an expressionist understanding of Cubism—a recognition of its eccentricity of vision, its troubled dialectical character as an anxious mode of art and anxious message about reality. No one today can say, with the confidence that they are speaking a fundamental truth, what is or is not normative in art, what is or is not eccentric—"distorted." For no one knows how to make the distinction convincingly in life. This is the point of Freud's assertion that the normal and the abnormal exist on the same continuum, are describable by the same concepts. We find ourselves in a situation, in art as in life, of discovering the normative within the eccentric, and the eccentric within the normative, with no sense of the priority of one to the other. The best Chicago art is a revelation of this simultaneity.

The anxieties of modern art are reflected in Chicago art through what I think is its basic concern: trying to tell a story. I experience most works of Chicago art as isolated episodes in an open-ended plot. They are moments in a tall story, which exists to make the point that there is a story to tell, and that there is a story still untold—that there is still more story to come. It is a sort of Thousand-and-One-Nights situation, trying to seduce us to the idea of the story itself—to the belief that understanding is still organized in terms of stories. Sometimes Chicago art offers us balladic tales—for me, much of the Hairy Who?—and sometimes its tales seem full of sound and fury signifying nothing, that is, the being of nothing, or the secret, frustrating nothingness of it all—for me, much of the post-Hairy Who? Expressionism—but it is always about the possibility of telling a story, always arguing that it still makes sense to think in terms of stories. Chicago art is a polemic in favor of storytelling, crucifying the story in order to resurrect it as valid beyond any possible doubt. There is a fundamental anxiety to hold on to the story in Chicago art—even when world and art history seem to have no plot to them, or no teleological point to their "plot."

I think this is true of all kinds of Chicago art that is stylistically different, but in which the difference expresses frustration with finding the proper way of telling a story in a world in which plot no longer takes a linear form, and in which an object or detail can act as or expand into a "character." Nicolas Africano, Ivan Albright, Roger Brown, Leon Golub, June Leaf, Gladys Nilsson, Ed Paschke, Irving Petlin, Seymour Rosofsky, Peter Saul, Hollis Sigler, H. C. Westerman, Karl Wirsum, and even, I submit, such abstract artists as William Conger, Miyoko Ito, Frank Piatek, Barbara Rossi, and Evelyn Statsinger are storytellers. The non-imagistic artists tell a story in abstract form, very much in the manner, if not with the same terms, as El Lissitzky's *Story of Two Squares* (1922). In general, much abstract art, if not disguised or subliminal narrative, treats various non-representational forms as "characters" in a dramatic plot, giving them added animus—adding to them a dynamic that they do not often have in themselves, supposedly thereby giving them more "human interest." In much of the current crop of Chicago Imagist work there seems to be a deliberate attempt to fuse representational and non-representational modes, but the narrative intention remains central.

In an art world in which narrative was for a long time *declasse*, even though much art was subliminally narrative, Chicago art's "mad" clinging to narrative seems to have paid off, in view of the new sense of narrative's potential—the new sense of "advanced narrative." Does the new narrative art look to Chicago for any of its standards? Is Chicago art in any way a model for neo-narrative art? I don't think so. The difference between Chicago narrative art and neo-narrative art can be stated quite simply in terms derived from Schulze. "Imagism," he says, "implies the summoning of figural/iconic symbols to convey personal psychic states and metaphorical responses to experience, as distinct from the organization of pictorial elements into formally expressive, psychically neutral configurations." The neo-narrativists want to deconstruct narrative, writing large the configurations that structure it. The Chicago narrativists don't want to deconstruct narrative; they want to use it to metaphorically convey psychic states. At the same time, the neo-narrativists want to use the neutralized, semiotically reconceived configurations, to ideological effect. The Chicago narrativists do not accept the semiotic neutralization of narrative configurations, and in fact seem to deny that there is any optimum form narrative can take. For them, narrative is in a state of flux, with no fixed conventions. That is, Chicago art seems to deny that narrative configurations exist as signs having a certain function in a certain kind of discourse before they exist as "moving" or as responses to experience. Kiefer's landscapes are semiotic restorations of an ideology before they are metaphors of experience. The Postmodernist/narrativists restate the double-edged anxiety of Modernism as a semiotic problem: the absence and conceptual nature of the signified conveys the problem of art's anxious relation to "positively" given modern reality, and the character of the stylistic signifier as part of a historical tradition of art discourse conveys the problem of art's unhappiness with its modes of articulation, leading it to become "revolutionary."

Is Chicago narrative art hopelessly antiquated? No, because it does one thing neo-narrative art doesn't do: it reminds us, through the insistent diversity of its stylistic modes, that there is no one privileged mode of narrative, and that the very idea of narrative is inseparable from art as an attempt to hold its own in a positivistic world that implicitly disbelieves in it, or believes in its "immaturity." Chicago narrative art's supposed reference to experience is beside the point of the larger issue it articulates, and that neo-narrative art subtly evades in its semiotic ostrich hole: the fact that art can only make a case as narrative—a kind of narrative of narratives?—in a world in which scientific theory has not only told the greatest story that can be told—the story of reality—but has incorporated aesthetics into itself by making aesthetic contemplation seem the appropriate mode of recognizing and respecting reality.

Neo-narrative art, for all the subtlety of its reflection of the basic anxieties of modern art, in a sense neutralizes those anxieties without working them through. It thus amounts to a repression of them. To see stylistic configurations as the signs of a kind of discourse called "art" is to ignore the question as to why we need that kind of discourse in the modern world. It is also to end art's self-doubt by assimilating it as one more kind of discourse, having the same nominal power as other kinds. Neo-narrative offers us a compromise position: art is anxious about itself and its place in the world, but it has a place (and so it can be less anxious) as one among many discourses—which is a sophisticated way of positivistically neutralizing it, denying its "difference," and treating it as another matter of fact.

Chicago narrative art makes a general point about the difference art makes: it tells a story in a world which seems to have no stories left to tell. Above all, it tells the story of the madness of making art in a world of science. That is, it tells us that we are still driven, caught up in plots while full well knowing there is no grand, over-all plot. It tells us that even in a society in which art has become another mode of simulation, that is, exists as no more than a sign of itself—in a world of neo-art—there is still art which is unwisely engaged in making up stories about the lifeworld that exists behind the various simulated ones.

The pathos of Chicago art is not that it is about pathos, but that it Still sees art as able to escape the institutional destiny which will invariably make it into a simulation—a sign of itself—by asserting itself as primary madness. To oppose the madness of the simulated world of signs with the madness of storytelling in a world in which all the stories seem to have been told over and over again—-this is truly to be psychotically realistic.

Ann Wiens EDITOR

1993–1997

INTRODUCTION

"We write about what artists talk about in bars."

That simple mantra, more than any other, informed my tenure as editor of the *New Art Examiner*. To the best of our ability, we covered the issues and influences affecting how art was being created, exhibited, transmitted and discussed, and we did so "without fear or favor," as founding editors Derek Guthrie and Jane Addams Allen had emphatically promised in the magazine's very first issue.

I initially became a subscriber to the magazine when I was an art student at the University of Oklahoma, and continued it without interruption as I moved around the country, to Chicago to attend the School of the Art Institute, to New York for graduate school, and back to Chicago to begin my career. I appreciated that the *Examiner* wasn't focused on collecting, or the New York scene, or art-making techniques. It was about the *ideas* that informed the making of art—which is, by and large, what artists talk about in bars.

I was 27 years old when I answered an ad in the *Chicago Reader* seeking an editor at my favorite art magazine. Armed with a new MFA in painting, a fledgling resume and a sheaf of graduate-school writing assignments that invoked the overbearing, pointlessly dense writing style favored at the time by self-important critics when contributing to the deconstructivist postmodern discourse, I somehow got the job. I loved it.

When Allison Gamble departed a year later, I ascended to the top of the masthead, becoming the first editor of the *Examiner* who had never worked under its founders, Derek and Jane. I had never even met them. This was significant. They were an incredibly strong presence in the Chicago art world in the '70s and '80s, and their influence was broad. They had moved to Washington, D.C. before I joined the *NAE*, so their significance was an abstraction to me—my allegiance was to the mission of the magazine as I understood it, not to its founders, despite my immense respect for their ideas and ideals.

By the time I took the reins, the economic downturn that had brought an abrupt end to the go-go days of art-world excess I'd witnessed as a graduate student in New York had made its way to Chicago. A few galleries had closed, and the giddiness of the '80s was waning—at least in terms of the market. But the market had never been a primary focus of the *Examiner*. My fellow editors—Kathryn Hixson and Deborah Wilk—and I looked at this somewhat more sober climate as a return to reality of sorts, a perfect opportunity to outline our philosophy for the magazine as it entered a new phase of its life, and a chance to clarify its relationship to artists. In an April 1993 editorial I wrote:

> While it's a serious mistake to buy into the "starving artist" myth and assume that difficult times produce better art, after a decade of viewing art surrounded by the context of money it's refreshing to look at art as art again, to think about things like form and content free from the distracting influence of a spectacular price tag.

I went on to discuss the approach we planned to take:

> It is a dedication to providing an open forum for the exchange of ideas based on a strident belief that our word should not be the final one, that not all the good ideas (or good art) come from urban centers, and that many diverse voices can describe a scene better than a few similar ones can. As the hegemony of New York and a handful of other major art centers dwindles and geography plays a decreasingly important role in artistic activity, the *New Art Examiner*'s established network of writers is already providing the framework to facilitate this open forum and to promote diverse critical viewpoints.

Looking back at what we were trying to do in 1993 from my perch here in the twenty-first century, I wonder what we might have done if we'd had the means to draw upon the wisdom of crowds and "facilitate an open forum" the likes of which we hadn't yet imagined in those pre-Internet days.

When we hired a new art director, Guido Mendez (with whom I again have the pleasure of working today), it seemed an apt time to redesign the magazine—to make it our own visually as well as editorially. The redesign was substantial—cutting the final threads that visually linked the magazine to its origins as a newspaper. Guido's vision had both strengths and flaws, but the torrent of negative criticism that greeted our updated design surprised us.

One morning I picked up the phone to hear, "I have no use for a cow on the table of contents," delivered with a gruff English accent. That was the first time I spoke with Derek, who clearly felt that I'd ruined the magazine, bastardized his vision and slandered his legacy.

We got letters, most complaining that the type was too small and the layout too trendy, criticisms I've since learned greet nearly every magazine redesign anywhere. Guido responded eloquently, shooting back that the magazine's form should undergo the same continual critique and questioning that its content was known for: "If this questioning can remain an ongoing process, resulting in both successful and questionable decisions—all the better. Becoming paralyzed in the headlights of continually changing ideas about aesthetics, both popular and academic, is undesirable. The *New Art Examiner,* at least as I understand it, is committed to fighting the idea that fascist standards of quality are desirable states."

The redesign reaction was one example among the many paradoxes that faced us every day as we tried to remain open-minded and multi-vocal in a milieu that was often as critical of change as it was of stasis. We saw no conflict in our dual roles as supporters and watchdogs of the art world, as both pundits and provocateurs.

The fall 1993 season premiere of the television program *60 Minutes* offered another opportunity to explain our ideals around the sanctity of critical dissent. It featured the infamous segment "Yes . . . but Is It Art?" in which Morley Safer led viewers, as I described in the November 1993 issue, "on a giddy romp through the standard, predictable litany of isn't-the-art-world-silly clichés," quoting P.T. Barnum ("There's a sucker born every minute") and portraying the art world as a vast conspiracy of conniving artists, unscrupulous dealers and unintelligible critics banded together to bury the gentle viewer under a deluge of gibberish and contrivance and depicting collectors as brainwashed cult members.

Although we were troubled by the knowledge that the art world's own complexity and lack of a united front bore much responsibility for the mainstream backlash against it, we saw it as our sacred duty to provide a platform that encouraged that very complexity, paradox and dissent. I remember Suzi Gablik's confusion when I called and asked her to write an article for the magazine shortly after I'd written a scathing review of her latest book, *The Reenchantment of Art.* "I thought you hated my work," she said. "I disagree with you," I answered, "but many of our readers don't, and they deserve to hear your ideas."

The magazine's staff was fully aware that whatever perceived "power" we had as editors of a national art magazine was mitigated by the fact that most people couldn't care less about art, *especially* contemporary art. We kept it in perspective and committed ourselves to carrying out the mission of the magazine with a purity of intent and clarity of purpose that amazes me to this day. We lived and breathed it, we worked long hours for little money, we put our ideas and reputations on the line daily.

We were dead serious in the pursuit of our project, but we seldom took our work, or ourselves, too seriously. When we put the magazine to bed, we would head over to Michigan Avenue, a short walk away, and make a game of putting our critical skills to use in a new context, weaving searing, theory-laden critiques of the displays in Jil Sander and Barney's as if they were gallery exhibitions. Then we'd head to the Ghirardelli shop for massive ice cream sundaes.

We kept a running list of potential band names on a whiteboard in our production room, most of them phrases snipped from manuscripts we were working on: "Fabric Tomato." "Discrete Hegemony." "The Murmerers." I think some kids from SAIC even used one for their band.

We published cartoons by Adam Green, who had preceded Guido as the *Examiner*'s art director. Green's cartoons poked at the art world with biting humor. For an issue devoted to arts education in January 1995, he drew a trio of infants under the caption, "My selfless dream of exposing children to art through novelty baby bibs has yet to be realized." Their bibs included the phrases, "Feed me yams, I'm Karen Finley!" and "Having a traumatic infancy, so I can one day produce mediocre art."

Another characteristic of the magazine in the mid 1990s was our fierce allegiance to Chicago, despite our frequent frustration with the city's seeming reluctance to rise up and take its rightful place among the great art cities of the world. A Chicagoan by choice rather than circumstance, I took to this mission with a convert's zeal.

I had moved to Chicago after completing my MFA at SUNY Stony Brook, commuting distance from Manhattan, where I took classes from Donald Kuspit, interned with Holly Solomon and had critiques and seminars with Holland Cotter, Robert Storr and Jacques Derrida. When I graduated I chose Chicago over New York. I explained my choice in a May 1994 editorial railing against Chicago's self-defeating tendency toward "second city syndrome": "In addition to good art schools and affordable studio space, Chicago has enough (just enough, sometimes) of the four components that are crucial to sustain a vital art community: artists (of course), curators/gallerists, critics, and collectors. You can think of these four components as the four legs of a table; take one away, and the thing falls over."

We at the *Examiner* saw ourselves as critical to maintaining the stability of that metaphorical table—without the *NAE*, the "critics" leg would splinter. Other than occasional coverage in the other national art magazines and localized reviews in the daily papers (always by the same few voices), the *Examiner* was the only source for smart, incisive, hard-hitting writing about contemporary art in the city.

So we continued, very deliberately, to position "Chicago art" within the context of contemporary art globally. We considered it central to our mission to discuss art in Chicago (and other underrepresented communities around the country) with the same criticality directed at art in the acknowledged cultural centers of New York, Los Angeles or London. We held firm to our belief that the art produced in our city was more than capable of provoking and responding to such criticism. We saw our role as critical supporters of the Chicago scene, providing thoughtful, pointed commentary on its inner workings, its successes and failures, to a sophisticated national and international readership. I wholeheartedly believed that it was only by being critical of ourselves as participants in both a local and global artistic discussion that we could function as serious members of that discourse, that only by being supportive of one another could we function as an artistic community. And I still do.

—Ann Wiens

ON VIEW

Chicago

May 1993

When the 1993 Whitney Biennial opened in March, it was greeted with the usual anguish, outrage, and expletives, followed, in a more apprehensive tone, by the observation that of the 82 artists included, only nine are painters. Could this possibly be an indication that painting really is, finally, dead? Did the inflated market of the '80s, the rejection of a Modernist hegemony, and the impulse toward more "reality-based" art forms—installation, film and video, even sculpture—form the lethal combination to finally do it in? Hardly. Given the number of times painting has been said to have died, and its equal number of miraculous resurrections (even the King of Kings and Lord of Lords only pulled off this trick once), it is probably safe to say that it never died at all. As an artist I know who has watched this "now-it's-dead, now-it's-not" phenomenon through several cycles recently suggested, painting travels its own road, a road that winds in and out of critical discourse and public attention, frequently crossing, or joining, paths with other art forms, continuing, steadily, regardless of what's hot and what's not. And regardless of what's currently enclosed by the granite walls of the Whitney, painting has been out in full force recently, not only alive, but relatively well.

This is due in part to economic necessity—abstract paintings look nicer in the home or office than, say, hunks of gnawed lard or pools of rubber vomit and are therefore easier to sell—especially here in Chicago, where the collector base is small and relatively conservative. Several dealers I spoke with recently acknowledged that they've opted to "play it safe" this season, and are necessarily reluctant to show much work they deem risky in terms of sales. But salability does not presuppose boredom, and although the voice of painting may have been drowned out by the din of more extroverted art forms it is still there, humming along. In fact, its voice has been steadily gaining volume over the last couple of years, providing harmony to (or a reprieve from) the prevailing didacticism of much current art.

Whatever the reasons, we have seen a surge in serious painting—often competent, sometimes even exciting—that makes for pleasurable, if peaceful, viewing. While such soothing adjectives as "pleasurable" and "peaceful" may be perceived as somewhat derogatory in the current climate, they shouldn't be. Confrontational is not always a synonym for compelling, nor is petulant one for provocative, and time spent pleasurably and peacefully observing quiet painting can remind one that innovation and interest are not the exclusive properties of the one who screams the loudest, and that painting is not always the safe harbor of conservative thought.

Conceptually astute, Jonathan Lasker's recent paintings at Rhona Hoffman Gallery (215 W. Superior St.) are also thoroughly enjoyable. They simultaneously parody and fulfill the legacy of artistic mark-making. They are about capital-"D"-Drawing and capital-"P"-Painting—the acts of drawing and painting reduced to their essences. In this reduction, this boiling-down of the painterly act, Lasker reveals its limitlessness. Each of the works shown here follows closely a format Lasker has been exploring for some time: A flat, monochromatic ground supports an arrangement of tangled black squiggles, absurdly thick swaths of paint, blocks of color, and/or any of several other painterly devices Lasker keeps close at hand. The allure of these works lies in their ability to be simultaneously satiric and genuine, to parody the tradition of Modern painting while functioning superbly within that tradition.

In *Artistic Painting,* even the title evidences Lasker's playful attitude toward the idea of art and artfulness, an attitude borne out in the painting itself. Here, a light blue ground is divided by rectangular blocks defined by a thin, Magic Marker-like black line and deliberately, but somewhat shakily, striped vertically, horizontally, or diagonally with the same thin line. This emphatically *drawn* line then turns scribbly, winding over and under itself in a tangled mass, a phone-pad doodle gone berserk, filling several of the rectangular blocks and escaping into the spaces between them. In the right third of the canvas, three fat, horizontal bars of very thick paint in lavender, red, and yellow are stacked one atop another, stridently declaring they have been *painted* there. These marks refer to the hand of the artist in the most tongue-in-cheek sense, taking the idea of artistic mark-making to such an obsessive extreme that it negates itself—both the thick, gooey bars of paint and the repetitive, hyper-deliberate masses of thin black lines become generic in their sameness, their choppy, awkward gesture taking on an air of cartoonish simulation. These works are saved from languishing in the realm of clever one-liners, however, by the fact that Lasker is very good at what he does—without taking himself or his project too seriously (there is, after all, something intrinsically goofy about the act of making paintings) he mounts a very serious attack against the seriousness of painting, with all the weight of its accumulated history, while at the same time making a strong case for the continuation of a history that brings us pictures as compelling, and enjoyable, as these.

The signature dots and dashes by which Richard Loving's paintings are immediately recognizable equal Lasker's squiggles and bars in deliberateness, but while Lasker's works are carefully wrapped in tongue-in-cheek irony, Loving's seem imbued with an almost naive sincerity, a faith that moves beyond their formal compositions and overall prettiness. At Roy Boyd Gallery (739 N. Wells), Loving showed a new series of large (70" x 50"), unabashedly decorative paintings which comprise the most recent chapter in a saga of dedication to the mark that has spanned at least three decades. In these works, chance merges with intention and repetition becomes ritual as Loving seeks an elusive spiritual experience—for himself via the ritualistic act of painting, of constructing an image stroke by stroke, dot by dot; and for the viewer in purely visual terms, via the relatively simple act of *looking*. This method, relying as heavily as it does on a near-absolute faith in the communicative abilities of painting as such, is entirely subjective in its effectiveness, but commendable in its mission.

Loving has remained remarkably steadfast in his disciplined, formulaic approach over the years, squeezing nuance from it drop by drop, at times trying the patience of viewers hopeful for a bigger splash, a jolt of incongruence or discord. The canvas is first stained with thin, matte, almost gritty paint (here in a palette limited to black, aqueous blues and purples, and mauve) poured and splattered onto its surface. Next, the careful process of building the overlying image through a series of methodical dots and dashes takes over. This Morse code of bright, often candy-colored marks at times imposes a seemingly unrelated image upon the background, whether recalling mathematical diagrams, as in *Parabola,* or stylized symbols for natural forces (like water), as in *Stretch,* where a series of symmetrical dashes spouts upward like a fountain. In other works, such as *Pathfinder,* the systematic dot patterns are held in check by large, coronal circles outlined in brushy paint or by the contours of the background splatters, which they alternately follow and avoid. Throughout, Loving flaunts his attraction to the decorative, to the extent that he has included a sprinkling of glitter in the backgrounds of these paintings purely for its sparkle. While these pretty, sometimes even sweet paintings may not push the envelope of either formal or conceptual innovation, they represent a faith, thoughtfulness, and completeness of intent worth considering.

"Rodney Carswell, Selected Works: 1975–1993" at The Renaissance Society (University of Chicago, 5811 S. Ellis Ave.) presented another, more comprehensive example of faith in painting and the relentless pursuit of subtle variation. The best of the 18 highly formal, unwaveringly geometric yet persistently quirky works included here divide their allegiance between process and presence. Purposefully crafted, the method of their facture laid bare, Carswell's elemental constructions quietly assert themselves, taking command of the spaces they inhabit while remaining paradoxically unobtrusive. Carswell is extremely generous to the viewer in his revelation of process: every step of the paintings' fabrication is outlined, from the careful construction of the stretchers (clearly visible from the sides, as the paintings project from the wall, or through holes or gaps in their surfaces) to the application of layer upon layer of paint (traces of often wildly varying colors are evident along the edges of the canvas, and subtle ghost images or flecks of color flicker on the works' dry, almost chalky surfaces). *Irregular Stack and Cross* (1993), one of the show's strongest works, is "built" with a series of small squares or rectangles stacked like out- of-whack building blocks or pieces of an ill-fitting puzzle. The placement of each piece appears highly calculated, resulting in a perfect, if precarious, balance. Each "block" is quartered by a faint cross which shimmers on the painting's milky green surface, like a score of afterimages of the single bright orange cross situated near the painting's center. Several rectangular gaps, or holes, punctuate the piece where the blocks refuse to interlock, again revealing the construction process, but also negating any attempts the painting might make to become the least bit pictorial—it is shown, clearly, to be an object on a wall.

Suzanne Caporael's series of 16 recent paintings at Richard Gray Gallery (620 N, Michigan Ave.) affirms the notion that terms traditionally applied to painting, such as "abstract" and "representational" and even "abstracted" or "referential," have become so relative as to be almost meaningless. Caporael's works combine issues of abstraction/representation and intuitive/rational consciousness prevalent in recent painting with parallel theories in current scientific practice (such as fractal geometry) which are finding order and rational meaning in systems formerly considered random or chaotic.

Caporael makes quiet, elegant paintings in a limited range of cool creams and umbers, that hover between the geometric and the organic. Most are composed of soft striations of dark and light paint, carefully applied in thin, somewhat translucent layers. The (usually vertical) stripes, or rays, are crossed by less well-defined horizontally arced bars, forming a loose, uneven grid. These pieces function well on a near-hermetic formal level, speaking to compositional structure, process, and the architectural environment in which they appear. They are completely recontextualized, however, by the exhibition's title—"Inside Trees"—and their individual titles—after various species of trees. Thus informed, they immediately shift to read as magnified cross-sections of tree trunks, and subtle variations in the color or grid structures reference characteristics of the particular species' wood. Several works, such as *Redwood* (*Compression Wood*) and *Arizona Cypress* (*Branch Section*) are more obviously referential, featuring complete, concentric rings, while others, most notably *Eastern White Pine* (*Crossfield*) only tenuously relate to our notion of what the inside of a tree looks like—these do not so much resemble the flat, hard surface of a cut tree as a moving, sinking space, perhaps the interior of a tree that has *not* been cut.

Of this group of work, Jackie Kazarian's at Klein Art Works, (400 N. Morgan) is by far the "loudest," providing a raucous counterpoint to the wry irony, cool elegance, and/or calculated craftsmanship of the others. In these acid-bright, visually active acrylic paintings, a concise vocabulary of related forms (dots and circles, squiggly intestine or rope shapes and writhing brush strokes) converses with an elaborate layering system and a disconcerting treatment of space to produce initially brash compositions which, over time, reveal a sophisticated formal sensibility. Sharp, cutout stenciled shapes (usually circles or leaf forms) over- and underlie the paintings' ground and other cutouts, each containing a complete painterly language and each given near-equal time in terms of activity.

They recall, in an offbeat way, James Rosenquist's works from the early '80s in which two or more individually complete images are stripped together, destroying conventional notions of positive/negative space or figure/ground relationships. In *Spring,* for example, the overall activity of loud, brushy passages in green and yellow, stenciled circles grouped to form clover shapes, and stenciled leaf shapes crisscrossed with quick brush strokes is interrupted by a single, nearly white circle that appears to float above the painting's surface, but is actually a "hole," a space masked out through much of the painting process so one of the very first layers is revealed. *Fire Work* gains a hint of narrative from its title; the left half of the canvas is engulfed in flickering, translucent orange-red brush strokes, a jolting contrast to the right half, in Play-Doh pink, yellow, and green, which features an intricate arrangement of layered and stenciled circles and web shapes echoed by swirling, arched brush marks and splatters. These works are both attractive and uneasy, and grow in interest over time as their more subtle elements slowly shine through their noisy surfaces.

It has been said that the Whitney Biennial serves as an accurate reflection of the art scene two or three years previous. If this is true, the 1995 Biennial may not go down as "The Biennial of Abstract Painters," but it will, if we're lucky, include more than nine.

STEVE HOHENBOKEN

COMFORT CUT ON THE (GENDER) BIAS

Out of the (Linen) Closet

September 1993

In 1976, when I was in the seventh grade at Western View Junior High, I was the only boy in Mrs. Farnes's needlecraft class. I spent the term latch-hooking a Mickey Mouse rug, laughing and yakking with the girls. Unsurprisingly, this was right around the time when I was branded a fag by boys more interested in metal shop. It was an accusation which I did not admit to be true until I came out a number of years later.

Now, in my nascent career as an artist, I'm experiencing a sense of déjà-vu. In my studies and in the textile shows I see or have work in, the gender ratio seems to follow that established in Mrs. Farnes's class: a few men, usually gay and always non-traditional; many women. I don't think it's coincidence that those of us who are working in this un-mainstream medium are so often those of us for whom the vernacular—be it American English or the most visible and promoted art of the day—does not speak. What is it that brings us to the field of textiles? In our diversity as men, women, stitchers, weavers, quilters—gay and straight—-what are the common threads in our work? To address these questions means making generalizations, and to do so risks exclusion and disagreement. But I'll forge ahead, for I feel the discussion is relevant and interesting, even central to our understanding of ourselves as artists.

In our culture it's women who are more likely to think of textile work as a viable activity in the first place—girls are more likely than boys to be steered into the realm of sewing and working with cloth at an early age. For men, the ways we come to see needlework as an option are less direct. Is there a natural tendency for future gay men to gravitate toward the gentler pastimes of childhood? It's an ancient debate, but for my part I know I quickly got tired of naked troll dolls and took to fashioning little tube tops and pants for them. Later, when I began to question what it meant to be gay, the first models I had in my smallish Oregon hometown were media caricatures, concerned with traditionally feminine pursuits. Like it or not, I think that kind of Mad Magazine stereotype of the homosexual thrilled with chintz led me to take a look at things I might not otherwise have paid attention to, some of them areas where I eventually found a genuine connection.

Then there's my friend Steph Hieston, a gay man who makes quilts and cross-stitched images, who says that one of his reasons for doing textile work echoes the reason some men say they are drag queens: "Because I can." There is a joy in defying traditional roles.

It's not that I believe that straight men are constitutionally less likely to feel an affinity for textiles. There are (a few) artists who prove otherwise. But I wonder whether in many straight men there is still, on some level, the fear that doing textile work means one is a fag. After all, back at Western View plenty of guys were willing to sign up for a half-sewing, half-cooking class when it was reassuringly titled "Bachelor Living." (Our sewing project: barbecue aprons.) Nor do I wish to imply, of course, that every woman and gay man will take to the Bernina with glee—only that, for various reasons, we're more likely to be introduced to it in the first place.

(While many of us remember fondly the relatives who taught us to sew, I regularly hear of textile artists well into their careers who learn of ancestors who were similarly inclined: Tom Lundberg discovered that his great-grandfather and great-uncle were tailors; Arturo Alonzo Sandoval found that the men in his family were weavers. One of my great-grandmothers was an avid quilter. I have heard artists wondering, tentatively, whether there might be something more than coincidence to this kind of lineage.)

But while there is often an early affinity with this medium, textile work seems to need to be discovered twice. I have talked to many people who loved working with cloth when young, but who, upon arriving at art school, picked up paintbrushes, the tools of Serious Art. Washington, D.C. artist Pat Autenrieth told me of her experience at the Kansas City Art Institute 20 years ago, when anything that "smacked of craft" was put down, "women's work" wasn't recognized, and art history texts were empty of references to female artists. In this climate, she became a painter. The rest of the story is familiar, I think, to anyone who has talked with textile artists. During a period of creative stagnation, Autenrieth came across some old, unfinished quilts she'd once bought. In working to complete them she rediscovered the connection to creating with cloth that she had known as a child, and she has been a quiltmaker ever since. Time and time again I hear of this "accidental" return to needle, thread, and cloth, and the simultaneous feeling of rightness; a   return to heart, home, self, and voice.

There's more to that feeling than the rediscovery of something deeply familiar from one's past, though that reconnection is profound in itself. I think there is also the instinctive understanding that this is a medium with which we can eloquently address who and where we are now. Certain personal and political issues have become central to us in this society. Textile artists are discovering—inventing—another language, one which brings to these issues the unique metaphorical and evocative qualities of fiber.

Consider a few of the many forms with which artists address issues of our bodies. Nick Cave's performances use costumes heavily embellished with bottle caps, wigs, sticks, and other objects to explore gender and identity. Beverly Semmes's bizarrely proportioned, empty garments evoke unease with the body and socialized gender roles. Norma Minkowitz's airy but self-supporting crocheted forms speak of the body as both a physical and spiritual vessel, and the stuffed, stitched ovoid shapes made by Magdalena Abakanowicz viscerally remind us that: *"It is from fiber that all living organisms are built—the tissues of plants, and ourselves. Our nerves, our genetic code, the canals of our veins, our muscles. We are fibrous structures"* (Exhibition Catalog, 94). Textiles, traditionally found in the domestic sphere, are uniquely suited to exploring personal history and that phenomenon we call family. By writing her personal histories on quilts, Faith Ringgold makes explicit the implicit storytelling aspect of quilts and in so doing brings resonance to the work. Autenrieth has offered another take on the quilt, using it as a canvas on which domestic objects are juxtaposed with unsettling intimacy to address the formation of identity within the family. Tom Lundberg's jewel-like embroideries are more contemplative meditations on the icons of home, lent a reverent quality by the tiny, richly colored stitches which form them.

Even in work that is overtly political, the textile medium can provide elements of the personal and intimate, reminders of the human side of issues. The Names Project quilt is a striking—perhaps the ultimate—example. Giving palpable form to the statistics of the AIDS crisis, its emotional impact is increased by the quilt's associations with solace, comfort, and sexuality.

But the feeling of tightness that is part of our discovery—or rediscovery—of textiles is more than the realization that we now have a broader vocabulary with which to speak of our lives. Underlying everything is the tactile, the intimacy and sensuality of the textile. Touch is integral to the processes of creating, as threads or cloth pass through the hands: stitches are made, fabric is cut and joined, fibers are brought together to create a new whole. Each is a deeply felt metaphor for the way we construct our lives.

It's not uncommon in some corners of the textile world to see bumper stickers of the "she who dies with the most fabric wins" variety; some trade magazines seem frequently to run essays with a self-deprecating "I'm just a kooky fabric-aholic" tone. These seem to me to come from a need to make a joke of, or to apologize for, the passion we feel for our materials and processes. We feel a little sheepish: it must be odd, we feel, to want to gather this stuff around us.

Comfort is, I believe, what we ultimately derive from this medium. Each of us, maker and viewer, senses the comfort that is so inherently a part of cloth—each of us who knows the feeling of having it caress the skin, night and day; who remembers lying with a loved one beneath a soft quilt; who perhaps even somewhere holds the sense memory of being sheltered in a blanket after that first nasty shock, birth. In a way it's embarrassing to admit to this deep, sensual discovery, at a time when Serious Art is for the most part colder, more ironic, more detached.

We don't, and shouldn't, all make plush Mickey Mouse rugs; unremittingly happy work. But even in our darkest themes I find a grace note of reassurance lent by the medium. In a world that's often difficult for us—women and men, gay and straight—there's comfort to be found here. And there's strength to be found in affirming our work and the voice it gives each of us; putting it into the world so it can give to others, too. It's a kind of coming out.

WORK CITED

Magdalena Abakanowicz, *Museum, of Contemporary Art, Chicago, exhibition catalogue,* (New York: Abbeville Press, 1982), p. 94.

PUBLIC DOMAIN

Frank Stella—The Town-Ho's Story

January 1994

Ralph Metcalfe Federal Building Clark St. and Jackson Blvd., Chicago

The fact that contemporary public art is extremely problematic is perhaps the very reason it has witnessed a surge of activity over the past decade. Originally the offspring of the museum/gallery discourse, public art has become largely independent of its parent, and as the diversity and depth of its projects attest, it has now reached puberty. But like those films shown in Human Development 101 told us, puberty is in many ways a nasty age, when the pubescent subject's actions oscillate between rebellion and reconciliation with the forces that are shaping it. In short, puberty signals an identity crisis. This is compounded in public art by an acute case of schizophrenia, with its two principle personalities, "Public" and "Art," each having its own identity crisis. With neither Public nor Art being able to define itself, the multitude of recent controversies seems unavoidable. And those involved on all sides have been left so defensive that it's hard to imagine the era that brought into being the Federal Art-in-Architecture Program and the host of state and local public art programs for which it served as a model. But the recent wave of public art projects hasn't so much resolved the dilemma between art and audience as it has further signified the problem.

Extending the analogy of public art's pubescence a little further and projecting this dilemma on to some of public art's recent high points provides the complex backdrop against which Frank Stella's *The Town-Ho's*

Story, a new public artwork commissioned through the Federal Art-in-Architecture Program, arrived in Chicago this fall. If Richard Serra's *Tilted Arc* fiasco announced public art's maturation with all the grace of a young boy's cracking voice, then Sculpture Chicago's "Culture in Action" series represents stages of guilt and denial about public art's privileged museum upbringing. These two contrary projects set an interesting context for three tons of discombobulated steel and aluminum to be heaped 22 feet high in the lobby of the new Ralph Metcalfe Federal Building in the Loop. Like a boy who revels in behaving like his father, *The Town-Ho's Story* unapologetically lays claim to its museum roots. Public art's earlier phase, circa 1972, when big abstract metal things were all the rage, has returned with a vengeance. But gone are the polished geometric forms that lulled audiences into forgetting or not even bothering to care about an artwork's existence.

If I were to liken *The Town-Ho's Story* to anything it would be a cross between an Anselm Kiefer and a John Chamberlain, although it makes Chamberlain's *Doorful of Syrup,* a work located just up the street in the lobby of the Leo Burnett Building, look tame. Stylistically, *Town-Ho* is a wake-up call much closer to Neo-Expressionism than straight abstraction-poles, planes, and sheets are crinkled, strewn, dipped, crunched, corrugated, and dented. Metal in every conceivable form is allowed to co-exist in a relaxed way to form a monotonous heap that resists an easy, immediate reading. Unlike *Knights and Squires* and *Loomings,* two of Stella's works installed nearby in the lobby of 181 W. Madison St., *The Town-Ho's Story* is relatively monochromatic, despite a pale swatch of color here and there. The two Madison Street works are wall pieces from 1990, and their allegiance to the wall, in conjunction with a series of repeating hoops and Nike-like swooshes gives them the look of a pair of gaudy corporate earrings, as well as a calculated wackiness reminiscent of MTV editing. With *Town-Ho,* Stella has resolved these problems by forsaking the wall and working in the round. An aggressively clunky, top-heavy composition, the sculpture never rests easy—from certain angles it appears to teeter, looming threateningly on a base that is conspicuously orderly and clean, with a zoo-like railing clearly designed to keep this beast at bay.

The piece actually consists of three components, *The Town-Ho's Story* being the largest. It shares a base with *The Gam* and *Postscript;* all three components take their names from chapter titles in Herman Melville's *Moby Dick.* Stella has been working on the *Moby Dick* series, which includes roughly 130 works so far, for the past few years. (*Knights and Squires* and *Loomings* are also in this series.) Such references to classic works of literature, mythology, or sites of significant historical events are common Neo-Expressionist ploys often used to lend an artwork a certain gravity that it might be unable to muster on its own. The weight of history, in all its drop-dead seriousness, is, of course, what museums market, and Stella, a big fan of the "series," has risen to the occasion by establishing the *Moby Dick Visual Interpretation Co.* With the weight of great literature behind him, all that remains is for Stella to streamline production. Spread out over 130 works, however, any meaningful reference to *Moby Dick* wears thin. Content and importance become givens, and the works assume a self-aggrandized posture demanding interpretation. This screaming demand, which inevitably relies on a text for any coherence, gives *The Town-Ho's Story* an unwarranted pretentiousness. (I must admit, though, that as a tale of mutiny and revenge, the chapter for which *The Town-Ho* is named made speculation as to the relation here between the site, the story, and the artwork a lot of fun.)

If the heyday of the metal monster has in fact returned, the best proof is to be found in the uneasy reception *The Town-Ho's Story* has received from Metcalfe Building tenants. Letters of protest refer to the work as a "statue" or "sculpture," these words appearing in quotes, betraying their authors' uncertainty as to what to call the thing. The cover letter of a petition demanding *Town-Ho's* removal read as though it were written shortly after the unveiling of the Daley Plaza Picasso; the issue of taxpayers' dollars, the dead horse that always manages to be resurrected and beaten yet again, was in fine form. In a *Chicago Sun-Times* telephone survey, 89 percent of the respondents felt that the sculpture was not worth its $450,000 price tag. Numerous petitioners declared it a rip-off, and one considered it a crime, given that there are starving children in the world. (I guess she forgot that's the reason U.S. troops are in Somalia, and that the Federal Government is probably shelling out $450,000 daily for that piece of performance art.) Some people thought the title was obscene, a reference, in dialect, to streetwalkers, prompting a pro-Stella tenant to put up posters throughout the building informing people of where the piece actually derived its tide. ("Town-Ho" refers to a ship named for an expression delivered by sailors upon sighting a whale.) There were also complaints that the work didn't reflect the spirit of the building's namesake, Ralph Metcalfe. As it turns out, Stella was selected to create the work before the idea of naming the building for Metcalfe even occurred. Hostility aside, these responses were at least lively compared to the anemic coverage *The Chicago Tribune* and *Sun-Times* provided.

When press releases and news articles mentioned that *The Town-Ho's Story* is Stella's first free-standing sculpture, perhaps theft use of the term "sculpture" should have been more conspicuous. Town-Ho does not simply represent a return to more conservative notions about public art, it also represents a return to conservative notions of sculpture. If sculpture from about 1960 onward began to question the autonomy of the freestanding object in relation to its site, then *The Town-Ho's Story*, in all its gleaming metal glory, has ignored the results, opting instead to expand autonomy into full-blown antagonism. An analysis of the piece using host/parasite relations as a metaphor would have to conclude that the sculpture is a hostile virus. But Stella, from his earliest, most sensitive works up to his latest undertakings (designing museums in Groningen and Dresden), has always championed autonomy. The keen awareness of edge that is the strength of his stripe paintings is the greatest extent to which Stella has ever been context sensitive. Stella's boundaries have always been defined by formal issues within the physical artwork, all the way out to its very edges. Where these edges end is where context begins, and in this domain Stella would indeed be a fish out of water. And while some fish left the water and learned to walk, the theory of evolution tells us, there are still fish, and everything in between, including whales.

> This is the first installment of "Public Domain," an occasional column addressing issues surrounding public art.

STEVEN C. DUBIN

ART'S DEMISE

Censors to the Right of Me, Censors to the Left of Me

March 1994

The impulse to censor art is not the exclusive domain of either the political Right or the Left. We *all* share the inclination to quash expression when our own buttons are pushed.

During the past few years a great deal of attention has been focused on a loose alliance of religious fundamentalists, conservative politicians, and neoconservative cultural critics who have assailed the cultural expressions of disenfranchised groups: African Americans, women, and gays and lesbians in particular. This is a symbolic attempt to blunt the social change of the past 35 to 40 years and roll society back to the standards of an earlier, considerably more oppressive time. But those very same marginalized groups are pushing back robustly, with a two-fold strategy. On the one hand, they hope to eradicate what they perceive to be residual signs of racism, sexism, and homophobia. On the other, they wish to substitute these with more acceptable images of themselves. In the process some of them, too, use a heavy hand in a somber crusade to make the world conform to their own vision. There is an element of magical thinking on both sides. Conservatives believe they can wipe out significant social advances by destroying cultural traces of them. Progressives believe that if they expunge symbols of oppression they will somehow eliminate oppression itself, even though they do not actually touch its structural causes. Each quest is chimeric.

The acceptability of art—high and low, contemporary and classical—is socially constructed, its reception contingent upon social time and place.

What is tolerated at one moment may become *verboten* the next. Controversies over art serve as markers of larger cultural crises, and their proliferation signals a society seeking to accommodate a great deal of change.

The same conflicts that have erupted in the art world since the late '80s have now flared up in many other domains. In fact, a line can be drawn from the arguments over what is good art, decent art, fundable art, or even art at all, to related debates in additional sites: the Republican ("family values") convention in August 1992; the anti-gay referendums in Oregon and Colorado in November 1992; and the ongoing conflict over public-school curriculums. Art battles, it turns out, have been simply the opening salvos in a much broader cultural war over what it means to be an American, and who is welcome within the scope of that vision.

While the frequency of these art controversies may have slowed somewhat from the frenzied events of 1988 to 1992, the conditions which incite them continue to smolder and ignite new blazes. In July 1993, for example, the House of Representatives approved a five-percent reduction in funding to the National Endowment for the Arts (NEA), a punishment imposed after the Christian Action Network sent congressmen and women distorted information. Barely a month later, Cobb County commissioners (in suburban Atlanta, Georgia) passed a resolution condemning homosexuality, and subsequently considered another which would require arts groups receiving county funds to meet "community, family-oriented standards." The Christian Crusade, angered by local productions of Terrence McNally's *Lips Together, Teeth Apart* and David Henry Hwang's *M. Butterfly,* launched this morality campaign. On August 23, 1993, after intense public debate, officials decided to sidestep the issue by prohibiting *any* county funds from underwriting the arts (see "Newsbriefs," October 1993).

My goal here is to examine the mindset and tactics of the ideologue, whichever end s/he occupies on the political spectrum. When ideas are deemed threatening—whether they be expressed through the written word, pop music, movies, theater, traditional painting and sculpture, performance art, or even fashion—a multiplicity of opponents is likely to dip into a common arsenal of counter-offensive weaponry.

Ideologues are absolutists. Confident of their reasoning, self-assured in their public manner, they are determined adversaries of whatever social evils they perceive. It would be a mistake to dismiss them as misguided or unpredictable zealots, however. Everything they do springs from an integrated world view.

Ideologues Insist on a Single Interpretation
of Works of Art or Popular Culture

For ideologues, there is only one correct reading of cultural expressions, and they are privy to it. Their version derives from pre-existing assumptions about the world, perhaps traditional, perhaps radically Utopian. When Reverend Donald E. Wildmon (of the Tupelo, Mississippi-based American Family Association) orchestrated protests against Martin Scorsese's film *The Last Temptation of Christ* in 1988, he and his followers were motivated by the intense desire to safeguard a particular view of Jesus and early Christianity. Based on the Nikos Kazantzakis novel of the same name—for which the author was excommunicated from the Greek Orthodox Church—the film presents a revisionist view, positing Jesus as both man and deity. But a demonstrator in Chicago objected that "You don't fictionalize the truth," and a sign carried during a protest at Universal Studios cautioned "Don't Change HisStory" (Cronin 4; Wildmon 191).

Moreover, when women reject ideas as sexist, when African Americans repudiate them because of alleged racism, or when lesbians and gays recoil from what they perceive as homophobic, they are all relying on their past experiences to understand and alter the status quo. They claim sensibilities which allow them a distinct perspective. The catchphrase, "It's a black thing, you wouldn't understand," captures the exclusivity of vision such groups profess to hold.

Ideologues Make Interpretations Which Are Concrete,
Literal; There Is Scant Appreciation of Subtlety

Absolutists have little tolerance for irony, complexity, or the multivalence of symbols. And why should they? Their ardent reactions are dictated by a perception of the social world as an arena where groups continually struggle for dominance and control. Not only that, but their own positions appear to be in jeopardy. In a contest where who controls impressions to a large extent controls reality, *any* expression which might weaken their image is deemed dangerous.

Their fervor can propel ideologues to commit preposterous blunders. A religious group once took issue with a book entitled *Making It With Mademoiselle*. Only later did they discover it was a sewing manual! And

Jean-Luc Godard's 1985 film *Hail Mary* attracted an ecumenical array of religious protesters, all because their leaders told them it presented Mary as a teen-aged basketball enthusiast and Joseph as a taxi driver. But for audiences actually viewing this film, its tedium and disarray were its most evident components. The story line and overhauled characters were submerged beneath a concoction of disparate elements, making it difficult to access what was happening—except for those who accepted only the literal, bare-bones outline.

Ideologues Decontextualize a Few Elements — Words, Titles, Part of a Design — And Present Them as if They Embodied the Whole Work of Art

Absolutists freely deconstruct and then reassemble new versions, highlighting exactly those elements they find the most distasteful. It is a clever, yet extremely cynical strategy. For example, Reverend Wildmon radically edited David Wojnarowicz's intricate collages to further his own agenda. Wildmon excerpted small circles of pornographic images from Wojnarowicz's "Sex Series," blew them up, and then sent them to members of Congress and to his followers as evidence of the sort of decadent work produced under NEA auspices. This was grossly misleading and exploitative. The selections ranged from two to 16 percent of the total image, hardly a fair representation. In addition, in the artist's version their meaning emerged from their context. And finally, the small sizes of the circles prevented even the most savvy observer of the originals from accurately identifying what was being depicted much of the time. But in 1990, with portions of Congress and the public already in an uproar over so-called immoral art, this was a calculated attempt to fuel the fire. Even though Wojnarowicz prevailed in a lawsuit against Wildmon, it was the reverend's point of view which secured greater public attention.

Political progressives employ similar tactics. In 1979, a gigantic brouhaha erupted over an exhibit at Artists Space in New York. The work consisted of non-objective charcoal drawings and enlarged photographs. The point of contention was not the art but the title, "The Nigger Drawings." The show's critics pronounced the title racist—automatically equating a racist word with a racist intent—while they dismissed alternative interpretations ("the student as nigger," or a bid to define the sting of the epithet).

Something similar happened in 1981, when individuals, many of them populating the same theatrical terrain, rebuked The Wooster Group for its production of *Route 1 & 9*. It, too, was condemned as racist when white actors performed in blackface in two sections of this complex work. Never mind that the troupe was renowned for its anti-naturalistic casting, crossing and re-crossing gender, age, and racial lines. Once particular sections were separated out, they were judged as complete in and of themselves, rather than deriving their meaning from their interaction with the whole. In both these instances challengers put pressure upon governmental funding sources to punish these "transgressions," years before the notion of "politically correct" gained wide currency.

Distortion of the artist's intentions are inevitable when small portions of cultural expressions are intentionally isolated from the whole. Signifiers become free-floating, endowed with fresh meanings and thus subject to being pressed into totally new types of service.

Ideologues Assume a Paternalistic Attitude

Because they understand what's truth and what's desirable, they wish to dictate what's best for others. In 1991, college writing instructor Nancy Stumhofer successfully pressured the administration at the Schuylkill campus of Penn State University to remove a reproduction of Goya's renowned *Naked Maja* from the wall of the classroom in which she was teaching. Her rationale? It was a sexist depiction, its presence intimidated female students and made it difficult for her to professionally manage the class, and it was therefore a form of sexual harassment. Stumhofer stated her case in terms which patronized her students and appropriated power for herself. Unilaterally claiming that her students weren't interested in art, Stumhofer stated, "They're not going to come up and complain. You have to do it for them" (Karolyi). The instructor cloaked her expulsion of the image in virtuous terms: "I'm fighting for human rights, for the ability to have a classroom where all of my students are comfortable" (Karolyi). Is such a state of affairs obtainable? Desirable? Many would argue that the goal of education is exactly the opposite: to shake up preconceived notions and to cause discomfort. At the very least, the classroom should be the one setting where alternative opinions may be freely voiced, to be rejected only if they fail to meet standards of credibility, internal consistency, logic, etc.

Ideologues wear their oppression as a badge of honor. Persecution stings, and it provides credentials which are difficult to dispute or discount. How does one sensitively counter the opinions of victims of the Holocaust or of hate crimes, for instance? When Jews denounce productions of Shakespeare's *The Merchant of Venice,* Rainer Werner Fassbinder's *Garbage, The City of Death,* the stereotyping of the Jewish American Princess, or the lyrics of certain rap singers; or when gays protest persistently unflattering depictions of themselves in the movies, their perceptions are obviously shaped by authentic experiences. Unfortunately, at times the world view of some segments of these communities is so molded by their past injuries that they may blur the line between reasonable concern and excessive paranoia.

Ideologues Overestimate the Effects of Exposure to Cultural Expressions, and Assume the Effects to Be Immediate and Direct

Those on the political Right believe that many elements in contemporary culture are menacing, capable of contaminating pure minds. Reverend Wildmon discovers these dangers everywhere, evidenced from his concern that Mighty Mouse was giving youngsters lessons on how to snort cocaine to his authoritative appraisal of what he labels pornography: this stuff is so powerful you may be "hooked with one look" (Wildmon 154). What he fears most is imitation with no reflection, no mediation.

From time to time, those on the Left uncannily reflect the same sentiments. For some anti-pornography feminists, the motto is "Porn is the theory; rape the practice." In pragmatic terms this led prominent feminists to condemn Bret Easton Ellis's 1991 novel *American Psycho* as a guidebook on how to brutalize women. And gays similarly protested *Cruising* (1980), *Silence of the Lambs* (1991), and *Basic Instinct* (1992)—to the point of disrupting the shooting of these films on several occasions—fearing that each movie perpetuated negative stereotypes and could provoke actual violence toward gays. These reactions are understandable but facile. They reflect a search for a "quick fix" to complex problems, and disregard the historical and structural roots of discrimination and violence toward "the other." If eliminating violence were as uncomplicated as eradicating representations of it, a large part of the populace would undoubtedly support such a drive. Absolutists comfort themselves by seeking a magic-bullet-type solution. Yet their assumptions about society and the individual are simplistic and not very flattering. Humans are far more enigmatic than Pavlovian dogs.

Ideologues Possess a Sense of Apocalypse

Many of the issues ideologues struggle over may seem trivial, but to them, they are not. Absolutists clutch a *Weltanschauung* which perceives the forces of darkness and light coming to critical blows. Even minor skirmishes are part of escalating hostilities. For those on the Right, the threat is the cumulative effect of the changes which have come about since the '60s, with various civil rights movements insisting on greater inclusion into society. The demands of these entitlement efforts have reshaped how we lead our lives, and have shifted power from some groups to others to a certain degree. African Americans, women, gays and lesbians, Hispanics, "secular humanists," and other constituencies have forced society to recognize their respective rights and talents, causing more established groups to feel left behind or left out. If you sample writings from a variety of conservatives, an over-arching theme which unites them is the sense that America has been steadily sliding into a moral sewer since the '60s. "Decadent art," the way conservatives so often describe the expression of these newly enfranchised groups, puts additional nails in society's coffin.

The political Left has been the beneficiary of many of the transformations the political Right abhors. But where the Right sees too much change, the Left feels that there has not been enough. The Left experiences a revolution of rising expectations: change *has* come, but accompanied by an impatience to speed the process along. Its goal, then, is to wipe out residual traces of prejudice and discrimination as quickly as possible. In the hands of absolutists, this means trying to enforce tolerance by eliminating or altering a wide range of offensive, archaic symbols.

Consider the humble crayon. Binney and Smith, manufacturers of Crayola, decided to "retire" eight traditional colors in 1990 and replace them with eight vibrant new ones. They did not anticipate the public uproar they would elicit by such meddling: scores of disgruntled people complained, and at least three grass-roots movements were initiated to symbolically restore order. The most telling, CRAYON: the Committee to Re-establish All Your Old Norms. Binney and Smith quickly saw the error of its marketing ways, reviving the old colors in a 1991 commemorative tin. Chastened by this breach, they demonstrated that they are attuned to contemporary sensitivities by next issuing a series of multicultural products, including a pack of eight hues embodying the skin colors of a broad sample of people, supplanting the antiquated, all-purpose "flesh" of the past. The smart shopper can now likewise find "adhesive bandages of color."

These examples are humorous, although they betray greater concerns. Absolutists from each end of the political spectrum are primed to spring into action whenever they see their interests at stake. The most casual remark, the most benign piece of art, even a well- recognized masterpiece such as the *Naked Maja* can trigger a confrontation. Analogous to the fears of the Right that we are "going to hell in a hand basket" because of an acute moral decline—no prayers in school, legalized abortion, homosexual rights, and sex education, for example—absolutists of the Left see any attempts to moderate expression as a sure slide down the slippery slope of censorship.

Further, absolutists of the Left are particularly thin skinned, quick to be offended by what they experience as slights. Sambo—or his or her religious, ethnic, gender, or sexual equivalent—might be lurking just beneath the surface in many situations. Absolutists are poised to cleanse the environment of linguistic or visual pollution.

This pursuit can be pushed to the point of absurdity. One letter-to-the-editor writer to the now-defunct gay magazine *Outweek,* wearied by protests over *Silence of the Lambs,* penned a witty parody of the "party-line" mentality which threatens to put a stranglehold on artistic expression. His claim? The main sacrilege of the film is the stereotypical depiction of the killer's dog: "The character of Precious, as played by the poodle Darla, was a complete and total lie. Another in a long and shameless line of yapping, brainless creatures with pom-poms for hair . . . An intensely spiritual dog, sensitive yet sprightly in movement, the poodle remains one of the most maligned creatures in fiction and film" (Outweek 7).

Ideologues Wish to Impose Their Own Sense of Morality onto the Entire Public

Senator Jesse Helms (R-NC) has distinguished himself as one of the most relentless crusaders against contemporary art. He declared in his book *Where Free Men Shall Stand,* "Our political problems are nothing but our psychological and moral problems writ large" (Helms 11). When he views Robert Mapplethorpe's photograph *Embrace,* in which a white man and a black man tenderly hug one another, it is probably difficult for him to regard this type of affection in positive (or even neutral) terms. Rather than viewing this as an alternative, legitimate relationship, it is likely that he perceives a dual challenge to the bedrock of his own life: the norms of racial segregation and heterosexuality. What's merely different can be quickly recast as immoral and unacceptable.

Helms's counterparts on the progressive side are legion. Black aldermen in Chicago could not tolerate an extremely unflattering portrait of the late Mayor Harold Washington in a 1988 student show at the School of the Art Institute of Chicago. They had it "arrested" to foreclose the chance it might "spark a riot." African Americans have similarly censured *The Adventures of Huckleberry Finn, Show Boat,* an outdoor sculpture by David Hammons (*How Ya Like Me Now?*), and a post-Civil War obelisk in downtown New Orleans. In 1991, the female director of the National Museum of American Art attempted to remove Sol LeWitt's *Muybridge 1* (1964) from an exhibit because it suggested to her the voyeurism of a peep show, what she judged to be "a degrading pornographic experience" (Gamarekian 11). In 1988, AIDS activists demonstrated outside the Museum of Modern Art against the work of photographer Nicholas Nixon. They believed that his portraits of people with AIDS (PWAs) captured isolated and defeated individuals. They wished to substitute images of PWAs who are "vibrant, angry, loving, sexy, beautiful, acting up and fighting back" (ACT-UP).

In all these cases there was a rejection of the belief that viewers in a free society have a fundamental right to draw their own conclusions about what they see. At the very least, this requires that the public have access to a wide range of material. Yet this is a scary proposition for those engaged in a high-stakes battle for hearts and minds. Such preemptive, protective responses reveal deep insecurities about the strength of the moral stances certain advocates espouse, and their urgent need to shore up their defenses lest people be lured away from "the right path."

The Result of Ideologues at Work —
The Restraint of Expression and the Shredding of the Social Fabric

Intergroup relations in America are in a disturbingly fragmented state at present. Those on the extreme Right wish to bury their heads in the sands of the past. If they could they would force the genie of civil rights back into the bottle and restore the verities of yesteryear. But those on the extreme Left insist on an "in your face" posture, guaranteeing that their demands be addressed in some manner or another. Each side shares the sense of these being momentous times, with the very nature of their world at risk at virtually every turn.

Ideologues see everything in black and white. The nuance, contradiction, and complexity which characterize so much contemporary art are destined to trouble them. In fact, a basic property of most of the art which has generated controversy is the *mixture* of sacred and profane elements, blending ingredients which generally are kept apart. This is evident in Andres Serrano's photograph *Piss Christ*, where a plastic crucifix was submerged in the artist's urine. It is manifest in many of Robert Mapplethorpe's photographs, and in the work of many other gay as well as feminist artists, where the attributes of "maleness" and "femaleness" may be deconstructed, merged, and/or reconfigured, and a heterosexual erotic preference cannot be taken for granted. And it is apparent in the work of performance artists who smudge the line between public and private, self and other, decency and morality.

Whereas some viewers enjoy the *frission* created by these novel combinations (for them the thrill is in the sense of fresh possibilities), these same efforts may cause immense discomfort for the absolutist. What, for one person, signals a laudable burst of creativity at most, or silliness at the very least, for another sounds a warning about a world gone terribly awry. It is then that the absolutist frame of mind is activated, engendering the types of results I've enumerated in the examples I've cited.

As I stated in the beginning, we all experience the impulse to censor cultural expressions at some time or another. Simply put, everyone holds certain beliefs to be normal and dear, and we feel the need to safeguard them. We have the latent capacity to be paragons of tolerance or tyrannical censors, based upon our biographies, the range of our experiences dealing with different forms of culture, our mood on a particular day, and a variety of other factors. A critical element that regulates how far an individual glides toward the Comstockian end of the scale is the capability to be guided by your head, not just your heart, in these matters.

A final image exposes the erroneous mandate of ideologues who take on the pain of others, who wish to shield them from perilous situations and influences, and self-righteously act as their mouthpiece. Ellen James is an intriguing character in John Irving's novel *The World According to Garp*. She was brutally raped by two men when she was an 11-year-old orphan. They also cut out her tongue so she couldn't say who did it. A cadre of women then repeat the mutilation on themselves in solidarity with the victim; the Ellen Jamesians become a confederation of silent partners in protest of the brutality of men. Garp is eventually murdered by a Jamesian after he writes about them critically. But Ellen James herself adamantly rejects her self-styled champions. She defiantly writes, "I hate the Ellen Jamesians. I would never do this to myself. I want to talk; I want to say everything" (Irving 508).

In an era of polarization, suspicion, and the fatigue which results when so many groups constantly challenge the rights and responsibilities of one another, the most important thing we can do is increase the dialogue—about past injustices and victimization, yes, but also about innovative ways to heal the wounds and move on to reconstitute the society—not decrease the speech, nor try to obliterate the types of displays with which we don't agree. Whenever we act on someone else's behalf, with neither their counsel nor permission, we inevitably deprive the supposed beneficiary of considerable autonomy, while we also ravage the contours of the cultural landscape.

WORKS CITED

ACT-UP. "No More Pictures Without Context."

Cronin, Barry and Tom Gibbons. "600 Picket as Christ Film Opens." *Chicago Sun-Times*, August 13, 1988.

Gamarekian, Barbara. "Show Closing Demanded at Washington Museum." *New York Times*. May 13, 1991.

Helms, Jesse. *Where Free Men Shall Stand*. Grand Rapids, MI: Zondervan Publishing House, 1976.

Irving, John. *The World According to Garp*. New York: Pocket Books, 1979.

Karolyi, Anne. "Maja Rehung at Campus: Schuylkill Nude-Art Issue Gains National Attention." *Pottsville Republican* (PA). November 16, 1991.

Outweek. March 20, 1991.

Wildmon, Donald E. with Randall Nulton. *Don Wildmon: The Man the Networks Love to Hate*. Wildmore, KY: Bristol Books, 1989.

PLEASE PAY ATTENTION PLEASE

January 1995

One of my favorite recurring lines from the *I Love Lucy* show is when Lucy, after getting caught in the act of one of her many hair-brained schemes, is confronted by Ricky. Hands on hips and head cocked, he always looks at her and says, "Loooooooosssseeee! 'Splain it to me!"

Educational programming: or "splaining" contemporary art, as I like to call it, has a very conspicuous and heavy barge to tow: namely the crisis of the audience. To whom, about whom, and for whom works of art speak translates directly into the question of who the audience is. Just as much contemporary art is obsessed with the notion of the viewer and the function of interpretation, institutional activities similarly reflect identification of and relevance to the visual art audience, an issue that has reached a crisis point. Typically when such a crisis is identified by reflective institutions, the search for a solution is deflected to the education department, which tries to provide a meaningful experience for viewers by better linking the audience to the work scheduled for exhibition. Is this more or less of a challenge with work that carries widely variable meaning? What about art that, for many people, resists being art? Trying to answer these, among the many other questions that arise regarding the definition of meaning, using existing educational strategies for contemporary art is like using o baseball bat to dice on onion. You can get the job done . . . sort of. The who, what, when, where, why and how that make up conventional institutional wall text (currently education's primary tool) take on slightly different proportions when "what" returns as the word that kicks off the question, "What makes this art?" And if you have ever had to deal with that question seriously, then you know how easy it is to end up sounding even worse than a parent trying to explain the facts of life to on inquisitive five-year-old.

At The Renaissance Society of the University of Chicago, renowned by the international art community as one of the foremost contemporary art-exhibition laboratories and the reflective institution at which I have the honor of being the director of education, the mission is "to encourage the growth and understanding of contemporary art. Through exhibitions, publications, and educational programs, the Society promotes the work of artists and movements that question, redefine, and expand the aesthetic boundaries of the visual arts": the key words in this statement being "question" and "redefine." To engage an audience in this type of thoughtful play is somewhat different than education that addresses traditional art forms. Trying to explain to someone what makes 2,000 pounds of hard candy placed on the floor in a perfect rectangle by Felix Gonzalez-Torres a work of art is different from engaging curious viewers in a discussion about, for instance, Odilon Redon's iconography. Viewers are wary of investing their interpretive skills in something they are not sure is art. If it doesn't look like a sign, then why bother to read it?

To recoup a gesture as art is o defensive maneuver that blurs the functions of education with those of the legal department. The audience says "Prove to us that what you're offering is art," and like an Alan Dershowitz with a significantly smaller fee, the education department begins to build a defense for its artwork/client. To hell with brokering knowledge, the hunt for clues is on. This search scapegoats artists as the guilty parties—guilty of creating objects that need both explanation and defense. Artists are accused of being guilty of obfuscating issues rather than revealing hidden truths, (And the artists' pointy-headed critic friends make the worst witnesses, so they are never called to the stand for fear that the case will surely be lost.) If you are a really brilliant lawyer, however, you manage to have the case thrown out of court. You know that you cannot argue when the law favors answers over questions, clarity over complexity, and sureness over uncertainty. Justifying something as a work of art is beside the point. The point is to get people to use analytical and interpretive skills outside the gallery. The term "art education" is exposed as redundant and "art as education" becomes more clearly operative.

I recently attended a meeting of my institution's public relations committee. On the agenda was the issue of education and its liaison to PR, leading to questions such as "How can we expand the audience for contemporary art that nobody understands?" The answer: "By getting them to understand it." Toward that end, all the conventional means of dissemination were discussed; text and more text, docents, tour groups, banners, publications, handouts, videos, and audio tours. As it stands, there is no shortage of paraphernalia designed to make people feel more socially adjusted when standing before a work of art. I would argue that such a plethora confirms the notion that people need to be properly oriented, initiated, or marinated, breaded, and fried before they deal with art. Which came first, the chicken or Colonel Sanders?

Artwork needs first to be acknowledged as having the ability to communicate. There is no substitute for looking, looking, looking, and then looking again. If "Cliff Notes" constitute education, then meaning becomes a chilly set of fat "facts." What I sensed from the PR committee was that the work was somehow not communicating and education could somehow turn up the volume. Then people could get it. Get it. I realized those words were bothering me and that I wanted to substitute get it with experience it. The issues, however, had already grown too diffuse and to raise that point would only have complicated matters. I nodded in complicity that perhaps something could be done, but exactly. what I did not say. In my secret mind, my wishing mind, the wall text for every exhibition would read as follows:

PAY ATTENTION DAMMIT!
Thank you, now enjoy the show.

M A R Í A   J O S É   B A R A N D I A R Á N

. . . IN A PLACE LIKE THIS?

What's a Contemporary Show Like 'About Place—

Recent Art of the Americas' Doing at

the Art Institute of Chicago?

September 1995

        As a survey of contemporary art whose dates roughly coincided with those of the 1995 Whitney Biennial, "About Place: Recent Art of the Americas," at the Art Institute of Chicago, could hardly escape comparison on some levels with that much-anticipated New York show. Each exhibition was tightly commanded by a single curatorial hand and each included works by Jeff Wall, Brice Marden, and Andrea Zittel. But all similarities end there. By including artists from Argentina, Brazil, Canada, Chile, Colombia, Cuba, and the United States in its survey, the Art Institute leapt beyond the idea of "American Art" to "Art of the Americas," moving toward the more international focus of contemporary art centers such as the Pompidou in Paris, the Reina Sofia in Madrid, and the Dia Foundation in New York.

        "About Place" marks the revival, after a nine-year hiatus, of the Art Institute's "American Exhibition" series. Instituted in 1888, these surveys of contemporary American art took place every year or two and featured up to 58 American artists and 500 artworks at a time. Since the '50s, as the North-American art scene grew in productivity and gained international critical and commodity status, the exhibitions decreased in size and, presumably, became more selective. This tendency continued in

"About Place," the seventy-sixth "American Exhibition," which included only 16 artists and 51 works; and, in response to the new cultural and economic climate of the '90s, featured work from North, South, and Central America.

The central theme of the exhibition was a definition of "place" as metaphor for the convergence of time, location, and ideology: place as local history; place in the canon of art, in ethnic displacement, and in political upheaval; place as a center/periphery relationship; place as the destruction of nature; place as social project; place as the economic condition; place as the poetic journey in search of self. By the curatorial hand, as critic Dave Hickey eloquently describes in his contribution to the catalogue, place is replaced by time, geography is replaced by history (Hickey 54).

While curators are often accused of not having clear and well-formed agendas for the exhibitions they create, "About Place" curator Madeleine Grynsztejn, the museum's Associate Curator of Twentieth Century Painting and Sculpture, might have overplayed her own. Throughout the support materials (catalogue, pamphlets, guided tours, wall labels, and press

releases), each artwork's reference to place was carefully sliced open and eviscerated for the viewer's contemplation. Given Grynsztejn's claim that the organizing concept of "place" came *after* the selection of the work, in the process of mounting the exhibition the internal narratives of the individual works were replaced by the metaphor of place: be it home, city, shelter, the Apocalypse, a garden, the land of the free, cultural regionalism, the universe, or the mattress as "primal dwelling." The narratives and metaphors operating within the pieces themselves were finessed to become "about place." In most instances the poetic sensibility of Grynsztejn's vision, as elucidated with great eloquence in the catalogue, complements and compliments the work, while in a few it becomes a case of the Emperor's new clothes. For Andrea Zittel's "perfect living units" (self-contained, hyper-efficient, portable interiors), for example, the issue of place—or, more accurately, lack of space in urban apartments—is not a metaphor, but a necessity, which the work addresses. On the other hand, applying a concept of "place" to Jeff Wall's Cibachromes, which mimic both commercial photography and European painting, amounts to little more than a strategy enlisted to impose theory on an aesthetic style that can barely reflect the splendor of Wall's original sources. The drama of two men fighting in an alley in *Fight on the Sidewalk* combined with the intellectual satisfaction of recognizing its Caravaggesque chiaroscuro effect still pales in comparison to that of advertising's perfect fictions.

In other artists' oeuvres, the concept/metaphor of place is historical, at times almost illustrative. There were two "Airmail Paintings" by Eugenio Dittborn in the exhibition: *Airmail Painting No. 95: The 13th History of the Human Face (The Portals of H.)* and *Airmail Painting No. 113: On la Grande Jatte, Final Version of a Sunday.* Dittborn started making these lightweight paintings and photo-silkscreens on non-woven fabrics as a cost-effective way of traveling his work the enormous distances between his home in Chile and the cities where he was invited to exhibit. The pieces are constructed in panels with grommet holes for efficient hanging, then individually folded and mailed in custom-made envelopes inscribed with sequential information about the travels and travails of each piece. All the works include reproductions of images of Chile and each painting contains images of its respective destination; *No. 113*, created for the Art Institute show, has reproductions of Seurat's *La Grande Jatte*, one of the museum's most famous holdings, and *No. 95*, which originally traveled to Antwerp, includes the image of a painting by Pieter Bruegel the Elder. Despite *No. 113s* potential local appeal, *No. 95* is the more compelling of the two: the relation between *Dulle Griet (Mad Meg)* returning from hell and an armadillo, some thieves, a handful of Ona women, and a toy boat creates a multi-layered narrative of colonialism, psychology, and religion that fully occupies—not metaphorically, but historically—the distance from Punta Arenas, Chile to Antwerp, Belgium. On the other hand, *No. 113* does not: Dittborn's images from the War of the Pacific (a border dispute between Chile, Peru, and Bolivia)—beyond the superficial irony that the dispute took place within a few years of Seurat's painting *La Grande Jatte*—fail to travel the distance between Africa, Chile and Chicago via Paris. Seurat's portrayal of Paris during the summer of 1884 has been superseded by its value as property of the museum. From Chicago, the cultural and historical distances remain unimaginable. On the opposite wall, though, the women of *No. 95*, Mad Meg and "La Guagua," have met at the edge of hell and shared heavy glances in the struggle for survival.

In the same room stood Jac Leirner's air-travel sculpture. Leirner "collects" flatware, blankets, luggage tickets, etc. during her travels and uses them as sculptural materials. The recycling of these objects, the refuse of modern transportation, into sculpture whimsically comments on the excesses of our economy. Though the process of collecting the airline paraphernalia is expensive and time consuming, that it can be done at all reveals the underside of the economic structure, evoking the growing landfills of disposable wares. This same excess in *Todos os Cem (All the one hundreds)*, a circular band of 80,000 outdated Brazilian bank notes winding across the museum floor, seems not all that extraordinary, though Brazilian inflationary rates, which quickly render currency worthless, may seem rather grotesque to Americans. While Leirner's sculptures are laden with these rather humorous commentaries on economics, the forks and spoons could be as easily replaced with common art materials, returning the form to more "traditional" art, unfazed by the consciousness of its own making yet still inscribed with the economic value of its production and circulation. "Place" in Leirner's art is equivocal: on a superficial level it might have come about as a result of traveling from São Paulo to other art-world centers, or as a reflection on the condition of the Brazilian economy, or from the subversive use of ordinary materials to make high art. While the work fulfills this laundry list of "place" metaphors, it most poignantly reveals the boundaries of the art world. As opposed to the comforting irony of Brice Marden's inclusion as the representative of New York-style painting for "About Place" (in an attempt to circumscribe modernism to an illusory provinciality), the sophistication of Leirner's work points out that art exists through more complex systems of experience than is accounted for by art history.

Leonardo Drew's *Number 43* also straddles a fine line between economics and aesthetics, but rather than being humorous and scandalous, his work is poetic and heroic. *Number 43* is a huge wall of wood boxes filled with rusting scraps of metal, hair, and cotton fibers. They look like remnants of a household-items manufacturing plant abandoned in the dawn of the industrial revolution; the workers are now dispersed and the natural elements have settled in to reclaim their piece of land. The installation is a metaphor for the labor of African Americans, as slaves in agriculture and as workers in urban factories: the tiniest nuances of the handling and "rusting" of the materials by the artist silently bear witness to the labor and suffering, the wanting and longing of a people. These socio-economic references are subtly inscribed in the fiber and structure of the piece, but it is its monumental scale, reminiscent of that of Anselm Kiefer's best work, that embodies melancholic abandonment.

Doris Salcedo's work strains to balance the particular beauty possible in art with the political concerns of historical painting and sculpture. The

"Atrabiliarios (Defiant)" series are 37 niches containing shoes, closed off with translucent animal intestinal fiber. The shoes belong to persons (in this particular installation, only women) who have been "disappeared" in Colombia: kidnapped, arrested, and possibly murdered in the violent struggles for land and power. While the obscured shoes painfully evoke the absence of the women, another series by Salcedo, "Casa Viuda," dramatically stages the forced evacuation of peasants and villagers from their homes by drug lords and *latifundistas:* the absence of its inhabitants literally collapses the spiritual meaning of the home, and the psychic fall-out of the terror renders it uninhabitable—whether in Colombia, Bosnia, or Kurdistan. Salcedo has been harshly criticized for using the pain of these families for her own gain—the oppressed are her own "other" and she exploits them for the sake of art. Some feel her work is too beautiful to be political, while others perceive the references to Colombia's political violence as irrelevant to the aesthetic experience. This is, I believe, a wonderful starting point for a constructive argument on the possibilities of political art beyond the conventions of historical painting or social realism. It is the beauty of the object itself that evokes in us, as viewers, a sentiment of loss and longing for what has been violated, for the terrible tragedy of losing something—somebody—intimate and unique. It is to the degree to which Salcedo's work etches itself in our memory that our political consciousness about Colombia changes, that we might understand better the human cost of producing bananas, coffee, and cocaine.

In both Drew's and Salcedo's work the singular histories, the individual names of the people whose pain is being evoked have been ultimately erased by the artist's aesthetic manipulation. Felix Gonzalez-Torres's work, represented here by *Untitled (America, dimmed for now),* uses similar strategies of symbolic representation, but his choice of materials—in this case, ordinary light bulbs—further sublimates or abstracts the relation of the subject to its condition, obliterating the emotional source. On the other hand, Larry Johnson heightens the personal experience through verbal narratives—egocentric fantasies in *Untitled (Winter Me),* muttered rage in *Untitled (Admit Nothing)*—to the point of their becoming everybody's words, regardless of the tightly codified gay, L.A. aesthetic. A similar "environmentalist" aesthetic is at work in Rodney Graham's photographs of inverted cedar trees, and more reflective in *Millennial Project for an Urban Plaza (with Cappuccino Bar).* To borrow Johnson's words, these artists' works are "realistically philosophical, poignantly cynical, and at times, hilarious" utopias, revelations, indictments (Johnson). Distilled of seductive engagement, the works might be reduced to signifiers of the aesthetic moment rather than of the events that inspire them.

It seems only proper that an exhibition which covers art practice from Montreal to Santiago would have as it *pièce de résistance* a local artist, that he would be a painter, and that he would say things like: "I was thinking to myself what would it be like if Matisse would have had a social consciousness" (Marshall). Kerry James Marshall's paintings of Chicago housing projects function within the city in ways similar to church frescoes in fourteenth-century Italy: not only are there enthralling similarities to the work of Duccio and Giotto in the treatment of figures and architecture, but it is the ideological significance of making pictures that the paintings rejuvenate. The characters are restrained in emotion and possess moral definition, actors in a nascent social order. Black Power, urbanity, industry, civil rights; fields of subsistence will be gardens of delight, public housing will be homes. The project gone awry is symbolized by the "nuked" vegetation that doesn't grow but stains the image of urban bliss. In an exhibition of sublimated obsessions and subdued passions, the audacity of Marshall's painting and the fortitude of his characters infuse Chicago with unexpected beauty and illuminated realism.

Ann Hamilton's *volumen* and Barbara Steinman's *Objects and Instruments* installations were disappointing, maybe because the ambitions and expectations that the scale of the works themselves demanded weren't met. While Steinman operates in reductive equivalences (object = idea), Hamilton's work uses excessive amounts of simple materials (floors covered in horse hair or pennies, stacks of shirts, gallons of honey, tons of tulip bulbs, and, in *volumen,* hundreds of yards of gossamer fabric hanging from a revolving, circular track) for metaphorical investigations of labor and Protestantism. Here, however, her Herculean efforts revealed only the inadequacies of the art machine to solve "real" problems, since the museum couldn't get the mechanical ceiling track to rotate consistently.

Vija Celmins's exquisite paintings of skies, webs, water surfaces, and desert floors are empty, seemingly lifeless pictures of "abstraction with representation." (Grynsztejn 28). Painted from photographs, the tireless details entrance our eyes unto the surface; we wake up maybe thinking we have seen nothing but an endless repetition of the universe. The certainty of reality—a place photographed and faithfully reproduced with brushstrokes on a canvas—fulfills the need—the expectation—for the locus of the spirit. Addressing the underlying content of her work, Celmins quotes Czeslaw Milosz: "Imagination can fashion a homeland," a statement Grynsztejn has attempted to equate throughout the exhibition with "art-making can fashion a place" (Grynsztejn 28). But what kind of place?

To different degrees, all the artists of "About Place" subscribe to what Dave Hickey calls a "post-Minimalist aesthetic," but it is also true that since colonial times Euro-North American trends have shaped the character of art in all of the Americas: as Matta, Rivera, Syzlo, Cuevas, Bravo, Tamayo, Lam, etc., worked from an European tradition. That center has shifted to New York City, where all the Latin American artists in the exhibition have commercial gallery representation. Grynsztejn nullified the possible political controversies of mounting a contemporary art survey by choosing not only works of compelling beauty, but works that intimately subscribe to the contemporary discourse. The cultural limitations of this discourse are evident, for example, with regard to Guillermo Kuitca's work: while he is not counted as a "white male" by American art critics, a forthcoming global vision of art and art history will offer new critical understanding of a piece like *San Juan de la Cruz*. One of Kuitca's mattress paintings, it shows a map of Poland, the land of Kuitca's ancestors, but the names of the major cities have been replaced with the fictitious name of San Juan de la Cruz. Alongside the aesthetic and theoretical fictions of "primal dwellings" and "truthfulness of human experience," there are cultural and historical issues in each Latin American country's art that remain uncharted. But as things stand now, if geography has indeed "subsumed history," as Hickey concludes, and "cultural urbanity" is permeated by a "mysterious anxiety," I am tempted to take Hickey's analysis a step further and say that aesthetics has subsumed culture. Too bad there wasn't any sex (Hickey 57).

The conceptual ambitions of "About Place" compare qualitatively to the Pompidou's "Les Magiciens de la Terre" and more recently, the Centro Reina Sofia's "Cocido y Crudo," exhibitions that, even if more politically autonomous than biennials, are no less controversial. Crossing the geographical *and* political borders of the United States might not mean crossing aesthetic borders, but this could be a limitation of the framework of large institutions, restrained by scholarship and economic interests. The cultural and thematic scope of "About Place" made it a very contemporary exhibition: whether it is or is not an "authentic" view of the North- and Latin-American art scene is beyond the grasp of one survey, but it was an impressive effort from an otherwise conservative museum. Between the scheduled Caillebotte and Monet exhibitions, the "place" that opened up the most was the Art Institute of Chicago.

WORKS CITED

Grynsztejn, Madeleine. *About Place: Recent Art of the Americas,* exhibition catalogue. 1995. p. 28.
Hickey, Dave. "A New World Every Day." *About Place: Recent Art of the Americas,* exhibition catalogue. 1995. pp. 54, 57.
Johnson, Larry. *Untitled (Classically Tragic Story).* 1991.
Marshall, Kerry James. "About Place: Recent Art of the Americas." 1995.

JEFF HUEBNER

BIGGER, BETTER, FASTER, MORE?

Chicago's New And Improved MCA

May 1996

With all the anticipatory hoopla, speculative press, and swelling drum rolls, it's easy to lose sight of a significant fact: Chicago will finally have a Museum, a building actually *meant* as a Museum, a Museum built specifically to house and display Contemporary Art. It will no longer be the museum founded essentially as a *kunsthalle*, a temporary exhibition hall, in a renovated office building nearly 29 years ago; it will no longer be a small place on a side street, a structure that had originally been built as a bakery and later served as the corporate offices for Playboy Enterprises. This is now something serious, something with institutional gravitas. Something that says: not only will we be a major player; we always have been.

"The new facility will do a great job of putting Chicago in a national context for contemporary art," says Kevin E. Consey, director and chief executive officer of the Museum of Contemporary Art (MCA) since 1989. "In the past we were at the margins of the international dialogue, and now we'll be in the middle. But we can't be all things to all people. We can't single- handedly solve a broad range of systemic social problems, or cause a resuscitation of the art market. But we can make contemporary art interesting, provocative, and appealing, emotionally and intellectually, to a broad range of people."

Whether or not one likes the "poetically rational" (as Berlin architect Josef Paul Kleihues calls it) limestone building fronting a street named Mies van der Rohe Way—is it too rational, too Miesian, or not poetic, not funky, enough?—most Chicagoans will agree that the new MCA is a spectacular advancement over the previous Ontario Street facility. When the long-awaited new building and sculpture garden, in the planning stages for a decade, formally opens to the public July 2 (following a Summer Solstice Celebration Weekend public preview in June), Chicago will finally get the spacious, stellar institution it has long deserved.

The new $46.5-million MCA, located in an urban canyon off East Chicago Avenue on a two-acre, lake-facing site previously occupied by the Illinois National Guard Armory, will encompass a total of 220,000 square feet, almost seven times the size of the previous facility. This, of course, will enable the museum to exponentially expand its exhibition and educational programming; for the first time since its founding in 1967, the MCA will be able to mount temporary exhibitions *and* show works from its 7,000-piece permanent collection at the same time.

There will be four times as much gallery space: two main, second-floor, "aircraft hangar"-size temporary exhibition galleries (5,800 square feet apiece); a third-floor gallery for video and media arts; and, on the fourth floor, four top-lit barrel- vaulted galleries for the permanent collection, three smaller suites suitable for exhibiting works on paper, and another space for the "Projects" series, which will feature solo exhibitions of new work by emerging artists. In addition to the 34,000- square-foot, terraced, outdoor sculpture garden, the building will have a museum store, a café, a special-events area, and an orientation gallery. Beatrice Cummings Mayer gave $7.5 million to establish the Mayer Education Center, which will include a 300-seat auditorium, classrooms, an art library, and a 100-seat space for lectures, symposia, films, performances, and conferences.

During the course of our recent conversation, Consey kept referring to the new MCA as a center of "contemporary culture." After a tour of the building, it soon became evident why: the museum won't simply be a place with art on the walls (or on the floor or in a garden), but a true cultural locus—perhaps even a type of community center, a place to meet, hang, discourse. It's really a straight-up but stunningly conceived public space: at no point do you feel that the interior (or exterior) design is compromising your ability to view art. Kleihues wanted to make a building in harmony with Chicago's pragmatic architectural spirit ("the naked concentration of the task at hand"), yet at the same time have it embody qualities of serenity, simplicity, openness, transparency, reserve. (While the 32-stair grand ceremonial entrance may evoke the notion of a Temple of Art, cynics may scoff at Kleihues's comparison of the MCA's floor plan to that of Louis Sullivan's Carson Pirie Scott & Co. building on State Street, a Temple of Commerce if there ever was one.)

Clearly, the new MCA will, conceptually and structurally speaking, join the ranks of the Big Leagues: it's the little museum that could—and did. The $37 million contributed by the board of trustees (toward an original fund-raising campaign goal of $55 million) certainly played a vital role. Set off amid a rich urban mix—high-rise rental residences, condominiums, hotels, offices, the Water Tower Place, the North Michigan Avenue retail district—the museum, Consey has commented, "has the potential to be enmeshed in the city's life."

But, psychologically speaking, there may be just as much at stake here. While Chicagoans interested in—and committed to—contemporary art have every right to feel smugly boosterish about the gleaming new institution, to what extent *will* the new MCA's offerings enmesh in the city's artistic and intellectual life, and contribute to the cultural dialogue locally—and beyond? How will it enhance or help legitimize Chicago's (and, potentially, Chicago artists') position in the art world at large? Can it work toward palliating Chicago's persistent Second City Complex— i.e., prevent the "paint drain" to New York? Does bigger always mean better? Does new necessarily mean improved?

The consensus among a number of Chicago visual-arts professionals— artists, dealers, curators, critics, collectors, educators—is that the new MCA unequivocally portends to be a positive force for the city and its art community. Some, however, express a more cautious sense of optimism regarding its overall vision, exhibitions programming, and its responsiveness—and responsibility—to the local "scene," as well as to emerging art currents (though the two shouldn't be seen as mutually exclusive). This is perhaps not an entirely unexpected attitude. As Wesley Kimler, a Chicago painter who had a solo exhibition at the MCA last fall, puts it: "The nature of Chicago is that a lot of people will find a way to tear the new museum down. Everybody's going to find something to complain about."

The museum will be in a "shakedown phase" for a while before it can really begin concentrating on programming, points out Dennis Adrian, art critic and art history professor at the School of the Art Institute of Chicago. "We'll have to wait and see what happens while the nuts and bolts are being tightened. But I don't see how [the new building] could not but help. More people will be able to see more things. How can that be bad?"

"It's not at all just that with the new building the MCA has the opportunity to be an international museum with an international profile," states Madeleine Grynsztejn, acting department head of the Art Institute of Chicago's Department of Twentieth Century Painting and Sculpture, "but rather that the building is now commensurate with its longstanding international programming. It was just a matter of the building catching up with the museum and its tremendously important history of programming."

Susanne Ghez, director of the Renaissance Society at the University of Chicago for 22 years, says, "It's wonderful and healthy for the city. It's a privilege to have such a great space. They now have a terrific team, and an outstanding leader in Kevin Consey, who has brought on smart and energetic curators. There's a good chance that [the MCA] will provide excitement and energy in the city." Citing a thriving young gallery scene, and recent exhibits such as the Art Institute's "About Place: Recent Art of the Americas," curated by Grynsztejn, as well as a plethora of exhibition spaces—the University of Illinois-Chicago School of Art and Design's Gallery 400, the Chicago Cultural Center, and the Renaissance Society itself—specializing in creative, national-caliber programming, Ghez says, "institutionally, it's a good moment in Chicago."

"Chicago has changed," notes Carol Becker, dean of faculty and interim president of the School of the Art Institute of Chicago. "It's no longer the industrial center it once was. It's become a service-sector city. It's also become a center of art and culture. But Chicago itself hasn't digested or ingested the idea that it has become much more like New York. It's never been articulated. I think that the MCA will hold that up as a mirror when it opens. It's going to bring a lot of people from the contemporary art world here, and they're going to find a truly cosmopolitan city. Then they're going to begin to understand that Chicago takes itself as a leader in art and culture more seriously."

"It's an amazing achievement being able to open a museum in a time of budget cutbacks," she adds. "People should celebrate that first, and then there could be discussions about what it represents later. I think it's going to be thrilling."

James Yood, an art critic and professor of art theory and history at Northwestern University, had been less than thrilled with the MCA in the past; he was often critical of the museum's exhibition programming in the'80s. "I didn't see eye-to-eye with its curatorial vision, and I found a lot of it uninteresting," he says. "I'd ask myself: 'Is the MCA showing the most interesting things in town this month?' No, it wasn't. Now they've gotten a little bit better. They've had good programming for five or six years now. They haven't been a player on the national scene, but [the new building] provides a platform for them to make a national splash. They should just do superb programming, and try to keep a finger on the pulse of what's going on."

Although the MCA has never ignored Chicago-area artists, it has frequently been criticized for not being regionally inclusive enough, for not keeping a focused enough eye on its own backyard. But many people involved in the local arts community feel that those now "running the show" have, on the whole, been taking a more proactive interest in what's going on around town than did previous curatorial staffs. Beginning in 1994, a series of one-person exhibits of artists living and working in Chicago was featured: Jeanne Dunning, Wesley Kimler, Jim Lutes, Dan Peterman, Kay Rosen, Vincent Shine, and Hollis Sigler have all been represented. Tony Tasset's work was shown as a companion to a recent Robert Smithson exhibition.

The MCA's current curatorial lineup includes: Richard Francis, the chief curator who's organizing the inaugural exhibition "Negotiating Rapture: The Power of Art to Transform Lives"; special projects curator Lynne Warren, who's working on the sure-to-be-controversial "Art in Chicago: 1945–1995," opening in November; curator of collections Lucinda Barnes, organizing the long-term "In the Shadow of Storms: Art of the Postwar Era from the MCA Collection"; and "Projects" manager and temporary-exhibitions curator Amada Cruz, who's putting together the interactive "Performance Anxiety" installation exhibit scheduled for 1997.

"I don't think they were giving the community its due at a time when it would've been more exciting and relevant, like when someone first hits and makes their mark," says Joel Leib, director of the up- and-coming Ten In One Gallery. "Now they're making up ground. [Before], they might wait a couple years until someone in another city gives [the artist] credibility so they wouldn't feel they were making a mistake by giving the artist an exhibition opportunity. My gut feeling now is that the new curators trust their own convictions more—not because they have to fulfill obligations or placate local artists, but because they see them as having a significant place in the art scene. I think that the new curators realize that a number of Chicago artists certainly stack up to artists nationally and internationally."

Leib was one of a multitude of local arts people invited to a series of five MCA-hosted community round tables throughout 1995 to freely discuss issues and concerns in preparation for "Art in Chicago."

Out of these meetings, guidelines and criteria were generated to aid in the research process, to set the parameters for the exhibition and catalogue, and to develop educational programming. "It's a good start, but it doesn't mean it won't continue," he says. "They've made a good foothold now, and they should continue to work at involving the arts community. The museum has to give artists the option that it's cool to be in Chicago."

The MCA is in the position to do that now, says Becker, because it literally "ups the ante" for local artists, many of whom have historically felt a "residual anger" at the museum because it didn't give them enough national exposure. "There have been some expectations that the museum would be showing Chicago artists all the time, which is an unreasonable expectation," she says. "When an artist reaches a certain level in his or her career, there hasn't been a next level to go to in Chicago, like there has been in Los Angeles. An artist at a successful mid-career level stops showing here because there's not a next level. Hopefully, [the new MCA] will provide that, and keep people in Chicago."

But will the MCA have the resources to take the work of Chicago artists on the road? The museum, as Yood points out, did not organize many traveling art exhibitions during the '80s, much less one that disseminated the local art community to the rest of the country. "I care about seeing Chicago artists in Chicago," he says, "but I also care about seeing Chicago artists in New York or L.A." The museum is committed to making strides in that direction: After its MCA debut, "Performance Anxiety" will travel to other institutions across the country.

Paul Gray, 13-year director of the 33-year-old Richard Gray Gallery, however, feels that the museum's exhibitions should remain in Chicago. "Then that makes the MCA a destination around the world, a place you can see original and unique programming you can't see anywhere else." He also says that "in the last six or seven years, the board of trustees and staff have been headed in the right direction, with a strong focus on the community and the art community at large. No longer can they be accused of being an elitist organization—something which is guided and influenced by a relatively small group of people."

Paul Klein, longtime director of Klein Artworks, however, believes that the MCA isn't doing enough. He thinks that if the museum cultivated a more symbiotic relationship with local artists, galleries, collectors, and other art venues, it could help contribute to an even more vital Chicago art scene—a reciprocity that would create an energy.

"The MCA has a reputation—earned or unearned—for being too elitist, and that's dangerous," Klein comments. "They've always had an incredible amount of potential, but they still need to do a better job of being more accountable and available to the public. With more space, maybe they'll be able to do that. Someone once asked George Burns what the secret to acting was. 'Sincerity,' he said. 'If you can fake that, you got it made.' Well, these people need to act like they care more, they need to seem sincere. They don't make enough studio and gallery visits, they don't have a visible enough presence in the art scene. They need to hone or develop their public image more."

Klein has tried to put his money where his mouth is. In recent years, he has, without attribution or fanfare, contributed funds to the MCA that went toward the publication of local artists' exhibition catalogues. Beginning two years ago, he met with curator Francis a number of times about the possibility of establishing a separate "Chicago Room" in the museum's completed quarters, a temporary exhibition space reserved for showing only local artists' work. The idea was considered but ultimately rejected. "They told me that Chicago artists do not want to be defined by their regionalism, that Chicago artists just want to be artists," Klein says. He doesn't totally disagree with this viewpoint. But, he says, "You've got to take care of your own. If you want a strong community, you've got to give something back to it."

Which brings up a cogent point: To what extent should the new MCA—or, for that matter, any large regional arts institution with the capability of exerting a national or even international taste- shaping influence (one thinks of the Walker Art Center in Minneapolis and the Hirshhorn Museum in Washington, D.C., for example, as well as recently completed facilities in San Francisco and Seattle)—be responsible for showcasing and promoting homegrown talent without appearing to patronize or "tokenize" local work?

This is an especially sensitive—and, for local curators, a conceivably tricky—issue in Chicago. This city has historically suffered from a "provincialized" mindset, an urban springboard from which many artists make the leap to New York, which potentially offers not only increased chances to show and to make connections and money, but also greatly enhanced opportunities to make a bigger art-world splash.

"Local artists are never going to be happy," states Kathy Halbreich, director of the Walker Art Center in Minneapolis, which has earned an estimable reputation for its world-class programming. "But a curatorial team has to be conscious of supporting the local ecosystem, and partnering with community organizations. It's important for an art museum to be deeply rooted in its local community as well as internationally—not in a mutually exclusive way but interdependently." While Halbreich says that it's "unusual for geographic shows to have any legs on the circuit," she mentions the Ed Paschke and Martin Puryear exhibits at the Art Institute of Chicago, each organized by former AIC contemporary curator Neal Benezra (now at the Hirshhorn), as examples of successful touring shows. But these were "extremely established" artists, she says, deserving of "broader focus."

States Grynsztejn, who succeeded Benezra at the Art Institute: "I think that local artists' inclusion in exhibitions should be based on the same criteria that would apply to artists living elsewhere, and to do otherwise is to the disadvantage of both the artists and the museum." She cites the inclusion of Chicago artists such as Kerry James Marshall in the "About Place" exhibition, for example, "because their work more than meets the criterion of great art, and it pays them the respect they deserve as serious artists."

"Even if everything is being done, there will be the perception that not a lot is being done," says Adrian, the accredited historian of the so-called Imagist Movement, which helped elevate Chicago—and a number of Chicago artists—to national prominence in the '60s and '70s. "Right now, the MCA can't be accused of ignoring local art, they've never shied away from it. An actor who doesn't get a part thinks the theatrical world is terrible and insensitive. Some people will always be left out. Sometimes things aren't shown because they aren't any good."

Tony Tasset, a UIC sculpture professor, feels that the MCA has the responsibility to exhibit local artists, but he also fears it could parochialize artists in the long run: The museum should treat them the same way it treats everybody else it shows. "But sometimes they don't treat them exactly the same," he says. "The way they should do that is treat them as they would any international artist, which, sometimes, I don't think they do." Then again, he says, "It's an impossible task."

Indeed. Though wearied from having to juggle several different job descriptions in recent years, museum director Kevin Consey is exhilarated to finally be settled in his new space: The MCA, he says, is now occupied territory. But from the circumspect nature of Consey's comments, it's clear he's given a great deal of thought to the museum's role in assimilating and dispersing "highly sophisticated visual culture," as well as to issues of local accountability. He likens the MCA to an import-export business.

"Visual art in the '90s is increasingly global," he says. "Ideas and visual imagery are traveling at an extraordinarily fast clip, and are absorbed and recontextualized in various cultures and put back in international culture. We want to bring ideas to the Chicago public and hopefully change their lives. But we also have something to export—to send visual imagery created by artists in this city to other parts of the world, [meaning that] local creative talent starts getting into the international exchange of ideas. There are a multiplicity of artists in this city, without question, creating work of international importance, and we're perfectly happy about presenting them as part of our exhibitions and collections.

"The experience of coming to the MCA shouldn't be different than going to the MOCA [in Los Angeles]. If you're a knowledgeable contemporary-art person and you went to a Los Angeles museum, you'd be disappointed if you didn't see [L.A. artists]. Similarly, if you spent time at the MCA and didn't see work by Jeanne Dunning, Ed Paschke, or Richard Hunt, you'd have to ask 'What does this place have to do with Chicago?' Part of the game here is to think about Chicago in the same way as Zürich, Milan, and Moscow. What is compelling and unique about Chicago? What does Chicago have in common with the rest of the world? An institutional agenda should be global in scope, but that's not to say there isn't sufficient talent and creativity in Chicago. But we'll not limit our talent to Chicago."

The new MCA's history dates back to March 1986, when nine trustees committed $5 million as seed money for the building of a new museum. The following year, the MCA submitted a proposal to the State of Illinois, after a task force appointed by then-governor James Thompson recommended the demolition of the Armory that stood on the site the new building occupies. In 1988, the State of Illinois awarded the MCA a 99-year, $1-per-year lease for the site, in exchange for a Near South Side warehouse. Chaired by MCA trustee and deputy chairman Jerome Stone, the Chicago Contemporary Campaign—the effort to fund, endow, and operate the MCA's new facility—was launched in June 1989, with the goal of raising $55 million. The museum's plans received a vote of confidence later in the year when the John D. and Catherine T. MacArthur Foundation awarded a $2-million grant to the MCA.

When Consey assumed leadership of the MCA in 1989, he organized the search for an architect. Kleihues was awarded the MCA commission in March 1991, and his conceptual design for the new building and sculpture garden was approved by the board in December. After "Art at the Armory: Occupied Territory" transformed the armory into a temporary art museum featuring 18 installations, the military facility was demolished. Groundbreaking for the new MCA was held in November 1993, and construction—funded through state-issued tax-exempt revenue bonds—began in April 1994. The old MCA (on the block for $4 million with a contract with Film and Tape Works, Inc. pending at press time) was closed for good on February 4, 1996.

The Chicago Contemporary Campaign exceeded its $55-million fundraising goal earlier this year. Given this huge endowment, to what degree will the MCA have to "mainstream" its mission, blunt the cutting-edge? Aside from the adventurous "Projects" series, how may the concept of "institutional risk-taking" be limited, if at all? As Chris Murray, director of MWMWM Gallery, who recently moved to New York, puts it: "It's not about ideas, but money. The economy of the whole thing dictates it to be benign. The dialogue is dictated by a handful of well-off people who are happy being driven by suburban culture."

Consey replies: "The type of art and ideas we deal with will be, by definition, disturbing to some people. It makes no sense to abandon our mission of delivering interesting, provocative new art; if we abandoned that, what would we be?" He mentions the 1989 Mapplethorpe and the recent Serrano exhibits, neither of which created a stir in Chicago. "It won't be necessary for us to sacrifice the edge. People should have certain expectations that they[1] re going to be challenged and provoked and experience a full range of emotions—from joy and beauty to pain and anguish."

One of the motivating factors in planning for the new museum was to make room for future donated collections and exhibition acquisitions. Since a number of MCA board members are major art collectors, they—as well as other area collectors—will now almost certainly be spurred to give more generously. The MCA's holdings include not only seminal works by such Chicago artists as Leon Golub, H.C. Westermann, June Leaf, and Paschke, but in-depth collections by such '60s and 70s Minimalist and Conceptual artists as Donald Judd, Sol LeWitt, Bruce Nauman, and Robert Smithson. There are also a number of key Surrealist works, Alexander Calder sculptures, and works by such '80s artists as Jeff Koons and Cindy Sherman. In addition, the MCA owns 3,000 artists' books.

"Nobody donated as extensively as they could have because [the MCA] didn't have space," says trustee Lewis Manilow, past board president (1976–81) and a prominent collector who has donated a number of works to the museum. "But now we'll be able to get far, far better pieces.

As the collection grows and grows, people will want to have their best things be a part of it. Once people see these beautiful upstairs galleries, they'll say, 'I want my major pictures in there.'"

Since the building cost more than $46 million, that leaves (at this point) $9 or $10 million in the MCA's coffers. Consey says that new art museums can expect a 30-percent drop-off in attendance after the first year, but he believes consistently strong programming will keep people coming again and again. More than just the turnstiles need to be turned, however, in order for the MCA to stay healthy—and relevant.

"The big immediate issue is whether there's enough money to fully program the museum right away, whether it'll get off to a good start," says Dr. John Hallmark Neff, director of the art program at First Chicago-NBD Bank and former MCA director (1978–84). "The hope is that people will be as enthusiastic about raising money for the operating program as they have been about the bricks and mortar. I hope the enthusiasm doesn't end with the dedication, and that the board will be able to use the enthusiasm of the event to enlist very sophisticated kinds of donors required for program endowments. Things are so difficult around the world, and any museum that has [money for programming] has an immediate leg up, and is in a primary position to let the staff do its function."

Particularly important, adds Neff, is the extent to which the new museum will be able to use its financial support to invest in its curatorial staff. "They need to be tended and taken care of," he says. "Curators should be seen as community resources, and they need time to develop. You want to do everything you can to help those people thrive personally and professionally. They need to travel, do research, and bring things back to Chicago. The world is waiting for institutions to have a vision, and if [curators] are given the resources they need to be venturesome and creative, then the world will sit up and take notice."

The whole world—or at least the whole art world in Chicago—will be watching when "Art in Chicago: 1945–1995" opens at the MCA in November. By that time, curator Lynne Warren, with the help of three full-time assistants, will have worked for five years on the project, the first exhibition to offer a comprehensive, historical survey of art-making in Chicago. Warren began her curatorial tenure under Neff—16 years ago.

Warren seems to possess the requisite amount of seasoned fortitude for the daunting task at hand. Think about it: Of the 100,000 or so artists who have lived and worked in Chicago since 1945, the decade-segmented exhibit will bring together about 200 works made by about 150 artists. Do you think for a Chicago minute that Warren's (and the MCA's) judgments won't provide grist for the critical mill? While she's aware of the exhibition's potentially politicized, damned-if-you-do- damned-if-you-don't hazards—rumors of who's in and who isn't are already circulating around town—Warren would much rather discuss the challenges and surprises inherent in the creation of such an exhibit, as well as the many stereotypical notions about Chicago art and artists that it will attempt to dispel.

Warren finds it ironic that for a city which has long defined itself in contrast to New York and Europe—as if our artists could only imitate or react to trends—Chicago art practice has actually been a lot more pioneering than even constituents of its visual arts community want to give it credit for. Chicago has historically (but not exclusively) been engaged in a socially and politically motivated art that's now embraced by the international art world, for example. While not ignorant of developments elsewhere, Chicago artists have evolved autonomously mainly because they had to rely on their own resources. And Warren says she didn't have to reach to include women artists and artists of color in the show: As a city with a history of social activism, a city of ethnic neighborhoods, Chicago has always had them.

So: The Second City Complex? Warren thinks the whole idea is greatly overstated. "Chicago really has this chip on its shoulder," she says. "To many people, the idea of being marginalized in the 'Second City' is more important than the factual reality. Chicago is so close to being a vital, exciting art center like New York, and Chicago can't taste it enough. As people look toward greener pastures, they don't see the green pastures around them. I hope that [the exhibition] brings out that elusive quality of civic pride. People have it in spades in other arenas, but they don't think it's cool when it comes to art. Artists have this complex, strange thing about the city. When you talk about civic pride in the art context, it's 'Let's get out of town and go to New York.'"

And that, perhaps, may be the new MCA's paramount message: New York? Don't even think about it.

ON VIEW

Chicago

May 1995

Sunday, February 4, 3:30–5:00 p.m., Museum of Contemporary Art

We begin with an ending, the day the MCA closes its Ontario Street operation to the public in preparation to move to its new ·Mies van der Rohe Way digs in June. Serving toxic-looking cake spray-painted with the mostly black museum logo, the employees wear nostalgic smiles, and take turns getting photographed pointing at their names painted on the mural at the museum's entrance.

A friend and I climb the stairs to view the museum's photographic history of itself. The exhibit amounts to an architectural version of a PR brochure, but sports some documentary gems—snazzy, blue-haired visitors attending one of the inaugural programs in '67, my hero Charlotte Moorman decked out in her TV bra, and this little pat on the back tacked up next to a self-portrait from the infamous Mapplethorpe show: "A lightning rod of controversy at other venues, the exhibition passed without incident at the MCA, where it set records for attendance."

Walking back down to the first floor, I say goodbye to the grating hum of the Max Neuhaus sound installation in the stairwell, not that I'll miss it. Neither it nor the tiny Charles Simonds cliff dwellings built into the basement bookstore wall will be making the trip to the new building.

After a sarcastic while spent with the Andres Serrano photographs downstairs—their slick, saturated colors and simple, perfect compositions remind me of nothing so much as a series of Benetton spreads—a friend and I sit in the lobby until close. I tell a polite guard that we're just waiting around to be kicked out and she complies, locking the door behind us without fanfare.

Monday, February 5, 4:06–4:38 p.m., Alan Cohen,
"Indelible Traces," Chicago Cultural Center

We call silver-gelatin prints "black and white," but these photographs are the color of ash. Focusing solely on the ground of concentration camps, Alan Cohen articulates a psychohistory spoken by ruts in the mud, crumbling concrete, scattered cobblestones, and creeping plants.

Outside, a Michigan Avenue bus pulls up, reflected into the grass at Bergen-Belsen. People get off and walk around it, through it, stomping all over the loneliest cigarette butt in the world. And, breaking my contemplation, a boorish man in the gallery says (loudly) to his wife (or at least the woman he calls "honey"), "You know what this reminds me of? When you're loading your camera and it accidentally goes off. He's got a whole year of sidewalks in here." And what sidewalks—intersections of nature and culture gracious in their very simplicity.

Tuesday, February 6, 1:08–3:34 p.m.,
Chez Jon Langford, Logan Square

The Leonardo of Leeds slides an old Hank Williams record out of its sleeve and puts on a song called "On No Joe," a curious indictment of Joseph Stalin. Jon Langford, guitarist for the beloved British punk diehards the Mekons, hands me his engraving that shares the song's title—a double portrait of the country crooner pointing his finger at the dictator, both of them enveloped by a garland of disjointed letters spelling "WE LIV E IN 2 D IFF F ER E NT W OR LD S."

I flip through frame after frame of lovely, allegorical effigies sanctifying the stars of country music. For example, a bare-chested Hank pierced by arrows becomes Saint Sebastian. Even though Langford printed these images last year, they feel as old and weary as a Carter Family dirge, making the good white paper they emboss dislocating; the timeless stories being told, of hard life and early death, call for brittle, yellowed newsprint.

A piece titled *Hank Signs His Contract* offers a remember-death skull, perched on a desk, staring out of a Dutch still-life set-up rife with morality. A slit-eyed, cigar-smoking angel in suit and tie witnesses the pact, a country-blues Faust update that is, like a long, high Hank moan, charming and gloomy at the same time, reminding me of Woody Guthrie's warning: "Some kill you with a six gun/And some with a fountain pen."

Wednesday, February 7, 1:00–4:00 p.m., Art Institute of Chicago

I take the students in two first-year art-history discussion sections I teach at the School of the Art Institute to the museum. While they're upstairs in the Impressionist galleries nervously racking their brains for something to say about Seurat and Degas (I give them 20 minutes to prepare short presentations), I go down to the gift shop to do some research among the Haystack coffee mugs and Caillebotte umbrellas. I plan to write a museum merchandise parody of H.W. Janson's classic art-history text. My title: *A History of Art As Illustrated By Meaningless Crap*. The sequel: *Lives of the Artists As Seen In Embarrassing Films*. Then I go back upstairs and plow through a history of art as spoken by talented teenagers who would rather be somewhere else.

Thursday, February 8, 5:00 p.m., John Buck lecture, University of Illinois-Chicago School of Architecture

Maybe it's just the crowd I hang with, but it's been a while (try never) since I heard an actual human being call himself a "profiteer" as a term of auto-endearment. The notorious local developer John Buck's most recent claim to fame is ripping down the entire 600 block of North Michigan Avenue to construct a mega-mall. Addressing the UIC School of Architecture, he adds "dreamer," "orchestrator," and "risk-taker" to his why-I-like-me list.

He clicks through a slide show of his architectural accomplishments (first image: his corporate logo)—big office buildings by Kenzo Tange and Philip Johnson, as well as the Sears Tower, which his company manages. He concludes with a rendering of the future 600 block (conceding that it has "not been without controversy"), a hideous, 300,000-square-foot, Block- buster-meets-Pompidou monstrosity that looks like some kind of robotic turtle.

When asked to defend his destruction of historic neighborhoods—he hopes to erase the McGraw-Hill building next—he responds that neither the McGraw-Hill nor any structure at 600 (including the Arts Club's Mies interior) was listed on the historic register, to which a frazzled woman in the audience who works for the register replies that they were eligible, and are/were on waiting lists, it's just that her office is understaffed and unable to keep up with applications.

I'm unsure why it is that we (and I'm just as guilty as anyone) celebrate the old brick charm of the monuments to early twentieth-century capitalism and denigrate the efforts of its recent glass-and-steel will to power. Maybe it's that the old warhorses—however grand—retain a sense of human scale. And those are two words that John "Profiteer" Buck might roll around his gold-plated tongue.

Friday, February 8, 7:30 p.m., Jo Carol Pierce at Schuba's

Performing the songs and stories from her wise and hilarious album *Bad Girls Upset By the Truth* (including the "Borderline Tango," which, she points out, happens to be a waltz), the Lubbock-born, middle-aged Jo Carol Pierce wears the frilly pink frock of a Texas prom queen. She recounts a Panhandle coming-of-age epic haunted by sex, mental illness, and religion, sometimes brilliantly confusing the three. Her words are dressed up in a seductive vernacular twang that almost undermines the profundity of her poetry. Almost. In the days and weeks after I first heard her record, I began having little Jo Carol epiphanies—on the bus, in the grocery store—sudden moments of satori in which a joke or an observation finally hit me in the forehead with the shock of recognition. Listening to her gritty laugh live only confirms my suspicions: Pierce is, like the country-music heroes Langford represents, a genius disguised as an ordinary woman.

Saturday, February 9, 2:30 p.m., N.A.M.E. Gallery, "15th Annual St. Valentine's Day Exhibition"

This multi-artist hodge-podge acts as a two-week preview to a benefit auction for this well-loved nonprofit space. There's only one thing the wildly diverse artists—from Yoko Ono to Buzz Spector—have in common: their generosity. Sometimes, that's more than enough.

JAN ESTEP EDITOR

1979–1982

A DAY IN THE LIFE

Editing and Writing for the New Art Examiner

Working as an editor at the *New Art Examiner* profoundly affected the course my life has taken, in terms of my knowledge base, art experience and, most significantly for me, my writing. It extended my art-world education in a way that would have been impossible to do on my own, putting me in daily contact with contemporary art at all points on the spectrum. From the behind-the-scenes view of a museum curator preparing a major exhibition to one-on-one interviews with visiting artists to the stealth street intervention around the corner, art editors along with critics in general have access to art events that greatly facilitates their ability to discern and discover the terrain. Though their approach is shaped by personal interests and background, all editors are concerned with information gathering, absorption and distillation. To do this well, they need to be always learning, looking and reading, open to what the world and artists have to show.

The other large part of being an editor concerns language and writing, as this forms the day-in/day-out substance of the profession. Paramount is a genuine love for art and the conversations it generates. I joined the magazine in 1997, the summer after I earned my MFA, fresh from the wringer of the studio arts program at the University of Illinois at Chicago (UIC). Primed by that curriculum, which followed years of studying and teaching academic philosophy, I found editing a natural occupation. The faculty at UIC introduced me to contemporary art and showed that it was far vaster and more complex than a neophyte might presume, Their expectation that art be more than personal self-expression attuned me to the broader significance of what artists do. In comparison, philosophy gave me a thorough understanding of argument and the process of putting ideas and thoughts into words as well as an appreciation for clarity. These two tracks of art and philosophy would prove invaluable for running an arts magazine and for working with—and in many instances training—individuals devoted to art writing.

A typical day at the office started with a round of correspondence, checking in with writers and skimming press announcements. The office was in a grungy basement space of a small building tucked directly under the El, one block north of Chicago Avenue in the River Loop District. Each day also included a morning meeting among the editors to coordinate our efforts and prioritize tasks, and occasionally a trip to see an exhibition or do an interview.

We also periodically devoted time writing grant applications to various public and private institutions that supported nonprofit arts organizations, which we were qualified for, and planning our yearly fundraisers for the magazine. However, the bulk of the day was spent reading and editing texts at various stages of readiness for print. In many ways editing is a desk job, routinely reading manuscripts and marking up texts for revision and writer approval. Working on a deadline and managing the workflow and production cycle call for practical skills, while finessing content requires more erudite leanings. There was always more work to do than one could plan for, incredible stress at the close of each issue and never enough money, but the opportunity to shape the content of the magazine was extremely rewarding.

While I was at *NAE* we made a concerted effort to situate Chicago within a national and increasingly international art-world context and also add a more philosophical perspective in the way we wrote about art and ideas. We also increased the number of first-person interviews with local artists and those coming through town for major exhibitions and expanded the geographical coverage of the Reviews sections. We did this while continuing to showcase what was special about Chicago:

the humor, the DIY spaces that continually crop up run by Chicago's never-ending supply of recent MFA students, and the burgeoning social-practices movement developing in the city (before they were even called "social practices"). Our approach reflected a desire to be understood for our independence and uniqueness but also to be respected by and included in the larger professional art world.

During my tenure at *NAE* we always had three editors—Editor, Senior/ Associate Editor, and Assistant Editor. I came on board as a part-time assistant editor working alongside Kathryn Hixson as Editor and Ann Wiens as Senior Editor. I graduated to a full-time associate editor in 1998 when Wiens left, and for my—and the magazine's—last two years was the full-time senior editor. Each position had primary responsibility for specific feature essays, exhibition and book reviews, and sundry regular sections such as the Newsbriefs and Scenes. Though each of us took the lead on specific texts, we worked as a team: all of us read everything before it was handed over to design and again in proof pages.

The proofing stage is fairly straightforward; by that point you are mainly looking for misspelled words, incorrect punctuation, dropped text and bad line breaks. The earlier editing of the writing submissions is the tricky part, both on the level of ideas and on the more personal level of dealing with the writer. The magazine rarely accepted anything sent to us on speculation, but writers were free to pitch ideas and exhibition reviews in advance and we also assigned features and reviews.

Each year the entire staff, which in addition to the three editors included a business manager, an advertising manager, an in-house de-signer (we sent our features to an outside design firm for layout) and our interns, would gather for an editorial summit, to develop themes for the upcoming year. Some of my favorites were Slummin' (November 1997), Painting and Performance (September 1998), Art and Public (April 1999), Appropriation (July August 1999), Heavy Emotion (September 1999), Play (October 1999), Animal Behavior (March 2001), our annual Education issues and our entire last volume: Midwesterness (May June 2001), Authenticity (July August 2001), Flat (September October 2001), Fear and Loathing (November December 2001), Talk (January February 2002), Social (March April 2002) and The Built World (May June 2002). We'd then send the list out to our writers with a request for submission proposals and also solicit specific essays directly from people we thought would do a good job with the topic. The exhibition reviews of current shows were divided into regions—Chicago, New York, Los Angeles, the

Midwest, and the rest of the country—and were not tied to the themes. Those too came about through a mix of writers' suggestions and editorial requests.

The primary editor of any given piece handled all communication with the writer. She did the first read of the original text and once it passed through the hands of the other editors it was her job to consolidate our comments into a singular, manageable response and send these to the writer. If the original copy was a bit of a mess and warranted it, the primary editor also did a "hard edit," working with the writer on the text before passing it over to the other editors for inspection. It was always a treat to receive submissions that needed little from us. These were well written and accessible, expressed a consistent voice, and shed new light on the topic or artist(s) discussed. Editors become accustomed to immersing themselves in the writing, sussing out the main through-lines and tone of the text, looking for contradictions and redundancy, anticipating points of confusion and distraction on the reader's behalf. When that editorial instinct to intervene doesn't kick in and one can simply be a reader rather than an editor, the job is relatively simple; just double check for house-style and grammar rules, and send to press.

Of course, as writing is such a difficult endeavor no matter how natural it appears when done well, we received our fair share of texts that needed far more editorial intervention. Sometimes it was a matter of writer laziness or presuming too much knowledge on the part of the reader: the points weren't connected very well, transitions were skipped, key terms or names were left undefined, and/or not enough historical or cultural context was given to anchor the argument. Sometimes it was necessary to reorganize the flow of the writer's thoughts, cutting and pasting sections in a different order and expanding where necessary to make more sense. These kinds of editorial requests, sent back to the writer, were fairly easy to address.

The hardest edits, those that require serious revision, are both the most challenging and the most rewarding. Given enough trust between editor and writer, most writers appreciate constructive criticism and feedback. But it can be hard when a writer gets defensive or thinks too highly of his or her own first impressions, which makes the writer unwilling to dive back into the text and make changes. This kind of rigid response was rare at the magazine, but when it happened it was as emotionally fraught as any sort of interpersonal conflict.

I write as someone who operates on both sides of the editor/writer relationship. While I was at the magazine training on the job as an arts editor I also became a writer, joining many other artists and critics who started their writing careers at the *New Art Examiner*. For me, one of the most significant accomplishments of the magazine was its support of quality arts writing and the mentoring of new arts writers. While we published experienced academic scholars such as Henry Giroux, Donald Kuspit, Susan Canning and Jennie Klein, and well-known art critics like Eleanor Heartney, Terry R. Meyers, Jan Tumlir and Polly Ullrich, we also created opportunities for newer and younger folks to enter the field. Fresh with their new art degrees in hand, Nato Thompson, Jenni Sorkin and Lori Waxman wrote some of their earliest pieces for *NAE* and have all gone on to become prolific writers and art-world regulars. I know in my case the writing-specific feedback and tutoring I received from the other editors whose tenures overlapped with mine—Hixson, Wiens, Kathryn Rosenfeld, Franklin Cason and Tony Neuhoff—all helped shape the writer I've become.

The magazine was especially friendly to artist-writers—David Robbins, Michelle Grabner, Nicholas Frank, Dan S. Wang, Matthew Girson, Mark Van Proyen and Shana Lutker, among many, many others. Artists who write make the connection between the two creative processes while also understanding that art and arts writing need each other. Every vital art community has this means of discourse and feedback.

However, this mutual dependence has its limits as to what it can accomplish. Eager to expand our impact even further, during the last volume of the magazine we grew the sponsorship and Board, in the process securing a generous but one-time investment by Lew Manilow, one of Chicago's premier art collectors. This allowed us to increase the business staff to help with further fundraising and also to initiate a redesign by Jason Pickleman of JNL Graphics, which along with stylistic changes included a larger page-size, higher page count and more color. However, unfortunately for us, we grew the magazine at exactly the wrong moment economically. Without continued external financing, and with nonprofit funding diminishing and the stock market falling, the magazine found itself in over its head and we could not sustain the higher costs the expansion entailed. The last six months at the magazine involved a slow, painful and inevitable entropic slip into chaos, as the magazine virtually imploded under the pressure.

Under the circumstances, it is a testament to our love of art and commitment to the magazine that the last volume reads and looks as good as it does. Some of our best work was done in terms of content and quality of the writing, and the magazine itself looks absolutely beautiful. And for the last issues we did this with a reduced staff and for no pay.

Since leaving the magazine and Chicago and moving to Minneapolis, where I now teach at the University of Minnesota, I have gotten over the upheaval and frustration of the last year at the magazine. I now view the experience of those last months as an incredible learning opportunity and choose to focus on all the good that occurred there: the high of putting an issue to bed and seeing the first copy in print, the nervous excitement of interviewing someone I admired artistically, the camaraderie among the staff, and the great fortune of having work that was both intellectually and creatively fulfilling. Working as an editor and writer for the *New Art Examiner,* I was surrounded by people who believe in art, and was thus able to cultivate an indelible sense that art is important. This belief is crucial given the myriad reasons to doubt art's social place and the economic obstacles facing most artists today, not to mention the curious infighting that occasionally flares up.

On this note I want to close by recalling my editorial published in the last issue of the magazine, which came out in May 2002. Regarding the issue's theme, The Built World, I began by ruminating on the idea of "nothing" and continued to describe the generative impulse artists have to create something out of nothing. Rereading the words today I am reminded of the incredible optimism of the creative fields and the remarkable feat writers and artists accomplish when given the space and context to do so. Though they come and go, outlets like the *New Art Examiner* provide such a place.

—Jan Estep

HENRY A. GIROUX

HEROIN CHIC, TRENDY AESTHETICS,
AND THE POLITICS OF PATHOLOGY

November 1997

Introduction

"It is the fear of what Jean Baudrillard calls simulations without referents, a Disneyland society in
which unanchored desires float from object to object
at the dictate of consumer capitalism. The body in
such a society loses its material reality; pain ceases
to be a teacher, and pleasure is degraded to mere
stimulation."[1]

In the Postmodern world described by Jean Baudrillard, daily life
consists of an endless series of simulations that lack any concrete referents.
Disneyland becomes a model for a sanitized society purged of politics, a
society in which representations become increasingly homogenized and
cease to be read critically as part of a broader strategy of understanding, struggle, and intervention.[3] In this Postmodern media-scape, images
bombard the senses, identities become transparent and one-dimensional,
space and time collapse and displace traditional understandings of place
and history, and concrete reality slips into a virtual society where "there is
more and more information, and less and less meaning."

Postmodern culture has become less a mode of cultural criticism
than a political and social condition marked by the rise of the national

entertainment state and the spread of corporate culture into every facet of life.[4] The concentration of apparatuses of cultural production, organization, and distribution in fewer and fewer hands undermines the possibility of culture as a dynamic zone of contention, an active public space prompting dialogue, dissent, and critical engagement. Culture becomes instead a commercial public sphere marked by the emergence, if not the triumph of stylized and superficial forms. Within such a society, "the social turns itself into advertising and . . . all current forms of activity tend toward advertising and most exhaust themselves therein."[5] As the social is emptied of all political and ethical referents, the tension between entertainment and politics becomes blurred, just as the relationship between art and commerce becomes less controversial.

It would be comforting to believe that Baudrillard's world of simulations exists simply as an arcane theoretical discourse endlessly replayed at academic conferences or Las Vegas retreats.[6] But the logic of the simulation—with its indifference to the distinction between representations of reality and actual experiences—operates in a variety of public spheres through which the social imaginary is redefined and reproduced within a commercial logic that renounces all claims to politics, moral compassion, and the obligations of public life. In such a society, art and commerce increasingly combine to package identities, commodity bodies, and organize desires to the dictates of the market. Creativity is given free reign as long as it sells goods, rather than connecting artistic transgression with political resistance or democratic struggle. As culture is increasingly corporatized, artists and other cultural workers can comfortably mortgage themselves to the logic of late capitalism and engage the larger society as public-relations intellectuals rather than as agents of social responsibility. For instance, film directors such as Francis Ford Coppola and Ridley Scott surrender their critical sensibilities and *auteur* status to work for corporate giants such as Disney, producing films that dissolve politics into either white-bread comedy or high-octane, military machismo (i.e., *Jack* and *G.I. Jane*). Numerous contemporary artists have followed in Andy Warhol's footsteps, using their talents to produce ads for Absolut Vodka.[7] Similarly, Benetton displays its ads in various galleries and employs a variety of actors and artists to either endorse or work for the company. Besides blurring the line between culture and society, they purge artistic production of any ethical referent while reaffirming the victory of capital over compassion: social responsibility loses out to "show me the money."

In a Postmodern world in which the focus of the "capitalist economy since the 1920s shifted from production to consumption,"[8] culture is more than commodified; it is emptied of resistance as critical reflection gives way to the reified image of the spectacle. Failing to discern between reality as a fact and reality as a possibility, between a morality committed to addressing forms of oppression and a representative politics in which oppression, suffering, and despair are translated into a stylized aesthetic, the commodified cultural realm demonstrates an apocalyptic emptiness. As the machineries of cultural pedagogy extend beyond the school into the largely corporate-controlled, electronically based media of communication, the realities of personal experience and collective memory are transformed into a "cartoon utopia" dressed up as entertainment.[9]

Within such a representational politics, commerce emerges as the bearer of a "refreshing" kind of art—a new form of cultural production with the aesthetic as its most important organizing principle. Culture and commodity become indistinguishable and social identities are shaped almost exclusively, within the ideology of consumerism. This is particularly clear in the way in which fashion designers such as Calvin Klein have used talented photographers, like Steven Meisel and Richard Avedon to recast or reframe indignation and resistance as no more than an attachment to a perfume, pair of jeans, shirt, or "something as distant, as decorative, as an alligator."[10]

The representational politics and relations of power that connect art and commerce veil how the operations of power work to produce a public sphere in which identities are shaped, values learned, and social relations legitimated. Of course, this is an issue that many artists, cultural critics, and social theorists have begun to explore in the second half of the twentieth century. What is new is not the intersection of art and commerce, but the degree to which in this intersection, as exemplified by "heroin chic," politics dissolves into pathology: I refer to an exclusively aesthetic sensibility in which the experiences of drug addiction and poverty become simply representations linking the emotionally charged stimulus of the spectacle to the free-floating desires of consumer capitalism. Within such a representational politics, aesthetic sensibility replaces any vestige of a moral sensibility, while simultaneously restricting the public space and sense of agency offered to young people and others. But the aesthetic of heroin chic legitimates not only a cynical disdain for human suffering, it also functions as a retro-aesthetic in which subcultural politics—however nihilistic and pathological—provide the new frontier for making profits. Transgression in this instance either reproduces uncritically or sanctions what Carol Becker has called "manifestations of psychic unhealth-malaise, racism, hypocrisy, despair."[11]

In what follows, I want to argue that the emergence of the heroin chic controversy in the popular press offers an important example of how art and commerce intersect to rewrite the politics of transgression as a domesticated mode of address designed to produce a consuming, rather than a critical, social subject. Not only does the heroin chic controversy reveal how transgression is purged of any semblance of political resistance, it demonstrates how such "transgression" becomes domesticated and complicitous by positioning its audience as voyeurs who can pleasurably consume prevailing sexist, racist, and class-specific stereotypes about youth and women. Richard Sennett signals the domestication of resistance by arguing that "the politics of transgression envisions a resistance to the norms of the dominant society which does nothing to change the social rules themselves. And even at best, the discourse of transgression evokes a familiar cultural trope: freedom as the mentality of alienation."[12]

I also want to argue that the "new art" of heroin chic in fashion photography points to a politics of representation that must be understood in relation to the current right-wing assault on working-class youth and women. Heroin chic does more than maximize the pleasure of viewing by glamorizing the aesthetics of cultural slumming, it also reinforces a cynicism that permeates large sections of the public sector in which the bodies of youth and women are no longer viewed within the privileged space of possibility. Bodies anorexic, physically abused, and paralyzed from substance abuse— such stylized representations do not evoke sympathy or compassion, but work largely to reinforce our image of youth as symbols of violence, crime, and social disorder and women as sexualized commodities.

Finally, I want to propose that the emergence of a society marked by an ever increasing commodification and homogeneity of culture does not and should not suggest that political resistance is meaningless. On the contrary, the sites of political struggle, as well as the strategies employed by progressive cultural workers, must be rethought and seized upon within new forms of struggle and resistance. Domination is never total in its effects; contradictions arise within all public spaces, even those that appear to be the most oppressive. While such a recognition in and of itself does not change anything, it is a precondition for pedagogical and political work that deepens our understanding of the role artists and other cultural workers might play, alone and collectively, as part of a broader attempt to revitalize democratic public life.

Heroin and the Politics of Popular Culture

"I saw the best minds of my generation destroyed by madness, starving hysterical naked, dragging themselves through the negro streets at dawn looking for an angry fix."—Allen Ginsberg, "Howl," 1956

"I've seen the needle and the damage done/A little part of it in everyone/But every junkie's like a setting sun."—Neil Young, *The Needle and the Damage Done*, 1972

The highs and lows of heroin use and addiction have a long legacy in popular culture and mass media. A lineage stretching from William Burroughs and Lou Reed to the Sex Pistols and the Rolling Stones gives heroin use a drug-cult status that extends from the '50s to the present. The drug's bohemian image was amplified as well as tempered by the deaths of such rock stars as Janis Joplin, Jimi Hendrix, and Jerry Garcia, along with the deaths of Hollywood actors such as John Belushi and River Phoenix. Grunge rockers find both an idol and a tragic example of heroin use in Kurt Cobain. But rock also produced an endless array of heroin survivors, such as the members of Aerosmith, who provided gruesome confessionals about addiction and abuse. Ironically, such confessionals seemed to testify to heroin's rising appeal to middle-class kids by suggesting that one could do the drug over long periods of time and still survive, thus undermining the equation of junk and death. The longevity of Patti Smith, Marianne Faithfull, Iggy Pop, and Keith Richards make them icons of junk culture, revered because of their personal journeys through the ultimate anti-establishment ritual.

Hollywood has offered its celluloid version of heroin's rhythms in films such as *Drugstore Cowboy* and *Pulp Fiction*. *Trainspotting*, one of the most controversial films to deal with heroin in the '90s, spearheaded its advertising campaign with the memorable line: "Take the best orgasm you ever had. Multiply it by a thousand. You're still nowhere near it." But drug films such as *Trainspotting* and *Gridlock'd* also show the downside of heroin addiction. In the art world, Nan Goldin produced numerous photographs chronicling the ups and downs of her friends' habits, addictions, and deaths in the '70s and '80s. The representational politics of junk culture before the '90s not only posited itself at the outpost of bohemian culture, it also paid lip service to creating or inhabiting new oppositional spaces where identity, place, and pleasure could be released from the demands of the dominant society.

There is no single narrative that does justice to the complexity of heroin use among a generation of bohemians and other outlaw subcultures that populated the cultural landscape of marginalized urban haunts before the rise of heroin chic in the '90s. Yet, I do think it is possible to suggest that the legacy of the '60s offered rationales for heroin use in which experience did not disassociate itself from meaning as much as it rushed headlong into a search for transcendence in which meaning and affect were redefined as part of a journey beyond middle-class norms and values. When not prompted by the social gravity of poverty and human suffering, heroin use found its rationale among intellectuals, artists, and other marginal groups not within the confines of fashion, but as a dead-end politics that weighed existential freedom against a potentially self-destructive act. The romance of heroin use was never that far removed from the recognition of the "damage done" and the lives it destroyed.

In the '90s, heroin re-emerged and became the drug of choice for members of the upper middle class who did not want to compromise their power or advantaged social positions, but wanted to escape from the boredom of their lives by appropriating the accouterments of a junk culture that romanticized the dangers and risks associated with the dispossessed and poor. Appearing as the ultimate form of transgression, heroin use in the mid-'90s became a cultural signifier among the rich, famous, and the trendy for combining the cool posture of alienation and the chilling willingness to appropriate what was considered the outlaw fashion accessory.[13] What is often left out of this narrative is that heroin has also become increasingly popular among young, middle-class kinds, especially high-schoolers and older teens.[14]

> Heroin Chic offers an important example of how art and commerce intersect to rewrite the politics of transgression as a domesticated mode of address designed to produce a consuming, rather than a critical, social subject.

Current heroin use has to be understood not just as the dangerous posturing of the bored and curious, but also as a symbol of the despair and pessimism that increasingly characterize a generations of young people for whom adult society appears to be not only morally indifferent, but vindictive. Seen as both troubled and troubling, youth appear as a burden, if not a threat, to public life. Deindustrialization, downsizing, and the dismantling of the welfare state have created fundamentally new realities for young people: a future of dead-end jobs, few social benefits, and the menacing image of a state composed of apparatuses of surveillance and containment. Under such circumstances, many young people find it difficult to embrace the future with either a science of hope or possibility.[15] Within this historical conjecture, heroin offers and allure difference from its romanticized image among intellectual and cultural renegades in the past. Ann Powers succinctly captures a sense of the social malaise many young people feel and hot it fosters an attraction for heroin. She writes:

> In the '90s, far from representing the carelessness of Generation Slack, heroin us surrounded by a strange seriousness—unlike the coke scene, this drug culture advertises its dangers as prominently as its pleasures, with a pessimism that must appeal to young people who have come to expect most satisfactions to carry their own layer of disaster. Its connection to AIDS drives home the message, it's not really possible to be casual, heroin says. It's not really sensible to feel free . . . As if so many promises—those offered and then betrayed by their ex-hippie parents, those contained within the faltering myth of the consumerist ideal, those seemingly their by right of hopeful youth, but poised at conception with a divided cynical, polluted world—had left these kids still starving. So they become seduced by the hunger, finding something that offers a way to be driven and aimless at the same time.[16]

Although the reasons behind heroin use among young people are complex, the simple reality is that heroin-related death rose significantly in 17 out of 25 major United States cites between 1991 and 1994. Moreover, according to Ginna Marston, vice president of the Partnership for a Drug Free America, "heroin use among . . . 8th-, 10th-, and 12th-graders, is on the increase . . . [and] the number of 12th-graders experimenting with heroin rose from 22,500 in 1991 to 40,000 in 1995."[17]

It is against the contradictory and complex legacy of heroin use as well as the changing context of its availability and its increasing use by middle-class professionals and young people that the use of heroin chic can be understood and analyzed in both aesthetic and political terms. Once heroin chic became an object of national attention, the underlying conditions that produce heroin use and the complicity of fashion advertising and art in legitimating junkie culture became part of a broader public discourse. Unfortunately, what was missing from this discourse were serious analyses regarding the limits that should be respected around the intersection of art and commerce, as well as any public debate about how heroin chic resonated with attacks in the media and a number of other public spheres on young people—especially minority and working-class youth—who are increasingly seen as the course of society's social problems. Underlying these concerns is the important issue, raised but largely ignored in the heroin chic debate, regarding the forces at work in a society (and not merely the fashion industry that reproduces a notion of the aesthetic that is predicated on moral indifference and a cynical disregards for social responsibility.

> The heroin chic crowd reduces representations of human suffering to a privatized, trendy aesthetic that defines the living present outside of a context of struggle, passion and hope.

The Public Politics of "Heroin Chic"

> "You do not need to glamorize addiction to sell clothes."—**President Bill Clinton, May 21, 1997**

On May 20, 1997, *The New York Times* ran a font-page story in which it reported on the heroin-related death of a 20-year-old fashion photographer Davide Sorrenti. The article also rebuked fashion-magazine editors and photographers for glamorizing what it called the "strung-out heroin look," and it charged that Sorrenti's death reflected wide-spread heroin use among young people working in the fashion industry. In effect, the articles charged that the fashion industry not only glamorized heroin use as an advertising gimmick, it was complicitous with, if not responsible for, promoting and condoning heroin use within its own ranks.

The following day, in a speech before 35 mayors from across the United States, President Clinton made "heroin chic" a household phrase by criticizing the fashion industry for glamorizing the use of the drug. Clinton asserted that fashion photography had sent the wrong message to the American public by making heroin appear "glamorous, sexy, and cool." More to the point, the President raised questions about the roles art plays in shaping public opinion and the dress to which it need to take responsibility for the consequences of its actions. Clinton challenged the assumption that the intersection of art and commerce can be understood exclusively in either the language of aesthetics or the language of profit margins. Accusing the fashion industry of being politically and morally remiss, Clinton made clear that the industry had over-stepped its freedoms and exercised its power in a way that was unethical and destructive. He summed up his critique by reminding the fashion industry that "The glorification of heroin is not creative. It's destructive. It's not beautiful, it's ugly. And this is not about art, it's about life and death."[18]

The photography to which Clinton referred had appeared in a wide range of fashion magazines, television ads, and fashion shows in the last few years.[19] But the heroin chic aesthetic became a dominant part of the cultural landscape not because of its emergence in cutting-edge fashion magazines such as *Detour, W, I.D.,* and *The Face,* but because Calvin Klein popularized the look in his advertising campaigns, especially his "just be" campaign for cK be cologne, which he launched in August 1996. Making a particularly important moment in the brief history of heroin chic, the cK be campaign not only pushed the look into mainstream advertising, but also prompted a public outcry from a number of anti-drug groups around the country, much of which went unreported and unnoticed. Klein's cK be ads features black-and-white images of blank-eyed models affecting the languid, sickly expression of "junk culture" teens waiting outside of a methadone clinic for their next fix. Inserted among the images appears a tidy summation—"be this, be that. Just be."—suggesting, if not glamorizing, the tragically hip posturing of the impoverished heroin junkie. "Just be" seems to offer an ironic alternative to a variety of ad campaigns" to the ultra-patriotic "Be All That You Can Be" army slogan, the ultra-jock "Just Do It" Nike slogan, and the insipid and moralizing "Just say no" slogan that inspired ant-drug campaigns launched during the Reagan era. In response to the latter, "just be" suggests junk culture in not dangerous, but fashionable and hip. The ads prompted angry and immediate protest, with a coalition of parent-led anti-drug groups leading the charge with the call for a national boycott of Klein's products. Paula Kemp, the associate director of National Families in Action, called upon "Klein's competitors to join [the organization] in refusing to glamorize addiction in any of their ads."[20] Klein's immediate response to the controversy was typical.

Company executives argues that they were selling products, not drugs, and that the kids in the ads were "based on real people and the emotions described by those people based on their lives."[21]

= = = =

Fashion photography in the mid-'90s lead the way in pushing the heroin chic style to its extreme. A number of young and talented photographers such as Corrine Day, Juergen Teller, Craig McDean, David Sims, Terry Richardson, Steven Meisel, Mario Sorrenti, and other became more popular because their work emulated the "new realism" that characterized heroin chic. For many of these photographer, what became known as the "heroin chic" look was in fact an attempt, through their work, to provide an alternative to the idealized, near-perfect images of beauty and glamour that appeared in magazines such as *Harper's Bazaar* or *Vogue*. Corrine Day's fashion photos in *The Face*, for instance, often consisted of young kids sitting in chairs or sprawled on second-hand couches in seedy rooms amid a clutter of empty soda cans, cigarettes, and crumpled newspapers.[22] Day justified her work by claiming it was a reaction against air-brushed, fantasy-like fashion images of men and women that served to undermine the truth of people's lives.[23] Stylized representations of the underclass as a counter aesthetic to idealized notions of beauty also figures prominently in Steven Meisel's photos of young males dressed in their underwear, sporting tattoos and black nail polish in seedy, wood-paneled basements—which appeared in Calvin Klein's famous 1995 advertising campaign for jeans. Meisel's aesthetic suggests images of "white-trash" kids on the make, selling their bodies for in cheap, trailer-park settings. Davide Sorrenti's photos for *Detour* and *I.D.*, which appeared in *The New York Times* shortly after his death, include a photo of model James King looking emaciated, disheveled, and hung over sitting on a couch surrounded by posters of Sid Vicious and Kurt Cobain. In the January 1997 issue of *W*, a gaunt, sullen model drenched with sweat sits huddled in a chair, an arm extended toward the camera. Commenting on the image, *Boston Globe* reporter Pamela Reynolds pointed out that "The only thing missing was the needle."[24] In many of these fashion photos, kids appear with eyes rimmed in dark eye shadow, sprawled on bathroom floors, across disheveled hotel-type beds, and in a variety of shabby and compromising settings.

The fashion industry's response to the charge that its use of heroin chic circulates an image of drug use as vogue and trendy appears, with few exceptions, largely disingenuous. For instance, Calvin Klein, appearing on the June 29, 1997 "Larry King Live" show, simply dismissed the charge by claiming that as a fashion statement heroin chic is both "old fashioned" and no longer has any credibility. Ignoring the ethical and political implications of such ads, Klein claimed that he was simply selling products. Terry Jones, an editor of *I.D.* magazine, which pioneered the druggy look, responded by claiming that he did not think that heroin chic as a style ever existed. Long Nguyen, style director at *Detour* magazine, claimed such images simply represented a window on life, echoing a defense used by a number of other fashion photographers.[25] In some cases, the "realism" argument was defended by fashion editors and photographers alike by invoking the photo-documentary work of Nan Goldin, Larry Clark, and Jim Goldberg. Another position representative of the fashion world's response to Clinton's speech was invoked by Laura Craik, fashion feature editor of *The Face* magazine. She argued that the fashion industry may seduce, but it doesn't peddle drugs. For Craik, it is the working-class pushers and drug-runners who bear the responsibility for the appeal of heroin to young people (a not too subtle form of racism that pathologizes urban, working-class whites and kids of color).[26]

Each of these defenses deserves a response. First, the work of Goldin, Clark, and Goldberg chronicles particular communities that were formative for each of the artists. In projects that combine narratives of personal experience, cultural specificity, memories, and historical contexts, each of these artists uses photography to register how the temporal, personal, and political intersect to reveal the "dangerous memories" that mark the social character of communities in which they have lived and, in part, shaped their own perceptions of society. Moreover, such work is usually accompanied by text that attempts to construct the viewer not as a distanced voyeur or consumer but as a moral witness. Goldin's narrations of her own experiences of drug abuse and physical battery and Goldberg's moving images of drugged-out, homeless teens do not appropriate the "other" in order to sell commodities in fashion magazines;[27] nor do they claim a specious realism that denies its own political and ideological location as a form of argument, disputation, and way of making the world intelligible.[28]

Unlike much of the fashion photography that is associated with heroin chic, in which viewers are positioned as voyeurs of stylized images of poverty, deprivation, and abuse, Goldin's and Goldberg's photographs depict the reality of pain and suffering experienced by those who neither have the resources to buy high-end fashion magazines and the clothes they advertise, nor the ability to fight back against the objectification of their lives in such magazines. The work of both artists strongly resists the objectifying posture of heroin chic photography and grapples with important considerations regarding how "reality and truth are constructed, both aesthetically and socially, in specific historical contexts."[29] Both artists construct images of the "other" within an ideological framework that integrates aesthetic and ethical sensibilities.

If Goldin and Goldberg attempt to reposition social violence in the collective consciousness as a disturbing pathology that undermines public life, the heroin chic crowd reduces representations of human suffering to a privatized, trendy aesthetic that defines the living present outside of a context of struggle, passion, and hope. Art in this case does not evoke violence, death, or human suffering as part of a strategy of moral witnessing and social engagement, but crudely represents it as simply more images linking desire and agency exclusively to consumerism. Within the Postmodern world of heroin chic fashion photography, the "other" is cast as an object of aesthetic consideration, a source of sensations rather than a serious object of moral evaluation and responsibility.[30] Realities melt into representations; aesthetic criteria replace considerations of history, politics, power, and morality. A chilling indifference to the experiences of human suffering allows moral apathy and cruelty to become central defining principles of artistic production and cultural work. Similarly, the intersection of art and commerce does not deny the political sphere, it simply appropriates it by creating a representational politics of the social that exists in harmony with the reductionistic, reifying demands of the market. Heroin chic may be "old fashioned," but the political and economic forces that legitimate it—hardly mentioned by President Clinton—are still in place. Similarly, the horribly tragic conditions that heroin chic chose to mimic are hardly endemic to the fashion industry, yet seem to be gaining ground in every aspect of our society.

Second, the argument that heroin chic photography in and of itself is wrongly accused of peddling drugs is not without merit. The drug industry cannot be understood outside of a complex set of institutional, political, and ideological relations of power. But the media, including the fashion industry, is crucial in shaping meaning, desire, and identity, especially among young people, in this society. Culture matters in both political and pedagogical terms. Politically, those who have the power to control the dominant machineries of cultural production set limits on what can be produced, legitimated, and distributed in a society even as they disproportionately control the conditions under which knowledge becomes accessible to specific groups and individuals. Pedagogically, the culture industry plays a crucial role in shaping public memory, in legitimating particular ways of knowing and specific forms of knowledge, and in producing identities and the discourses that inform them. By legitimating particular forms of identity and identification, the fashion industry and other cultural sites play an important, though far from strictly deterministic, role in shaping "how we get to know what we know and the moral life we aspire to lead."[31] The fashion industry is not responsible for causing heroin addiction in this country among young people, but it is politically and morally responsible for legitimating the culture of addiction as a vehicle for selling a lifestyle. At the same time, it is culpable for legitimating a type of moral insensitivity that has become widespread, in which images of the poor, oppressed, and disadvantaged are reified and those depicted scorned as such—rather than as victims of an often cruel and exploitative social system. Similarly, the fashion industry should be roundly condemned for failing to provide anti-drug programs for those who work within its ranks—such programs are well established in the music and film industries. Pedagogically, the fashion industry appears to embrace the heroin chic lifestyle it sought to legitimate to a larger public culture; this suggests that rather than merely reflecting the larger society, it actually seeks to play a role in constructing values and ideologies that shape social identities.

Confusing the reality of human suffering with an aesthetic that celebrates a politics of despair and pathology, heroin chic does more than generate images in which the lure of cheap sensation is tied to fast money and quick notoriety. Heroin chic also bespeaks a privatized space where art and commerce can withdraw to shield themselves and their viewers from any sense of public accountability. Heroin chic also must be read in more general terms as symptomatic of a society that encourages a representational politics and cultural pedagogy which views young people as symbols of social degeneracy while simultaneously treating them as both disposable and as an industrial reserve army of consumers. Heroin chic celebrates a society that mocks the poor, increasingly incarcerates its youth, and wages war against people of color. Its brief rise in prominence signals a broader, retrograde public discourse that shares its mocking indifference and celebrates its cheap appropriation of the "other" as an amusing spectacle. Heroin chic offers a Postmodern form of cultural slumming as cheap titillation for its yuppie audience, whose members imagine themselves being reckless and edgy as they appropriate the behaviors, dress, discourse, and experiences of those who occupy the most tragic margins of society.

NOTES

1. Richard Sennett, "The Social Body," *Transition* 71, 1997, 80–98.

2. This theme is taken up brilliantly in Michael Sorkin, "See You in Disneyland," in Michael Sorkin, ed., *Variations on a Theme Park* (New York: The Noon Day Press, 1992), 205–232.

3. Jean Baudrillard, *Simulacra and Simulation* (Michigan: University of Michigan Press, 1994), 87.

4. For a series of articles on the national entertainment state, see the June 3, 1996 issue of *The Nation*.

5. Baudrillard, 87–88.

6. I am referring here to the infamous conference of artists and academics at Whiskey Pete's Casino in Stateline, Nevada that included Baudrillard's debut as a Vegas nightclub act. See M. Corrigan, "Vive Las Vegas," *The Village Voice*, November 19,1996,13.

7. For an insightful piece on art and commerce, see Luis Camnitzer, "Absolut Relativity," *Third Text*, Spring 1997, 86–91.

8. Mark Poster, The *Mode of Information: Poststructuralism and Social Context* (Chicago: University of Chicago Press, 1990), 56.

9. I address this issue in detail in my *Disturbing Pleasures* (New York: Routledge, 1994). The term "cartoon utopia" is from Michael Sorkin, op. cit., 232.

10. Camnitzer, 87.

11. Carol Becker, "The Art of Testimony," *Sculpture*, March 1997, 28.

12. Sennett, 90.

13. For a personal narrative of heroin use among trendy intellectuals, see Ann M., "Listening to Heroin," *The Village Voice*, April 23, 1994, 25–30; and Mark Ehrman, "Heroin Chic," *Playboy*, May 1995, 66–68, 144–147.

14. For example, in Seattle between 1986 and 1994, heroin fatalities increased by nearly 300 percent, primarily among young people. For an analysis of the heroin drug scene in Seattle, see David Lipsky, "Junkie Town," *Rolling Stone*, May 30, 1996, 35–62.

15. See my *Fugitive Cultures: Race, Violence, and Youth* (New York: Routledge, 1996).

16. Ann Powers, "The hunger," *The Village Voice*, August 23, 1994, 29.

17. Cited in Pamela Reynolds, "A Fashion World Hooked on 'Heroin Chic,'" *Boston Globe*, July 26, 1996, CI.

18. Clinton cited in Robert A. Rankin, "Clinton Rebukes Fashion Industry for 'Glorification' of Drug Addiction," *Centre Daily Times*, Wednesday, May 21, 1997, 6A.

19. Amy M. Spindler argues that "In the last three years some version of the look has

been seen in almost every fashion magazine." See Amy M. Spindler, "A Death Tarnishes Fashion's 'Heroin Look,'" *The New York Times*, Thursday, May 20, 1997, A25.

20. Cited in Warren Richey, "Boycott Groups: Klein Ads Carry Scent of 'Heroin Chic,'" The *Christian Science Monitor*, October 25, 1996, 3.

21. Robert Triefus, a senior vice president at Calvin Klein, cited in Warren Richey, ibid.

22. Corrine Day's work can be seen in Camilla Nickerson and Neville Wakefield, eds., *Fashion* (Zurich: Scalo, 1996).

23. Day says "I like beauty the way I find it, and I don't want to disturb it." Cited in Holly Brubach, "Beyond Shocking," *The New York Times Magazine*, May 18, 1997.

24. Pamela Reynolds, "A Fashion World Hooked on 'Heroin Chic,'" *Boston Globe*, July 26, 1996, CI.

25. Both Jones and Nguyen are cited in Richard B. Woodward, "Whither Fashion Photography?" *The New York Times*, Sunday, June 8, 1997, 58.

26. Laura Craik, "Heroin Chic? Just Say No," *The Guardian*, May 23, 1997, 19.

27. See Nan Goldin, *I'll Be Your Mirror*, Elisabeth Sussman, ed. (Zurich: Scalo, 1997), and Jim Goldberg, *Raised by Wolves* (Zurich: Scalo, 1995).

28. See Richard Harvey Brown, "Realism and Power in Aesthetic Representation," in Richard Brown, ed., *Postmodern Representations* (Bloomington: Indiana University Press, 1995), 134–167.

29. Brown, 135.

30. I am drawing in this case on the work of Zygmunt Bauman, *Life in Fragments* (Cambridge: Basil Blackwell, 1995), especially "Violence and Postmodernism," 139–162.

31. Geoffrey Hartman, "Public Memory and Its Discontents," *Raritan*, Spring 1994, 28.

ART IS DEAD

Long Live Aesthetic Management

April 1999

> "Here the sociology of art overtly enters
> into the theory and practice of creation."
> —Harold Rosenberg[1]

> "The only person who is in touch with the whole
> product is the manager, but to him the product is an
> abstraction, whose essence is exchange value . . ."
> —Erich Fromm[2]

Compare two works of art, both of which represent Marilyn Monroe. One is by Willem de Kooning, the other by Andy Warhol. They are separated by only eight years—de Kooning's *Marilyn Monroe* was painted in 1954, Warhol's *Gold Marilyn Monroe,* a combination of silkscreen, oil, and synthetic polymer paint on canvas manufactured in 1962—but they are worlds of art and attitude apart. I believe that the de Kooning image is *artistically created,* while the Warhol image is *aesthetically managed.* It is a momentous distinction, for "art" seems to be on the way out, while "aesthetic management" is here to stay. The general interest in art today has largely to do with its high exchange value, and the transformation of the artist into an aesthetic manager is the perhaps unavoidable consequence of this powerful capitalist fact. The term "aesthetic management" is that of Bernd Schmitt and Alex Simonson, two professors of marketing, who explicate it in one of the most important books of our time about the astonishing convergence of art and business: *Marketing Aesthetics: The Strategic Management of Brands, Identity, and Image.*[3]

In the years between de Kooning's Marilyn and Warhol's Marilyn, there was a heightened consciousness of the soaring exchange value of art. In 1957, Meyer Schapiro observed that works of art "are perhaps the most costly man-made objects in the world. The enormous importance given to a work of art as a precious object, which is advertised and known in connection with its price, is bound to affect the consciousness of our culture. It stamps the painting as an object of speculation, confusing the values of art."[4] In 1955, Erich Fromm published *The Sane Society,* observing that in capitalistic society "the essential point in the description" of any and every thing is its cost.[5] This holds for works of art as well as bridges, cigars, watches—and people. The "concrete (use) value" of the thing (and people are simply more or less costly things in capitalistic society, according to Fromm) is "secondary to its abstract (exchange) value in the way the object is experienced . . . In other words, things are experienced as commodities, as embodiments of exchange value, not only while we are buying or selling, but in our attitude toward them when the economic transaction is finished." People will speak of the extraordinary price a de Kooning or Warhol picture brings at auction, not of what, concretely and humanly, the picture is about and how it is experienced.

The difference between the troubled way de Kooning pictures Marilyn Monroe and the garish way Warhol pictures her symbolizes the difference between the painting as an embodiment of *artistic value* and the painting as an embodiment of *exchange value.* Their difference in technique—de Kooning vigorously painting Marilyn's picture by hand in contrast to Warhol silkscreening ink over a photograph of her—signals this difference in kind. It is symptomatic of the sea change that occurred in American art from the 1950s to the 1960s, from Abstract Expressionism, a subjective, existential, relatively esoteric art, to the more conspicuously collective orientation of Pop art. It is also symptomatic of the emergence of the aesthetic manager, exemplified by Andy Warhol, as an alternative to the creative artist, epitomized by de Kooning, who, indeed, was one of the last of a dying breed.

Marcel Duchamp was probably the first artist manager: his intellectual management of ready- made objects made them artistically significant. But he was not yet an aesthetic manager, because he still worked with actual things. The readymades Warhol worked with were pure appearances—celebrity images that had already been "abstractified," to use Fromm's term, by being commercially and socially celebrated—which he quantified by serializing them, repeating them indefinitely, as though cloned. The peculiarly inhuman character of the appropriated appearance is conveyed by its machine-made look of automaton conformity and indicates the absence of any real selfhood or individuality represented in the subject.[6] Warhol declared that he himself was nothing but an appearance, a pseudo self. "The pseudo self," Fromm writes, "is only an agent who actually represents the role a person is supposed to play but who does so under the name of the self . . . [F]or many people . . . the original self is completely suffocated by the pseudo self."[7] Similarly, a pseudo artist plays the role an artist is expected to play, and as such loses his original feelings and thoughts, that he thinks and feels for himself outside of an adopted role.[8] Warhol seemed to be deliberately suffocating his original self, and in his work, his aesthetic management of human appearances seems to suffocate the original self of the persons pictured. Successfully marketed, commodities acquire the aura of personhood for Warhol, just as successfully marketed "personalities" became expensive commodities.

While the struggle between the creative artist and the aesthetic manager persists to this day—the difference between the German Neo-Expressionists and the American Conceptualists carried it forward in perhaps a new way—the latter type seems to be winning, at least in this particular capitalistic society. If high exchange value is the highest absolute value, then images that apotheosize this monetary value—which imply that exchange value is immanent in life and that its total commodification is its climax—will inevitably triumph over images on which no obvious price can be placed, because they are too full of life and all too human.

What values do de Kooning's expressionistic *Marilyn Monroe* embody? They are values of art absent from Warhol's fabricated *Gold Marilyn Monroe,* which presents the star as the ultimate golden girl, the perfect embodiment of the "bitch goddess of success," her seductive sexuality the very symbol of exchange value itself. The values in de Kooning's painting, rather, embody the emotional achievements possible in genuine art. "The work of art," Alfred North Whitehead writes, "is a message from the Unseen," or the unconscious. "It unlooses the depths of feeling from behind the frontier where the precision of consciousness fails.[9] This is the credo and intention of all true artistic creativity—to reach into the unseen depths of the psyche and bring back a pearl of original feeling. T.W. Adorno says something similar. "Works of art," he writes, "do not, in the psychological sense, repress contents of consciousness. Rather, through expression they help raise into consciousness diffuse and forgotten experiences without 'rationalizing' them."[10] The primary artistic accomplishment is the convincing, original expression of a unique, and hitherto unfelt feeling. As such, the artistic expression therefore undermines the pseudo self and restores the original self. Diffuse feelings arise spontaneously, as though experienced for the first time, a surprise that cannot readily be explained, which makes it all the more resonant, urgent, and profound.

De Kooning's *Marilyn Monroe* expresses his deep, contradictory feelings about women. There is no attempt to rationalize this ambivalence by accommodating the representation to traditional rendering. Rather than risk that his feelings lose their traumatic intensity and pathos—their overwhelming expressivity—and become decorative or cosmetic, de Kooning overthrows the familiarity: of convention. In his agitated gestures, it is as if the loving desire that originally, irresistibly led de Kooning to the female figure fuses with a protective hatred that keeps him from surrendering to her completely. Some gestures seem to caress and soothe her flesh, while others seem to sadistically gnaw at it, as though to violently strip her flesh from her body. Whether grandly aggressive or touchingly tender, de Kooning's raw, raucous painterliness distorts Monroe's familiar appearance and all but destroys any resemblance to her voluptuous body. Under pressure from his powerful gestures, the icon of her body loses cohesiveness and coherence, lacks unity and integrity, and defies clarity and logic. In psychological terms, de Kooning turns a benign external object—a collectively conceived image of the ideal woman—into a malevolent internal object, bizarre and grotesque yet exciting and seductive. De Kooning's *Marilyn Monroe* is the anxiety-arousing figment of an overheated, nightmarish imagination.

De Kooning took a mass-produced, standardized image of a woman and treated it in a personal, idiosyncratic, almost absurd way, making what was socially precise emotionally imprecise. By irrationally generalizing her glamorous appearance until it is all but unrecognizable—a comic beast rather than a superior star—de Kooning threw a monkey wrench into the Hollywood dream machine. Expression of his unconscious feelings not only declares the image of the conventional dream girl a fraud, but slashes the potency of the photograph, the most precious instrument of her fame and fortune. Hollywood images such as Monroe's are carefully manufactured simulations of seductive beauty rather than emotionally and physically realistic representations of living women. They betray women as well as mislead men. In attacking Monroe's photograph-a social treasure-he attacks the whole entertainment industry's system of creating stardom.

The difference between de Kooning's crude, splashy, all but nihilistic picture and Warhol's slick, self-contained, carefully composed one is that Warhol preserves the public image of Monroe. Unlike de Kooning, Warhol modifies it but does not destroy it. Moreover, the means by which he alters Marilyn's image are the same cosmetic mechanisms used to invent it. Monroe's features remain clear and decipherable, however garishly accentuated, as though she had on too much make-up. This is perhaps Warhol's most extreme, heavy-handed transformation-but the image remains unmistakably the glamorous Marilyn Monroe, elevated to iconic, idolatrous status by being framed in gold, as heavenly as the golden sky of a medieval altarpiece.

Where de Kooning defied socially manufactured appearances, Warhol celebrated them, however ironically. Usually, irony implicitly negates what it explicitly affirms, but Warhol's ironical treatment of Monroe's appearance does nothing to undermine her celebrity. Irony usually reminds us that things are not what they seem, but Warhol's presentation of Marilyn suggests that appearance *is* reality. His rendering may seem satiric, but reducing Monroe's face to a simple two-dimensional surface does not expose the representation as a farce, but rather acknowledges the ingenuity and persuasiveness of its presence. He strengthens the cosmetic foundation of appearance. To render Monroe as purely a matter of surface is to make it impossible to experience it as the representation of any real person. There is no need for a real self-cosmetics, generating a sense of pseudo self, will do quite well in a world of appearances and role-playing. Monroe died prematurely, a great commercial loss, and Warhol brings all his brilliance as a make-up artist, his cosmetic creativity and wizardry—as great and as morbid as that of any Egyptian embalmer—to bear on her appearance, in an effort to make it enduring, and of continuing commercial value and use.

Thus, Warhol does not so much satirize the details of Monroe's beauty as animate and levitate them. Warhol cunningly suggests Monroe's immortality by cosmetically accentuating her deathmask, making it seem transcendentally expressive. Does not the mystifying, stiff, unreal, aloof, mummified look Warhol gives Monroe resemble the saints in Byzantine art? The static rigidity of her face, and its conspicuously composite, pseudo-mosaic character, confirms her more-than-mortal existence—a shimmering, martyred intermediary between this world and another. Warhol's picture makes Monroe into more of a star—a more transcendental star—than she was in Hollywood.

= = = =

De Kooning's painting of Marilyn Monroe is a creative discovery and an expression of feelings that seek to violate the social barrier of repression. Warhol's painting of Marilyn Monroe keeps the social repression barrier in place and reinforces it—by suppressing the real beneath the imperative of appearance—and thus amounts to its instrument. This confirms that Warhol's picture is a product of aesthetic management, while de Kooning's is a product of original art, to recall Fromm: an original psychic act. Aesthetic management always serves and reinforces social repression, while artistic expression cannot help but contradict and undermine it by reason of its originality.

De Kooning's emotional, physically primitive vision of a woman may have been enacted before. But we sense that it is original to him, because of its seemingly inexhaustible intensity, excruciating complexity, and ultimate unintelligibility. There is something about de Kooning's Marilyn that is ultimately unverbalizable, however much its physical properties can be described. It is as if it has been derived from a preverbal, infantile experience of the mother. De Kooning uses the image of Marilyn Monroe as an occasion to raise to consciousness a diffuse and forgotten experience of the mother in all her primary majesty: overwhelming and confrontational. It is a remarkable achievement: a profound regression handled in an artistically progressive way. While it may have affinities with previous paintings of women—the Willendorf Venus, Rubens' nudes, contemporaneous pinups—its expressive radically gives it an emotional edge and uncanniness that is unique.

Warhol's image may be equally uncanny, but for very different reasons: his makes clear the manufactured, devious, even outright deceptive character of Monroe's commodified image. Warhol strongly suggests its socially repressive character: ironically sublime, it stimulates and manipulates its worshipper's desire even as it mocks and negates it. The image is manifestly fake, evident in the all too emphatic embellishment of the features of Monroe's face, and so the desire it arouses must also be fake. The eyes, nose, and mouth remain in place but are ingeniously exaggerated, suggesting the malleability and artificiality of the image. Warhol's picture of Monroe is a summary of abstract sensory details, predetermined and stereotyped by the media that add up to a fore-ordained whole.

This is exactly the character of an aesthetically managed product, as Schmitt and Simonson make clear in their aforementioned *Marketing*

Aesthetics. Everything that they say about aesthetic management and its purpose can easily be applied to Warhol's *Gold Marilyn Monroe* and his oeuvre as a whole. Their book deals with "corporate and brand aesthetics, i.e., attractive visual and other sensory markers and symbols that represent the organization and its brands appropriately and dazzle customers through sensory experiences."[11] It is a study of aesthetics as "the new marketing paradigm," a new way to sell a product by transforming it into "an appearance center." Aesthetics gives the product "an irresistible appeal" and "an attractive and lasting identity," thus differentiating it from all other products. Aesthetics presents the product as pure surplus value. "Value," Schmitt and Simonson write, "is provided only by satisfying needs. In a world in which most consumers have their basic needs satisfied, value is easily provided by satisfying customers' experiential needs-their aesthetic needs."

Aesthetic positioning can establish product uniqueness and market dominance. As Schmitt and Simonson say, "the willingness to market its aesthetics moved Absolut [vodka] into its enviable market position."[12] Without its "artistically imaginative" identity-its association "with, a fashionable, arty scene"- it would be simply another vodka. Absolut's "aesthetic image as part of an upscale culture" and its hiring a whole host of artists such as Andy Warhol and Keith Haring to create "artistic visions of the bottle marked by their own easily identifiable visual styles" was an "aesthetic strategy" that "revolutionized liquor marketing."

Today retailing relies heavily on aesthetics, not only because the "look and feel" of a product establishes its identity, but because it also establishes "tangible benefits": aesthetic identity "increases productivity, creates loyalty, allows for premium pricing, saves costs, affords protection from competition, cuts through information clutter." Moreover, the authors emphasize, the "aesthetic management" of a product is not a matter of hit-or-miss guesswork, but is the result of scientific research, measurement, and planning. Aesthetic management assumes that it is possible to control, manipulate, and exploit aesthetic experience, and attempts to do so on the basis of factual knowledge about its constituents.

Schmitt and Simonson demonstrate that aesthetics can be quantitatively analyzed into basic elements, and its qualitative effect—the impressions it generates—can be precisely measured. "All perceptions start with the eye," they write in emulation of Aristotle, and proceed to list and describe in detail the primary factors in visual perception: "color, shape, line, and pattern." But, they assert, such physical or stylistic elements alone are "insufficient to express an identity," and must be combined with content or human-interest themes. Schmitt and Simonson try to make aesthetics easy, and their reductive analysis is useful: The goal of aesthetic management is to establish a rich, seductive "associational network" causing easy recollection—or "higher recall"—of the product.

As Schmitt and Simonson say, the secret of commercial success has nothing to do with the function of the product, or the communication of any central message about it, or the way people actually use it, but rather with its form, the peripheral messages associated with it, and its often subliminal symbolic meaning. These seemingly secondary features give the product an aura of significance that makes the consumer invest in it emotionally, which is what triggers sales. Aesthetically manipulated, it is no longer simply a product, but a "life experience," and it is only when it is such a presumably unique experience that its commodification is complete.

Marilyn Monroe's appearance is a consumer product, and Warhol's further aestheticization of it adds to its irresistible appeal. Warhol adds value to what is already socially valuable by making it more aesthetically satisfying—more visually dazzling and attractive than a Hollywood movie—and thus more marketable. But the image of Marilyn is already overvalued, made banal by its ubiquity. Paradoxically, Marilyn Monroe's oversold image *needs* the surplus value of the high-art aesthetics that Warhol brings to it, to continually resuscitate its popularity. Conversely, Warhol's artwork becomes more marketable by association with Monroe. His aesthetics add to her aura, and her aura makes him a star by association.

Warhol works with the same assumptions outlined in Schmitt and Simonson's marketing manual. He conceives of sensory features as quantitative units, each having a specifiable qualitative appeal. Thus Monroe's hair, eyebrows, eyelids, eyes, nose, lips are each a distinct, measurable sensory feature, with its own particular emotional appeal. There is nothing intrinsically marketable about the basic features of a face. But aesthetically isolated, enhanced, and individualized they can be made mysterious and seductive enough to be marketable. Thus Monroe's face becomes a desirable commodity, which both men and women want to possess, it is the need to market the face that makes both Hollywood and Warhol abstractify and quantify it so that it can be aesthetically managed. *Gold Marilyn Monroe* seems to even be prefabricated, assembled on the site of the canvas, its basic parts shipped from the Hollywood beauty parlor, with a few embellishments thrown in from the art scene. Warhol may be parodying both, but his complete dependence on them indicates that his so-called art has no substance without them.

Whatever contradictory or spontaneous personal feelings Marilyn Monroe's appearance might arouse seem to be beside the point. In fact, the introspective awareness of such feelings might hinder effective marketing. Emotional confusion would distract from the appearance's seemingly objective, self-evident appeal and make one critically reflect on its character, construction, and purpose, in effect distancing oneself from the product. The feeling of control, calculation, and pre-meditation—the major components of successful *management*—evident in Warhol's picture is quite different from the feeling of spontaneity, insecurity, and delirium, or *expression*—evident in de Kooning's picture of her. Warhol uses colors in measured amounts, and turns the features of Monroe's face into fixed gestures, taking up just so much expressive space and not more. In contrast, de Kooning does not try to predict and control his feelings.

Warhol gave Marilyn Monroe's face what Daniel Bell calls "the new look [that] creates an 'avant-garde' identity,"[13] according to Schmitt and Simonson the most desirable product identity there is. It looks the most different, draws the most attention, and is the riskiest. Of course, it is never risky enough to be unnerving, only enough to pique curiosity. Thus, artists who once enjoyed "special recognition," as Ernst Kris said, because they "had power over memory and could eternalize human appearance,"[14] now enjoy special recognition because they labor on the consumer frontier, creating new looks that facilitate marketing and can be marketed in their own right. As Bell says, the avant-garde artist "swiftly shapes the audience and the market, rather than being shaped by them."

Kris notes that the work of art was once thought to have "magic power" and was in some sense sacred. The use of aesthetics as the ultimate marketing strategy—as in Warhol's work- suggests that the work of art, as the ultimate aesthetic identity, still has magical power, now more vulgar than divine. The "magic potency of images," as Kris calls it, which involves the notion that "images give power over what they depict," has been transferred to the product by way of a simplified aesthetics. The art/product has magical power over the consumer, who finds his or her innermost wishes symbolized and simplified—and probably parodied—by it.

Warhol's Marilyn is pure exchange value, in both its aesthetic character and its social purpose. Fromm writes in *The Sane Society*, that "in capitalistic society exchanging has become an end in itself." For Fromm, this "need for exchange" is not "an inherent part of human nature," as Adam Smith thought, but "a symptom of the abstractification and alienation inherent in the social character of modern man." In Warhol's *Gold*

Marilyn Monroe, aesthetics has become alien and abstractified, a means to an economic end but also an economic end in itself. Rather than generate passion for what it informs, or an empathic feeling for what it adorns, in Warhol's image aesthetics is used dispassionately and indifferently, confirming the alienation embodied in his subject matter. Warhol's Marilyn is beautiful only in so much as she costs a great deal of money, which alone signifies pure beauty in capitalism.

In short, Warhol's *Gold Marilyn Monroe* fuses and confuses aesthetic value and exchange value. And this is exactly what aesthetic management is supposed to do. It turns consumption into aesthetic contemplation, and aesthetic contemplation into consumption. It degrades art by equating it with exchange value, while glorifying exchange value with its association with art. This amounts to the dumbing down of art and the smarting up of commerce.

The aesthetic manager packages exchange value under the guise of making art, which is why the result cannot help be a failure as art-as expression. Warhol is the aesthetic manager par excellence. Idolizing Marilyn Monroe, who was already an idol, Warhol aestheticizes alienation. As Fromm writes, "idolatrous man bows down to the work of his own hands. The idol represents his own life forces in an alienated form." Warhol normalizes the worship of an image, as if to urge us to waste our life forces on a clearly fabricated fantasy. The aesthetically managed avant-garde work of art is the capitalist idol par excellence, the ultimate commodity.

Warhol is not alone. Aesthetic management has become a dominant mode of art making in this post-Postmodern moment, a matter of manipulating prefabricated stylistic and thematic variables, according Schmitt and Simonson, to predictable aesthetic and emotional effect. Confirmation that one is an artist comes when your aesthetic product is marketable. This is a kind of decadence, and the core of the Postmodernist condition of art. The artist has become a product designer, and his or her specialized products exist to supply new ideas for marketing. In short, art making has become fused with marketing chic. All the irony with which it seeks to defend itself only makes it more marketable.

I see this trend in the works of Alexis Smith, Richard Prince, David Salle, and any number of photographers, installation artists, and Conceptual artists. They gain their credibility, such as it is, through the identity and celebrity of their sources. Their art gets its aesthetic value from the exchange value of the images they appropriate. Many of these aesthetic managers think appropriation as such is ironical, and they are certainly right in thinking that irony has become standard aesthetic strategy in the Postmodern situation. But the subliminal point is that ironically enhanced images have high exchange value, for the speculative character irony gives the images confirms the speculative character of exchange value.

Even Duchamp, the beatified role model of the aesthetic managers, was not above commercialism, as his project to market the readymade word "dada" in the form of silver, gold, and platinum ornaments—a product for each pocket—suggests. It was the last Dada joke: these precious materials, ironically used, would no doubt enhance the value of Dada, which had become a stale, boring joke. Duchamp's heir is Steve Wynn, a Las Vegas entrepreneur, who is filling his new casino with blue-chip art—art no longer known for its aesthetics, but for its exchange value— in the hope of attracting high rollers. Wynn has clearly understood the capitalist destiny of art, as did Duchamp. Was the epistemological problem Duchamp made of art really a ploy for using "art" to make ordinary things—readymades—more commercially valuable than they would otherwise be? He, too, saw that art had its price, and that by associating everyday products with art, their exchange value would be enhanced and increased. They would become expensive avant-garde idols, confirming our mounting alienation from the life force, however inescapable.

NOTES

1. Harold Rosenberg, "De-aestheticization," *The De-definition of Art* (New York: Collier Books, 1973), p. 29.

2. Erich Fromm, *The Sane Society* (New York: Fawcett, 1965), 105.

3. Bernd Schmitt and Alex Simonson, *Marketing Aesthetics: The Strategic Management of Brands, Identity, and Image* (New York: Free Press, 1997).

4. Meyer Schapiro, "Recent Abstract Painting" (1957), *Modern Art: 19th and 20th Centuries* (New York: George Braziller, 1980), 224.

5. Fromm, 106.

6. Erich Fromm, *Escape from Freedom* (New York: Avon, 1965), 208–30.

7. Ibid., 229.

8. See ibid., 267 for Fromm's discussion of "the elimination of spontaneity and . . . the substitution of original psychic acts by superimposed feelings, thoughts, and wishes." As Fromm says, "by original I do not mean . . . that an idea has not been thought before by someone else, but that it originates in the individual, that is, it is the result of his own activity and in this sense is his thought." The same holds for feelings and actions, he argues, I would add to this that original thoughts, feelings, and actions originate in an original experience of life—in experience that, if truly lived, cannot help but be original.

9. Alfred North Whitehead, *Adventures of Ideas* (New York: Mentor, 1955), 270.

10. T.W. Adorno, *Aesthetic Theory* (London: Routledge & Kegan Paul, 1984), 82.

11 Schmitt and Simonson, xiii. All subsequent quotations are from this book.

12. Their excited discussion of Absolut vodka's avant-garde image (176) also implies their advocacy of avant-garde identity as the most marketable identity. There is an odd reciprocity between the avant-garde art appropriated and the newly avant-gardized product: the product gains a new avant-garde lease on commercial life, and the art gets its avant-garde credentials extended beyond the normal short duration avant-garde art has. Art cannot help but benefit from lending itself to a product in quest of market dominance, for if and when the product achieves dominance and becomes a household name, so will the avant-garde artist, by reason of his association with it. (Warhol is a case in point.) Each rides on the coattails of the other, and both have much to gain by their association.

13. Daniel Bell, *The Cultural Contradictions of Capitalism* (New York: Basic Books, 1978), 39. Aesthetics managers are not the only ones concerned to create a superficial new look of avant-garde identity, in lieu of making substantial material and social changes. But they remain the implicit model for all image managers, for aesthetic artistry becomes absolutely essential when the old ruling class feels that its authority, power, and wealth are threatened by those who lack authority, power, and wealth. A new avant-garde identity helps the old ruling class maintain its monopoly by giving it a new look that "proves" it to be fresh, vigorous, and competent even when it isn't, seducing those without power into complacent acceptance of the status quo. It excites, exhausts, distracts, and narcotizes them with spectacular appearances, leaving them with little critical consciousness to rebelliously think about their social misery and inferiority, let alone to act on that awareness. Warhol's avant-garde adumbration and reification of Marilyn Monroe's glamorous appearance strengthens the authority, power, and wealth of the entertainment industry, and, more insidiously, confirms that it presents an ideal path to social authority (whatever the existential and emotional expense). In general our society is image-management conscious, differentiating between the image manager and genuine character. I believe that the more a society lets itself be taken in by images, the more extreme its underlying conflicts are, that is, the riper it is for existential and emotional disaster. The better designed the images the greater the existential and emotional horror they mask. Thus, presidential historian Michael R. Beschloss argues that "the core of (President] Clinton's authority is political management, not character." Political management includes the creation of a new avant-garde look for politics, supposedly giving politicians such as Clinton fresh credibility. Quoted in Dan Balz, "Clinton's Confession," *Washington Post National Weekly,* August 24, 1998, 8.

It is worth noting that British Prime Minister Tony Blair was regarded as little more than an image manager on first taking office. He undertook a "style offensive" to give Britain a new avant-garde identity. "It was time to 'rebrand' Britain as 'one of the world's pioneers rather than one of its museums,'" asserted "Demos, a social policy research center close to Mr. Blair." Quoted in Warren Hoge, "Blair's 'Rebranded' Britain Is No Museum," *The New York Times,* November 12, 1997, A1. Successful image making or aesthetic rebranding adds to the power, authority, and wealth of the image maker, for he seems to be an efficient, competent, knowledgeable manager of reality, even if he is not.

14. Ernst Kris, *Psychoanalytic Explorations in Art* (New York: Schocken, 1964), 48.

HA HA HA

Ray's A Laugh

September 1999

"I've always wanted to move people as much as I can,
so much that they cry. Sometimes women look at the
book and they cry and I think, 'I've done it.'"
—Richard Billingham[1]

Since I first picked up the 1997 publication *Ray's a Laugh,*
I've had an uneasy relationship with Richard Billingham's work: both
with the artist's intent, and with its emotional resonance. The book
features snapshot pictures of the artist's family taken over a six-year
period from 1990 to 1996: the alcoholic father Ray, the obese mother
Liz, and the fidgety younger brother Jason. They live in what appears to
be a cramped, dimly lit apartment that lies just outside of Birmingham,
England. They seem to spend most of their time drinking and hanging out in this crowded domestic space. In one image Ray slumps on
the floor next to a toilet, dark stains running down the porcelain. In
another a cat whizzes through the air toward Ray's head as he ducks
for cover. Syringe in hand, Liz feeds a tiny, newborn kitten enveloped
by the heavily tattooed folds of her arm. She pieces together a jigsaw
puzzle of a picturesque town, wearing a voluminous, floral housecoat.
A stack of white bread sits on a dresser next to a rumpled bed on which
Ray perches. There's evidence of domestic warfare: in a couple of pictures Liz threatens Ray with her fists, cheeks puffed out in anger, then,
in a later shot, offers him a tissue to wipe up the blood. We see their

unwashed hair and pimples and yellowed, crooked teeth. And, despite the occasional fun and games, the group looks worn out and resigned.

When showing the book to other people I've witnessed the "Make 'em laugh, make 'em cry" response that the artist describes: people nervously chuckle and point their finger, with the gesture seeming to shake off some excess of feeling. Or they get really quiet and sad, sort of closed in. The emotions seem to come quickly, clearly, and distinctly. But I've always felt a complicated mess of feelings: I don't particularly want to look, but I'm fascinated; I can't say I *like* them, but they linger with me; there is humor and intimacy, but also a kind of clinical coolness in the artist's stance. I have a strong reaction, but one borne more out of am-bivalence than anything else. And it's precisely this lack of simplicity—so seemingly at odds with the straightforward response the artist wants to elicit—that keeps me interested.

Putting aside the complicated emotional tone of the work for a mo-ment, something more readily articulated and understood (by me) is the way one might question the artist's intent. What is the purpose in pub-lishing and exhibiting pictures that are so private, that seem to breach a bond of confidence? Many people have family secrets, more or less trau-matic, but most people shy away from revealing them in such a public way. It's not always prudent to disclose one's troubled history, especially to someone in a position of power; someone who is deciding whether or not you'd make a good parent or a fit employee, for example. Collectively, we're of two minds. On the one hand, we don't seem too accepting of other people's emotional excesses. The fact that experimental geneticists are eagerly searching to locate the chromosome markers for alcoholism, depression, and obsessive-compulsive disorder with the intent to con-trol and ideally eliminate these so-called "defects" from the gene pool, hints at the lack of tolerance for emotional "imbalances" or "problems" in the culture. On the other hand, we encourage the identification and disclosure of illness in order to fight its debilitating effects and as enter-tainment. We live in a time of abundant emphasis on self-help programs and psychotherapy; there are even public venues in which to proclaim our desperation and unhappiness, daytime talk shows being one of the most popular arenas. The book publishing industry has seen a virtual spate of autobiographical memoirs describing excessive drinking, eating disorders, incest, sex addiction, bad marriages, etc. But these books are about survival and recovery. There's public ridicule if your case is too extreme or too far out there, as if compassion is called for only when the emotional problems reach a certain degree of intensity, yet have a palatable resolution. Again, daytime-talk-show audiences lambast and attack anyone they deem too ignorant or too mired in bad habits to change.

Many people also feel the stigma of growing up poor or in a social class that's not given much credit. Midst the ideals of the American dream and the current political rhetoric slamming welfare we're urged to raise ourselves out, pulled up by our proverbial bootstraps. Other than the occasional bell hooks essay, there's no encouragement to dwell there; we can only claim it if and when, like Oprah, or Madonna, Suze Orman, or Billie Jean King (classic poor-girls-done-good), our early poverty is far behind us. But Billingham put his work out there, displaying his poverty and family troubles, *before* he was a rich and famous artist. How was he able to override these social inhibitions and prohibitions, and more importantly, *why* does he do so *in his art?*

Logic warns us against falling prey to the intentional fallacy, the mistake of attributing ideas and moral positions found in a work of art back to the artist him- or herself. We may fault Friedrich Nietzsche for his concept of the all-powerful *Übermensch* or Paul de Man for his fascism, but we don't necessarily ascribe the wrongs and failures of the Karamazov brothers back to Fyodor Dostoevsky. We tend to give fiction writers more moral latitude (Salman Rushdie aside), as if the acknowledged exercise of the imagination safeguards the private life of the writer. But how does the artist fare in this respect? Do artists inevitably engage in autobiography when creating an imagined world? Usually, knowledge of an artist's personal beliefs helps a viewer understand the work. Knowing their relationship to the people they photograph, for instance, is an important bit of information that may shift one's response. Yet I would also warn against limiting a work's significance simply to what an artist says it means. The gap between the artist and the work as it has meaning in the world allows for multiple interpretations. In other words, the artist's self-conscious understanding about what he or she makes shouldn't constrain a viewer's experience. This means that it's not enough to erase the question of intent just because an artist professes *good* intentions or a lack of awareness about what they're doing or how it may come across to others.

Of course, whether or not we'll raise such questions depends on the crime. When artists use their own family or friends in their work, it's hard to resist this intentional backtracking, because we all know you can get things from your close intimates that you can't get from a stranger. You know which buttons to push, where the boundaries are normally set, what makes someone comfortable or anxious. You know the weaknesses and flaws, and the point at which a person's narcissism will crowd out their dignity. Trust in a relationship allows for this knowledge, and thus the exploitation of that trust becomes a concern when artists turn their gaze to their inner circles. We can talk about Larry Clark photographing his friends shooting up or teenagers having sex, Catherine Opie photographing fellow lesbians in various transgendered states and self-scarring acts, Jeff Koons and Cicciolina staging and photographing their sexual adventures. Or we can talk about Nan Goldin hanging out with her hard-won gangs of heroin junkies, drag queens, and Japanese prostitutes, and her friends dying of AIDS, camera always in hand. With every picture snapped, there's a moment where the friendship is taken into the arena of art that makes me pause. What is the larger purpose, other than memorializing your friends for your own record? We know the subjects are aware of being photographed; the artists "have permission"; some of the subjects are even performers, so it's not a matter of voyeurism without consent. In many of the photographs there is a sense that the subjects *want* to feel the camera on them, they *need* to be seen; the artist is just giving them what they want. And in all of these cases, we're welcomed into worlds that are not often documented with such care and loving detail. But these are the same worlds that are sensationalized in tabloids and talk shows: titillating, shocking, *transgressive*. This stuff sells; looking at it makes people feel risky, sexy, sophisticated. Displaying a Robert Mapplethorpe print from the "X Portfolio" on your corporate walls makes for a pretty bold statement.

I overstate the case a bit to make a point: despite whatever powerful sense of recognition an insider may feel looking at these images, and despite whatever political impact a thoughtful, nuanced image of "alternative lifestyles" may have, to outsiders these images are shocking, and it's often the shock value that draws people to them. Does this mean artists shouldn't make such images? I'm not saying that, but it does mean that such images come with a lot of baggage that's not easily dismissed, baggage that can prevent people from seeing the work on other levels. It just comes with the territory when you treat and represent your friends this way.

The charge of exploitation and sensationalism can be applied to Billingham's photographs but it doesn't quite stick. His images are not transgressive in a sexual, gender-politics way, so I don't get the sense that he's working that particular angle, either directly or incidentally.

And his subjects are not friends he's hooked up with as one social misfit/ revolutionary to another, a "created, chosen family" with its own political agenda for inclusiveness and positive change. The photographs are literally and emotionally closer to home. This is his family of origin, his own stock, for better and definitely for worse, and it's as if he's seeing them for the first time in all their glory; in turns nonchalant, appalled, stunned, and amused. When asked what his family thinks about his work, Billingham asserts their naïveté. While he is acutely self-conscious, they remain unflustered by the filming,[2] so I wonder if they can perceive how others apprehend the images and thus what the status of their consent actually is. Do they realize the way the art world glamorizes poverty or the way an image of social despair often displaces and undercuts social action? How can you consent to something you don't understand? And if they can't imagine it, and don't care, does it matter anymore? They're adults, right?

The point of entry to Billingham's work is family: utterly familiar family drama, and this is a much less sensationalized topic than women who look like men or children having sex in front of grown-ups. The emotional resonance of the images is not easily overtaken by a question of exploitation. Yet, still there is an awkward tone to them. Caught somewhere between empathy and cruelty, honor and anger, acceptance and disdain, they push and pull the way family ties do. When experiencing them I'm not sure if these images are expressing emotions closer to love or to hate.

Billingham quit taking still photographs of his family in 1996, then started to log over 40 hours of videotape of' them, resulting in the 45-minute, made-for-TV *Fishtank*. Commissioned by Artangel, a British charity arts organization, it aired on the British Broadcasting Corporation (BBC) in England last December. The video footage is similar to the photographs: the same people the same house. Jason dances around catching flies. Ray watches the fish in his aquarium and sneaks beer. Liz plays with a snake, puts on makeup. There's a sickly beautiful scene in which Liz, mesmerized by a video game, glows blue in the otherwise orange-lit room, beads of perspiration slowly bulging up and rolling off her face. The saddest scenes are when Liz and Ray tell each other how much they are sick of it, sick of each other; they both threaten to leave but they've got nowhere to go. The video, which is so slowly paced and trying—and thus so unlike the shock tactics of the "Jerry Springer Show" with its escalating "surprises" and surges of adrenaline—convinces me further that this work does not sensationalize what it pictures. If anything, the approach elicits boredom. The camera lingers for minutes on the contours of a face, holds steady while the domestic quarrels fizzle and slowly peter out. You don't get the sense that anyone is acting for the camera or exaggerating their behavior for effect. Even though it is photographic and thus detached and mediated, the gaze feels attentive, patient, and, above all, tolerant. It's painful to watch, you feel a violation of privacy, and I still wonder about an artist, who, rather than protect his dysfunctional, poverty-stricken family from scrutiny, exposes them, but I get the sense that there is something else at work here than simply "gawking at the freaks." That something else is the sheer complicated emotionality of it.

After all of the analysis I am left with an ambivalence that revolves at its core around two poles: shame and pride. The overwhelming emotional response I have to Billingham's images is not compassion, not love, not ridicule, not indifference, not laughter but shame. It is a difficult feeling to experience, and not one I tend to seek out, but I recognize the power of its universality. Billingham's images seem universal because like ciphers we can project our own family issues onto them, whatever they are and whatever they make us feel. This is what makes his work so timely and so accessible. But feeling embarrassed or disgraced is essentially a public act. Shame is based on external judgments (however internalized), what others think or say. And as a viewer I cringe at the thought of putting myself in the artist's place, that this were my family, and the world had a peek into its particular dysfunction.

However, akin to this feeling of shame I also imagine an odd pride behind Billingham's images, as if to say, "Who cares if these are my parents and they're poor and screwed up. I'm no less a person for it. I am who I am, they are who they are. Deal with it." There is an intrepid self-confidence that flaunts itself regardless of such socially inculcated shame. In the end, the question of how Billingham could exploit his parents by disclosing their shameful private life becomes, "How could he reveal these things about himself with such honesty and blind confidence?"

If we give Billingham the benefit of the doubt, his daring may have been due in part to his youthful inexperience. The artist was 20 when he started taking the photographs of his family, and since they were originally taken as reference photos for his figurative paintings, he didn't consider them to be art. Since the conclusion of *Fishtank* he's moved off taking pictures of his family, claiming, "I was innocent then. If I carried on, it would be exploitation." More recent videos, which have been exhibited in London, show super close up views of his friends smoking. And his latest photographs feature cool urban landscapes taken in his home town of Stourbridge: an old pickup parked near a garbage can, a brick wall fence, an overgrown gated drive, a windswept empty beach. Billingham has likened them to places he might have seen as he was walking to school, but they feel anonymous.[3] The earlier images seem to be taken by an incredible someone. And his implicit presence complicates the work. Any number of artists could have taken Billingham's new photographs. They feel less specific and less driven by personality. They are most curious and make the most sense to me as a polar reaction to the *Sturm and Drang* of Billingham's family images, but I wonder how they would stand on their own.

Devoid of people the loneliness of the urban landscapes is palpable, though the subtlety of the feeling is still too easily overshadowed by the ominous cloud of the earlier work. The implied waiting in them reconnects with *Ray's a Laugh* and *Fishtank*, but I'm not sure who or what he's waiting for now.

NOTES

1. In an interview with Oliver Bennett, "My Family and Other Animals," *Independent Magazine.* November 28, 1998.
2. Ibid.
3. Ibid.

TEST FAMILY

Children in Contemporary Art

October 1999

Last spring I volunteered our family to be test subjects for a physiological study on working families. Arriving Fed Ex from the Alfred P. Sloan Family Center at the University of Chicago to our home in Oak Park, the study's test-kit included labeled Zip-lock Baggies stuffed with sanitary plastic syringes, teeny-tiny medical vials, pre-programmed wristwatches, Trident gum, and Kool-Aid crystals.

After filling out pages of questionnaires, sitting through several interviews conducted by a barrage of project assistants, and signing multiple release forms, we were ready to strap on the watches. The study worked like this: the watches would beep at random times throughout the day. The first beep signaled parents to fill out a journal entry that asked questions like "Do you feel caring? Stressed? Proud? Hardworking?" Twenty minutes later the watch would beep again and we'd each collect a saliva sample generated by chewing a piece of Trident or sucking on some Kool-Aid crystals. Then we'd label the vial and stick it in the refrigerator.

In 1992, Deborah Bright stated that "The myth of the dominant nuclear family purveyed through the media and conservative rhetoric" does not mesh with "the reality that fewer than 25 percent of families conform to that type."[1] This means that the so-called "norm" or "ideal" of the white, middle-class, heterosexual family has been replaced by a changing slurry of social relationships; ethical, religious, sexual, and physiological identities; and conflicting patterns of self-expression, consumption, leisure, and education. So, given the changing, complicated nature of the modern family, why are parenting issues, kids, and pedagogy so largely unexamined by today's artists?

At a lecture in 1992 Vito Acconci acknowledged that he has a great fear of the notion of home and family. Was he referring to the outdated notion of "family values" as touted by right-wing politicians and Christian organizations? Or did he mean to invoke the stereotype of the three-bedroom nursery in the suburbs governed by women obsessed with decor, or the ego-charged product of this domestic institution: kids? Regardless of the root of his fears, at least Acconci is up-front with his confession. The rest of the art world, like a cranky old coot, has grown away from a utopian belief that art and progressive social change can go hand in hand. The idea that children and family constructs operate as a premier emblem of the health and welfare of the nation or even as the most representational form of daily banality is for the most part overlooked in contemporary art production. Today's art world may be enamored with Modernism's retro-chic anxiety about domestic concerns, and contemporary painting may be infatuated with decoration, but few artists take on the subject of family directly.

Obviously the few artists who *are* working to focus attention on new family constructs and children's welfare have something more dear at stake than just their political identity. And although it is not a prerequisite to be a parent to effectively delve into these issues, the following artists (with the exception of Rirkrit Tiravanija) weave their firsthand experience as parents negotiating cultural values and stereotypes with their children into their art.

In the 1960s, many conceptual artists enthusiastic for the ordinary and concerned with non-objects and non-art sites happily embraced their own families, wife, kids, and dogs, working to reconfigure various social and pedagogical structures at play in an imperfect world. In the late '60s, Vancouver's N. E. Thing Co.—the name under which artists Iain and Ingrid Baxter and their children did things together—explored their favorite urban and suburban destinations on regular Sunday drives. They also took numerous family vacations throughout the United States and Canada disrupting what curator Nancy Shaw calls the "unidimensional, unidirectional hegemonic annexations of landscape."[2] N. E. Thing Co.'s aesthetic records take the form of photographic documents, geographic maps and drawings, as well as products like life-size balloons with images of Prime Minister Pierre Trudeau, and activities such as frequenting "family" restaurants and eating an abundance of "family" food. These occupy the gaps left between established institutions like art, the nuclear family, informational technologies, and the taken-for-granted. In one adventure this bohemian family drove around the North American continent in a truck re-evaluating everything and "anything." In a 1969 piece titled *1/4 Mile Landscape*, N. E. Thing Co. mounted three signs alongside a highway cutting through wooded terrain. Passing traffic would first see a sign that read "START VIEWING." The next sign down the road read "YOU ARE NOW IN THE MIDDLE OF A N. E. THING CO. LANDSCAPE" with the final sign reading "STOP VIEWING."

"The Company poked gentle fun at existing boundaries in order to improve the quality of life for themselves and others while inadvertently leaving a partial social document of their hybrid and polymorphic milieu," Shaw explains.[3] They functioned more like tourists in the strange, wonderful land of the ordinary, taking notes along the way, instead of artists theorizing and recomposing their discoveries. Whether it was organizing a PeeWee hockey team or traveling through 31 states in 40 days, the Baxters integrated corporate, domestic, and artistic activities with earnest participation, good humor, and play.

At the same time N. E. Thing Co. was taking Polaroids of roadside kitsch, Danish artist Palle Nielsen transformed Moderna Museet in Stockholm into a colorful, romping playground for children. Outfitted with dress-up clothes, carnival masks, jungle gyms, foam blocks, record players, art supplies, and construction materials, Nielsen's 1968 *Modellen for ett kvalitativt samhalle* (*Model for a Qualitative Society*) incited the kids of Stockholm to free, expansive play. Curator Lars Bang Larsen explained, "Through the means of *Modellen*, Nielsen was putting into practice the notion that it is the child's early social relations which form the person as an individual in society."[4] This same intersection of creative pedagogy and art has been turned on its head in the late 1990s.

Rirkrit Tiravanija's *Untitled, 1997* (*Playtime*), a scaled-down, child-size version of Philip Johnson's Glass House installed at the sculpture garden at Museum of Modern Art and later at Williams College was similar to Nielsen's *Modellen*, complete with the raw materials for creative play. But in comparison, Tiravanija's social dynamics are a bit disingenuous and very redundant. Tiravanija's miniaturizing of a Modernist icon to house educational programs that are already in place in museums throughout the United States, as Francesco Bonami argues, "succeeds in a kind of cultural nemesis."[5] In this educational pavilion, the kids, like the pom-poms and pipe cleaners, become the raw material for examining the public dimension of Modernism by humanizing the institutional nature of the exhibition space. Less concerned with the broader social ramifications motivated by creative learning, *Untitled 1997 (Playtime)* illustrates institutional paradoxes; art asking questions about art without reforming social or aesthetic dynamics.

Epitomizing Lucy Lippard's concept of art's "dematerialization," the championing of the idea over the object, Dennis Oppenheim relied on a fairly explicit set of conceptual conventions, creating work that frequently and radically involved his children. As curator Peter Spooner describes it, his research into "sensory substitution, translocation (the relocation of events and space), and transmogrification (the shifting of shaped into different forms)" makes sense of the use of his offspring as the perfect conduit to draw out his shamanistic experimentation.[6] Thomas McEvilley called it "genetic extension."[7] Simply, Oppenheim regarded his children as an extension of his own body.

Two-Stage Transfer Drawings. (Returning to a Past State). Dennis to Erik Oppenheim, and *Two-Stage Transfer Drawings. (Advancing to a Future State). Erik to Dennis Oppenheim* both from 1971 established a re-orientation of mark, body, and father-son relationship. In (*Returning to a Past State*), Oppenheim senior runs a Magic Marker over his young son's back as the boy attempts to duplicate the line's path on a wall. They then reverse the roles in (*Advancing to a Future State*) and Erik draws through his father. Oppenheim describes the process:

> My activity stimulates a kinetic response from his memory system. I am therefore, drawing through him. Sensory retardation or disorientation makes up the discrepancy between the two drawings, and could be seen as elements that are activated during this procedure. Because Erik is my offspring, and we share similar biological ingredients, his back (as surface) can be seen as an immature version of my own . . . in a sense, I make contact with a past state [of myself].[8]

In a piece involving his daughter, Oppenheim developed another system of events in which he channeled his voice and cognitive abilities through his child. In *Color Application for Chandra* from 1971 Oppenheim taught his two-and-a-half-year-old daughter to identify seven basic colors with their names using projected light and repeated verbal cues. Again Oppenheim describes,

In three hours she is able to associate the color symbol with the word symbol . . . Individual tape loops of Chandra's voice repeating the color names are then played twenty-four hours a day to a parrot in a separate room. The parrot eventually learns to mimic the color names . . . It is a method for me to throw my voice.

His kids, their art work, and even his father's technical drawings provided Oppenheim with the tools to achieve a decentered presence, a practice of ruptures, starts, and stops. In contrast, artist Tony Tasset employed his familial structure in order to look at his own sense of upper-middle-class identity. *I M U R ME* is a looped video made in 1998 of the Tony Tasset-Judy Ledgerwood family: mom, dad, and son Henry, sitting at the breakfast table eating oatmeal. Facilely computer morphing into one another, this idealized family unit is unbearably perfect: blond hair, blue eyes, polite as can be, as Tony becomes Judy becomes Henry becomes Tony. Fortifying bathetic normative family values made trite in Norman Rockwell prints and 1950s sitcoms, this family-related work seems to embrace the clean-cut aura of a conservative lifestyle. However, like Charles Ray's *Family Romance,* an invisible thread of suspicion cuts through the pretensions of normalcy, thereby destabilizing the idea of the model family.

In soap-opera vogue, Tasset's 1996 video *Better Me* also poignantly examines his paradoxical relationship to his bourgeois lifestyle. The lead character interacts with his wife, son, art dealer, and an enamored student in such affluent settings as a courtyard on an ivy-league campus, a high-tech office/studio, and in front of a crackling fire with a glass of wine. The clash between career and passion, between recklessness and domestic responsibility are played out in four short vignettes. As the actor ambivalently adopts the role of husband, artist, father, and teacher, each successive scenario reveals more evidence of a false integrity in increasingly regressive interpersonal relationships.

Unsatisfied with a static art product, New York artist Ben Kinmont creates new applicable models for artists who happen to have family responsibilities. As the son of California conceptual artist Robert Kinmont, Ben and his sister were often the subjects of their father's search for raw experience. Like Oppenheim, the social gulf between parents and children represented divisions of power, which Kinmont senior and his colleagues where interested in dissolving. This philosophy was not only played out in their work but within the way they experienced the everyday. Since their artist parents often affirmed their direct guttural and inquisitive behavior, some kids of this generation had an unprecedented involvement in making family decisions.

Losing a tooth at a baseball game or taking a new route home from school were inter- family experiences that showed up publicly in Robert Kinmont's art. Today, Ben continues some aspects of his father's investigation into domestic life through his "social sculptures," but unlike his father, he chooses to keep his wife and children out of the public aspects of his performances. His most recent work integrates his art activity with his occupation as an antiquarian book dealer, naming it *Sometimes a nicer sculpture is to be able to provide a living for your family*. In this way, the business becomes an art work, which provides for his family, simultaneously building a foundation for a shared domestic life. Where Tasset identifies many hats in his daily round, Ben Kinmont struggles to successfully wear just one hat at all times.

Ben Kinmont is a consummate researcher, and other models of fatherhood in the art world have been sources of his work. In 1989 he made a multiple based on an obscure family photograph of Joseph Beuys with his wife and kids. Curious why Beuys rarely acknowledged his family, Kinmont wrapped copies of the Shel Silverstein book *The Giving Tree* with paper bands that read "I wonder if Joseph Beuys ever explained the meaning of art to his son and daughter?"

Whether it is dealing in rare books, serving waffles, or washing dishes in stranger's homes, Kinmont is one of a few male artists interested in creating a new working model for his family that is neither bohemian nor conventional. Women artists, on the other hand, have been actively examining notions of family and child well-being since Mary Kelly analyzed her son's fecal stains in the early '70s. Today, artist mothers like Myrel Chernick, Judy Gelles, Gail Rebhan, Marion Wilson, and Sarah Vanderlip continue to "tactically (re)conceptualize family relations as children, parents, couples, siblings, lovers, and members of extended, non-biologically based kinship systems."[9] Following closely Kelly's lead in researching mother-child relationships, New York artist Myrel Chernick's multi-media works fuse text by Julia Kristeva, Hélène Cixous, and Virginia Woolf with clean, crisp graphic design and occasional appearances by her twin sons. Instead of answering Sigmund Freud's question "What does a woman want?" Chernick's projects radically, and persistently re-phrase it, over and over again.

Philadelphia-based artist Judy Gelles integrates pictures from her childhood with the photographic history she, as a dedicated mother, has secured for her family. Like Palle Nielsen, she is interested in children as agencies of socialization and sites for the development of notions of gender. *When We Were Ten* from 1997 is a photo/text book presenting the physical and psychological growth of Gelles and her son Jason from the age of six to 18. She walks us through the tooth fairy and second grade, then later makes us uncomfortable with straightforward discussion of jock straps, menstruation, and Jewish stereotypes. In a photo essay she did for *Ms.* magazine in 1990 titled *A Family Portrait: A Wife/Mother/Photographer's Revenge,* Gelles reprints a family snapshot from 1978 depicting her sitting on the toilet surrounded by toddlers. The accompanying text reads, "I would love to be able to go to the bathroom alone, but I don't dare. David could put his finger in the socket."

Casting a replica of her one-year-old son in white sugar is a metaphorical albeit classical art move by young New York artist Sarah Vanderlip. But in a recent exhibition, the gesture gains expanded meaning when juxtaposed with a homemade wood playroom bedecked with all the best toys. Needing to occupy her son's time while she makes art is a much more urgent and real gesture than playing "cultural nemesis." Another New Yorker, Marion Wilson also asks real questions about the practical nurturing of children. Her concern is popular culture's exaggerated representations of masculinity as evidenced in her 1998 piece *Guns for Newborns,* a collection of six small bronze squirt guns poised on wire mounts. "The silhouettes of the gun holds the less logical portions of our protective psyches forever hostage."[10]

Washington D.C.-based artist Gail Rebhan layers the often irrational, convoluted, and profound dialogue she has with her two sons with graphic images that edify the frequent expanding exchanges. For example, she includes a discussion with her sons on what "gay" means in *Mother-Son Talk,* a book published at the Visual Studies Workshop in Rochester, New York in 1996. Imposed over colorful Twister-like dots filled with dictionary definitions of "gay," the conversation reads:

Son (age seven)—"Does gay mean stupid or crazy?"
Mom—"It doesn't mean either."
Son—"What does gay mean?"
Mom—"It means happy."

Son—"No, when it means something bad. Like you're gay."

Mom—"It means homosexual."

Son—"Ooooooh. Sexy!"

Mom—"No, it doesn't mean sexy. It means men who are attracted to men."

Son—"What?"

Mom—"You know how men and women get married. Gays are men who are attracted to other men."

Son (uncomprehending)—"Oh."

These little stories from home are the social and cultural basis of our future. Starting as simple discussions within the relative obscurity of the domestic world, Rebhan's daily interaction with her kids is more affecting than a resulting image or object could ever be.

If Oppenheim and his generation of artists worked to level the social and cultural privileges reserved for adults, some contemporary artists like Aura Rosenberg appear to be shoring up the parental/child, artist/subject hierarchy. Inviting respected art-world figures to paint on children with face paint, her own kids and others, Rosenberg mocks the plethora of Anna Gaskells and Kim Dingles whose work is spurred by a non-threatening self-indulgence with childhood seduction and fantasy. By re-introducing an actual child into our cultural fixation with play, dress-up, and pretend, Rosenberg's photographs create an environment in which artists like John Baldessari, James Siena, Haim Steinbach, Dan Graham, and others can assume exploitative roles familiar to dysfunctional family dynamics and artist/subject relationships. Coming close to crossing an unacceptable ethical line, Rosenberg's 1996 C-print titled *Jim Shaw/Joe Siena* documents Shaw's red-and-black grizzly gesture drawing on the pre-teen boy Joe Siena, looking much like the handiwork of a drunken fratboy before the big game. *Mike Kelley/Carmen Rosenberg-Miller*, Mike Kelley's transformation of a pre-pubescent girl into a ghastly innocent, ventures into a place where even Benetton wouldn't dare to go.

I have slim hope that the Sloan spit study in which my family participated will yield any real changes in how our culture (re)defines family values or socializes its children. The fact that these issues do not pose a viable concern with most of today's art world is less puzzling when we examine the demographics of its whole. Art has always offered a refuge from social norms. Perhaps it will take the efforts of gay men and lesbians interested in altering domestic arrangements to bring questions about family to the foreground. Or perhaps the issues surrounding family structures and pedagogy are simply thought to be too commonplace, too boring, too tied to the political right wing to be bothered with. As parents, my husband and I form a collaborative art practice out of examining our clumsy, middle-class, suburban domicile, churning our observations and questions into projects (the group is called CAR). Like Ben Kinmont and his father, the N. E. Thing Co., and a handful of others, we are interested in new models of what family and art can be. But for now this family is off to Blockbuster to cash in the gift certificate the Sloan Family Center sent us as a token of their appreciation.

NOTES

1. Deborah Bright, "Family Practices," *Views*, Summer 1992, 7.

2. Nancy Shaw, "Siting the Banal: The Expanded Landscapes of the N. E. Thing Co.," in *Start Viewing* (Vancouver: UBC Fine Arts Gallery, 1993), 25.

3. Ibid., 33.

4. Lars Bang Larsen, "Sometimes I'm Up. Sometimes I'm Down. Sometimes I'm Underground Making Social Aesthetics Operative," in *Like Virginity, Once Lost: Five Views on Nordic Art Now* (Sweden: Proplex, 1999), 42.

5. Francesco Bonami, "Spotlight: Rirkrit Tiravanija," *Flash Art*, October 1997, 112.

6. Peter F. Spooner, "Drawing Delirium," in *Dennis Oppenheim: Drawing and Selected Sculpture*, exhibition catalogue (Normal: Illinois State University, 1992), 6.

7. Thomas McEvilley, "The Rightness of Wrongness: Modernism and Its Alter-ego in the Work of Dennis Oppenheim," in *Dennis Oppenheim Selected Works 1967–1990* (New York: P.S, 1 Museum and Abrams, 1992), 33.

8. Dennis Oppenheim, quoted in ibid., 72.

9. Bright, 8.

10. Bill Arning, *Marion Wilson: Playing War* (Buffalo, New York: Hallwalls Contemporary Art Center, 1999), unpaginated.

KERRY JAMES MARSHALL

Agent of Change

February 2001

What did Sam Cooke's mother's house look like? If Mercy Dee had a sister, how did she decorate her living room? If you have a likely idea, then chances are good that you are black. Whites, especially of a certain age and class, are more often than not familiar with the songs, but not the people. If you are white, Aretha Franklin's recorded voice may hold a prominent place in the soundtrack of your life, but how often do you hang with your black neighbors, over at their house?

Kerry James Marshall paints images of those people. His "Mementos" show, first exhibited at the Renaissance Society in 1998 and traveling throughout the United States since then, takes the 1960s as its subject; collective historical memory is its obvious theme. But a different consideration of this Chicago-based artist's "Souvenir" paintings included in the show reveals a consequence of that decade and the gap between a culture and its products still felt very vividly today. Each of these domestic tableaux is based on the actual interior of one of the artist's relatives or relative's friend's houses. In representing these specific environments, Marshall renders visible the problem of being intimate with a cultural product but not its producers, of knowing a culture through its expressions but not its members.

In the wall-sized painting *Souvenir IV,* Marshall depicts an interior based on his mother-in-law's friend's living room, over which emerges a heavenly array of deceased musicians all identified in their day as "Negro" or "colored." Marshall screenprinted the names and faces of these figures in a zone outside the perspectival space of the room, thus rendering visible the non-corporeal realm of memory. And yet this roster of black cultural greats belongs in this room—together they establish the territory of the painting's surface. By situating a black cultural memory—now in the process of mainstream canonization—within the sweep of a black living space alien to most non-black people, Marshall exposes that white people's media consumption is not a valid substitute for social interaction.

This is a significant point when one realizes that Marshall—whose work has in recent years been shown in such prestigious exhibitions as the Carnegie International, the Whitney Biennial, and documenta X—chooses to reside and make art in the Third Ward on Chicago's South Side, in what many would say is the heart of the near south ghetto. The specificity of indigence and segregation to this location is an essential consideration in drawing a thread of continuity between this place where he lives and Marshall's artistic and pedagogical practice. (Marshall is a tenured faculty member at the School of Art and Design at the University of Illinois at Chicago.)

Marshall's commitment to a skill-based foundation accounts for his varied early works on paper, canvas, and board, using collage, charcoal, tempera, woodcut, and acrylics. As a whole, these works stand as a record of Marshall's earnest pursuit of mastering the manipulation of materials. At the same time as he honed his painterly skills, Marshall also laid the groundwork for what has become a sort of personal hallmark: the image of the jet-black figure. *A Portrait of the Artist as a Shadow of His Former Self* from 1980, in which Marshall paints a figure almost too dark to be seen but flashing a gap toothed Cheshire cat grin, predicts by a decade the powerful use of non-valorized black figures by artists such as Thom Shaw and Kara Walker. And by enunciating his racial identity as a given, Marshall clears a path toward conceptual and art-historical concerns early on, rather than dwelling on narrowly autobiographical narratives.

Marshall's rejection of the strictly autobiographical means that he has chosen to dispense with the artist as storyteller in favor of the artist as critic, theorist, and historian. The resultant seriousness of inquiry has allowed him to work in representational styles not historically associated with the narratives of any marginalized population. In fact, much of his output aims for a stylistic position updating that most hallowed of visual traditions, the painting of the pre- and early Modern European masters. It may be that only an artist with Marshall's seemingly contradictory commitments to an unflinching investigation into the sociopolitical conditions of black American life, on the one hand, and to a painterly prowess in the Western vein, on the other, can make paintings in the classical traditions vital. It is apparent that what is conventionally thought of as the art world's indifference or even hostility to the artist of color has not stopped Marshall from inserting himself into the European representational lineage, and thereby extending it.

A typical example is the mural-sized *Bang* from 1994, in which Marshall scrambles religious motifs, dramatic historical themes, and pastoral ideals of different classical genres into a starkly melancholy view of twentieth century American secular faith. In the painting, three staid children mournfully conduct what seems to be an impromptu pledge to a flaccidly draped American flag. They stand in a backyard complete with garden hose, barbecue grill, and white picket fence, but whose idealization is marred by streaks and gestural splotches of paint. The image effectively links middle-class aspirations to national rituals and to segregated realities. The group of paintings from 1994 and 1995 known as the "Garden Project" continue these investigations. Titled after public housing projects that have "Garden" in their names, the group consists of epic paintings that present an amalgam of classical elements, mixing Renaissance composition with pastoral themes and Mannerist detail. The overt classical vocabulary in each painting is proportionally balanced by Postmodern elements, including the foregrounding of one or several super-dark figures, and perhaps chiefly, the public housing projects themselves as setting and subject. The overlaid, obviously Modernistic drips and gestural strokes not only complete the nearly encyclopedic painter's lexicon Marshall employs in these works, but also blunt attempts to force the work into Socialist Realism, except, again, by enlivening and extending that category.

Stateway Gardens and Wentworth Gardens—two of the housing projects pictured in the "Garden Project"—are a short walk from Marshall's studio. But the projects are only half the story of this part of town. The "interaction" between races on the South Side of Chicago can be described by a term that only now, decades after the population movement reached its fever pitch, can be used without evoking a torrent of fear, guilt, and sadness: white flight. This demographic shift left to black people vast tracts of the city—neighborhoods later made known to the white mainstream through the nightly news, to the liberal white elite through social science, and to neither through actual contact.

If there is a linchpin to the narrative of modern urban segregation, it must be education. Education, as the nation eternally intonates in unison, is a ticket out of the ghetto. And yet underfunding and mismanagement of urban school systems have become the clearest example of institutional failure and inequality in the United States. Ask Marshall about deficiencies in the educational experience and he'll launch into the usual litany of woes: students can't read well, can't write at all, can't think, and lack a host of fundamental skills. All of these are predictably understood as problems, except for one thing: he is not talking just about the grade schools several blocks from his studio which serve an impoverished black neighborhood—he's also talking about undergraduate universities and graduate art education and the privileged class of students these programs serve.

For Marshall, the integral continuity between the two worlds he inhabits—art schools and inner-city environments—is that both suffer from an absence of expected excellence. That this should be the case when history abounds with exemplary models of behavior challenges Marshall to formulate a practice through which he can articulate a politics of excellence.

In one of a set of murals done for the hallways of a middle school in Chicago in 1994, his assertion of excellence takes the straightforward form of celebrating Frederick Douglass as an exemplar of self-educated black American power. As someone who literally had to beg, borrow, and steal his education, and then wielded it against the system that would keep him enslaved, Douglass represents that combination of elements Marshall finds so lacking in both academia and the social universe outside his studio: a powerful imagination wedded to practical self-discipline. Moreover, judging from our conversations, Marshall's notion of excellence consists fundamentally of a strong work ethic. The high quality of an artist's technical skills, understanding art history, and critical thinking will all follow his or her refusal to cut corners.

As part of the "Mementos" exhibit, the "We Mourn Our Loss" paintings reach an art world audience different from neighborhood middle-school students, but can be interpreted similarly. Composed of images of the modern-day trinity of Martin Luther King and the Kennedy brothers in differing arrangements against flat dark backgrounds along with the solemn words "We Mourn Our Loss," the series historicizes a remembrance that has become so important to the generation of black Americans who lived through the Civil Rights era as to have become emblematic.

Marshall, however recalls the three figures as symbols not only of an idealism lost, but, just as importantly, of an ability to meet the challenges of circumstances, to excel despite political obstacles and personal flaws, and to inspire others to commit their own acts of greatness.

In an age in which the demonized liberal and the ultra-cynical conservative define the poles of the political spectrum, Marshall's message takes on added resonance and depth. He insists that the impulse and ability to change the world arises most powerfully from a will to excellence. Paradoxically, it may be the marginalized who are best positioned to advance new standards of excellence, since they have the most to gain in a changed world.

Marshall's work speaks the language of contemporary art confidently, having lately moved into video, sculpture, and installation. It also amplifies two long-standing black traditions. The first is politicized self-reliance, the icons of which range from Marcus Garvey to the Black Panthers. Interestingly, Marshall's unique contribution to this legacy is the generalized application of a peculiarity belonging to the art world: the anticipation of critique. To give one case, in his suite of five "Black Power" prints from 1998 Marshall enlarges the subject of critique to include the strategic orientation of the Black Power movement itself, and not simply the objects that make up the suite. Each piece bears a dated slogan such as "Black is Beautiful" or "By Any Means Necessary" simply printed in block letters in quotation marks but without other adornment, thereby memorializing a crucial chapter of struggle without erasing the movement's flaws. Just as artists anticipate critical reception from friendly audiences, these prints suggest that partisans likewise ought to interrogate the strategies of their own political movements and histories, and remove the blockages that prevent self-critique. The strikingly neutral presentation of such once- incendiary expressions sufficiently reopens critical reassessment of, for example, the Black Panther Party. As he travels parallel socioeconomic spheres both suffering from normalized underachievement, it is the kind of ethic—an independence that takes responsibility for its own self-reflection and dispenses with blind loyalties (whether political or aesthetic)—that Marshall seeks to instill in young people.

The second black aesthetic tradition employed by Marshall is that of the artistic imaginary: from Sun Ra to DJ Spooky, black artists have always used available linguistic and technological tools to project into the sci-fi future, to envision a changed world. One of Marshall's current ventures fits right into this strain of black culture. He's developing a comic strip called *Rythm Mastr,* in which his twin concerns of art history and urban black society continue in a futuristic setting with the added layer of narrative development over time. As with his painting, in which he masters the language of the canonized traditions in order to spotlight the deficiencies of those same traditions, Marshall began this enterprise with his own learning process. A dozen or more books about animation, cartoons, and comics sit near his drawing tables and on his shelves. After researching the medium, Marshall put time-tested comic book devices such as the unlikely superhero and the dramatic visual sequence to work telling the story of a crew of young black people discovering superhuman powers in a not-so-imaginary time of social distress. The result is an apocalyptic world filled with lots of fine and popular art-historical references and a hip-hop sensibility.

Rythm Mastr is the latest example of Marshall's artistic and educational philosophies in action: he works to possess a knowledge of art-historical precedent (in this case, the popular art of cartooning), a command of materials, and the ability to gauge one against the other in the course of producing a work of art. In combination, these skills allow Marshall to rightfully claim status as an agent of change within the field. This level of empowerment is also the goal he sets for his students, and a model which he hopes to present to those of his inner-city neighborhood.

Already having had a limited run in the *Pittsburgh Post-Gazette* as an extension of his contribution to the 1999 Carnegie International, and with future comic-book installments forthcoming, *Rythm Mastr* promises to solidify the bridge between Marshall's worlds in mass-media form, and will undoubtedly question the established reach of the art world. As always, for Marshall, the quality of the product will determine the potency of its questioning.

NOTES ON A MIDWEST MAKEOVER

May/June 2001

Rumors There'd Been, But Still the News Jolted

The Onion, beloved free weekly deadpan satirical newspaper extraordinaire, had relocated, departing its long-time base in Madison, Wisconsin for New York City! How could they? How dare they? Had *The Onion* really no grasp of how essential to our fragile regional pride it had become? Disappointment was instantly supplanted, however, by a welling feeling of, gulp, *patriotism*, rendered in the style of an *Onion* headline: "Wisconsin's Loss Is Corrupt Nation's Gain." Let them go. They *should* go. Over the course of the next four years (the new Administration's efforts to blur the line between church and state making it easier for us to pray publicly it'll be only four) Americans will need a ruthless retailer of hard truths operating from *some* quarter, and nothing currently in circulation more expertly pinpoints the delusions we inhabit or the lies deployed against us than does *The Onion*. Scaling up the weekly's hilariously bracing observations about Who We Are, Right Now, Like It Or Not for the New York market and positioning its mercy-unencumbered writers before the shiny bouquet of microphones comprised of the book, TV, and radio deals they so evidently yearn to ink and, more importantly, richly deserve, ought to do a lot to deflect the Bush-league inequities certain, to flow our way. So let them go. If their move from Madison is a blow to the renewal of indigenous contemporary Midwestern culture—and we shouldn't kid ourselves, it is—well, doesn't their departure just make room for the next configuration, whatever it might be, to take shape?

That one needn't feel altogether cockeyed in indulging such optimism is attributable to the fact that the American Midwest is, thankfully, in a fascinating period of renewal and re-invention. It's true that in recent years the entire stratum of this nation's "mid-cap" cities has bloomed, seeded and watered by a decade of economic boom; the dispersal of power sponsored by the personal computer and the Internet; cable TV, which has piped into homes everywhere a sophistication that's broken the deadly sleeperhold long applied by local media outlets; and, more amorphously, the indie, DIY aesthetic, unbottled by punk 25 years ago and still permeating modern life to glorious effect—the accretion of these forces working to blur any simple distinction between province and capital. While widespread, this happy evolution of America's second- and third-tier burgs (our versions of Rotterdam, Antwerp, Naples, Stockholm . . .) is perhaps most compelling—because perhaps most unexpected—in those cities lodged in the belts of rust and of corn.

The cultural makeovers currently underway in towns like Milwaukee, Cleveland, Des Moines, Pittsburgh, and Indianapolis were hardly elective. Crisis and pain spurred their innovation. With America's transition away from the family farm gradually eroding the region's cultural import, its vitality was already on the wane when, during the 1970s, the proud industrial era that had underwritten America's transition from rural to urban at last petered out. As, one by one, the manufacturers of the machine tools, farming equipment, and mining equipment that had literally *made* those rust-belt towns went down the tubes, big chunks of indigenous cultural identity were carried along with them. Through the subsequent decades, the region's cities mostly limped along—wounded, stunned, famously "out of it," semi-somnambulant. Although they remained for the most part physically pleasant and livable places, such "local culture" as these cities offered their residents came drawn from increasingly stagnant wells of nostalgia for heydays of harvesting, brewing, smelting, and welding. A genuine and vibrant contemporary indigenous culture was, for all intents and purposes, here nonexistent, which absence appeared to doom the cities of the Midwest to be ever receivers, never senders. Anyone who required a snazzier life split, or yearned to.

Fortunately these were, always had been, pragmatic places; whatever they'd absolutely *had* to do they'd done well and seriously. Forced now to play serious catch-up lest they shrivel up and blow away, the more progressive Midwestern towns gradually groped their way onto the post-industrial grid of the emerging information/service economy. In doing so, they discovered a bonus, of an unanticipated high: a sense of exhilaration at being liberated from pasts defined so exclusively and dogmatically by their earlier, stubbornly earthbound agrarian and industrial phases. Today, despite lousy weather half the year, there's a newfound lightness to these places, a flexibility mirroring that of the new arrivals who work for the new capital-unintensive companies that don't manufacture anything. Environments with greater give and play in them have always held more appeal, obviously, for the more purely inutile types who dedicate themselves to the invention of reflective culture. Throw cheap rents into that mix and, presto, we're talking primed agar. And so, although it's taken a long time—nearly 30 years of gestation and muted mutation—today some mighty interesting critters can again be observed walking fully erect through the cities of the plains. The progressive concentration of such people—artists of every stripe—is fundamentally, and likely permanently, altering the experience of the hinterlands.

Take Milwaukee. Those of us currently living in Milwaukee can hardly believe our eyes and ears, so long had little save sports and nature appreciation and racism and money-making and taverning gone on here. Today, a quite vibrant and original *something* else is brewing. The city's image of itself is changing—appropriately enough, as it's becoming a different place. It's always been well-managed and clean, but now it's both more hospitable to ideas and less hostile to the sort of people who prefer to organize their lives around them. Good young filmmakers, musicians, writers, poets, and visual artists no longer automatically flee in pursuit of the glittery tantalizations allegedly paving the streets of New York or Los Angeles. More novel yet, good artists who've done time in New York or LA are choosing to move *here*. That's news, and it'd *be* news in any of the smaller American cities. Milwaukee isn't a town to everyone's taste—maybe some get turned off by the old Lawrence Welk shows broadcast on local public television Saturday nights—but those who are neck-deep in its re-invention actually use words such as "magical" to describe both it and this moment they're living through. And when strong imaginations love the place they're working in, even the ghost of Lawrence Welk can't keep good things from happening.

Whenever anyone takes up a new medium, it's a while, of course, before they're able to put any personal imprint on it, and in many places in the Midwest the very idea of a "contemporary indigenous culture" is just that: a new medium. This whole exciting shmear I'm gassing on about is just beginning to come into focus. Already, though, certain distinct attributes can be identified.

Now as ever, the city fathers' approach to culture is to think big, write big checks, and import works by big names who are based in the capitals. That is unquestionably a contribution. Still, the hardcore re-invention of indigenous culture so crucial to a city's continued renaissance isn't something that transpires at the macroscopic level but, rather, the micro-, deep down in the trenches of behavioral innovation. As usual, then, the organisms currently returning nutrients to the region's soil are a few dozen smart young-ish adults with forceful imaginative lives and no money, a type who might once have been labeled "bohemian" but here aren't because a) within the context of the Midwest's friendly innocence the dark allures of bohemian excess appear, even to those who might have been most susceptible to them, several shades too silly to be actively indulged, and b) these folks are in synch with the region's work ethic. They're industrious as hell. Some boast Master's degrees, others are disciplined autodidacts. Teaching some, running clever shops, holding down part-time gigs interesting or dreary or ridiculous, they get by, and save a deeper commitment for their real work; having seen something of the world, both physically and virtually, they're not thrown by close, continual proximity to existential uncertainty. From their art, films, music, and poetry they derive little or no income (in the new Midwest, monied people haven't yet established any connection to the strange new culture springing up around them), but that's okay because these artists are disposed to identify self-interest broadly, unselfishly: what's good for their community of like-minded comrades is, they figure, in the long run good, too, for their own lives. So far, anyway, they're unafflicted by career- or money-madness.

Probably this communitarian attitude grows out of the all-for-one-and-one-for-all, working-class mentality of the region (Milwaukee, for instance, elected a socialist mayor, and it did so twice). Another, less sanguine influence is the fact that it's still quite difficult to make any sort of living as a professional reflective imagination in markets like Pittsburgh, St. Louis, and Des Moines. But it's a mistake to paint anyone anywhere as a mere expression of some historical force. Midwestern imaginations are *choosing* the Midwest. It's not as if they don't know where the airport is. They like, for one thing, that in towns of smaller consequence it's harder to treat people as opportunities, something all too easy to do in New York or Los Angeles (or, for that matter, Chicago). They *want* to treat the people around them, and to be treated, decently—a life-preference sometimes difficult for the success-obsessed in the capitals to grasp.

More than this, the most advanced Midwestern imaginations are quite conscious that they represent and embody an alternative to the dominant models of culture-making celebrated in and promoted by the magazines and television shows produced in the current centers. Having been officially "out of it" and in the middle of the country for much of their lives, Midwesterners enjoy a natural, deep-dyed perspective on the seamlessly managed professional culture of often-dubious commercial product that is ceaselessly lobbed at them from the coasts. The model of Midwestern contemporary culture emergent is based in part on plasticizing, activating, and exploiting that perspective to risk the creation of something different.

Post-Professionalism?

When the likelihood of anyone paying for your product shows itself, year in and year out, to be slim at best, equating "professional product" with culture *per se* starts looking pretty foolish. Smart artists contending with chronically insalubrious market prospects might be wiser to devote themselves instead to making the *process* of producing culture as pleasurable as possible. The Midwestern sensibilities currently making things happen do elevate process—here defined existentially, as centering oneself in an inventive life and *living an inventive life for its own sake*—over product. Indeed the more extreme among them regard process—how something might be made, and what experience might be had while making it—as their true product. The now standard contemporary strategy (dictated by the coastal centers) of consciously streamlining one's life in order to produce a neat, saleable package of culture doesn't hold great appeal for these people.

Moreover, the region's most highly evolved artists recognize that their creative stance also contains a political dimension, one which pushes "alternative culture" past the merely decorative status it has fallen into. Revamping that worn phrase, they pursue a positivistic, quotidian construction, a day-to-day creativity. The binding agent in their ongoing collaboration isn't the prospect of making money together but, instead, the wilder prospect of together inventing powerful creative lives that are not organized around the psychological enslavement to an iconic content or style for commercial purposes. Closely linking experience and invention, they do what they do without the expectation of being offered a contract to do it. (When I tried to pay a local artist for participating in a project of mine, he refused, saying "Participating is just something we do.") Having done what they do without attention, i.e. invisibly, all these years, their lack of concern about being "noticed" or "discovered" or "celebrated" by a profoundly flawed, fickle, and duplicitous cultural eye is genuine, ingrained, and resolute—*especially* now that portions of the Midwest are enjoying semi-"in" status.

Creative activity that can't be bought off is inherently political.

Send Us a Tape, Why Don't You?

Essential to the new and undeniable vigor of the Midwestern scene is the fact that its artists are able to make work that easily connects to like-minded pockets of the wider world; the fruit of what's happening here can be and is getting exported to parallel scenes in New York, Los Angeles, and beyond. Undiscovered talents are able to catapult their ideas outside the region for the same reason that talents with national and international reputations are able to retain Midwestern locales as their bases: the lingua franca of the Midwestern renaissance isn't high-art media but pop-format media—film, video, CDs, Web sites.

Artists who work out of the Midwest today utilize the same formats and the same distribution networks as artists living in New Jersey or, for that matter, New Delhi. An artist who wants to communicate a sense of what it's like to live in Wisconsin is no longer restricted to painting a picture of a Wisconsin marsh. That artist now can make a video of that Wisconsin marsh, add voiceover, music, and animation effects, and then join the media flow, popping his or her creation in the mail or posting it on a Web site. Today the artists of the Midwest celebrate two landscapes: the local, natural landscape, and the synthetic, international one. Like their counterparts in Stockholm or Seattle or Taiwan, these artists use pop culture as a platform on which they invent experience, for themselves and others. So far, the strongest stuff showing up in these parts isn't destined for galleries but for screens and stereos.

Whereas, The Green Bay Packers Are The Grateful Dead of the NFL . . .

Artists anywhere are involved in a search for authenticity. For many years now this search has been complicated by the fact that, especially in America, authentic experience is substantially comprised of the synthetic realm known as "mass media." The confusion between what's natural and what's synthetic is deeply ingrained in the regional artist who works in pop media formats. An artist so located lives with internal dialogues that are unlikely to visit an artist who is based in one of the capitals. In the mind of the former, contradictions between what's indigenous and what's an import, what's regional and what's international, what's contiguous with the ideas that issue from the capitals and what isn't, demand to be negotiated. How does a place go about advancing into a future that clearly breaks with its origins? Which aspects of the past get preserved, and in what form? What model do progressive people employ?

Un/Cool 1

Only a certain sort of person finds such questions as these remotely attractive or "cool," it should be said. Only a certain sort of person is attracted to this particular manifestation of the frontier—or, frankly, even recognizes it to *be* one. Setting aside the comparative rarity of such people, the idea remains that cities which had done years of service as punchlines should suddenly be perceived as cool—in any way, by anyone—says a lot about the complex status of "cool" today.

In New York or LA a person can go to work for Sony or Gucci, MoMA or MoCA, or some other officially cool place, and by so doing be cool by association. Aspiration toward that status draws many people to the coasts; jobs with one or another officially cool institution are actively competed for. For many of those who win one of these coveted positions, the privilege of being cool-by-association allows them to avoid undertaking the hard work of establishing a handmade cool that's truly indigenous to themselves. That's okay, as that work is too hard for many people. In the Midwest, by contrast, it's much harder to be cool by association because hardly any institutions here participate in the official line of cool (there's one less, now, with *The Onion*'s departure). Anyone who wants to live close to the glamour that the life of the imagination can lend existence must generate that glamour all by themselves.

Un/Cool 2

But of course the official line of cool has been both oppressive and rather lame for years now. Anyone not personally employed by the cool industry grasps this, but some imaginations feel compelled to go further, actually seeking out places that have been, if not exactly outside the cool industry's influence, at least seriously insulated from it. (On the coasts, cool evolves by negotiating with earlier incarnations of its manufacture; something—a manifestation of fashion, art, music, whatever—used to be cool, but is no longer. In the Midwest, cool negotiates instead with certain cultural conditions and artifacts that have never been cool—quite a different phenomenon.) Suddenly all those years of being "out of it" become an advantage to a place; it reads now, to some, as an *oxygenating* place. Of course, irony—"They're so out they're in!"—subverts the native uncoolness; irony enables cool to annex the uncool. But that's by no means the limit of the negotiation; the densely corny Lawrence Welk matter which has defined these Midwestern places for so long doesn't give up quite that easily. Unmoved and unmoving, it remains as indifferent to cool as it ever was. "What's irony?" it asks, watching as cool slides right off it, just as had happened during all those years prior.

It turns out that this hardcore, genuine disregard for cool incidentally generates an interesting context for creative action. An important kind of freedom is attained when nobody's certain anymore what moves are going to make them look bad or, for that matter, good.

Dahmer and Gacy Had to Have Come From Somewhere. Y'know

In so sunny a portrait of the New Midwest, is all darkness banished? Not by a long shot. To those who have not already secured for themselves passports to the free zone that the imagination represents, the Midwest's greatest threat remains, now as ever, the narrow range of models presented, to children and adults alike, of how life can be lived. This is not a slight danger, nor is it a small offense. Schools and local media—print and broadcast both—still contribute shamefully to a chronic, stifling narrowness of the human imagination. According to local institutions, we're all still supposed to be quarterbacks who cart our brood to the annual boat show. Disdain for, fear of, and repression of the complex needs of the imagination still permeate the region's psychology. Furthermore, local institutions and media, which still can't imagine that any really first-rate creative minds would actually choose to stay here, or, God forbid, return here, still fail to offer to living local imaginations any real support; promotion and advocacy are simply unheard of. The local newspapers need to reserve that space for printing the weekly Nielsen ratings. Little wonder that culture has had a hard time taking root in this part of the world.

Certain unhealthy constructs exist among progressive Midwesterners, too. Until I moved back to this part of the country (after 25 years away), I'd never heard artists so frequently use the term "unpretentious" to favorably describe someone's aesthetic, presentation, or character. I've heard it often since then—much *too* often. The word unconsciously expresses suspicion of and hostility toward anyone who dares to separate themselves from the pack. (A communitarian ethos can be as oppressive as any.) If being "unpretentious" means restraining oneself from pursuing ambitious degrees of abstraction or refinement, then all I can say is, "Viva pretentiousness." Another note that gets hit too automatically in the Midwest is the phrase "down to earth." Meant as a compliment, through overuse it's become a term that puts that set of life-possibilities achievable only through ambitious, unreasonable imagining on, to my mind, a frighteningly short tether. It's a phrase that undermines the value and the contribution of anyone who *isn't* "down to earth." My objection to its overvaluation isn't just based on the fact that, in my experience, "down to earth" has usually meant dull as hell. Human beings define and extend their humanness through artifice and imagination.

The struggle over modernization, so classic to Modernism, is the story of this moment in the Midwest. The out-of-it-and-proud-of-it who oppose modernization of their cultural experience are still around, insisting on their right to remain fossilized, fighting to protect What They Worked So Hard To Achieve (or something) from making contact with the future. By leveraging their inertia and suspiciousness, the enfossiled, still plentiful in number, can retard the evolution of the area under their control, just as they'd managed to do for so long. But this can work only for a while, because there's no going back. Agriculture and heavy industry are unlikely to make a comeback as dominant cultural signifiers. Dotcoms may come and dotcoms may go, but the electronic infrastructure they're a part of is, for better or worse, with us from here on out. The good people of the bygone world have had their century (and a half). Now it's someone else's turn to say what Mid-western culture's going to be.

The trick, in life as in art, is to respect the past without being constrained by it. Is something lost amid the "progress"? Of course. There'd been a genuine virtue to places that in the honest pursuit of their own reality went blind to such trivial matters as style or concept, to being "in" or "out"—and not only because the dominant, mainstream culture that cares about these distinctions arrives at them through a fearsomely heavy investment in a mechanism that's consistently cheap, degrading, and mercenary. But it would be a mistake to indulge too deeply in nostalgia. The fact is, it's painful to live too long in places that are too cut off from the possibilities of the present. No one benefits from prolonged immersion in that sort of frustration. In the final analysis it's better for the health of people, region, and nation that those who reside in quieter places feel there's a future in staying right where they are and working to open right where they are to more of what life offers. That sort of sentiment is, I suppose, classically Midwestern in its wholesomeness. If it is, then congratulations all around.

BIOGRAPHIES

Jane Addams Allen (1935–2004) was an art critic and co-founder of the *New Art Examiner*. She wrote art criticism for the newspapers *Chicago Tribune* and *The Washington Times* in addition to publications such as *Art in America, American Craft, Insight,* and *Studio International.* Allen received two art critic's grants from the National Endowment for the Arts, a Renwick Fellowship from the Smithsonian, a Manufacturers Hanover award for excellence in art criticism, and a Chicago Art Award for investigative reporting.

Derek Guthrie is an artist, art critic, and co-founder of the *New Art Examiner.* From 1971–73, Guthrie wrote art criticism for the *Chicago Tribune.* He and his wife, Jane Addams Allen, co-founded *The New Art Examiner* to create an alternative voice in Chicago with a national view of the art world. As a result, the magazine nurtured and brought to view a new generation of art critics, including Eleanor Heartney, Jerry Saltz, Robert Storr, Grant Kester, Suzi Gablik, Howard Risatti and Alice Thorson. He is currently an Editor-at-Large for *Proof* magazine.

Contributors

María José Barandiarán was born in Argentina and grew up in Chile and the U.S., where she studied art and printmaking at the Corcoran School of Art (BFA), Cranbrook Academy of Art (MFA), and Il Bisonte, in Florence, Italy. She moved to Chicago in 1992, and while interning at the *New Art Examiner*, she was given the opportunity to write art reviews. She truly enjoyed writing. Since then, she moved back to Chile, where she runs a small bakery and coffee shop, enjoys her art collection and reads a lot.

Steven C. Dubin is Professor of Arts Administration at Teachers College, Columbia University and a Research Affiliate of the Columbia Institute of African Studies. He has written extensively on controversial art, censorship, museums, and the art and politics of South Africa. He is the recipient of a Fulbright fellowship and has been a visiting professor in Israel, Iceland, and South Africa. He is the author of five books, including *Arresting Images* (Routledge, 1992), *Displays of Power* (New York University Press, 1999), and *Transforming Museums: Mounting Queen Victoria* (Palgrave Macmillan, 2006), and his writing appears regularly in *Art in America*, *Art South Africa*, and *African Arts*.

Jan Estep [www.janestep.com] has an expanded creative practice that comprises critical writing, creative writing, and a range of visual media including sculpture, photography, video, and independent publishing. In her writing and art projects she is concerned with the relationship between art and language and the ways humans connect to social and natural environments through images and words. Estep exhibits nationally and internationally and her critical writing has been published in *Bomb*, *Afterall*, *Frieze*, *Modern Painters*, *InterReview*, *Rain Taxi*, and *New Art Examiner*. She has been awarded a McKnight Visual Artist Fellowship, a Jerome Foundation NY Artist Residency, a Jerome Foundation Travel and Research Grant, a research commission from Breaking Ground, Ireland, and in 2008-2009 Estep was the inaugural arts practitioner/writer fellow at the Stanford Humanities Center. In December 2009 she was awarded a Creative Capital/Warhol Foundation Arts Writers Grant for short-form writing. Estep is currently Associate Professor and Director of Graduate Studies in the Department of Art at the University of Minnesota, Minneapolis.

Joanna Frueh is a writer, a performance artist, and a scholar whose work expands into photo, video, and audio pieces. Her most recent book is *Clairvoyance (For Those In The Desert): Performance Pieces, 1979–2004* (Duke University Press, 2008). She is Professor of Art History Emerita at the University of Nevada, Reno.

Henry A. Giroux currently holds the Global TV Network Chair Professorship at McMaster University in the English and Cultural Studies Department. His most recent books include: *The University in Chains: Confronting the Military-Industrial-Academic Complex* (Paradigm, 2007); *Youth in a Suspect Society: Democracy or Disposability?* (Palgrave Macmillan, 2009); *Politics Beyond Hope: Obama and the Crisis of Youth, Race and Democracy* (Paradigm, 2010); and *Hearts of Darkness: Torturing Children in the War on Terror* (Paradigm, 2010).

Michelle Grabner is an artist and writer. She is a Professor and Chair of the Painting and Drawing Department at The School of the Art Institute. Grabner is the co-founder and director of The Suburban, an artist-run project space in Oak Park, Illinois, which over the past ten years has hosted projects by numerous major and emerging artists. With her husband, Brad Killam, she is also the co-founder and director of The Poor Farm, an exhibition space in Northeastern Wisconsin.

The Guerrilla Girls are feminist masked avengers in the tradition of anonymous do-gooders like Robin Hood, Wonder Woman, and Batman. They use facts, humor, and outrageous visuals to expose sexism, racism, and corruption in politics, art, film, and pop culture. They undermine the idea of a mainstream narrative in visual culture by revealing the understory, the subtext, the overlooked, and the downright unfair. They are authors of stickers, billboards, many, many posters and street projects, as well as several books including: *The Guerrilla Girls' Bedside Companion to the History of Western Art* (Penguin, 1998); *Bitches, Bimbos and Ballbreakers: The Guerrilla Girls' Guide to Female Stereotypes* (Penguin, 2003); and *The Guerrilla Girls' Art Museum Activity Book* (Printed Matter, 2004). They've unveiled anti-film industry billboards in Hollywood just in time for the Oscars, dissed the Museum of Modern Art at its own Feminist Futures Symposium, and created a large scale project for the Venice Biennale. Their work is passed around the world by their tireless supporters, who use it as a model for doing their own crazy kind of activism.

Carole Harmel is a photographer, writer and retired Professor of Art from the Chicago City Colleges, where she taught film and photography for 37 years. She holds a BA from Antioch College, an MFA in photography from the School of the Art Institute of Chicago, and a PhD in film studies from Northwestern University in Evanston. The title of her dissertation was *Strategies of the Still: Minor White's Theory of Reading the Photograph Extended and Applied to Still Images in Experimental Film*. She has always been interested in the differences between how the word and the image interpret the world. Currently she lives in Chicago, where she is working on a project of portraits of Chicago artists.

Jeff Huebner is a Chicago-based art journalist, freelance writer and critic who writes frequently on public art. His articles have appeared in dozens of publications, including *ARTnews*, *Sculpture*, *Public Art Review*,

Art Papers, Landscape Architecture, Labor's Heritage, Greenmuseum, Ceramics Monthly, and *Michigan History,* as well as the *Chicago Reader, Chicago* magazine, *Chicago Tribune* and *Chicago Art Magazine,* along with many other local publications. He is the author or co-author of several books, including *Urban Art Chicago: A Guide to Community Murals, Mosaics, and Sculptures* (Ivan R. Dee, 2000); and *Murals: The Great Walls of Joliet* (University of Illinois Press, 2001).

Steve Hohenboken was the Indiana State editor and Craft editor for the *New Art Examiner* in the mid-90s. He is a photographer and works as an art therapist with adults who are developmentally disabled and/or have mental illnesses. He lives in Portland, Oregon.

Joshua Kind is a retired art history professor from Northern Illinois University in DeKalb, Illinois. He earned his BA from the University of Pennsylvania, Philadelphia, and holds a Ph.D. from Columbia University. Previously he has taught at Northwestern University, University of Chicago, The School of the Art Institute of Chicago, and Illinois Institute of Technology. He has served as Midwest correspondent for *ARTnews* as well as contributing editor for *The New Art Examiner.* A critic, essayist, and lecturer, his interests include Contemporary Art, Print History, and Architectural Design.

Hilton Kramer began publishing literary criticism in 1950, and art criticism in 1953. He was appointed chief art critic of the *New York Times* in 1973 and remained in that position until he resigned in 1982 to become the editor and publisher of *The New Criterion,* which he founded with the late Samuel Lipman. From 1987 until 2006, Kramer was also the art critic for the weekly *New York Observer,* and for many years wrote the "Critic's Notebook" column in *Art & Antiques* magazine. He has served on the faculties of Indiana University, Bennington College, the University of Colorado, and Yale University. He has lectured widely at museums and universities in this country and abroad. He is the author of *The Age of the Avant-Garde* (1973; Transaction Publishers, 2009), *The Revenge of the Philistines* (Free Press, 1985), *The Twilight of the Intellectuals* (1999; Ivan R. Dee, 2000), and most recently *The Triumph of Modernism: The Art World, 1985–2005* (Ivan R. Dee, 2006).

Donald Kuspit is one of America's most distinguished art critics. Winner of the prestigious Frank Jewett Mather Award for Distinction in

Art Criticism (1983), given by the College Art Association, Professor Kuspit is a Contributing Editor at *Artforum*, *Sculpture*, and *tema
celeste* magazines, and the editor of *Art Criticism*. He has doctorates
in philosophy (University of Frankfurt) and art history (University of
Michigan), as well as degrees from Columbia University, Yale University, and Pennsylvania State University. He is Distinguished Professor
of Art History and Philosophy at the State University of New York
at Stony Brook, and has been the A.D. White Professor at Large at
Cornell University (1991–97). He has received fellowships from the
Ford Foundation, Fulbright Commission, National Endowment for
the Arts, National Endowment for the Humanities, Guggenheim
Foundation, and Asian Cultural Council, among other organizations.
He is the editorial advisor for both European art 1900–50 and art
criticism for the *Encyclopedia Britannica* (16th edition), and wrote its
entry on Art Criticism. He is the author of numerous books includ-
ing: *The Rebirth of Painting in the Late Twentieth Century* (Cambridge
University Press, 2000); *Redeeming Art: Critical Reveries* (Allworth
Press, 2000); *The End of Art* (Cambridge University Press, 2005); and
A Critical History of Twentieth Century Art (Artnet, 2006).

Ann Lee Morgan is the author, most recently, of *The Oxford Dictionary
of American Art and Artists* (Oxford University Press, 2007). Other
publications include *Arthur Dove: Life and Art, with a Catalogue Raisonné* (University of Delaware Press, 1984) and *Dear Stieglitz, Dear
Dove* (Delaware University Press, 1988), an edited collection of the
letters between Arthur Dove and Alfred Stieglitz. A specialist in early
twentieth-century American art, she works as an independent scholar
in Princeton, New Jersey.

Keith Morrison, artist, curator, art critic, art educator and administra-
tor, has contributed articles to journals, periodicals, arts institutions
and museums across the US and abroad. He is author of *Art in Washington and Its Afro-American Presence: 1940–1970* (WPA, 1985). He
has curated exhibitions for many galleries and museums across the US
and in other countries. His paintings and prints have been collected
and exhibited in galleries and museums worldwide. His paintings
were also selected to represent his native country, Jamaica, at the 2001
Venice Biennale. A monograph of his work, titled *Keith Morrison*, by
Renee Ater, was published by Pomegranate Press in 2004. He has held
the rank of Professor and served as dean at several art schools and

universities. Among the awards and grants Morrison has received are a Ford Foundation, Danforth, African OAU, Chicago Bicentennial Award for Painting, and a Fulbright. Keith Morrison also represented the US as cultural envoy and critic to the 2008 Shanghai Biennale. See: www.keithmorrison.com.

Frank Pannier born in Florida in 1946, grew up in Brazil and Argentina, attending American schools where his father worked overseas. From the time he could hold a pencil, he began drawing. At 16, he moved to Chicago to live with his uncle, fellow artist and mentor, Herbert Pannier. He studied art at the University of Illinois, Chicago Circle campus. Dedicating his life to creating abstract art, he had 60 exhibitions in Chicago in the 1970s. Large diamond-shaped canvases, painted concurrently, in a series devoted to one subject matter, are typical of his art. Often the subject was Chicago architecture, or encompassed architectural elements in the structure of the paintings. A series could be up to a dozen canvases of similar shape, technique and color palette. He layered a myriad of colors of acrylic paint, rendering his art three-dimensional. Pannier also stretched canvas over wood blocks giving it depth, and making it structurally similar to architectural design. A mostly ignored Chicago abstract painter, he has just one painting hanging publicly in Chicago. "Ahrinsko" has hung at Blackies on Clark Street ever since it settled a bar tab. In 1996 at age 50, Pannier lost his life-long struggle with alcoholism, never realizing his dream to relocate to New York where he believed his art would find acceptance. Five years after his death, his work was shown in New York in an exhibit overshadowed by the tragedy of September 11th.

Ed Paschke was born in 1939 in Chicago. His childhood interest in animation and cartoons led him toward a career in art. As a student at The School of the Art Institute of Chicago he was influenced by many artists, in particular the work of Gauguin, Picasso and Seurat. Although Paschke's interests leaned toward representational imagery, he learned to paint based on the principles of abstraction and expressionism. Between his graduate and undergraduate work Paschke traveled and worked a variety of jobs amassing the experiences that would shape his artistic style. During a brief period in New York, he was exposed to Pop Art philosophy and began to incorporate elements of this style, borrowing images directly from the print media and other elements of popular culture. But unlike most of his Pop predecessors with their unthreatening embrace of popular culture, Paschke gravitated toward the images that exemplified the underside of American values—fame, violence, sex and money. Although long considered to be an artist of his own time and place, his explorations of the archetypes and clichés of media identity prefigured the appropriative gestures of the "Pictures Generation," and for a new generation of global artists his totemic, colorful eye-popping paintings have come to embody the essence of cosmopolitan art.

Michael Rabiger, now Professor Emeritus, was Chair of the Film/Video Department at Columbia College Chicago and wrote three manuals on filmmaking. The best known is *Directing the Documentary*, originally published in1987, now in its fifth edition (Focal Press, 2009) and translated into ten languages.

David Robbins was born in 1957 in Whitefish Bay, Wisconsin. Robbins is an artist and writer who was one of the first to investigate the art world's entrance into the culture industry. After attending Brown University, Robbins was employed in the early 1980s by Andy Warhol, George Plimpton and Diana Vreeland, during which years he educated himself about art by interviewing emerging artists such as Richard Prince, Jenny Holzer, Keith Haring and Allan McCollum. His work reflects on the spectacle, the transformation of the position of the artist in the visual system, and areas of overlap between art, entertainment, and comedy. As an artist he is best known for his 1986 work entitled *Talent*, eighteen "entertainer's headshots" of contemporary artists including Cindy Sherman, Jeff Koons, Jenny Holzer, Allan McCollum and others. As a writer he is known for his essays about entertainment and comedy. Robbins was an early contributor to *REALLIFE Magazine*, *Purple* magazine, and *Art issues*. He has published numerous books including: *The Velvet Grind: Essays, Interviews, Satires 1983–2005* (JRP/Ringier, 2006), which collect several of his early interviews; a novella, *The Ice Cream Social* (Purple Books/Feature, 1998); and *The Camera Believes Everything* (Edition P. Schwarz, 1988).

Connie Samaras is an artist and writer based in Los Angeles. Working primarily in photography and video her subjects include mapping political and psychological geographies in the everyday, future imaginaries and speculative landscapes, art as historical artifact, and the shifting membrane between fiction and real world. Recent published writings include, "America Dreams," *Gender on Ice, The Scholar & The Feminist Online* (Barnard.edu, 2008) and "The Magician," for the exhibition *Remix: Santiago Bose,* Yuchengo Museum, Makati City, the Philippines (2010). She is a Professor in the Department of Studio Art at University of California, Irvine and is represented by de Soto Gallery, Los Angeles.

Peter Schjeldahl was born in Fargo, North Dakota and now lives in New York City. He has authored several books of art criticism such as *Let's See: Writings on Art from The New Yorker* (Thames and Hudson, 2008), and *De Kooning and Dubuffet: The Late Works* (Pace Gallery,1993), as well as a collection of poetry entitled *Since 1964: New and Selected Poems* (Sun, 1978). Schjeldahl is a recipient of the Frank Jewett Mather Award for art criticism and in 1995 won a Guggenheim Fellowship. In addition to his work as staff writer for *The New Yorker*, his writing has appeared in *Artforum, Vanity Fair, The Village Voice, Art in America,* and of course, the *New Art Examiner.*

Michael Starenko [michael.starenko@gmail.com] is a faculty developer and online education specialist in the Teaching and Learning Center at the Rochester Institute of Technology. He is the former Editor of *Afterimage: The Journal of Media Studies and Cultural Criticism,* and editor of *Reflections on Blended Learning: Rethinking the Classroom* (Rochester Institute of Technology, 2008). He has published more than 100 reviews and articles on topics ranging from photography history to video art to online pedagogy. Michael and his wife, the writer and teaching artist Dale Davis, live in Fairport, New York; they have two grown children: Christopher, a Hollywood film and TV production designer; and Catherine, Managing Editor of NYC-based *Spin* magazine.

Alice Thorson, trained in art history at Northern Illinois University and the University of Chicago, has been the art critic for the *Kansas City Star* since 1991. She began her career in 1982 as managing editor of the non-profit *New Art Examiner,* first in the publication's Chicago office and later in Washington, D.C. In D.C., Thorson taught at the

Corcoran School of Art, and was the gallery columnist for the *Washington Times* and later *The City Paper*. She has contributed articles on art to numerous national publications and presently contributes reviews of Kansas City art to *Art in America*.

Stephen and Donna Toulmin—A native of England, **Stephen Toulmin** (1922–2009) earned degrees in physics and philosophy from Cambridge University. He wrote 17 books, contributed to another 20, and wrote for numerous journals and reviews including *Encounter*, *Minerva*, *Synthese*, *Daedalus*, *Hastings Center Report*, *Critical Inquiry*, *The American Scholar* and the *New York Review of Books*. After moving to the United States he held professorships at a number of universities including, Columbia, Brandeis, Michigan State, the University of California at Santa Cruz, the University of Chicago, Northwestern University and the University of Southern California. **Donna Toulmin** earned degrees in Comparative Culture and Law, and has spent her professional career teaching and writing about legal topics to non-lawyers. She is presently the Director of Training at University of Southern California Center on Child Welfare. They spent 35 happy years together viewing, acquiring, and talking about art.

Sarah Vowell is the author of six books including *Assassination Vacation* (Simon & Schuster, 2005) and *The Wordy Shipmates* (Riverhead Books, 2008).

Hamza Walker has served since 1994 as Director of Education/Associate Curator for The Renaissance Society at The University of Chicago—a non-collecting museum devoted to contemporary art. He was the recipient of the 1999 Norton Curatorial Grant, the 2005 Walter Hopps Award for curatorial achievement, a 2006 Emily Hall Tremaine Award for the exhibition *Black Is, Black Ain't* and the 2010 Ordway Prize. In addition to serving on panels and juries throughout Europe and the United States, he has written for numerous artist's monographs in addition to publications such as *Artforum* and *Parkett*.

Dan S. Wang was born in the American Midwest in 1968 to immigrant parents. His texts have been published in *SITE* magazine, *Whitewall*, *Art Journal*, *ArtAsiaPacific*, the *Journal of Aesthetics & Protest*, and in catalogues for the Smart Museum of Art, the Milwaukee Art Museum and Documenta 12. Along with seven others, he co-founded

Mess Hall, an experimental cultural space in Chicago. He regularly collaborates with a range of art groups, activists, and researchers in creating exhibitions, publications, and events. He teaches printmaking at Columbia College Chicago.

Lynne Warren is Curator at the Museum of Contemporary Art in Chicago where she has organized over 25 solo exhibitions of artists ranging from *Robert Heinecken: Photographist* of 1999 and 2004's *Dan Peterman: Plastic Economies* to *Jim Nutt: Coming Into Character* of 2011. Major exhibitions include *Alexander Calder: Form, Balance, Joy* of 2010, the *H.C. Westermann* exhibition and catalogue raisonné projects of 2001, and the *Art in Chicago, 1945–1995* exhibition of 1996 which produced the first comprehensive book of Chicago's unique art history. She has also realized numerous smaller exhibitions including those in the *MCA's 12 x 12: New Artists/New Works* series of emerging Chicago artists. She was the curator-in-charge for the MCA presentation of *Gordon Matta-Clark: You Are the Measure* in 2008 and organized the exhibition *Everything's Here* in conjunction with MCA's *Jeff Koons,* also 2008, which presented those Chicago-based artists Koons had admired and been influenced by. Her publications are wide-ranging and numerous, including over 30 exhibition catalogues published by the MCA and such publishers as Harry N. Abrams and Thames and Hudson. As well she has contributed to *Masterpieces of 20th Century Art* (The Art Institute of Chicago, 1988); *The Grove Dictionary of Art* (Groveart, 1995); *Photography After Photography* (Siemans AG, 1999); and is the editor for the three-volume reference book *The Encyclopedia of 20th Century Photography* published by Taylor and Francis Books, London and New York. Warren has taught courses at the University of Chicago, The School of the Art Institute of Chicago, Northwestern University, and The University of Illinois at Chicago, and has lectured throughout the United States.

Ann Wiens served as East Coast editor, then managing editor of the *New Art Examiner* from 1991 to 1998. As a writer, she is a regular contributor to *Chicago* magazine, was formerly the art critic for *Newcity,* and has written for *CS,* the *Chicago Reader, Art and Antiques, dialog, Lake,* the *Chicago Collection,* and other periodicals. She has authored numerous catalogue essays. With Dr. Carol Becker she co-edited the book *The Artist in Society: Rights, Roles, and Responsibilities* (New Art

Examiner Press, 1995), and in 2004 wrote a monograph on artist Darrel Morris (Telos Art Publishing, 2003). Wiens, a painter, is represented in Chicago by Byron Roche Gallery. Her public commissions may be seen in Chicago's Mount Greenwood branch library and the Chicago Center for Green Technology. In 2010, Wiens joined the School of the Art Institute of Chicago as executive director of marketing, public relations, and graphics. Prior to that she served as director of communications for Columbia College Chicago, where she was founding editor of *DEMO*, Columbia's award-winning alumni magazine. Wiens holds a BFA from The School of the Art Institute of Chicago and an MFA from the State University of New York at Stony Brook.

James Yood directs the New Arts Journalism program at the School of the Art Institute of Chicago, and teaches modern and contemporary art history there. He writes regularly for *Artforum*, *GLASS*, and *Aperture* magazines, and used to do so for *tema celeste* and *American Craft* and some gone but not forgotten publications such as *Dialogue*, *Art on Paper* and—sniff, sniff—the *New Art Examiner*.

Editors

Kathryn Born is an artist, writer, film maker, poet, publisher and art critic. She is the Editor-in-Chief and founder of *Chicago Art Magazine*, an online publication that is part of Chicago Art Machine, a media company that publishes articles and creates software related to the topics of independent film, technology and art. She is a graduate of Indiana University, receiving a degree from the Individualized Major Program for a dual major in both Creative Writing and English.

Terri Griffith is the author of the novel *So Much Better* (Green Lantern Press, 2009). Her fiction and criticism has appeared in the magazines *Bloom*, *Suspect Thoughts,* and *BUST*, as well as in the anthologies *Without a Net: The Female Experience of Growing Up Working Class* (Seal Press, 2003), *Are We Feeling Better Yet?* (Penultimate Press 2008) and *Art from Art* (Modernist Press, 2011*)*. Since 2006, she has been the literary correspondent and blogger for the contemporary art podcast *Bad at Sports*. She teaches writing and literature at The School of The Art Institute of Chicago.

Janet Koplos wrote for the *New Art Examiner* in the 1970s and '80s. Currently based in New York City, she is co-author of *Makers: A History of American Studio Craft* (University of North Carolina Press, 2010) and author of *Contemporary Japanese Sculpture* (Abbeville, 1990) and other books. She has written extensively on crafts and on American, Japanese, and Dutch contemporary art and has published about 2,500 articles, reviews and essays in approximately two dozen periodicals over the last 30 years, writing on Richard DeVore, Lesley Dill, Oliver Herring, Teun Hocks, Gyöngy Laky, Ed Moses, David Nash, Rona Pondick, Martin Puryear, Hiroshi Sugimoto, Ursula von Rydingsvard and Betty Woodman, among others. She lectures, critiques, and juries frequently, and occasionally teaches and curates. She was for 18 years a staff editor at *Art in America* and is currently a contributing editor to the magazine. She is a Phi Beta Kappa graduate of the University of Minnesota and holds a master's degree from Illinois State University. She was recently named an honorary fellow of the American Craft Council.

ACKNOWLEDGMENTS

The editors would like to thank the many people who helped craft this book into its finished form. Anne Roecklein single handedly managed all of the permissions. Jay Crenshaw digitally converted and proofread nearly every article contained within these pages. Robin Dluzen helped check the accuracy of the hundreds of proper names. John McKinnon offered excellent editorial suggestions and compiled many of the author biographies. In addition, we had permissions assistance from Maya Marshall and Susan Tweed, as well as technical help from Dave Ward. Many thanks to our proofreaders, Ian Taylor, Rachel Earls, Sharon R. Emeigh and Kate West. Thank you to our intern Minami Furukawa.

www.ingramcontent.com/pod-product-compliance
Lightning Source LLC
Chambersburg PA
CBHW020853180526
45163CB00007B/2492